Grounding

Cognitive Linguistics Research
21

Editors
René Dirven
Ronald W. Langacker
John R. Taylor

Mouton de Gruyter
Berlin · New York

Grounding

The Epistemic Footing of Deixis and Reference

Edited by
Frank Brisard

Mouton de Gruyter
Berlin · New York 2002

Mouton de Gruyter (formerly Mouton, The Hague)
is a Division of Walter de Gruyter GmbH & Co. KG, Berlin

The extract from MASON & DIXON by Thomas Pynchon on page xi, originally published by Jonathan Cape, is used by permission of The Random House Group Limited

Copyright of extract © 1997 by Thomas Pynchon, reproduced by permission of Rogers, Coleridge & White, 20 Powis Mews, London W11 1JN, UK.

∞ Printed on acid-free paper
which falls within
the guidelines of the ANSI
to ensure permanence and durability.

Library of Congress Cataloging-in-Publication Data

Grounding : the epistemic footing of deixis and reference / edited by Frank Brisard.
　　　p.　cm. − (Cognitive linguistics research ; 21)
　Some of the papers presented during the 7th International Pragmatics Conference, held in Budapest, Hungary in July 2000.
　Includes bibliographical references and index.
　ISBN 3 11 017369 7 (alk. paper)
　1. Cognitive grammar.　2. Grammar, Comparative and general − Deixis.　3. Reference (Linguistics).　I. Brisard, Frank.　II. International Pragmatics Conference (7th : 2000 : Budapest, Hungary).　III. Series.
　P165 .G76　2002
　415−dc21
　　　　　　　　　　　　　　　　　　　　　2002033656

ISBN 3 11 017369 7

Bibliographic information published by Die Deutsche Bibliothek

Die Deutsche Bibliothek lists this publication in the Deutsche Nationalbibliografie; detailed bibliographic data is available in the Internet at <http://dnb.ddb.de>.

© Copyright 2002 by Walter de Gruyter GmbH & Co. KG, D-10785 Berlin

All rights reserved, including those of translation into foreign languages. No part of this book may be reproduced or transmitted in any form or by any means, electronic or mechanical, including photocopy, recording, or any information storage and retrieval system, without permission in writing from the publisher.
Printing: WB-Druck, Rieden/Allgäu
Binding: Lüderitz & Bauer, Berlin
Printed in Germany

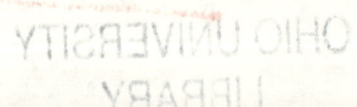

Acknowledgments

I should like to thank the editors of the "Cognitive Linguistics Research" series, René Dirven, Ron Langacker, and John Taylor, for the interest they expressed in the theme of the present volume, as well as for the time and energy dedicated to reading and sometimes rereading the individual contributions presented here. I also thank the staff at Mouton de Gruyter for their professional help in dealing with the practical sides of the publication process, and especially Birgit Sievert, who has graciously guided me through this process without ever, or so it seems, putting me through the wringer.

In addition, I am grateful to a number of people who have allowed me, in one way or another, to put all worries aside and focus on the completion of this enterprise. For one, Dominiek Sandra's continuous support and affable companionship remain a source of inspiration to me. On a more practical note, most of the work going into the preparation of the manuscript has been carried out at the University of Alberta (Edmonton, Canada), which I have had the pleasure to visit during the academic year 2001–2002. In particular, my thanks go to Gary Libben and Sally Rice at the Department of Linguistics, for their hospitable reception and quite simply for putting up with me.

Finally, I also appreciate the opportunity granted to me by the organizers of the 7th International Pragmatics Conference, held in Budapest, Hungary in July 2000, to put together a panel on "Grounding". Some of the chapters included in the present volume have first been presented during that conference, which offered a wide-ranging platform while allowing a sharp focus on matters of grammar and grounding within the confines of our panel.

I have been able to work on this project as a Postdoctoral Fellow of the Fund for Scientific Research – Flanders (Belgium).

List of contributors

Michel Achard
Rice University
Houston, Texas, U.S.A.

Frank Brisard
University of Antwerp
Antwerp, Belgium

Walter De Mulder
Université d'Artois
Arras, France

Aintzane Doiz-Bienzobas
University of the Basque Country
Vitoria-Gasteiz, Spain

Richard Epstein
Rutgers University
Camden, New Jersey, U.S.A.

Theo A. J. M. Janssen
Free University
Amsterdam, The Netherlands

Agata Kochańska
Warsaw University
Warsaw, Poland

Ronald W. Langacker
University of California at San Diego
La Jolla, California, U.S.A.

Ritva Laury
California State University
Fresno, California, U.S.A.

Tanja Mortelmans
University of Antwerp
Antwerp, Belgium

Jan Nuyts
University of Antwerp
Antwerp, Belgium

Carl Vetters
Université du Littoral
Dunkerque, France

Table of contents

Acknowledgments   v

List of contributors   vii

Introduction: The epistemic basis of deixis and reference   xi
   Frank Brisard

Deixis and subjectivity   1
   Ronald W. Langacker

Remarks on the English grounding systems   29
   Ronald W. Langacker

Part I: Nominal grounding

Grounding, subjectivity and definite descriptions   41
   Richard Epstein

Interaction, grounding and third-person referential forms   83
   Ritva Laury

The French *imparfait*, determiners and grounding   113
   Walter De Mulder and *Carl Vetters*

Deictic principles of pronominals, demonstratives, and tenses   151
   Theo A. J. M. Janssen

Part II: Clausal grounding

The meaning and distribution of French mood inflections 197
  Michel Achard

The English present 251
  Frank Brisard

The preterit and the imperfect as grounding predications 299
  Aintzane Doiz-Bienzobas

A cognitive grammar analysis of Polish nonpast perfectives 349
and imperfectives: How virtual events differ from actual ones
  Agata Kochańska

"Wieso sollte ich dich küssen, du hässlicher Mensch!" 391
A study of the German modals *sollen* and *müssen* as
"grounding predications" in interrogatives
  Tanja Mortelmans

Grounding and the system of epistemic expressions in Dutch: 433
A cognitive-functional view
  Jan Nuyts

Subject index 467

Introduction: The epistemic basis of deixis and reference

Frank Brisard

> "As if... there were no single Destiny, ... but rather a choice among a great many possible ones, their number steadily diminishing each time a Choice be made, till at last 'reduc'd,' to the events that do happen to us, as we pass among 'em, thro' Time unredeemable, — much as a Lens, indeed, may receive all the Light from some vast celestial Field of View, and reduce it to a single Point. Suggests an optical person..."
>
> Thomas Pynchon, *Mason & Dixon*

1. Grounding and grounding predications

Grounding is proposed as a technical term in Cognitive Grammar[1] to characterize grammatical predications that indicate the relationship of a designated entity to the ground or situation of speech, including the speech event itself, its participants, and their respective spheres of knowledge. By definition, grounding predications are obligatory grammatical elements needed to turn nouns into full *nominals*, and verbs into *finite clauses*. When this happens, the resulting nominal designates an instance of the thing type presented by the head noun, just like a finite clause is taken to designate an instance of the process type expressed by the main verb. This selection of instances is made possible by the very nature of the grounding function, which incorporates some relation between the ground and a designated process or thing whose main import can arguably be called "deictic" (Langacker 1994).[2] The relationship in question can be one of straightforward inclusion in the ground, but of course it need not be. Typical of grounding predications is that the conceptual relationship which they specify is left "offstage" or "unprofiled", in contrast with some of the more "objective" deictic expressions in lexicon and grammar (such as *I*, *here*, or *now*). In a language like English, the class of grounding predications includes demonstratives, articles, and a number of quantifiers for nominals, and tense and modals for finite clauses. Other languages will usually display a similar range of grounding predications, including the same or related morphemes in both the nominal and the clausal realms, although it is not always clear where exactly the line should be drawn between strict grounding predications and those grammatical predications that appear to aspire to grounding status (always through a process of grammaticalization) without quite having reached it as yet.

In proposing an initial approximation of the function of grounding predications, the first volume of Langacker's (1987: 126–129) *Foundations of Cognitive Grammar* sets the scene for a truly meaning-oriented approach to the fair number of ramifications that deixis presents in the context of grammar. It is maintained that all grammatically elaborated "phrases"[3] — full nominals and finite clauses — are necessarily deictic, or grounded, in some way or the other, making reference to an element of the ground that is meant to enable a more or less unique identification of the entity that is at issue in the nominal or clause (i.e., its head, or rather what it refers to). Prototypically, those aspects of the ground, and thus of grounding predications, most likely to establish the conditions that lead to the successful communication of intended referents are restricted to such abstract domains as space and time. Space is most relevant for the nominal paradigm, which is often concerned with things that can be located relative to a deictic center. By contrast, time is more relevant for the verb paradigm, with its systematic insistence on the temporal location of processes. More schematically, issues that are raised by the interpretation of grounding predications revolve around the *(non)existence* of processes and the *accessibility* of things (which are presupposed to exist in some space, if not in reality). In addition, when we are considering grounding predications as necessarily contributing to the formation of nominals or finite clauses (whether in a phonologically overt way or not), the conceptualization involved in such grammatical, as opposed to lexical, manifestations of deixis is more of a subjective nature (Langacker 1993). This means that the grounding relation itself is not what motivates the expression of the relevant nominal or clause, and it is reflected in the nonfocal status of true grounding predications, which can generally be found quite literally in the margins of the "phrases" they ground (English nominal determiners are a case in point here), or even take on the form of bound morphemes (as in the case of tense/agreement inflections on finite verb forms).

Interestingly, the same introductory volume to Cognitive Grammar primarily speaks of *epistemic grounding* as the most directly pertinent frame for explicating the meanings of deictic expressions falling under this definition. Thus, deixis, which has traditionally been taken to be concerned essentially, if not absolutely, with reference and identification, loses the aura of "objectivity" that has been bestowed upon it by the many logical treatments of grammatical function words and morphemes. (These treatments invariably rely on a correspondence theory of meaning, in which deictic expressions merely reflect physical properties of the worlds they describe.) Instead, for all grounding purposes deixis is now being presented as a psychological concern marking a grammatical category that is also, and perhaps more basically so, aimed at the qualification of referential contents (in terms of their accessibility and/or degree of reality). This epistemic turn in Cognitive Grammar imposes a perspective on the functions of deictic grammatical expressions that acknowledges the significance of how referents are assessed with respect to the knowledge repertoires of discourse participants, rather than focusing on so-called objective properties that relate referents directly to coordinates in the outer world. Thus, it is the participants' knowledge systems, whether construed at a local or more global level of deliberation, that constitute reference points for the successful interpretation of simple and syntactically complex, grounded expressions. It is the shared responsibility of the discourse participants to provide and/or identify anchors that allow the relative positioning of such expressions with respect to some negotiable frame of knowledge. This grounding process happens on top of the recognition of decontextualized semantic contents as contained in the nongrounding elements of grammatical "phrases" (e.g., in nominal expressions that are not determiners or quantifiers, and in nonfinite verb forms). The layered conception of linguistic representations, in which grounding occupies the topmost (epistemically oriented) level, is, incidentally, quite compatible with earlier work in Space Grammar (Langacker 1975, 1978), where the constituency of clauses is tackled from a functional-stratigraphic perspective. There, the *epistemic path*, reflecting various conceptual steps involved in the construction of an *objective content*, represents an essential quality of the compositional trajectory that leads to fully interpretable and contextually situated utterances.[4] This type of construction is also called *construal*, a notion which is essential to the general enterprise of a conceptualist semantics (as in Cognitive Grammar), and in particular to the description and analysis of highly schematic grammatical meaning types.

Quantity and (in)definiteness serve as the main measures for the grounding of nominals, while reality, as defined within the *dynamic evolutionary model* (Langacker 1991: 277), provides the benchmark against which the substance of full clauses is checked. In accordance with their highly grammaticalized status, grounding predications always constitute the final step in the formation of contextually transparent (if not always totally unequivocal) utterances.[5] They do this by relating a designatum, defined as the profile or point of focal interest within a given predication, to (an element of) the ground without, importantly, having this relation itself be profiled. This implies that the act of grounding is not one that exhibits a referential character per se. Rather, it builds upon an already presupposed act of reference as contained within the profiled portion of a predication and, in a way, qualifies a designated referent's relation to the physical, mental, or social world that is at issue at a given moment in discourse. The stuff of reference (or profiling) itself is established entirely through the semantic content of the head of a predication, whether nominal or clausal. When combined with the specific instructions provided by a grounding predication, discourse participants equipped with a knowledge of which *type* of nominal or clausal referent they are looking for, are able to select fairly specific (or even individual) instances in the "real world" or some other cognitive domain, but not as the direct result of what the grounding predication in question has specified through its own profile. Grounding predications, in other words, tend to set up a path and point out a region in which to look for intended referents, but they never indicate these referents as such, or only schematically.[6]

The conceptual implication here is that nongrounded profiles can, at best, suggest possible referents only at the level of the type which they are supposed to instantiate. Following Langacker, grounding predications allow the identification of a particular token that is to be selected on the basis of such type specifications, precisely because they can delimit the range of referents through their intimation of singular reference points that more or less pinpoint the relevant region of the ground (or outside it) that needs to be searched. Accordingly, one could say, grounding predications *situate* things or processes that are themselves *designated* by the lexical heads that also describe them, and more often than not this situating is seen as taking place in space and time, two of the more conceptually salient dimensions of the ground. Unfortunately, it is exactly the latter tendency to thoroughly spatialize or temporalize deictic meanings which could insinuate that the practical work of arriving at a grounded nominal or clause is still primarily framed in terms of the *location* of entities with respect to the (physical) speech situation, as upheld in orthodox studies of deixis.[7] The fundamentally epistemic character ascribed to these predications in Cognitive Grammar should prevent such a move, however. At least at the ultimate level of explanation, it is not necessary that grounding predications *directly* incorporate notions of, say, a referent's spatial and temporal proximity/distance, or of its unique identifiability in the case of definite descriptions (including the so-called definite tenses), even if they tend to do so prototypically.

The aim of grounding a predication is to establish mental contact with, or direct someone's attention to, a referent which discourse participants are presumably able to determine, given 1) the semantic content of the "phrase" to which the grounding predication attaches, and 2) the nature of the grounding relation proper. For this, it does not suffice to point out that the ground, as the locus of physical and mental events, is composed of several dimensions in which things and processes can be located. Rather, discourse participants need to call upon certain cognitive abilities, crucially mediated by the assumption of a shared repertoire of background knowledge, that should enable them to find out which dimensions are attended to and how exactly these can do the job of singling out the "right", intended instance of reference. This is called the *coordination of reference* (Langacker 1991: 91), which again stresses the notion that a grounding act is not particularly concerned with reference itself, or with the more specific location of referents with respect to the ground. Instead, grounding appears to be about the procedures that allow an interpreter to address such referential concerns on an inferential basis (with locations in space and time as potential physical correlates to the schematic instructions that grounding predications proffer). In line with the epistemic orientation noted above, grounding predications, as they are actually used in discourse, are not, or not exclusively, concerned with the location of specified instances in space, time, or even discourse. Indeed, the functional range of this type of predication is overwhelming, including many modal and even affective meaning nuances, and it would not only be theoretically but also empirically flawed to treat such uses as fundamentally "secondary", or derived from the purely referential function which many grounding predications obviously also exhibit.

Examples of nonreferential uses of grounding predications abound, both in the realm of the noun and in that of the verb, and we will see many such cases in the course of the following chapters. Thus, neither demonstratives nor articles function exclusively as expressions of the spatial proximity or distance of an intended referent, or of its unique identifiability within a (mentally constructed) space, respectively. Likewise, tense is by no means to be taken as dealing with locations in time only. The ubiquity and creativity of modal and discourse uses of tenses challenge the popular conception that basic temporal frames (past, present, and future) can always serve as source domains for the attested variety of such meaning "extensions". In fact, the main difficulty with these and other allegedly deviant cases is not that linguists have not been aware of their attestation or choose not to include them within the scope of their analyses (although this does constitute an accepted strategy, especially within formal-semantic and -pragmatic accounts of deictic constructions). It is the insistence to treat such recognizably nonprototypical meanings of grounding predications as in any way untrue to their referential origins that is the theoretical reason for the analytical problems that typify many studies of deixis and related phenomena in grammar. In such cases, the decision to resort to pragmatics for the explication of so-called "secondary" uses only shows that an auxiliary discipline is called in *faute de mieux*, treating all cases that do not conform to an a-priori conception of what a grammatical category should logically (as opposed to empirically) indicate.

2. Grammatical implications

Perhaps the time has come to turn the tables and ask whether referential (possibly locative) meanings, as important components in the use of grounding predications, are not themselves subservient to more basic concepts that are not intrinsically domain-specific. Thus, attempts to ground the meaning of grounding itself in schematic, procedural categories might present promising alternatives to the idea that (grammatical) deixis is only concerned with the identification of referents. Such categories, whatever their exact nature turns out to be, may then point in the direction of a general notion of *control* governing the use of grounding predications and generating, in turn, concrete inferences in specific domains like time and space, but also modality and discourse. Conceived along these lines, a comprehensive overview of grounding should address such diverse topics as *definiteness* (in articles, demonstratives, and tenses), *quantification* (both in nominal quantifiers[8] and in the realm of modal verbs), *tense* (plus certain grammatical manifestations of aspect, such as [im]perfectivity), and *mood*. Finally, a whole range of modal expressions can be taken into account as well, including auxiliaries but also other grammatical and lexical categories, if only to establish a clear dividing line between actual grounding predications and the non-grounding expression of epistemic modality.

The chapters included in the present volume are divided into two parts, dealing with nominal and clausal grounding, respectively. Both grammatically and conceptually, there is no denying that there are important ways in which the two types of grounding diverge, depending on the different "basic cognitive models" they invoke. For nouns, the preexistence and relative permanence of the things they designate is typically taken for granted, such that the selection of nominal referents needs to separate the intended targets from potential competitors in the same search domain. This is not true for processes (as designated by finite clauses), instances of which are typically transient and in any case unique to a specific configuration of events in time. These basic, and other more subtle, differences account for the fact that issues of nominal and clausal grounding tend to focus on different reflexes of the cardinal concerns that seem to be involved in grounding, viz., definiteness, quantification, and proximity vs. distance. What unites these concerns in a grammatical sense is that grounding predications, whether nominal or clausal, always seem to be about a speaker (iconically) indicating the amount of "effort" that goes into determining the epistemic status of a referent (in terms of its definiteness, its proximity/distance vis-à-vis an *origo*, or its quantificational evaluation with respect to some reference mass). Thus, "[i]n both the nominal and the clausal realms, overt marking signals an attempt by C [the conceptualizer] to bring matters "under control" with respect to what is primarily at issue" (Langacker 1994: 140).

Part I of the present volume, on nominal grounding, concentrates on the interpretation of definite descriptions. The first two chapters, by *Richard Epstein* ("Grounding, subjectivity and definite descriptions") and *Ritva Laury* ("Interaction, grounding and third-person referential forms"), propose a radical break with the presumption of identifiability for definite nominals and turn to alternative models — all of them in principle compatible with equivalent analytical work in Cognitive Grammar — that leave room for dynamic and jointly creative uses of these expressions in discourse (including naturally occurring conversation). The latter usage types may cover issues of salience, role/value status, and perspective that do not exactly reflect preexisting configurations of the objective world but that, instead, rely on the subjective ability of speakers to construe referents, including other discourse participants, under a range of specific "guises" and impose those construals on their audience. Above all, Laury also questions the assumption of an "egocentric" arrangement underlying the use of third-person pronouns and definite nominals, since the coordination of reference that is at stake here is typically not one that simply asks the hearer to "extract" a corresponding representation of the intended referent from the speaker's mind (or to reconstruct such a representation on the basis of information that is exclusively speaker-oriented). Rather, many and possibly all facets of grounding reveal something of a "sociocentric" (or "allocentric", or even "ecocentric") structure, in line with treatments of indexicality in ethnomethodology and Conversation Analysis, where definiteness is a property of referents that needs to be negotiated in interaction and is thus not entirely given at the outset of any interactional episode. In these chapters, it is also remarked that qualifications of definiteness and the subjective concerns of construal that go with it are not restricted to acts of judging the availability of nominal referents (things), whose existence can be taken for granted globally or constructed locally, but appear in clausal environments as well. In the latter case, the notion of definiteness, as applied to the temporal domain, only seems to matter to the conception of "real" (i.e., "nonquantified") processes, just like for nominals.

Despite the clear differences between instances of nominal and of clausal grounding, there also appears to be an extensive parallelism in the notions that operate throughout the category of grounding predications. This symmetry has been noted by Langacker (1994) and is developed in detail for a number of concrete grammatical domains in the chapters by *Walter De Mulder* and *Carl Vetters* ("The French *imparfait*, determiners and grounding") and *Theo Janssen* ("Deictic principles of pronominals, demonstratives, and tenses"). The first of these deals with the *imparfait*, one of two past tenses in French. It examines close links between this tense and some of the procedures underlying the use of definite articles (including their so-called partitive counterparts). In this case, anaphoricity, as a property related to the recovery of an antecedent entity for the interpretation of an expression's particular "viewpoint", ties phenomena of grounding in the domains of tense and determiners together. Also, De Mulder and Vetter's analysis makes extensive use of Fauconnier's (1994) "Mental-Space" approach to define the relevance of constructing accessible spaces or planes different from the ground (and from which the process designated by the *imparfait* should be seen as "actual"), a tendency which is mirrored in other contributions to this volume — notably, in the chapters by Achard, Brisard, and Doiz-Bienzobas.[9] Janssen's chapter, on the other hand, investigates the wide-ranging symmetry that can be postulated for the deictic meanings of personal pronouns, demonstratives, and tenses in a variety of languages. For this, he puts forward a central analytical metaphor, that of a mental field of vision divided into specific regions that can then be associated with distinct forms within a single paradigm of grounding predications. Implicit in this approach is the idea that deictic elements always express some kind of "referential concern" that is obviously related to their purely referential functions but does not exhaust them. Janssen is careful to include many "attitudinal" uses of certain grounding predications within his scope of analysis as well.

Part II, on clausal grounding, features analyses of tense, mood, and aspect in various languages. In Cognitive Grammar terms, the interest that unites these divergent categories is to be found in the dynamic evolutionary model of reality to which they all orient. Starting with (inflectional) mood, a marginal phenomenon in English grammar, *Michel Achard* ("The meaning and distribution of French mood inflections") points out that the selection of different moods is related to the speaker's effort to signal a state of affairs' status with respect to reality and other, locally constructed mental spaces. In fact, it turns out that French mood resembles English grounding modals to a large extent in this respect, even if the grammatical mechanics of the two systems tend to differ considerably. Still, both inflectional mood and modal auxiliaries can be said to focus on a conception of the "structure of the world" and on how the knowledge of that structure directly affects the expression of real and less than real "propositions".

Of course, indicating the likelihood of an event's occurrence is what modals in general, including nongrounding ones, seem to do if they have acquired any kind of epistemic range as part of their meaning at all. Consequently, one of the problems conjured up by this account is the question to what extent one could entertain the possibility of also including non- or semi-grammatical predications in the discussion of grounding. In other words, the extent to which grounding status is a binary or a gradient notion is still in dispute. *Tanja Mortelmans* ("A study of the German modals *sollen* and *müssen* as "grounding predications" in interrogatives") seems to go for the gradient interpretation of grounding, which in her case makes good sense in light of the highly grammaticalized status of the German modals under consideration. The crux of the argument here is that some *uses*, in restricted contexts, may qualify as grounding in the strict sense of the term, even if there is not one German modal in its entirety that can claim such a status. *Jan Nuyts* ("Grounding and the system of epistemic expressions in Dutch") appears to follow these very same lines of reasoning when he looks at lexical expressions of epistemic modality, but actually goes much further and effectively argues for a conceptual, not grammatical, definition of grounding. It remains to be seen whether or not the separation of a conceptual layer of representation from a strictly linguistic one is legitimate in Cognitive Grammar, which assumes the relevance of a conceptual semantics that is directly linked to phonological form.

Tense and aspect are traditionally, and often rightly, seen as intricately intertwined. The same picture emerges from the remaining chapters in the second part of this volume, which stress the heavy interaction that goes on between tense predications and various aspectual notions, in particular that of the contrast between a perfective and an imperfective construal of events. *Frank Brisard* ("The English present") adopts a nontemporal definition of tense and tries to show how present-time and other meanings of the English present tense emerge from a more basic epistemic concern with the structure of the world (as represented through the ground). In his account, (im)perfectivity, as a matter of semantic aspect, imposes a global split between "states" and "actions" in the English lexicon. The interaction of the present tense with this aspectual category results in a peculiar distribution of simple and progressive marking, which reflects a preoccupation with revealing certain states of affairs as constitutive of the ground (pretty much extraneous to any temporal point that might also be made), and others as nonconstitutive or incidental. The Polish verb system, like the English, contrasts a past with a nonpast tense as well, but it adds to this a grammatical manifestation of (im)perfectivity that is responsible for very specific inferences in futurate contexts of nonpast tense uses. *Agata Kochańska* ("A cognitive grammar analysis of Polish nonpast perfectives and imperfectives") explains such inferences by referring to Cognitive Grammar's distinction between actual and virtual planes of reference within which to locate designated processes, in conjunction with the better-known contrast between projected and potential reality. All of these notions, as it turns out, are ultimately epistemic. Finally, *Aintzane Doiz-Bienzobas* ("The preterit and the imperfect as grounding predications") observes similar effects in analyzing the two past tenses in Spanish, which differ mainly in their assignment of (past) states of affairs to an actual or structural plane of conceptualization. Her analysis of the Spanish preterit and imperfect is first and foremost rooted in a Mental-Space approach to "discourse tracking devices", which implies that the "viewpoint" from which states of affairs are set up (and their accessibility is determined) takes on a central role in defining the meanings of these clausal grounding predications.

Fauconnier's (1994: xix) statement, cited in Epstein's chapter, that "unusual cases reveal the general nature of the operations at work, whereas the typical cases do not" serves as a key methodological principle adhered to in many of the present contributions. Especially for grounding predications, relatively atypical modal, affective, and also generic usage types happen to illustrate the basic epistemic workings of this grammatical class in a much more revealing way than the so-called referential uses, which can be seen as parasitic upon the "coordinating" function of grounding. Related to the concern with uncovering "marginal" usage types, then, is the decision, also respected in many chapters, to shy away from introspectively constructed linguistic examples and concentrate on the actual use in context of grounding predications. That, too, constitutes a practice of "grounding", be it at a metatheoretical level and as applied to the analysis of language, rather than to linguistic structure per se. In combination with the vast range of crosslinguistic observations and the recourse to various distinct analytical methods (from psycholinguistic experimentation, over corpus analysis, to the qualitative analysis of spoken and written discourse), the present volume hopes to offer a diversified picture of the many routes that grounding theory, as formulated within Cognitive Grammar, can lead us onto.

Both the subjective character and the strictly grammatical status of grounding predications present themselves as crucial to any adequate understanding of the nature of grounding. This is precisely why grounding predications form a separate class in grammar, even if they share an attentiveness to epistemic modality with many other items and constructions in language. The fundamental question that needs to be answered in this respect touches on the very essence of grounding, insofar as there is no more or less discrete and universal phenomenon of grounding to begin with, if the quality of its modal concerns does not differ from that of (less grammaticalized and) lexical expressions of epistemic modality — see especially the chapters by Laury, Mortelmans, and Nuyts. In the words of Nuyts (this volume: 458), we might ask "why languages tend to grammatically code qualificational dimensions, but not dimensions of the "object world"", where "qualification" is to be understood as a subjective sensitivity to how objects are linguistically presented (rather than to what is actually being presented). Although no division between lexicon and grammar should be assumed to derive from this, it is probably appropriate to see grammar as the locus of a world view that transcends local concerns with "accidental" properties of the world to be described (in any case much more so than lexicon, which tends to be easily affected by concrete cultural models that have no claim to any kind of transcendental status in language). Grammar, in other words, seems to offer a collection of metaphysical questions (or an ethnometaphysics, for that matter) that need to be addressed time and again in the course of any structured episode of symbolic interactional behavior, and it is very unlikely that lexicon might be up to the task of providing elements that are sufficiently general to be able to fulfill this function. In this picture of grammar, it surely looks as if the notion of the ground has a privileged and even primitive status, so that the next step would be to substantiate this conception, in the face of its fundamentally abstract and schematic makeup, and ask how and why it has developed in the first place.

3. Theoretical implications

Space and time, as important correlates to the meanings of many grounding predications, can be said to belong to the realm of immediate sensations (see, e.g., the "Transcendental aesthetic" section of Kant's *Critique of Pure Reason*). They are the stuff that is always already given in our conceptual (propositional, argumentative) dealings with the world and upon which we build the substance of rational understanding. Any representation presupposes the restrictive dimensions of space and time as the forms in which the brute matter of experience is cast, and these forms are always immediately available, here and now. Thus, space and time cannot be treated as concepts in their own right but rather as modes or modalities of presentation. (Conceptual) re-presentations are presentations that have been fitted into these modes. But the modes themselves are not so much conceptual as they are procedural, providing instructions on how to treat and integrate representational content. Now, in grammar it is not representations that are of primary concern, in the sense that a representation pertains to the construal of an *objective scene*. What lies behind this relation of construal, and what is correspondingly indicated by grammatical means, is something of a "directing" instance, a role that might conceivably be performed by all sorts of constructions, including grounding predications. This, of course, is also a matter of construal (or of *constituting the world*), but it is crucially one of subjective import, in that it relates whatever content there is to express to the ground.

In a Husserlian vein, we might say that the fundamental crisis of Western civilization does not primarily pertain to the foundations of reason, but rather to the scientific project of defining "real" objects in the world, i.e., that which is given in the sensibilities of space and time (Husserl 1970).[10] In contrast to what science itself might pretend, the formation of intelligible objects, or concepts, does not proceed *sui generis* but needs to be "prepared". Space and time perform this preparatory work. Husserl contended that, in modern civilization, we are "losing ground" (and the sense of community that goes with it). That is to say that the "here and now" of our experiences, the actuality and immediacy immanent in the feeling of "belonging" that is conjured up by the ground (*Grund* or *[Ur-]Erde*), are somehow fundamentally affected by this loss. The problem of the ground in Husserl's phenomenology, then, is one of modality and not of content. It is intimately connected with his notion of the "lifeworld", specifying a "pre-understanding sedimented in a deep-seated stratum of things that are taken for granted, of certainties, and of unquestioned assumptions" (Habermas 1998: 236–237), so as to absorb and regulate the risk of disagreement — an "epistemic" risk (on the transcendental relationship between the ground and acts of communication, see also Lyotard 1991: chapter 8).

It is to this conception of a "ground" that grounding predications can be taken to "refer" when they indicate degrees of epistemic certainty or control (over objects in space and time), and for this it is absolutely necessary that grounding predications operate in the realm of the subjective, i.e., in grammar. For the "pre-predicative knowledge" that forms the horizon of a massive background consensus is not about objects of deliberation, but about ways in which to present such objects. In other words, the categories and meanings that grounding predications have to offer are unthematic and cannot accurately be seen as explicit topics of reflection. That would be like questioning the frame of a picture, when what people normally do is focus on its (referential) contents. Of course, it is possible to thematize, as it were, the meanings expressed by grounding predications, but then such a process would need to convert the background character of this information into something of a foregrounded, or "objective", status, which might involve lexicalizing grammatical meanings. Thus, one does not typically question the pastness of a situation, as presented in an utterance like *He graduated with honors*, by merely repeating the utterance in a contrastive tone of voice: *What? He **graduated** with honors?* (with heavy stress on the past-tense morpheme, to indicate something like 'What? His graduation [with honors] is located at a time prior to the time of speaking?').[11] Instead, one typically resorts to lexical means in order to indicate where exactly the problem with the utterance at hand is to be located: e.g., *What? He **already** graduated? (I thought he was still in high school...)*. Questioning and (re)negotiating the position of elements within or outside the ground is in principle always possible, but it is not primarily perceived as going on in grammar and whenever it does happen, chances are that objectifying predications are called in to signal the fact that the information at stake is (temporarily) removed from the ground — or, from another perspective, that (some element of) the ground itself is put "onstage".

If the ground, as a privileged domain that provides a baseline for grammatical expressions, is a collection of (nonpropositional)[12] "statements" of the immediately familiar (as well as, by implication, one that negatively defines the surprising), it should be obvious that this entity is neither static nor completely private. The metaphysical objects involved are not eternal, and their constitution is a matter of intersubjective praxis, rather than theoretical debate (cf. Laury's use of the label "sociocentric" in this volume to characterize grounding practices). In this light, the importance of related research into issues of deixis needs to be more fully appreciated. As grounding affects all structural levels of language, it also interacts with the discursive and argumentative organization of *text*. Thus, the same term covers a similar concept in discourse analysis, where it designates the relationship between (discursive) foreground and background (incidentally also assigning a discourse-pragmatic function to "syntax"; see, e.g., the contributions to Tomlin 1987). Furthermore, grounding is directly drawn into any discussion of *indexicality*, which has received considerable attention from linguistic anthropologists and critical linguists alike. In the so-called Chicago School, including Goffman and the work of Silverstein and Hanks, indexical or deictic categories figure among the foremost indicators of reflexive or meta-linguistic awareness, and grammar is seen as the primary locus in which to look for strategies resorted to by language users to communicate their assessment of the overall status of what is being said. (Goffman [1981: 325–326] talks of the speaker shifting alignments, "a combination of production format and participation status".) The assessment/alignment can be made in epistemic terms, and such epistemic judgments are central to the organization of grammar.

As should be clear by now, there is nothing to prevent concrete grammatical analyses of grounding predications from focusing on discursive, interpersonal (social), or affective functions, as long as these are not treated as mere connotations pragmatically derived from an "essential", truth-conditional semantics of the predications in question. The status of referential usage types as somehow essential to the meaning of functional categories is quite understandable from a "native" angle, yet there is no compelling reason to adopt the same referentialist stance in the analytic techniques and formal descriptive machinery that linguists have at their disposal (Silverstein 1976; see Epstein, this volume). Referentialism, thus defined, may be a worthy object of psychological investigation in its own right, considering how language users themselves conceive of the functions of language, but as a presupposition governing the systematic study of language it is unmistakably misguided. Obviously, considerations of strategy and alignment apply most pertinently to those instances of grounding that are traditionally taken as deictic, such as demonstratives (for space) and tense (for time). Still, it can be reasonably hypothesized that other constructions like moods/modals, determiners, and quantifiers, which belong to the same class of grounding predications in Cognitive Grammar, operate in comparable ways on the semantic contents of clauses and nominals, respectively. One of the *theoretical* challenges for a genuinely unified account of grounding, therefore, is to offer possibilities of linking the various linguistic and paralinguistic paradigms involved, thereby effectively creating a trans-paradigmatic concept of grounding. The general intuition behind this is that, throughout different disciplines, uses of the same term, "grounding", point to a general property of symbolic interaction that is differentially manifested in the range of paradigms where this term surfaces. Attempts at such an interdisciplinary approach can be witnessed in the chapters by Brisard, Epstein, Janssen, and Laury.

One way of responding to this challenge, from the grammatical perspective, is to abandon the specific modalities of the domains in which the different grounding predications function and formulate parameters of grounding in terms of general frames for the organization of experience (and, hence, of linguistic meaning). Cognitive Grammar provides just this scenario when it proposes grounding as situated in an epistemic "stratum" of grammatical structure, i.e., as epistemically motivated. In his repeated observations of the many parallels between clausal and nominal grounding, Langacker emphasizes the unitary aspect of this grammatical phenomenon and accordingly suggests an integrated phenomenology that is not domain-specific for tackling individual constructions. In this respect, the many symmetries between conception and perception (especially vision), as noted in Langacker (1999: chapter 7), provide some extremely useful guidelines for the development of a cognitive approach to grammatical structure that is motivated by generalized conceptual capacities — rather than specialized, encapsulated symbolic skills.[13] Notably, through the postulation of different "viewing arrangements" underlying the construal of configurations that are otherwise identical, Cognitive Grammar manages to capture many of the more subtle meaning distinctions in grammar, which do not necessarily reflect a difference in objective content. This same analogy is stressed in the present volume by Janssen and Kochańska, and it is also present in accounts of mental-space construction processes, where the notion of a "viewpoint" plays a central role — see the chapter by Doiz-Bienzobas and, to a lesser extent, those by Achard, De Mulder and Vetters, and Epstein. These, and other, mechanisms offered in Cognitive Grammar allow analyses to move away from the seemingly unproblematic premises that have typified "referentialist" thinking on grounding predications, i.e., the assumption that expressions whose meanings depend on situated properties of the ground do nothing but relate the referents they designate to that ground as a physical speech event.

Grounding theory offers at least two major objections against this view. The first is that the relation which a designated entity, be it a nominal thing or a clausal process, entertains with the ground of the speech event is not exclusively, and perhaps not even primarily, of a physical or logical nature (in the sense of a spatial or temporal "logic", for instance). The main point of the conceptual models proposed in Cognitive Grammar is exactly that a schematic characterization can be given of *all* grounding predications, and that this characterization is not a matter of locating things or processes in (physical) dimensions of reality, but of qualifying the status of things or processes with respect to the structure of reality *tout court*. In this light, particular features of the meanings of grounding predications derive from such general epistemic considerations, instead of the other way around. Technically speaking, moreover, grounding predications only designate *schematic* things or processes, as we have seen. And when they combine with nouns or verb forms, the actual relationship with the ground is an aspect of subjective construal rather than an objective focus within the scene that is being described.

The focus on the subjective nature of grounding predications implies a conception of grammar that is not reflexive of contextual properties "out there" but of the speaker construing a context, possibly even creating it, and in any case designing it in function of the interaction with an addressee (i.e., also drawing on assumptions regarding what she knows or would be in a position to know). The subjective status of grounding predications, in other words, highlights the active role that a speaker plays in organizing the contents of linguistic communication. In this capacity, it is obviously related to similar organizing principles at the discourse level, as indicated above: the foreground/background distinction (corresponding to figure/ground organization in Cognitive Grammar), as well as the construction of relevant discourse spaces, where accessibility relations between space elements indicate the epistemic status of these elements. In this strand of enquiry, deictic (or grounding) elements are seen as fundamentally challenging the viability of viewing language as a self-contained, autonomous system (see also Duranti and Goodwin 1992).

The emphasis on a unifying approach to the class of grounding predications, itself comprising a number of different construction types, leads to an integrated analysis in which a limited number of cognitive principles of information structuring, attention management, and "ception" may motivate comparable linguistic observations over various domains. Thus, at an abstract level of grammatical structure, clauses and nominals make use of the same strategic concerns, apply them in similar ways, and therefore also function similarly in accordance with the semantic options projected by these strategies. This methodological preference for unification can be extended to include all possible forms of "grounding" at higher levels of organization, notably those that involve the constitution of a ground for the patterning of text and discourse as a whole, or for the construction of participant status (footing) and "framing". Also, the need to start semantic analyses of grounding predications from a perspective that is not domain-specific (i.e., not temporal, or spatial, or otherwise "objectively" framed in terms of some direct measure of identifiability) calls for a reappraisal of peripheral usage types. Against the rising hegemony of "frequency" thinking in much of current linguistics and cognitive psychology, peripheral uses, *qua* limiting cases, can indeed be seen as instantiating general principles of cognition in a more transparent way, as their functioning is not obscured by the specifics of the domains which grounding predications are often presupposed to instantiate. The resulting analyses are to be free from any logically inspired hierarchy and do not implement a strict distinction between semantic ("true") and pragmatic ("derived") meanings.

Notes

1. The name "Cognitive Grammar" will be used exclusively to refer to Langacker's (cf. 1987, 1990, 1991, 1999) semiological theory of grammar. The term "grounding", too, is used exclusively in the technical sense given to it in Cognitive Grammar, although some of the contributions contained in the present volume do indicate plausible links with certain broader conceptions of the "ground" (as an implicit background invoked in the production and comprehension of linguistic expressions). This particular focus is not to be con-

fused with some of the outstanding and obviously related endeavors of other cognitive linguists, in which the relevant terminology seems to be deployed in a somewhat looser, less structure-oriented fashion (see, e.g., Dirven and Radden's [2002] paradigmatic use of the notion of a "cognitive grammar").
2. References to Langacker (1993) and (1994) provide the respective bibliographical details for the first publication of these two papers, "Deixis and subjectivity" and "Remarks on the English grounding systems", which are cited in most of the subsequent chapters in the present volume as well. Langacker's papers are reprinted here, following this introduction, under the same titles as their originals.
3. The term "phrase" is necessarily qualified in Cognitive Grammar, as the theory does not assume any phrase-structured organization of natural language. Noun and verb phrases might emerge from grounding (conceptually grouped) units of phonological material, if the resulting structures display the appropriate heads, but they are not essential to the structured inventory of symbolic assemblies that makes up a language.
4. In Space Grammar, the ground is in effect separated from an epistemic layer of conceptualization, as the former pertains primarily to the "performative" aspects of utterance production. It should be clear, however, that the eventual integration of these two levels ("ground" and a kind of "epistemic" concern) does not go against the spirit of the earlier analyses and in fact broadens the range of semantic import that "grounding predications" may display.
5. The "chronology" suggested here is more of a procedural nature. As such, it does not necessarily reflect the relative orderings of processing stages that might be relevant to a "real-time" (or online) model of language production. Also, "utterance", here and elsewhere, may refer to full finite clauses as well as to interpretable parts thereof (insofar as these parts are themselves grounded).
6. Technically, a grounding predication also displays a profile "onstage", and thus a referential focus, just like any other predication. The profile of a grounding predication, though, is extremely schematic (merely specifying the conceptual availability of a thing or process) and therefore immediately filled in, as it were, by the nominal or clausal head that it modifies. The latter process relies on perfectly mundane relations of correspondence between the elements of the semantic poles of predications that are syntactically integrated.
7. Location is a special type of situation and, as such, canonically tied to an act of reference. Reference is thus a special type of situation, too (i.e., one among various possible acts of situating or "contextualizing" things and processes).
8. Nominal quantification is conspicuously absent in the present volume. In fact, except for work by Langacker and some analysis of quantification by Israel (1996) in the context of polar sensitivity, I am not aware of any substantial discussions on the topic within Cognitive Grammar.

9. In Fauconnier's model, it is the conception of the "base (space)" that comes closest to illustrating what the function of the ground could be in discourse. If a base space is a starting point for the construction of mental spaces and sets up discourse elements which can be linked to various other frames "by background knowledge and previous meaning construction" (Fauconnier 1997: 42), then this might be seen as a direct manifestation of knowledge springing from the ground. Note that the base *is not* the ground, but a construction whose import is shaped by what discourse participants are locally seeing as belonging to the ground. This neither implies that the ground is a static repertoire of knowledge, nor does it even presuppose that there is any other independent means of getting at the ground, because the only way to access its contents, analytically speaking, is exactly by looking at the behavior and function of base spaces in contextually anchored instances of discourse. Still, it is useful for grammatical purposes to maintain a distinction between the ground and the base, if only because the two notions apparently pertain to epistemic concerns that differ considerably in their scope as well as in their degree of contextual relevance. Furthermore, it should be clear that the ground is definitely not to be equated either with a kind of "focus space" (like a "belief space"), which presents what is actually at issue in an utterance. Even though the ground can be seen as made up of countless beliefs, it does not present any of them as a focus of attention.
10. We are talking about the natural sciences "of space and time" here, including, crucially, arithmetic (time), geometry (space), and mechanics (space and time). Note that the conception of space (and time) that is entertained in most cognitive-linguistic thinking about grammar is topological, not geometric (Talmy 1988; cf. Langacker 1994 for a mild critique).
11. In principle, such a contrastive strategy is indeed possible and may sometimes be resorted to, but in any case, as a marked option, the meaningful use of heavy stress alone seems to involve a kind of "objectifying" force, then.
12. This is, crucially, how the ground differs from the notion of "context", which is equally pervasive in the organization of interaction. Context, as it has been traditionally defined in formal semantics, is a collection of propositional beliefs used to "enrich" or "complete" the (semantically underspecified) contents of "what is said" in an utterance. This conception of context is useful in its own right, but it does not directly tackle the theme of the ground, which is nonpropositional and in fact shapes the very form in which to address the specifics of context.
13. The idea of "ception" as a general mode or "module" of cognition, comprising principles of con- and perception, should be attributed to Talmy (e.g., 1996).

References

Dirven, René and Günter Radden
    2002   *Cognitive English Grammar*. Amsterdam: John Benjamins.
Duranti, Alessandro and Charles Goodwin (eds.)
    1992   *Rethinking Context: Language as an Interactive Phenomenon*. Cambridge: Cambridge University Press.
Fauconnier, Gilles
    1994   *Mental Spaces: Aspects of Meaning Construction in Natural Language*. Cambridge: Cambridge University Press.
    1997   *Mappings in Thought and Language*. Cambridge: Cambridge University Press.
Goffman, Erving
    1981   *Forms of Talk*. Philadelphia: University of Pennsylvania Press.
Habermas, Jürgen
    1998   *On the Pragmatics of Communication*. Edited by Maeve Cooke. Cambridge, MA: MIT Press.
Husserl, Edmund
    1970   *The Crisis of European Sciences and Transcendental Phenomenology: An Introduction to Phenomenological Philosophy*. Translated, with an introduction, by David Carr. Evanston: Northwestern University Press.
Israel, Michael
    1996   Polarity sensitivity as lexical semantics. *Linguistics and Philosophy* 19: 619–666.
Langacker, Ronald W.
    1975   Functional stratigraphy. In: Robin E. Grossman, L. James San and Timothy J. Vance (eds.), *Papers from the Parasession on Functionalism*, 351–397. Chicago: Chicago Linguistic Society.
    1978   The form and meaning of the English auxiliary. *Language* 54: 853–882.
    1987   *Foundations of Cognitive Grammar*, Volume 1: *Theoretical Prerequisites*. Stanford: Stanford University Press.
    1990   *Concept, Image, and Symbol: The Cognitive Basis of Grammar*. Berlin: Mouton de Gruyter.
    1991   *Foundations of Cognitive Grammar*, Volume 2: *Descriptive Application*. Stanford: Stanford University Press.
    1993   Deixis and subjectivity. In: S. K. Verma and V. Prakasam (eds.), *New Horizons in Functional Linguistics*, 43–58. Hyderabad: Booklinks.

1994 Remarks on the English grounding systems. In: Ronny Boogaart and Jan Noordegraaf (eds.), *Nauwe betrekkingen: Voor Theo Janssen bij zijn vijftigste verjaardag*, 137–144. Amsterdam: Stichting Neerlandistiek VU.
1999 *Grammar and Conceptualization*. Berlin: Mouton de Gruyter.

Lyotard, Jean-François
1991 *The Inhuman: Reflections on Time*. Translated by Geoffrey Bennington and Rachel Bowlby. Cambridge: Polity.

Silverstein, Michael
1976 Shifters, linguistic categories, and cultural description. In: Keith H. Basso and Henry A. Selby (eds.), *Meaning in Anthropology*, 11–55. Albuquerque: University of New Mexico Press.

Talmy, Leonard
1988 The relation of grammar to cognition. In: Brygida Rudzka-Ostyn (ed.), *Topics in Cognitive Linguistics*, 165–205. Amsterdam: John Benjamins.
1996 Fictive motion in language and "ception". In: Paul Bloom, Mary A. Peterson, Lynn Nadel and Merrill F. Garrett (eds.), *Language and Space*, 211–276. Cambridge, MA: MIT Press.

Tomlin, Russell S. (ed.)
1987 *Coherence and Grounding in Discourse: Outcome of a Symposium, Eugene, Oregon, June 1984*. Amsterdam: John Benjamins.

Deixis and subjectivity

Ronald W. Langacker

If the task of devising a linguistic theory were just beginning, and linguists were free to imagine some basic properties of an optimal theoretical framework, what might they come up with? What might they offer as reasonable grounds for judging a theory to be natural, elegant, and revelatory?[1]

They might very well imagine a linguistic theory conceived in full harmony with the semiotic function of language, that of allowing conceptualizations to be symbolized by phonological sequences. Such a theory would posit only the minimal apparatus required for this function: semantic structures, phonological structures, and symbolic links between the two. It would recognize that all grammatical constructs are meaningful, thereby reducing grammar to symbolic relationships between semantic and phonological structures. By viewing grammar and lexicon as a continuum of symbolic structures, it would thus achieve a fundamental conceptual unification. It would further recognize conventionalized aspects of pragmatics — including deixis — as constituting an integral part of linguistic semantics, treated in the same fashion as any other aspect of semantic structure. Finally, such a theory would be founded on a view of meaning that acknowledged its conceptual basis and fully accommodated our capacity for construing a situation in alternate ways (e.g. as seen from different perspectives). A theory of this sort would obviously be of great interest from both the linguistic and the semiological standpoints.

A theory with these properties has of course been available to the theoretical linguistic community for over two decades. It goes by the name of Cognitive Grammar (CG), and has been successfully applied to a substantial, ever-widening array of languages and linguistic phenomena.[2] Reasonably precise semantic characterizations have been proposed for a large number of grammatical markers, and for such basic grammatical notions as noun, verb, head, complement, modifier, coordination, subordination, subject, object, auxiliary verb, transitivity, unaccusative, and ergativity. Our interest here is the conceptual characterization of deictic elements, in particular those essential to the formation of nominals (i.e. noun phrases) and finite clauses. A revealing semantic analysis of these elements, one that explains their special grammatical properties, pivots on the phenomenon of subjectivity, which pertains to vantage point and the relationship between the subject and object of conception. Subjectivity proves to have substantial linguistic significance, both synchronic and diachronic.

1. A symbolic view of grammar

CG posits just three basic kinds of structures: semantic, phonological, and symbolic. Symbolic structures are not distinct from the other two, but reside in the symbolization of semantic structures by phonological structures: [[SEM]/[PHON]]. The most obvious examples of symbolic structures are lexical items, e.g. [[PENCIL]/[pencil]]. A central tenet of CG is that morphology and syntax are also symbolic in nature. It claims, in other words, that only symbolic structures are required for the full and proper characterization of grammatical structure. A further contention is that lexicon, morphology, and syntax form a continuum; only arbitrarily can they be divided into separate and discrete "components".

The basic import of this symbolic conception of grammar is that all grammatical elements have some kind of semantic value. The inherent plausibility of this claim is most evident for "grammatical morphemes" and "function words", many of which are clearly meaningful (e.g. prepositions). These form a gradation with lexical items, and markers toward the nonlexical end of the scale are better analyzed as having an abstract or redundant meaning than none at all (cf. Langacker 1988). I have argued elsewhere (1987a, 1987c) that basic grammatical categories such as noun and verb can be attributed not only prototypical semantic values, but also highly abstract characterizations applicable to all class members. The same is true for such grammatical notions as subject, object, clause, subordination, and transitivity. Whereas a subject, for example, is prototypically both an agent and a topic, I believe that every subject is correctly described more abstractly as a clause-level figure (Langacker 1991, 1999b, 2001a). What about grammatical rules? These are just patterns for the integration of simpler symbolic structures to form progressively more complex ones. These patterns are themselves complex symbolic structures; they can be thought of as templates used for assembling and evaluating expressions. Structurally, such a template is directly parallel to the expressions it characterizes, but abstracts away from their points of divergence to reveal their schematic commonality.

This symbolic account of grammar presupposes an appropriate view of linguistic semantics. I assume, first, that meaning is correctly identified with conceptualization (or mental experience), in the broadest sense of that term. It includes, for example, both sensory and motor experience, as well as a speaker's conception of the social, cultural, and linguistic context. I further assume that linguistic semantics is properly regarded as being encyclopedic in scope (Haiman 1980; Langacker 1987a: chapter 4; cf. Wierzbicka 1995). There is no precise delimitation between semantics and pragmatics (or "linguistic" vs. "extralinguistic" knowledge).[3] As the basis for its meaning, an expression invokes an open-ended array of conceptions pertaining in some fashion to the entity it designates. Any facet of this knowledge (essentially anything we know about the entity) may prove important on a given occasion or for a specific linguistic purpose. Finally, I assume that meaning is critically dependent on construal, i.e. on our capacity for conceptualizing the same situation in alternate ways. Owing to construal, expressions that describe the same objective situation and convey the same conceptual content (or have the same truth conditions) can nevertheless be semantically quite distinct.

Numerous aspects of construal have been identified. One aspect is our ability to conceive of an entity at various levels of specificity and detail, as witnessed by hierarchies such as *thing* > *creature* > *insect* > *fly* > *fruit fly*, each term being schematic for the one that follows. With respect to their meanings, grammatical elements (including the templates describing grammatical constructions) cluster toward the schematic end of the spectrum, but crucially, this lack of semantic specificity is not the same as meaninglessness. A second aspect of construal is our capacity for conceptualizing one structure against the background provided by another. Under this heading fall such varied and essential phenomena as metaphor, presupposition, and discourse continuity. Three additional aspects of construal are especially significant for present purposes: scope, prominence, and perspective.

An expression's scope comprises the full array of conceptual content that it specifically evokes and relies upon for its characterization. Essential to the meaning of *lid*, for instance, is the schematic conception of a container, and also that of one object covering another. Likewise, the characterization of *knuckle* relies on the conception of a finger, while the latter in turn invokes the notion of a hand. The concept of a finger thus constitutes the immediate scope for *knuckle*, and the concept of a hand, its overall scope. Indirectly, of course, *knuckle*'s overall scope can further be thought of as including the conception of an arm and even the body as a whole (since hand evokes arm, and arm evokes body). An expression's scope need not, then, be sharply or precisely delimited. It must however be attributed not only a certain minimal inclusiveness but also some kind of bounding — it does not extend indefinitely (cf. Casad and Langacker 1985; Langacker 1993b, 1995, 2001b).

Of the various types of prominence having linguistic significance, two stand out as being especially important for grammatical structure. The first of these is profiling: within its scope (the array of conceptual content it evokes), every expression singles out a particular substructure as a kind of focal point; this substructure — the profile — can be characterized as the entity which the expression designates. For example, with respect to the conceived relationship involving a container and its cover, the noun *lid* profiles (designates) the cover, as shown in Figure 1(a). (Note that heavy lines indicate profiling.) Similarly, the verb *arrive* evokes the conception of an entity moving along a spatial path to a goal, but within that overall conception (its scope) it profiles only the final portion of the trajectory, as sketched in Figure 1(b). These examples illustrate a fundamental contrast between nominal and relational expressions. A nominal expression (such as a noun or pronoun) profiles a thing, given a highly abstract definition of that term (see Langacker 1987a: part II, 1987c). A relational expression (e.g. a verb, preposition, adjective, or adverb) profiles a relationship, also abstractly defined. For our purposes here, we can simply represent a thing by means of a circle, and a relationship by means of a line connecting the entities it associates, as shown in Figure 2(a).

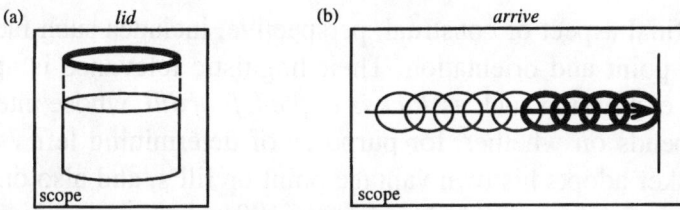

Figure 1. Profiling

A second type of prominence, which I analyze in terms of figure/ground organization, involves the participants in a relational expression. Consider the semantic contrast between *X is near Y* and *Y is near X*, which evoke the same conceptual content and profile the same relationship. What, then, is the nature of their difference? In *X is near Y*, the concern is with locating X — which is thus the figure within the profiled relationship — and Y is invoked as a reference point for this purpose. The reverse is true in *Y is near X*. Adopting the term trajector (tr) for the relational figure, and landmark (lm) for an additional salient participant, we can say that the two expressions impose alternate trajector/landmark alignments on the scene they invoke.[4] Their subtle semantic contrast does not reside in conceptual content (or truth conditions), but is rather a matter of construal (choice of relational figure). Expressions invoking the same conceptual content may also differ in meaning due to other aspects of construal, notably profiling. Thus, if Figure 2(a) represents the verb *employ*, we obtain the nouns *employer* and *employee* by restricting the profile to its trajector and landmark, respectively, as shown in (b) and (c). The imposition of these nominal profiles constitutes the semantic value of the suffixes *-er* and *-ee*.[5]

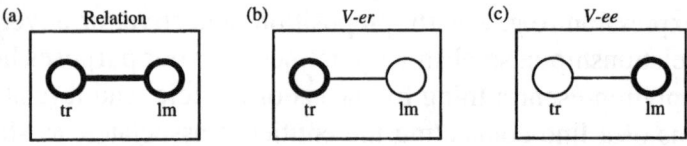

Figure 2. Trajector/landmark alignment

The final aspect of construal, perspective, includes such factors as vantage point and orientation. Their linguistic relevance is apparent from an expression such as *Jack is to the left of Jill*, whose interpretation depends on whether, for purposes of determining left vs. right, the speaker adopts his own vantage point or Jill's, and also on which way they are facing (cf. Vandeloise 1991; Casad and Langacker 1985). A related factor, subjectivity, will be the primary focus of our later discussion.

2. Nominals and finite clauses

A basic tenet of CG is that grammatical notions are susceptible to semantic characterization. For sake of discussion, let me simply take it as established that every noun profiles a thing (abstractly defined), whereas every verb designates a particular kind of relationship called a process (in which a profiled relation is followed sequentially in its evolution through time). The problem I want to address is how to characterize the related notions nominal (my term for "noun phrase"[6]) and finite clause. There is no disputing their fundamental linguistic importance — these constituent types figure prominently in the description of every language. Yet the nature and even the possibility of viable semantic definitions is less than obvious.

The problem can be posed in the following manner: what is the semantic distinction between, on the one hand, a simple noun like *dog*, and on the other, a full nominal such as *a dog*, *this shaggy dog*, *every dog*, or *the dog in the driveway*? Likewise, what semantic factor consistently distinguishes a simple verb stem like *jump* from a full finite clause such as *He jumped, He will jump, He might not jump*, or *Jump!*? It is not a matter of profiling. If we consider a simple noun (*dog*), an intermediate-level structure (*shaggy dog*), and a full nominal (*this shaggy dog*), we find that each of them profiles a thing. By the same token, the verb *jump* and the finite clause *He jumped* are alike in that each profiles a process. The semantic basis for these distinctions must therefore lie elsewhere.

I suggest that, whereas a simple noun or verb stem merely specifies a type, a full nominal or finite clause designates a grounded instance of that type. Of the terms that figure in this definition, I will not say much here about the type/instance distinction (see Langacker 1991 for extensive discussion). Let me simply note that, by itself, a noun like *dog* fails even to evoke a specific number of instances. For example, the compound *dog hater* does not specifically indicate whether one or multiple dogs are involved, let alone refer to any particular instance of the *dog* category. A noun or a verb stem serves only the minimal semantic function of providing an initial type specification, which undergoes refinement, adjustment, and quantification at higher levels of organization in the assembly of a nominal or a finite clause. Grounding constitutes the final, criterial step in their assembly. The essential property of a nominal or a finite clause is that it not only profiles an instance of the thing or process type in question, but indicates the status of this instance vis-à-vis the ground.

I use the term ground for the speech event, its participants, and its immediate circumstances. In one way or another, the elements that serve a grounding function specify the relationship between some facet of the ground and the entity profiled by the nominal or clause. For nominals in English, grounding elements include demonstratives (*this, that, these, those*), articles (*the, a,* unstressed *some,* zero), and certain quantifiers (*all, most, some, no, any, every, each*). One aspect of the grounding relationship they express is either definiteness or indefiniteness, where definiteness implies (roughly) that the speaker and hearer have both succeeded in establishing mental contact with the profiled thing instance (i.e. they have singled it out for individual conscious awareness).[7] For English finite clauses, the grounding elements are tense (so-called "present" and "past") and the modals (*may, will, shall, can, must*). The former specify whether or not the designated process is immediate to the ground (either temporally or in a more abstract sense), while the absence vs. the presence of a modal indicates whether this process belongs to reality (where the ground is located) or is merely potential.

3. Deixis and grounding

A deictic expression can be characterized as one that includes the ground within its scope. Grounding elements are therefore deictic in nature, since they specify a relationship between some facet of the ground and the nominal or processual profile. However, not every deictic expression serves a grounding function in the sense of being criterial to the formation of a nominal or a finite clause. The adverb *now*, for instance, is deictic because it makes reference to the time of speaking, but a clause is not rendered finite by its presence; note its occurrence as part of an infinitival complement: *She would really like to be here now*. We thus face the task of ascertaining what is special about grounding elements. What is it that distinguishes them from other deictic expressions and makes them capable of deriving a finite clause or a nominal?

Deictic expressions can be classified in various ways. One basis for classification is the nature of their profile: a deictic element can profile either a thing or a relationship. In fact, many deictic expressions can assume both nominal and relational values, representing different grammatical classes accordingly. Consider *yesterday*, which has both nominal and adverbial function. Its nominal meaning (as in *Yesterday was pleasant*, or *I thought of yesterday*) is depicted in Figure 3(a). As a noun, *yesterday* evokes the conception of a sequence of days extending through time (t) and profiles (designates) the day immediately prior to the one containing the ground (G). When *yesterday* is used adverbially (e.g. *It arrived yesterday*), it has the value sketched in Figure 3(b). It evokes essentially the same conceptual content as in its nominal use, but profiles the relationship between some event (e.g. *It arrived*) and the day in question, which respectively serve as trajector and landmark. Observe, however, that *yesterday* is deictic in either capacity by virtue of invoking the ground as a point of reference.[8]

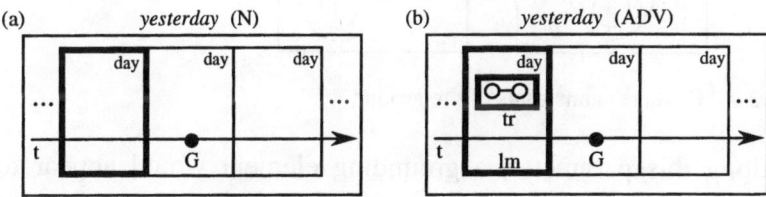

Figure 3. Nominal and relational construal

An alternate basis for classification is the salience of the ground's role within the conception that constitutes a deictic element's meaning. An expression that does not invoke the ground at all is of course nondeictic for that very reason; considered in isolation, a simple noun or verb (e.g. *dog* or *jump*) has this character. The ground does fall within the scope of expressions like *yesterday*, but there it remains implicit and nonsalient, serving only as an "offstage" reference point. It can however be put "onstage" and made a specific focus of attention. One option is for some facet of the ground to be singled out as the profile of a nominal expression; examples include the pronouns *I* and *you*, as well as *here* and *now* in their nominal uses. The pronoun *you* is sketched in Figure 4(a), where S and H represent the speaker and hearer, and the dashed-line rectangle delimits the onstage region. A second option is for a ground element to function as one of the focal participants in a relational expression (i.e. as its trajector or primary landmark). Thus a prepositional phrase like *near you* involves the configuration diagrammed in Figure 4(b). Finally, the speech event itself can go onstage as the process designated by a finite clause, as shown in 4(c). That is the distinguishing property of an explicit performative (e.g. *I order you to desist!*).

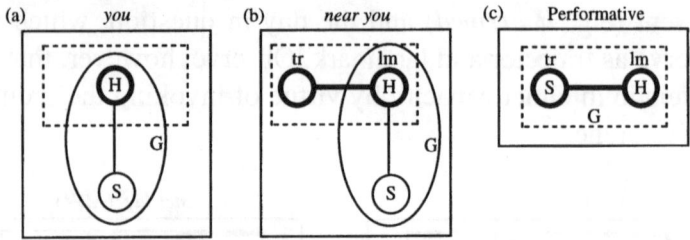

Figure 4. "Onstage" construals of the ground

Along this parameter, a grounding element would appear to be most similar to expressions like *yesterday*. A demonstrative or tense marker, for example, certainly does include the ground within its scope, but it is not explicitly mentioned nor is it particularly salient — rather than being profiled (as in the case of *you*, *now*, or *here*), the ground remains implicit and serves as a reference point. Yet a word like *yesterday* is insufficient by itself to ground a clause in the sense of making it finite. Observe the felicity of using it to modify an infinitival clause: *I would like **to have finished** yesterday*. We must therefore address the question of why certain expressions invoking the ground as an offstage reference point function as grounding elements while others do not. What is it that crucially distinguishes *yesterday*, for instance, from the past-tense morpheme?

A true grounding element, I suggest, is grammatical rather than lexical in nature and has a particular kind of meaning.[9] Like other grammatical elements, grounding expressions tend to be abstract and schematic semantically, and to have a "relativistic" or "topological" nature as opposed to indicating a specific shape or value (cf. Talmy 1988). Moreover, their characterization pertains to fundamental cognitive notions whose import is not unreasonably described as "epistemic": notions such as reality, time, immediacy, and mental contact. Thus the definite article specifies mental contact by the speaker and hearer, while the demonstratives make a further specification regarding proximity. The presence or absence of a modal indicates whether a process falls within reality. The opposition between "present" and "past" tense is best analyzed in terms of whether a process is immediate to the ground or distant in either time or reality (see Langacker

1991: chapter 6). By contrast, *yesterday* invokes a higher-order conceptual structure and has more of a metric character. It presupposes a conception involving a succession of days — a series of discrete metric units superimposed on the temporal axis — and confines a process to one specific unit within the sequence (whereas the past-tense morpheme merely indicates removal from the time of speaking, or at most temporal anteriority).

Grounding elements can therefore be distinguished from words like *yesterday* owing to their grammatical status and the nature of their conceptual content. There are however other expressions that seem quite comparable in terms of conceptual content yet do not serve a grounding function. For example, *possible* offers a reasonable paraphrase for the modal *may* (in its epistemic value). Likewise, *before now* would appear to be equivalent to a past-tense morpheme. And for the two components of the demonstrative *this*, namely definiteness and proximity to the speaker, the glosses *known to us* and *near me* may at least be in the ballpark. Despite their apparent semantic equivalence, these expressions show very different grammatical behavior from the corresponding grounding elements. The reason, I will argue, is that they are not in fact semantically equivalent. Even if we attribute to them precisely the same conceptual content, they nonetheless differ in meaning by virtue of how they construe that content. We will see that the crucial factors are profiling, subjectivity, and the salience accorded the ground. Especially interesting are the interrelationships among these factors.

4. Grammatical behavior

At least five grammatical properties are characteristic of grounding elements and collectively distinguish them from other kinds of expression, including their seeming paraphrases. In CG, such properties are taken as being symptomatic of underlying conceptual differences. The first two properties suggest a difference in profiling. The remaining three pertain to subjectivity.

Property 1: Strikingly, the expressions that come to mind as paraphrases of grounding elements are headed by adjectives, prepositions, and participles. These are all analyzed in CG as belonging to the broad class of what I will call atemporal expressions, which are distinguished by their profiles from both nouns and verbs.[10] As shown in (1), atemporal expressions are typically able to follow the verb *be* as the lexical head of a clause:

(1)a. *That they will ultimately prevail is **possible**.*
   b. *Probably the filing deadline was **before now**.*
   c. *The culprit is **known to us** and **near me**.*

However, the corresponding grounding elements cannot occur in the same position:[11]

(2)a. **That they will ultimately prevail is **may**.*
   b. **Probably the filing deadline was **-ed**.*
   c. **The culprit is **this**.*

Note further that many quantifiers serve as clausal heads, as in (3a), but we see from (3b) that the ones identified as grounding elements cannot:

(3)a. *His problems are {few/many/three/several}.*
   b. **His problems are {all/most/some/each/every/any/no}.*

From these observations, we may draw the conclusion that the grounding elements are not atemporal expressions (i.e. they do not profile atemporal relations).

Property 2: Many grounding elements are capable of functioning as nominal or clausal pro forms. For example, *this* can stand alone as a full nominal with possible anaphoric reference (e.g. *This bothers him a lot*). The same is true of *all, most, some, each, any*, and the other demonstratives. By the same token, the modals can stand alone as finite clauses (except that they are not immune to the general requirement that a finite clause have an overt subject): *She may; They must*; *You should*. The proper conclusion is that a grounding element is itself either a schematic nominal, in which case it profiles a thing, or else a schematic finite clause, which implies a processual profile.

Taken together, properties 1 and 2 motivate the analysis sketched in Figure 5. A pivotal feature of the account is that a grounding element profiles only the *grounded entity*, not the *grounding relationship*. The grounded entity is a thing or process that corresponds to the profile of the nominal or clausal head. In the nominal *this dog*, for instance, the profile of *this* corresponds to that of the head noun *dog*, and in the clause *She jumped*, the process designated by the past-tense morpheme is equated with *jump*. The grounding element itself is highly schematic in regard to the profiled thing or process — its essential content resides in the grounding relationship (R_g) that locates the profiled entity vis-à-vis the ground (e.g. a relationship of definiteness, proximity, or temporal anteriority). But like the ground itself, the grounding relationship remains offstage and unprofiled. It is only the grounded entity, the one whose epistemic status in relation to the ground is being specified, that goes onstage as the focus of attention.

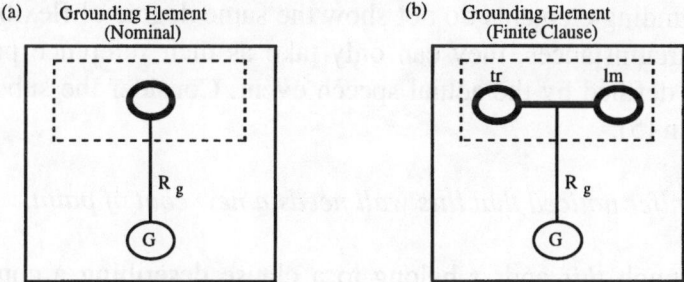

Figure 5. Nominal and clausal grounding

Property 3: A grounding element does not specifically mention the ground, despite invoking it as a reference point. In contrast to such paraphrases as *before now*, *near me*, and *known to us*, a grounding element does not explicitly refer to any facet of the ground (e.g. the speaker, the addressee, or the time of speaking) and cannot be made to do so. Observe, for example, that the reference points of *near* and *known* can either remain covert or be spelled out overtly by a first- or second-person pronoun: *It is near* vs. *It is near me*; *a nearby store* vs. *a store near us*; *a known criminal* vs. *a criminal known to us*. However, a demonstrative does not take a complement that would specify its reference points. There is no direct way to expand a nominal such as *this dog* to allow explicit mention of the speaker and hearer: **this me dog*; **this (to) us dog*; **(the) dog this me*; **(the) dog this (to) us*.[12]

Property 4: Many expressions that take the ground as a default reference point allow some other entity to assume this function in particular circumstances. Thus, whereas *across the street* in (4a) is interpreted as meaning across the street from the speaker, and *immediately* as referring to the time just subsequent to the time of speaking, in (4b) these same expressions take as their reference points the main-clause subject (*Jennifer*) and the time of the main-clause verb (*notice*):

(4)a. *The shop **across the street** is going to close **immediately**.*
   b. *Jennifer noticed that the shop **across the street** was going to close **immediately**.*

Grounding elements do not show the same degree of flexibility. In most circumstances, they can only take as their reference point the ground defined by the actual speech event. Consider the subordinate clause in (5):

(5) *Jennifer noticed that **this** wall needs a new coat of paint.*

Although *this* and *-s* belong to a clause describing a conception entertained by the main-clause subject, it is not Jennifer and her perception that they invoke as reference points, but rather the actual speaker and the time of his utterance. The wall in question must be in proximity to the actual speaker (Jennifer's present location being irrelevant), and the situation of its needing a new coat of paint is construed as extending through the actual time of speaking.

Property 5: The final property is the one with which we started, namely that a grounding element (which may be zero phonologically) is prerequisite to the formation of a nominal or a finite clause. From a noun like *dog*, for instance, a full nominal can be derived just by adding a demonstrative (e.g. *this dog*), but not its relational paraphrase — to constitute a nominal, *dog near me and known to us* still requires grounding.

If properties 1 and 2 reflect the basic structure of grounding elements, the remaining properties raise more fundamental questions: Why do they have such a structure? What is the nature of the grounding function? The key to the matter is the notion of subjectivity, to which we now turn.

5. Subjectivity

I will use the terms subjective, objective, and their derivatives in special, technical senses that are most easily described and understood in regard to perception. They pertain to the inherent asymmetry between the roles of subject and object of perception, i.e. between the perceiving individual and the entity being perceived. Diagrammed in Figure 6 is a canonical viewing arrangement, which has the following components: V is the viewer; the box corresponds to the visual field, and thus encompasses the full range of perception at any given moment; the dashed rectangle indicates the general locus of viewing attention (the onstage region); P is the perceived entity, the specific focus of attention; and the dashed arrow represents the perceptual relationship. Suppose, now, that the respective roles of V and P as the subject and object of perception are maximally asymmetrical. This is so when (i) V and P are wholly distinct; (ii) P is sharply delimited and perceived with full acuity; and (iii) V's attention is directed outward, so that he does not perceive himself in any way — V is exclusively the subject of perception, not at all its object. With respect to this ideally asymmetrical viewing arrangement, I say that V construes P with maximal objectivity, and construes himself with maximal subjectivity.

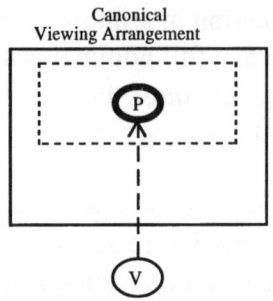

Figure 6. Canonical viewing arrangement

Thus subjective and objective construal are respectively characteristic of the entities serving as the source of a perceptual path and as its target. An entity is construed objectively to the extent that it is external yet fully accessible to the perceiver, and salient by virtue of being put onstage as the specific focus of viewing attention. On the other hand, the viewer is construed subjectively when he directs his gaze outward and focuses exclusively on an external region, so that he himself is left offstage and unperceived; although his role is crucial to the perceptual relationship, the viewer remains implicit and nonsalient for essentially the same reason that a flashlight fails to illuminate itself, and the eyeballs can never see themselves directly. There are, of course, many kinds of departure from this idealized viewing arrangement, each having some effect on the degree of subjectivity/objectivity with which the participating entities are construed. For example, if I glance down and look at myself (as best I can), the object of perception receives a less objective construal than when I attend to an external object. Or suppose that I am watching a television monitor, and being televised doing so, with the picture being fed to that same monitor. The effect of this special viewing arrangement is to objectify both the perceptual relationship and my own (normally subjective) role within it, with the consequence that both are objectively construed.

Our concern here is with conception overall, not just the special case of perception. I believe, however, that the foregoing perceptual notions all instantiate general conceptual phenomena which have substantial linguistic import (Langacker 1995, 2001b; cf. Talmy 1996). The conceptualizations that interest us are the meanings of linguistic expressions. The relevant conceptualizers are thus the speaker and the addressee. Moreover, the viewing arrangement depicted in Figure 6 can be given a linguistic interpretation, such that each element corresponds to a particular linguistic construct. Corresponding to the viewer (V) are the speaker and hearer, whose conceptualization of an expression's meaning is represented by the dashed arrow. The solid-line box delimits the expression's overall scope, and the dashed rectangle, its immediate scope. Lastly, P can be identified as the expression's profile, which is by definition the focal point in its immediate scope.

The notions subjectivity and objectivity also have a general conceptual interpretation, with respect to which their perceptual manifestation constitutes a special case. An entity is construed objectively to the extent that it is distinct from the conceptualizer and is put onstage as a salient object of conception. Being the focal point within the onstage region, an expression's profile has a high degree of objectivity. An entity receives a subjective construal to the extent that it functions as the subject of conception but not as the object. The highest degree of subjectivity thus attaches to the speaker and hearer, specifically in regard to those expressions that do not in any way include them within their scope. Of course, they only achieve this maximal subjectivity in simple or fragmentary expressions, such as a noun or a verb taken in isolation (*dog*; *jump*). By virtue of grounding, any expression that contains a full nominal or a finite clause necessarily has the ground within its scope, with the consequence that its subjectivity is in some measure diminished (cf. Figures 5 and 6). Let me suggest, however, that with grounding elements this diminution is quite minimal. An important characteristic of grounding elements is that, although they necessarily invoke the ground in some fashion, they construe the ground with the highest degree of subjectivity consistent with its inclusion in their scope. By recognizing this essential property of grounding elements, we can start to explain their grammatical behavior.

Properties 1 and 2 follow from the generalization that a grounding element profiles the grounded entity rather than the grounding relationship. This in turn is a consequence of the fact that a grounding element construes the ground itself with maximal subjectivity (given that the ground falls within its scope). Suppose one did attempt to profile the relationship (R_g) between the grounded entity and the subjectively construed ground. The resulting configuration, diagrammed in Figure 7, turns out to be impermissible when one considers the characterizations of certain constructs. The profile necessarily has a highly objective construal, for it is characterized as the focus of attention within the onstage region. Moreover, the trajector and landmark of a relational expression are focal points within its profile, so that they too are highly salient and objectively construed. It would therefore be contradictory for the ground to serve as the landmark of such a relationship and at the same time to be offstage and construed with extreme subjectivity. Hence the ground's subjectivity entails the configuration of Figure 5, where only the grounded entity is onstage and in profile.

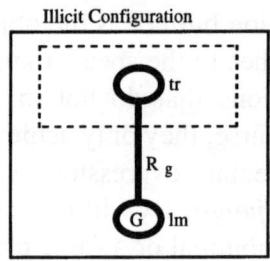

Figure 7. Illicit grounding configuration

Property 3 — the failure of grounding elements to take complements that mention the ground explicitly (e.g. **this {me/[to] us} dog*) — also follows directly from the ground's subjectivity. I have argued elsewhere (1985) that entities construed subjectively tend to be left implicit, because explicit mention has an objectifying impact. Hence the sentences in (6) are semantically distinct, even assuming that in (6b) the locative reference point is known with certainty to be the speaker:

(6)a. *Mulroney was sitting across the table from me.*
b. *Mulroney was sitting across the table.*

Whereas (6a) describes the scene in more or less neutral terms, and is quite compatible with an external vantage point (as in describing a photograph), (6b) is more readily construed as portraying the scene from the speaker's vantage point within it (i.e. as describing what the speaker actually saw at the time), which makes his role a subjective one. Granted this correlation between implicitness and subjective construal, property 3 is both motivated and predicted: the ground cannot simultaneously be mentioned overtly and construed with maximal subjectivity.

The contrast in (6) underscores the importance of perspective to semantic and grammatical structure, and suggests that the ground should perhaps be taken — almost in a literal sense — as the vantage point from which a scene is viewed. Certainly I regard it as the vantage from which a scene is conceptualized, primarily by the speaker and secondarily by the hearer. A sentence will have rather limited communicative utility unless the situation it describes is somehow related to these conceptualizers. To accomplish more than simply evoking a situation type as an abstract contemplative exercise (e.g. *girl like cat*), a sentence must specify the epistemic status vis-à-vis the ground of both the profiled relationship and its central participants (as in *The girl liked the cat, A girl likes this cat, Any girl would like that cat, No girl can like any cat,* and so on). Grounding elements serve this function, and by doing so they necessarily extend an expression's scope to encompass the ground, even when the speaker and hearer are solely concerned with the external situation. To the extent that their own role is limited to this grounding function, the conceptualizers construe themselves subjectively from the scope's periphery as they direct their attention to the objective situation onstage.

These notions afford the basis for understanding properties 4 and 5. Property 5 — that grounding is prerequisite to the formation of a nominal or a finite clause — is partly just a matter of definition: nominal and finite clause are simply the terms that we apply to grounded constituents. There remains, however, the question of why such constituents should be both universal and central to grammatical structure. The answer lies in the fundamental importance of the grounding function. It is of great cognitive and communicative utility to the conceptualizers to relate a situation to their own circumstances, whereas merely contemplating a situation type in the abstract, with no indication of its epistemic status, is essentially pointless.

Property 4 is the fact (illustrated in [5]) that the grounding relationship is anchored by the actual speaker and speech event even in a finite clause describing the conception entertained by another individual. Let us first note that such a conception is also entertained by the speaker — it represents his own conception, construed from his own vantage point, of what someone else conceives of. Why should the speaker construe it from his own vantage point, instead of adopting that of the other conceptualizer? We can plausibly speculate that maintaining a common deictic center, defined by the "here-and-now" of the speech event, is essential to the coherence of a complex sentence. Were the deictic center to shift on a clause-by-clause basis, always reflecting the vantage of the last conceptualizer introduced (or the one whose conception is being described), keeping things straight might be extremely difficult in a sentence of even moderate complexity. The speaker and hearer need to establish a coherent view of a complex situation involving multiple perspectives. The easiest way to do so is by directly assessing — from their own vantage point — the basic epistemic status of each profiled process and major participant (rather than jumping repeatedly from one perspective to another). By viewing each salient entity from this stable platform, they impose a fundamental reference frame which enables them to keep track of those shifts of perspective that do occur.

6. Subjectification

Having shown the linguistic significance of subjectivity, let me now call attention to its diachronic relevance. Many instances of semantic change involve subjectification, whereby some notion that is originally construed objectively undergoes a kind of semantic "bleaching", leaving behind a comparable notion, subjectively construed, that was originally immanent in the objective conception. In particular, subjectification often figures in the semantic evolution of grammatical elements from their lexical origins (Langacker 1990b, 1999d).[13]

For an initial example, consider two senses of the preposition *across*. Figure 8(a) diagrams the meaning of *across* in a sentence such as *Mulroney jumped across the table*, in which the trajector traces a spatial path leading from one side of the landmark object to the other.

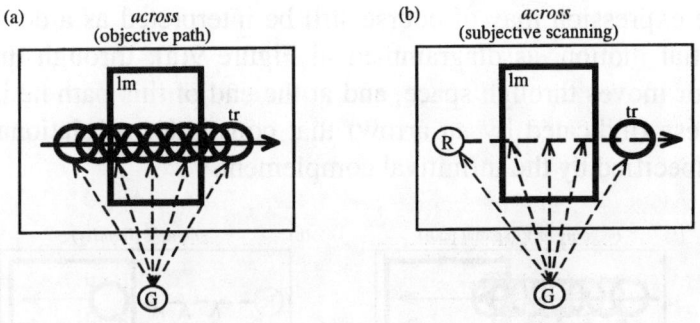

Figure 8. Objective and subjective construal

The speaker construes this path objectively; he conceives of the trajector (also objective) occupying each successive position along it, as indicated by the dashed arrows. Diagrammed in Figure 8(b), on the other hand, is the meaning that *across* assumes in a sentence like (6b), *Mulroney was sitting across the table*. Here there is no objective motion or path — the trajector's position is static vis-à-vis the landmark. Subjective analogs of these notions can however be discerned. In lieu of the subject (or trajector) moving objectively along a path, the speaker (or conceptualizer) follows the same path subjectively: he traces along it mentally in order to specify the trajector's location with respect to some reference point (R). Of course, this subjective motion by the speaker was there all along, immanent in the speaker's conception of the subject's objective motion. It becomes more evident when the original objective conception fades away, so that only this mental scanning remains.

The role of subjectification in grammaticization (i.e. the evolution of grammatical morphemes) is exemplified by the well-attested phenomenon of verbs meaning 'go' evolving into markers of futurity (cf. Givón 1973; Bybee and Pagliuca 1987; Langacker 1986). Illustration is afforded by either the French example in (7) or its English translation:

(7) *Il va fermer la porte.*
 'He is going to close the door.'

The expression may of course still be interpreted as a description of spatial motion, as diagrammed in Figure 9(a): through time, the trajector moves through space, and at the end of this path he initiates a process (indicated by an arrow) that constitutes a relational landmark specified by the infinitival complement.

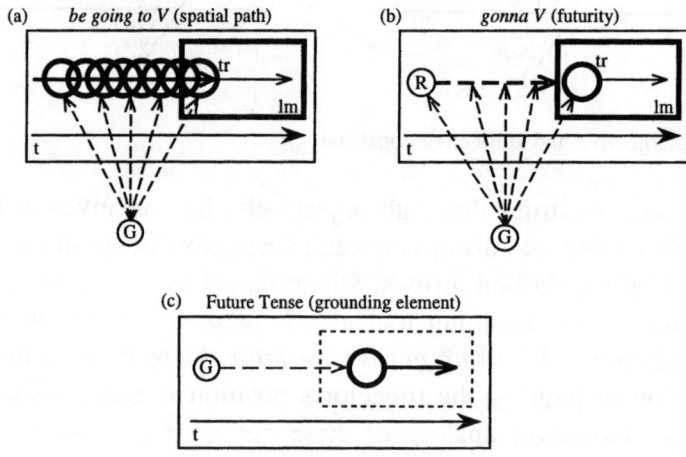

Figure 9. Grammaticization and clausal grounding

More likely, however, is the 'gonna' sense depicted in 9(b), which comes about through subjectification of the sort just described. The conception of the subject moving through space fades from the picture. What remains, originally immanent in this conception, is the conceptualizer's mental scanning through time up to the time of the landmark process. By tracing subjectively along this path, the conceptualizer situates the infinitival process with respect to a temporal reference point (R).

It should be noted that French *aller* and English *gonna* are not grounding elements, even with their future value — they are themselves main verbs that require grounding to form a finite clause. Observe that the temporal reference point (R) need not coincide with the time of speaking:

(8)*Il allait fermer la porte.*
 'He was going to close the door.'

Moreover, Figure 9(b) indicates that the future 'go' profiles the relationship of temporal posteriority, whereas a true grounding element profiles the grounded entity instead of the grounding relationship. An actual future-tense grounding element, as in *Il finira* 'He will finish', has the form sketched in 9(c). The reference point is specifically identified with the ground, and the profiled entity is not the relationship of posteriority but rather the temporally posterior process itself (cf. Figure 5[b]). The evolution leading from 9(b) to 9(c) amounts to a further subjectification. R becomes more subjective by being equated with G, and as a consequence, the temporal relationship it anchors winds up offstage and hence unprofiled.

7. Conclusion

By way of conclusion, I wish to emphasize the critical importance to linguistic structure of our multifaceted capacity for construing a conceived situation in alternate ways. Certain aspects of construal — such as profiling, scope, and perspective — have both synchronic and diachronic relevance, and are not just semantically significant but have a pivotal role in grammatical structure. A subtle yet crucial aspect of perspective is the possibility of an entity receiving a subjective construal, analogously to a viewer whose gaze is directed outward so that he himself remains unseen. It seems quite natural that subjectivity should figure in the characterization of deictic elements, for these make reference to the speaker and hearer, who serve as viewers (or conceptualizers) with respect to the meanings of linguistic expressions. In particular, the speech-event participants receive a subjective construal in grounding elements, which are essential to the formation of nominals and finite clauses.

Notes

1. This paper is a slightly revised and updated version of Langacker (1993a).
2. The first accessible presentation of the framework was Langacker (1982). For a comprehensive description, see Langacker (1987a, 1990a, 1991, 1999a). References provided in these volumes lead to what is now a vast CG literature.
3. Judging from their misinterpretation by Levinson (1997), my comments on this point have evidently lacked sufficient clarity. It is not denied that pragmatics exists, and that many pragmatic phenomena are "extralinguistic". It is only denied that a precise boundary can be drawn nonarbitrarily in any particular place. It seems to me that a noncircular delimitation of what counts as "linguistic" has to depend on two factors: the extent to which something is familiar to speakers (entrenchment) and established in a speech community (conventionalization). Since both factors are matters of degree, we must recognize a gradation leading from what is definitely linguistic to what is definitely nonlinguistic.
4. The notions subject and object are special cases of trajector and landmark. Whereas subject and object pertain primarily to participants in the relationship profiled at the clausal level, trajector/landmark asymmetry is characteristic of relational expressions at any level of organization.
5. This is, of course, just a first approximation. For more extensive and detailed descriptions, see Barker (1998), Ryder (1991), and Panther and Thornburg (2001).
6. Though well entrenched, the term noun phrase is inappropriate: a nominal need not contain any element traditionally regarded as a noun (consider *this, you, any two, those working steadily*), and its phrasal character is inessential (it may consist of a single word or a full clause).

7. With certain nominal expressions, notably personal pronouns and proper names, a specification of this sort is intrinsic. Such expressions can therefore function as full nominals without incorporating a separate grounding element.
8. Other examples include *today, tomorrow, {next/last} {week/month/year}, now, then, here, there*, and the names of the days of the week. It is worth investigating an alternative account that does not posit relational variants of these elements, but rather describes them as elaborating settings or locations evoked as part of clausal frames (Langacker 1987b, 1993b, 1999c). This would not affect the analysis of grounding elements.
9. I do not mean to imply a rigid dichotomy between lexical and grammatical elements, nor that grounding elements constitute a homogeneous or sharply delimited class. The characterization is aimed specifically at exemplars plausibly considered prototypical.
10. A noun profiles a thing, whereas both verbs and atemporal expressions designate relationships. The difference between a verb and an atemporal expression is that the former profiles a process, comprising a series of component states scanned sequentially along the temporal axis. An atemporal expression profiles a relationship that is atemporal in that it is not scanned sequentially along the temporal axis (hence it is nonprocessual). (See Langacker 1986, 1987a, 1987c.)
11. Sentence (2b) is bad even ignoring the morphological peccadillo of leaving a suffix unattached (observe that *do* support does not help: **Probably the filing deadline was did*). In the case of (2c), *this* must be interpreted as a relational expression analogous to *known to us and near me*. It is true but irrelevant that the sentence is marginally acceptable when *this* is construed instead as a predicate nominative.
12. Explicit mention can of course be achieved indirectly via periphrasis (e.g. *this dog near me*). What matters is that a grounding element does not itself take a complement expressing its reference point.
13. My use of the term subjectification is not equivalent to Traugott's (e.g. 1982, 1989), although they are not unrelated (and both are valid). In her sense, subjectification pertains to the cognitive domain in which an expression is interpreted, whereas in my sense, it pertains to perspective.

References

Barker, Chris
    1998   Episodic *-ee* in English: A thematic role constraint on new word formations. *Language* 74: 695–727.

Bybee, Joan L. and William Pagliuca
    1987   The evolution of future meaning. In: Anna Giacalone Ramat, Onofrio Carruba and Giuliano Bernini (eds.), *Papers from the 7th International Conference on Historical Linguistics*, 109–122. Amsterdam: John Benjamins.

Casad, Eugene H. and Ronald W. Langacker
    1985   'Inside' and 'outside' in Cora grammar. *International Journal of American Linguistics* 51: 247–281.

Givón, Talmy
    1973   The time-axis phenomenon. *Language* 49: 890–925.

Haiman, John
    1980   Dictionaries and encyclopedias. *Lingua* 50: 329–357.

Langacker, Ronald W.
    1982   Space grammar, analysability, and the English passive. *Language* 58: 22–80.
    1985   Observations and speculations on subjectivity. In: John Haiman (ed.), *Iconicity in Syntax*, 109–150. (Typological Studies in Language 6.) Amsterdam: John Benjamins.
    1986   Abstract motion. In: Vassiliki Nikiforidou, Mary VanClay, Mary Niepokuj and Deborah Feder (eds.), *Proceedings of the Twelfth Annual Meeting of the Berkeley Linguistics Society*, 455–471. Berkeley: Berkeley Linguistics Society.
    1987a   *Foundations of Cognitive Grammar*, Volume 1: *Theoretical Prerequisites*. Stanford: Stanford University Press.
    1987b   Grammatical ramifications of the setting/participant distinction. In: Jon Aske, Natasha Beery, Laura Michaelis and Hana Filip (eds.), *Proceedings of the Thirteenth Annual Meeting of the Berkeley Linguistics Society*, 383–394. Berkeley: Berkeley Linguistics Society.
    1987c   Nouns and verbs. *Language* 63: 53–94.
    1988   Autonomy, agreement, and cognitive grammar. In: Diane Brentari, Gary Larson and Lynn MacLeod (eds.), *Agreement in Grammatical Theory*, 147–180. Chicago: Chicago Linguistic Society.
    1990a   *Concept, Image, and Symbol: The Cognitive Basis of Grammar*. (Cognitive Linguistics Research 1.) Berlin: Mouton de Gruyter.
    1990b   Subjectification. *Cognitive Linguistics* 1: 5–38.
    1991   *Foundations of Cognitive Grammar*, Volume 2: *Descriptive Application*. Stanford: Stanford University Press.
    1993a   Deixis and subjectivity. In: S. K. Verma and V. Prakasam (eds.), *New Horizons in Functional Linguistics*, 43–58. Hyderabad: Booklinks.
    1993b   Grammatical traces of some "invisible" semantic constructs. *Language Sciences* 15: 323–355.

1995 Viewing in cognition and grammar. In: Philip W. Davis (ed.), *Alternative Linguistics: Descriptive and Theoretical Modes*, 153–212. (Current Issues in Linguistic Theory 102.) Amsterdam: John Benjamins.
1999a *Grammar and Conceptualization*. (Cognitive Linguistics Research 14.) Berlin: Mouton de Gruyter.
1999b Assessing the cognitive linguistic enterprise. In: Theo Janssen and Gisela Redeker (eds.), *Cognitive Linguistics: Foundations, Scope, and Methodology*, 13–59. (Cognitive Linguistics Research 15.) Berlin: Mouton de Gruyter.
1999c A study in unified diversity: English and Mixtec locatives. *RASK* 9/10: 215–256. Also published in: Jacob L. Mey and Andrzej Boguslawski (eds.), *"E Pluribus Una": The One in the Many (For Anna Wierzbicka)*. Odense: Odense University Press.
1999d Losing control: Grammaticization, subjectification, and transparency. In: Andreas Blank and Peter Koch (eds.), *Historical Semantics and Cognition*, 147–175. (Cognitive Linguistics Research 13.) Berlin: Mouton de Gruyter.
2001a Topic, subject, and possessor. In: Hanne Gram Simonsen and Rolf Theil Endresen (eds.), *A Cognitive Approach to the Verb: Morphological and Constructional Perspectives*, 11–48. (Cognitive Linguistics Research 16.) Berlin: Mouton de Gruyter.
2001b Viewing and experiential reporting in cognitive grammar. In: Augusto Soares da Silva (ed.), *Linguagem e cognição: A perspectiva da linguística cognitiva*, 19–49. Braga: Associação Portuguesa de Linguística and Universidade Católica Portuguesa, Faculdade de Filosofia de Braga.

Levinson, Stephen C.
1997 From outer to inner space: Linguistic categories and non-linguistic thinking. In: Jan Nuyts and Eric Pederson (eds.), *Language and Conceptualization*, 13–45. (Language, Culture and Cognition 1.) Cambridge: Cambridge University Press.

Panther, Klaus-Uwe and Linda L. Thornburg
2001 A conceptual analysis of English *-er* nominals. In: Martin Pütz, Susanne Niemeier and René Dirven (eds.), *Applied Cognitive Linguistics*, Volume 2: *Language Pedagogy*, 149–200. (Cognitive Linguistics Research 19.2.) Berlin: Mouton de Gruyter.

Ryder, Mary Ellen
    1991   Mixers, mufflers and mousers: The extending of the *-er* suffix as a case of prototype reanalysis. In: Laurel A. Sutton and Christopher Johnson with Ruth Shields (eds.), *Proceedings of the Seventeenth Annual Meeting of the Berkeley Linguistics Society*, 299–311. Berkeley: Berkeley Linguistics Society.

Talmy, Leonard
    1988   The relation of grammar to cognition. In: Brygida Rudzka-Ostyn (ed.), *Topics in Cognitive Linguistics*, 165–205. Amsterdam: John Benjamins.
    1996   Fictive motion in language and "ception". In: Paul Bloom, Mary A. Peterson, Lynn Nadel and Merrill F. Garrett (eds.), *Language and Space*, 211–276. Cambridge, MA: MIT Press.

Traugott, Elizabeth
    1982   From propositional to textual and expressive meanings: Some semantic-pragmatic aspects of grammaticalization. In: Winfred P. Lehmann and Yakov Malkiel (eds.), *Perspectives on Historical Linguistics*, 245–271. Amsterdam: John Benjamins.
    1989   On the rise of epistemic meanings in English: An example of subjectification in semantic change. *Language* 65: 31–55.

Vandeloise, Claude
    1991   *Spatial Prepositions: A Case Study from French*. Chicago: University of Chicago Press.

Wierzbicka, Anna
    1995   Dictionaries vs. encyclopaedias: How to draw the line. In: Philip W. Davis (ed.), *Alternative Linguistics: Descriptive and Theoretical Modes*, 289–315. (Current Issues in Linguistic Theory 102.) Amsterdam: John Benjamins.

Remarks on the English grounding systems
Ronald W. Langacker

Following Chafe (1970: 96), I consider nouns and verbs to be conceptually based universal categories of fundamental linguistic importance. Each projects to a higher-level constituent — a nominal (i.e. noun phrase) and a finite clause — that is likewise both basic and universal. As analyzed in cognitive grammar (Langacker 1987a, 1987b, 1990a, 1991), the internal organization of these constituents shows extensive parallelism. A noun profiles (i.e. designates) a thing and a verb profiles a process (each in an abstract sense of the term). By itself, however, a simple noun or verb merely specifies a thing or process type, whereas a full nominal or finite clause designates a grounded instance of that type.

The term ground is used for the speech event, its participants, and its immediate circumstances. A nominal or a finite clause incorporates some element which specifies a relationship between the ground and the thing or process it designates. There may be a number of such elements, all describable as "deictic", but the ones identified as grounding predications have certain additional properties. First, grounding predications constitute a small set of highly grammaticized elements, one of which has to be chosen as the final step in forming a full nominal or finite clause. Second, their specification of how the designated thing or process relates to the ground involves some very basic notions reasonably considered "epistemic" in nature: notions such as time, reality, immediacy, and identification (i.e. the "mental contact" established by directed attention). Third, grounding predications profile (designate) the grounded entity rather than the grounding relationship which provides their essential conceptual content. The demonstrative *this*, for example, does not profile the relationship of identification and of proximity to the speaker, despite their importance to its meaning; what *this* actually designates — its conceptual referent — is the *thing* related to the ground in this fashion. The "onstage" profile (or referent) of *this* is consequently a schematically characterized thing (typically specified by the head noun), whereas the ground and the grounding relationship are "offstage" and unprofiled. This analysis accounts for various grammatical properties of the grounding elements (Langacker 1985, 1990b, this volume).

The elements identified as the nominal grounding predications of English are the demonstratives (*this, that, these, those*), the articles (*the, a, sm* [unstressed *some*], *Ø*), and certain quantifiers (*some, most, all, no, each, every, any*). The clausal grounding predications include the "tense/agreement" inflections (*Ø, -ed, -s,* etc.) and the modals (*may, can, shall, will, must,* and the "distal" forms *might, could, should, would*). Langacker (1991) provides semantic descriptions of all these elements, as well as initial characterizations of the grammatical constructions they participate in. My purpose here is to examine more closely the organization of the nominal and clausal grounding systems, to note their parallelism and certain ways in which they diverge, and to explicate their points of difference in terms of basic cognitive models that motivate essential features of nominal and clausal structure.

The organization I propose is summarized in the following table:

Table 1. Nominal and clausal grounding in English

	Definite	Quantificational
Nominal	th + prox/dist (*-is, -at,* ...)	*Ø, sm, a, some, most,* ...
Finite clause	*Ø* + prox/dist (*Ø, -ed,* ...)	*may, will,* ... + prox/dist

In both the nominal and the clausal realms, grounding predications divide naturally into two groups labeled "definite" and "quantificational". For nominals, the definite grounding elements are limited to the definite article *th(e)*, optionally expanded by a proximal or distal marker to form a demonstrative (*this, that,* and their plurals). For finite clauses, "definiteness" is signaled by the absence of a modal; the table thus represents the counterpart of *th* as zero (*Ø*). Clauses without a modal show a proximal/distal contrast which is prototypically manifested as "present" vs. "past tense" (*Ø* vs. *-ed*). The nominal grounding predications labeled "quantificational" include the indefinite articles *Ø*, *sm*, and *a* (e.g. *She drank {Ø/sm/a} beer*), together with various elements traditionally recognized as quantifiers. For clauses, the quantificational grounding elements are the modals, which — except for *must* (Langacker 1991: section 6.2.2.3) — show a contrast between their basic "proximal" forms (*may, will*, etc.) and the longer "distal" forms (*might, would, could, should*).

I will address three questions that arise in regard to this organization. The first concerns the status and distribution of "zero" elements. In particular, why should definiteness be associated with overt marking in the case of nominals, whereas a comparable notion is signaled by zero (the absence of a modal) in the case of finite clauses? The other two questions pertain to the proximal/distal contrast. Although the table does not reveal it, there are grounds for believing that the unmarked member of the opposition is "proximal" for clauses, but "distal" for nominals. What is the source of this difference? Moreover, the table clearly shows that the proximal/distal contrast holds in the clausal realm for both definite and quantificational grounding elements, but only for definites in the nominal realm. Why is there no such contrast with nominal quantification?

My attempt to answer these questions starts from a fundamental premise of cognitive linguistics, namely that certain idealized cognitive models (Lakoff 1987) with the status of conceptual archetypes underlie the prototypical meanings of basic grammatical constructs and provide the functional motivation for unmarked nominal and clausal structure (Langacker 1991). One archetypal ICM is the billiard-ball model: we conceive of our world as being populated by discrete physical objects, which move around in space and interact with one another; in canonical interactions, one object makes forceful physical contact with another and thereby induces an observable change. Another archetypal ICM is the basic epistemic model, whose essential notion is that a given conceptualizer (C) accepts certain "occurrences" (primarily "events", but also including "states") as being real, whereas others are not. Reality — C's view of what has happened up through the present — is an ever-evolving entity whose evolution through time continuously augments the complexity of the structure defined by its previous history. To the basic epistemic model, the elaborated epistemic model adds C's realization that reality as C knows it does not exhaust the world and its evolutionary history, and that other conceptualizers have overlapping but partially different views of each. Finally, the dynamic evolutionary model incorporates force-dynamic notions (Talmy 1985) and the idea that the world has a stable "structure" (cf. Goldsmith and Woisetschlaeger 1982). Together these notions permit C to assess the future evolution of reality on the basis of its history to date: since the world "works" in a certain way, its evolution up through the present amounts to a kind of evolutionary momentum that constrains the possible paths of its future evolution and allows certain projections to be made.

These archetypal conceptions are reflected in the organization of the English grounding systems. These systems have developed to accommodate a canonical situation implied by the archetypes: that of a conceptualizer trying to construct and communicate a comprehensive, coherent, and accurate picture of evolving reality. In so doing, C confronts a basic asymmetry between "objects" and "events". Inherent in the billiard-ball model is the *pre-existence* and relative *permanence* of objects, as opposed to the *transience* of events. Because objects endure, at a given moment C is surrounded by many objects, including multiple instances of the same object type. Events, by contrast, take a certain span of time to occur and then are gone forever. If we understand an event as including its participants, multiple instances of the same event type (with a specific set of participants) can only occur at different times. Were they to occur at the same time, they would constitute the same event instance, just as two objects occupying the same space at the same time have to be the same object.

From this asymmetry between archetypal objects and events, it follows that different factors are primarily at issue in the nominal and the clausal realms. Because the existence of objects is basically taken for granted, for them the key issue is *identification*: the simultaneous existence of many objects (even of the same type) requires that particular objects be singled out for purposes of describing events. For events, on the other hand, *existence* (occurrence) is precisely what is at issue. Moreover, since multiple instances of the same event type do not occur simultaneously, identification is not a factor.

We can now observe a basic iconicity, whereby the extent of a grounding predication's overt phonological realization roughly parallels the amount of effort C exerts in attempting to construct a coherent picture of evolving reality. In both the nominal and clausal realms, overt marking signals an attempt by C to bring matters "under control" with respect to what is primarily at issue. This is most apparent in the case of finite clauses, where the elements with the greatest phonological substance — the modals — derive historically from force-dynamic verbs of power, desire, and ability. In their "root" senses (permission, obligation, etc.), the modals still often represent the speaker's attempt to "gain control" over the evolution of reality by directly influencing its future course. When used epistemically, the modals remain force-dynamic, but in a different way: here the speaker asserts control intellectually, by trying to determine where the evolutionary momentum of reality is likely to lead it (cf. Talmy 1985; Langacker 1990b; Sweetser 1990). By contrast, the zero form — the absence of a modal — iconically indicates the absence of effort to gain control over the designated occurrence. It has already been accepted as part of the speaker's conception of reality, so there is no further need or effort to control it.

In the nominal sphere, where existence is taken for granted, gaining control resides in directing attention to a particular instance of a type, out of all the possible candidates. Here the prime examples are demonstratives. I basically accept their characterization (e.g. in Kirsner 1993) as instructions to "seek out" the intended referent, i.e. as verbal acts of pointing. The definite article is phonologically weaker and also weaker in its directive force, for it carries the supposition that the intended referent is contextually unique, so seeking it out requires no effort. The quantificational grounding elements represent other ways of establishing nominal reference. Certain quantifiers (e.g. *most*) characterize the profiled entity as comprising some proportion of the total set of instances of the type specified by the head noun. Others profile a single (arbitrary) instance somehow portrayed as being *representative* of the class as a whole (e.g. *any* implies random selection from the class). The articles have much less phonological substance and, iconically, embody less effort to identify a referent. The indefinite article *a* merely instructs the addressee to evoke an arbitrary instance of a count-noun class (any specificity it might have is contributed by factors external to the nominal), and *sm*, an arbitrary but small instance of a mass-noun class. The zero form indicates a mass but makes no specifications whatever concerning identity or even magnitude: the interpretations it allows range from small quantities (e.g. *She sipped beer*) to full generics (*Beer is alcoholic*). Hence Ø indicates the least effort to establish control.

Let us turn now to the proximal/distal opposition. It seems evident that in the clausal realm the proximal forms are unmarked. For non-modal clauses, the proximal form is generally zero phonologically and indicates that the designated process is not only *real* but immediate to the ground (hence "present"). The distal form is usually overtly marked and specifies the nonimmediacy of the profiled occurrence; distance within reality normally amounts to "past tense". Indications that the "distal" forms of the modals are likewise marked relative to the basic forms include their greater brevity (*may* vs. *might*), the nonexistence of a distal counterpart for *must*, and their lesser semantic complexity (*might*, for instance, assesses the potentiality conveyed by *may* from a reference point removed from the ground, whereas *may* assesses it directly from the ground). It only stands to reason that markedness should correlate with departures from immediate reality, the location of the ground.

Other factors have greater import in the nominal realm, where the archetypal conception presupposes the reality of the entities concerned (a population of physical objects). Here there are reasons for believing that distal forms are unmarked relative to proximal ones. In Dutch, for example, the distal demonstrative *die* involves "lesser urging" to seek out the noun's referent than does the proximal form *deze* (Kirsner 1993). Moreover, it is generally the distal demonstratives that undergo further grammaticization to yield semantically weaker forms such as definite articles and subordinators (e.g. English *that*).

The explanation I suggest is rather obvious: the proximal forms are marked because the proximity of an object to the ground is more noteworthy. At a given moment, the conceptualizer's view of reality comprises myriad objects most of which lie at some remove; those within reach constitute just a small proportion of the total and thus depart from the normal expectation. This explanation runs mildly counter to Talmy's generally valid observation that "grammatical" elements specify "topological" as opposed to metric (or "Euclidean-geometric") ones (Talmy 1988). Whereas Talmy describes demonstratives in terms of a conceptual partition through space (the speaker side and the nonspeaker side), a simple partitioning predicts no quantitative asymmetry leading to the unmarked nature of distal forms — why should roughly the same number of objects not occur on both sides of the line? We must instead construe the partition as a circle enclosing the speaker, dividing space into an "inside" and an "outside" region. Beyond this, the circle has to be conceived as relatively small, for otherwise there is no basis for anticipating that most objects will fall in the outside region. It is only when this egocentric configuration incorporates the (geo)metric notion of relative size that the occurrence of an object in the speaker's domain comes to represent the marked situation.

The final question to be addressed is why, in the case of nominals, the quantificational grounding elements do not manifest a proximal/distal contrast. The answer, I think, is quite simple: the referents grounded by these elements have no particular spatial location, hence they cannot be either proximal or distal vis-à-vis the speaker. They represent *arbitrary* instances of the thing type specified by the head noun, instances "conjured up" for the purpose at hand, as opposed to specific objects that pre-exist in the context of speech and need only be pointed to. Let us briefly consider three cases, one for each basic kind of quantificational grounding predication. The forms *most*, *any*, and *a* respectively exemplify the *proportional* quantifiers, the *representative-instance* quantifiers, and the *indefinite articles*.

A nominal such as *most ducks* designates a set of ducks characterized only as a large proportion of the set of all instances. No particular ducks are singled out as necessarily belonging to the profiled subset — so far as the internal structure of the nominal is concerned, the choice is arbitrary. Because no specific ducks are involved, they have no specific location. In response to the statement *Jill likes most ducks*, asking *Where are they?* makes no sense. Whether considered individually or collectively, the referent of *most ducks* has no particular location with respect to the speaker. Likewise, *Any duck has webbed feet* cannot be followed felicitously by the question *Where is it?*, for there is no specific referent. *Any* serves to conjure up an arbitrary instance of the class construed as being chosen randomly from the set of all instances. The randomness of the selection is conceived as assuring that the instance chosen is representative of the class as a whole.

It might at first seem problematic to claim that an indefinite article always evokes an arbitrary instance of the noun class, for it is generally claimed that the referent can either be specific or nonspecific: *Jack is looking for a duck* may mean that Jack will be content with any duck he comes across, but it can also mean that he has a specific duck in mind. Moreover, *Jack found a duck* can only involve a particular duck. We must however distinguish between the internal structure of the nominal, on the one hand, and information contributed by external factors, on the other. Definiteness appears to hinge on the information supplied internally. Observe that the contextual uniqueness required for the use of *the* has to be established via the content provided by the nominal itself, not the rest of the clause or sentence containing it (Hawkins 1978; Langacker 1991: section 3.1.1). Thus in *Jack found a duck* the indefinite article appears even though the property of being found by Jack is sufficient to single out a unique instance of the *duck* class; that property is not supplied by the object nominal itself, whose content fails to assure uniqueness. By contrast, in a sentence like *Jill hates the duck Jack found*, the nominal-internal relative clause does provide the requisite information.

In uttering the sentence *Jack found a duck*, the speaker already possesses information that singles out a unique instance of the *duck* category: the duck in question is the one Jack found. Definiteness however requires that the nominal be sufficient to direct the *addressee*'s attention to the intended referent. Since the addressee is not presumed to have prior knowledge of the event described by the clause as a whole, the object nominal alone fails to single out a unique instance of the class. From the addressee's standpoint, *a duck* merely serves to conjure up an arbitrary instance of the *duck* category, which the remainder of the sentence may render specific. This account therefore does not attribute the specific/nonspecific contrast to polysemy of the indefinite articles, but rather to factors external to the nominal (see also Fauconnier 1985). At the nominal level of organization, the indefinite articles always serve an evocative function for the addressee: they call to mind an arbitrary instance of the nominal category, which as such has no particular location with respect to the speaker.

References

Chafe, Wallace L.
    1970   *Meaning and the Structure of Language*. Chicago: University of Chicago Press.
Fauconnier, Gilles
    1985   *Mental Spaces: Aspects of Meaning Construction in Natural Language*. Cambridge, MA: MIT Press.
Goldsmith, John and Erich Woisetschlaeger
    1982   The logic of the English progressive. *Linguistic Inquiry* 13: 79–89.
Hawkins, John
    1978   *Definiteness and Indefiniteness: A Study in Reference and Grammaticality Prediction*. London: Croom Helm.
Kirsner, Robert S.
    1993   From meaning to message in two theories: Cognitive and Saussurean views of the modern Dutch demonstratives. In: Richard A. Geiger and Brygida Rudzka-Ostyn (eds.), *Conceptualizations and Mental Processing in Language*, 81–114. (Cognitive Linguistics Research 3.) Berlin: Mouton de Gruyter.
Lakoff, George
    1987   *Women, Fire, and Dangerous Things: What Categories Reveal About the Mind*. Chicago: University of Chicago Press.
Langacker, Ronald W.
    1985   Observations and speculations on subjectivity. In: John Haiman (ed.), *Iconicity in Syntax*, 109–150. (Typological Studies in Language 6.) Amsterdam: John Benjamins.
    1987a   *Foundations of Cognitive Grammar*, Volume 1: *Theoretical Prerequisites*. Stanford: Stanford University Press.
    1987b   Nouns and verbs. *Language* 63: 53–94.

1990a   *Concept, Image, and Symbol: The Cognitive Basis of Grammar.* (Cognitive Linguistics Research 1.) Berlin: Mouton de Gruyter.
1990b   Subjectification. *Cognitive Linguistics* 1: 5–38.
1991   *Foundations of Cognitive Grammar,* Volume 2: *Descriptive Application.* Stanford: Stanford University Press.
this vol. Deixis and subjectivity.

Sweetser, Eve E.
1990   *From Etymology to Pragmatics: Metaphorical and Cultural Aspects of Semantic Structure.* (Cambridge Studies in Linguistics 54.) Cambridge: Cambridge University Press.

Talmy, Leonard
1985   Force dynamics in language and thought. In: William H. Eilfort, Paul D. Kroeber and Karen L. Peterson (eds.), *Papers from the Parasession on Causatives and Agentivity,* 293–337. Chicago: Chicago Linguistic Society.
1988   The relation of grammar to cognition. In: Brygida Rudzka-Ostyn (ed.), *Topics in Cognitive Linguistics,* 165–205. Amsterdam: John Benjamins.

Part I
Nominal grounding

Grounding, subjectivity and definite descriptions

Richard Epstein

1. Introduction[1]

The purpose of this chapter is to examine the ways in which definite articles are used for grounding — how speakers employ definite articles to relate the thing profiled by a nominal to the ground. Most previous work on definiteness focuses on the logico-referential aspects of grounding, i.e. the factors that permit the hearer to pick out, or identify, the exact (unique) thing to which the speaker intends to refer (the *referent* of the nominal). Accordingly, the basic meaning of definite articles in English and many other languages is usually said to involve the notion of (unique) identifiability. Under this referential view of definiteness, speakers choose a definite article when they assume that the hearer is able to identify the intended referent (see Abbott 1999; Chafe 1994; Chesterman 1991; Du Bois 1980; Givón 1984; Gundel, Hedberg, and Zacharski 1993; Hawkins 1978, 1991; Kleiber 1992; Lambrecht 1994; Löbner 1985; Lyons 1999; Searle 1969; *inter alia*).

Identifiability is, of course, an important aspect of nominal grounding. However, a key goal of this chapter is to demonstrate that speakers do not employ definite articles solely to indicate that a referent is uniquely identifiable. In particular, the referential view omits the relatively subjective aspects of grounding, i.e. features whose existence "inheres solely in the conceptualizing activity itself and thus no longer depends on any objective ... "input" from the outside world" (Brisard, this volume: 277). Nominals are not used for evoking objective, preexisting, homogeneous entities. Rather, speakers must *construct* discourse referents before they can call the hearer's attention to those referents (this is especially crucial when a nominal is first introduced into the discourse). Moreover, referents are set up under a range of specific guises. Speakers employ various grounding predications — including definite articles — to facilitate the construction of discourse and, at the same time, to induce hearers to accept each referent into the discourse under the desired guise. As I will argue, other important aspects of nominal grounding are: the conceptual status of a discourse referent (is it a role? a value?), the referent's relation to the broader discourse context (is it in focus? is it a new topic? from which conceptualizer's point of view is it to be construed?), and the organization of background knowledge (which specific elements, general domains, frames, etc., must be accessed to arrive at a coherent interpretation of the nominal?). I agree with Nuyts (this volume: 456) that these sorts of "qualification" ought to be viewed as aspects of grounding, since knowledge of an object cannot be "fully anchored in one's conceptual system until all dimensions of its status are clear".

This chapter, then, concentrates on speakers' epistemic assessments of discourse entities and their characteristics, that is, on the more subjective ways in which speakers use definite articles to relate discourse referents to the ground. Such an orientation is in keeping with Cognitive Grammar's basic commitment to the epistemic nature of grounding (see Langacker 1991: 90, this volume b; Brisard, this volume; Nuyts, this volume). I present data, drawn mostly from English, illustrating some of the guises under which referents may be constructed, and I argue that such data show that definite articles can be used to introduce discourse entities that hearers are manifestly not able to identify. I also propose a unified account of the meaning of definite articles in terms of *accessibility* (Ariel 1990; Fauconnier 1994). Under this view, the coordination of reference (identifying referents) is treated as just one element of nominal grounding, just one of the reasons why speakers select definite articles.

2. Nominal grounding and definite articles

One of the main semantic functions of a nominal is to ground the instance designated by the nominal (Langacker 1991: 53). That is, a nominal indicates how its discourse referent relates to the *ground*, where the ground is defined as "the speech event, its participants, and its immediate circumstances" (Langacker, this volume a: 7). Nominals accomplish their grounding function by virtue of the fact that they contain elements, known as *grounding predications*, whose purpose is to specify the nature of the relationship between the ground and the discourse referent. As Langacker points out, it makes perfect sense that grounding predications should be a universal and central feature of nominal structure, because it is only natural that people should seek to connect the things they talk about to their own interests and experiences: "It is of great cognitive and communicative utility to the conceptualizers to relate a situation to their own circumstances, whereas merely contemplating a situation type in the abstract, with no indication of its epistemic status, is essentially pointless." (Langacker, this volume a: 20) Nominal grounding predications include such elements as articles, demonstratives, and certain quantifiers (Langacker, this volume b).

Given the crucial role of grounding in the organization of nominals, it is worth examining this notion much more closely. In particular, we would like to know exactly *how* grounding predications relate designated instances to the ground — what is the nature of the relationship between instances and the ground? Langacker (this volume a: 7) gives a preliminary response when he notes that "[o]ne aspect of the grounding relationship ... is either definiteness or indefiniteness, where definiteness implies (roughly) that the speaker and hearer have both succeeded in establishing mental contact with the profiled thing instance". By *mental contact*, Langacker means that a person has singled out the instance for individual conscious awareness. But what else, if anything, is involved in nominal grounding? In the rest of this chapter, I will try to sketch some answers to this question by closely examining the grounding effected by definite articles.

To begin, there is wide agreement that one of the chief functions of definite articles is to aid in the coordination of reference. The speaker and hearer constantly "confront the challenge of directing their attention to the same instance" (Langacker 1991: 89–90), i.e. they must assure that they are talking about the same thing. In particular, it is the speaker's job to "direct the hearer's attention to the instance he has in mind" (Langacker 1991: 91). If both the speaker and the hearer can achieve mental contact with the designated instance, the speaker may choose a definite article to ground the nominal.[2] Frequently, the hearer can achieve mental contact with an instance if that instance is the only one of its type in the current discourse context (or, with respect to plural and mass nouns, if the designated entity is the maximal instance of its type in the context). It is for this reason that linguists analyze the definite article as specifying a relationship of unique identifiability between the designated instance and the ground. This function of the article may be labeled its *referential function*.

There is no doubt that singling out instances and coordinating reference is a very important function of definite articles. However, calling attention to a discourse entity implies that the entity exists, though often this is not so until the nominal itself is actually uttered. Many nominals do not refer to preexisting entities but, rather, create entities which are to be entered into the discourse for the first time (see also Laury, this volume). In these cases, grounding predications (e.g. definite articles) still help call attention to the entity, but they may also evoke for the hearer various characteristics of the previously unknown entity. Most research on definiteness has overlooked the fact that discourse referents are not all constructed in the same way. For instance, some referents are more prominent than others (say, because they are new topics); some referents are set up as roles, others as values; referents can be construed from distinct points of view, etc. Speakers frequently employ definite articles to prompt the hearer to infer that a newly created discourse entity possesses these relatively subjective properties.

In brief, definite articles can be used to ground discourse referents in a number of ways. Unique identifiability is important, but so are other factors pertaining to the construction of discourse referents. Speakers choose definite articles to help coordinate reference, as well as to communicate their assessment of the overall status of an entity. The bulk of this chapter (section 3) will be concerned with elaborating different nonreferential uses of definite articles, i.e. it will describe relationships between the ground and designated instances other than unique identifiability. First, though, in the rest of section 2, I will briefly discuss the better-known referential use; then I will sketch an alternative framework for understanding the meaning of definite articles, one based on the notion of accessibility.

2.1. Referential use of definite articles

Most theories, whether formal or functional, assume that definiteness is essentially a matter of reference. They typically focus on the use of *the* to pick out or distinguish a discourse referent from other entities in the universe of discourse: "Speakers code a referential nominal as definite if they think that they are entitled to assume that the hearer can — by whatever means — assign it unique reference." (Givón 1984: 399; in addition to the references given in the introduction, see also Barwise and Cooper 1981; Birner and Ward 1994; Chafe 1976; Givón 1992; Halliday and Hasan 1976; Hintikka and Kulas 1985; Ojeda 1991)

Two main referential explanations concerning the meaning of definite articles are commonly found in the literature. One is based on *uniqueness*, or *unique identifiability*, and the other is based on *familiarity*. Uniqueness theories claim that definite articles refer to the unique entity or set of entities in the relevant domain of discourse (e.g. Russell 1905; Kadmon 1990; Hawkins 1991). Familiarity theories claim that for a definite description to be felicitous, it must refer to an entity, unique or not, that is already present in the discourse domain (e.g. Christophersen 1939; Heim 1982). The centrality of reference and reference coordination is manifest in the widespread agreement amongst both uniqueness and familiarity theorists regarding the core facts for which any theory of definiteness should be responsible. Research into the definite article has concentrated, for the most part, on the following factors exerting an influence on definiteness: anaphora (*We saw a film... the film was great*), deixis (*Look at the bird!*), a larger situation (*I heard the Prime Minister give a speech yesterday*; the term *larger situation* is from Hawkins 1978: 115), and bridging (*I have an old car, but the motor is new*; also known as associative anaphora, inferrability, or accommodation; see Hawkins 1978; Clark and Marshall 1981; Prince 1981; Heim 1982; Schnedecker et al. 1994). Each of these factors renders a discourse referent uniquely identifiable (or familiar) and thereby justifies the appearance of a definite article.

The problem for referential approaches to definiteness is that factors unrelated to uniqueness and familiarity may also justify the appearance of a definite article. Consider first the examples in (1), where the definite articles are motivated by the prominence (importance) of the referents.

(1)a. With Louisville clinging to a 61–59 lead, Tick Rogers made a turnaround jumper from the right baseline with 2:04 remaining and the Wildcats never got closer ... "Tick Rogers's turnaround was **the shot of the game**," Villanova Coach Steve Lappas said. "Eric Eberz was all over him. He made a tough shot." (*The New York Times*, 3/18/96, p. B9)
   b. Dinkins is doing his best to convince New Yorkers that he burns with unfinished ambitions for remaking the city. He announces that he will release a series of "future-prints" detailing his plans for reform; he says he will demand "intense and radical change." And he declares: "It's time to let New York know that not only do we have the vision, we have **the plan to keep New York great**." (*Los Angeles Times* magazine, 10/17/93, p. 16)

Referential accounts claim that definite descriptions in predicate position, such as *the shot of the game* in (1a), represent a "uniquely determining" property, that is, they imply that the subject is the only entity (in the given context) to which the property may be ascribed (Declerck 1986: 30). However, in (1a), we do not understand that Rogers's turnaround jumper was the only shot of the basketball game (many shots, of course, are attempted in a typical game such as that one). Nor do we infer from Dinkins's statement in (1b) that he possesses the unique plan to keep New York great. These definite descriptions carry no implication of uniqueness. On the contrary, the interpretation of these nominals with *the* requires that there be other shots and other plans in the relevant contexts, because they suggest that the referents in question are more important than other referents of the same type — in (1a), Rogers's shot is more important than the other shots of that game and, in (1b), Dinkins's plan is superior to those of the other politicians running for Mayor of New York at that time.

Nonunique discourse entities may also be introduced by a nominal with *the* in order to indicate that the entity should be set up as a *role* (see section 3.2 for details), as in (2).

(2) Researchers who reported in July that family history appeared to play a slightly smaller role in breast cancer than previously believed backed off, saying they had erred... "We took **the wrong number** and multiplied it by **the wrong number**," said Dr. Graham A. Colditz, a co-author of the study. (*Los Angeles Times*, 10/7/93, p. A20)[3]

The definite articles in (2) are felicitous because both occurrences of *the wrong number* are interpretable as salient, though nonunique, roles within the frame evoked by the verb *multiplied*. This interpretation is possible because multiplication problems are stereotypically associated with slots (roles) for two numbers, regardless of the specific values of those numbers in any given context.

The next example shows that *the* can equally well occur in nominals introducing unfamiliar (or unidentifiable) entities into the discourse. In (3), *the* serves as a signal to the hearer that the new discourse referent *jealousy* is about to become the topic of the next stretch of talk.

(3) "His mother? Died in 1983... Yeah, they were poor... Patrick had a lot of brothers and sisters. I don't even know how many.

"The biggest problem was **the jealousy**. People were jealous of our team. Some hated us. Because we were *good*. We were 74–1. We won three Massachusetts state titles at the highest level. A lot of that jealousy and hatred went against Patrick." (*Sports Illustrated*, 1/17/94, p. 56; italics in the original)

To this point in the discourse, *jealousy* has not yet been explicitly mentioned, nor can the presence of this referent be inferred from contextual considerations. Thus, when the speaker first utters *the jealousy* in (3), we cannot know what he is referring to. Nevertheless, this definite article is felicitous since it implies that *jealousy* is a new topic. The analysis of *the* as an indication that the referent will be highly topical, or prominent, in the subsequent discourse is supported by the recurrence of the notion of jealousy twice more shortly after its initial mention.

In sum, previous explanations of the meaning of *the* (unique identifiability, familiarity, and other related notions based on referential considerations) do not correctly account for all uses of the article.[4] As we will see in section 3 below, definite articles exhibit a range of usage types in which the coordination of reference is not the primary factor motivating their selection. Before turning to a discussion of these usage types, in the next section I present an analysis of definite articles that unifies the different usage types under a single schematic meaning, namely *low accessibility*.

2.2. Accessibility

The aim of this section is to sketch the outlines of a theory in which the various functions served by definite articles — both referential and non-referential — are treated as the discourse manifestations of a common basic meaning (see Epstein, forthcoming, for a more detailed exposition of the theory). This theory is situated within the broader framework provided by Ariel's (1990) *Accessibility theory* and Fauconnier's (1994, 1997) *Mental Spaces*, which both regard grammatical elements as discourse processing instructions. In line with this view, I propose that definite articles, in general, serve as instructions to hearers to set up domains, elements, and the conceptual connections between them in specific ways, in accordance with speakers' communicative and rhetorical intentions.

Under the mental spaces view of language, the production and interpretation of discourse results from the construction of a hierarchical network of mental spaces, or cognitive domains. These spaces are mental models of discourse that we structure with elements, roles, properties, relations, and strategies. A central precept of mental space research is that "[l]anguage does not carry meaning, it guides it" (Fauconnier 1994: xxii). Sentences are underspecified forms that prompt us to construct appropriate meanings by drawing on a variety of background and contextual knowledge. In particular, grammatical morphemes are seen as instructions for the construction of spaces, the introduction of elements into the spaces, the distribution of knowledge over a given set of spaces, the establishment of links and relationships between spaces, and the accessibility of knowledge in a given space with respect to other spaces. The notion of accessibility is especially relevant for understanding definiteness. An accessible mental space is defined as one that is linked via some type of conceptual connection to another mental space. As a result, knowledge contained in an accessible space is available for interpretation in the current discourse space, even if the accessible space is not the most active in current processing.

My understanding of the term accessibility builds upon, and extends, the work of Ariel (1988, 1990, and elsewhere). Accessibility has to do with the degree of activation of information in memory.[5] The basic insight of Accessibility theory is that highly accessible mental entities — those which are most active in consciousness — require less processing effort to be retrieved than entities of low accessibility. Moreover, relatively "heavy" nominals (e.g. full noun phrases, proper names) tend to be used to retrieve entities that are of low accessibility, while "light" nominals (e.g. pronouns, zero anaphors) tend to be used to retrieve entities that are of high accessibility, i.e. highly active in memory (see Ariel 1990 for details; similar accessibility hierarchies can be found in Givón 1983 and Gundel, Hedberg, and Zacharski 1993). Accordingly, definite descriptions mark low accessibility and are typically employed when referring to entities that are not highly active in memory.

Bringing together all these pieces, I claim that *the basic (schematic) meaning of definite articles is low accessibility*. The article simply conveys that the knowledge required for interpreting a nominal in the current discourse space is accessible — either already active or if not, then currently available and able to be activated — somewhere in the dynamic configuration of spaces. At the same time, the article indicates that the requisite knowledge is currently not easily accessible and must be sought out by the hearer (it is of low accessibility).[6] Thus, the main function of a definite article is to signal the availability of an *access path* because, along with contextual cues, it helps guide the addressee through a network of mental spaces, so that she can construct the elements and connections allowing access to the appropriate space(s). Some conceptual connections between spaces are set up on the basis of the identity of elements in each space, as in the anaphoric use of the article. Other nominals with *the* trigger the construction of connections to spaces containing information about the deictic situation or relevant background knowledge. And as we will see in section 3, spaces can also be constructed and accessed through the use of viewpoint and viewpoint shifts, or through the attribution of differing degrees of prominence to elements. It is important to note, however, that the article itself does not specify the details of the access path, i.e. it does not spell out the precise connections that should be constructed in the process of interpreting any individual nominal. The exact space configuration — and, by the same token, the exact interpretation — set up by a sentence containing a definite description is always underspecified and can only be determined from the circumstances of the broader context of utterance (see section 3.4). Often, it is necessary for the hearer to discern the speaker's local communicative intentions in order to arrive at the proper access path. The complexity of the path may vary considerably, from relatively simple to highly complex, but in all cases, the article merely represents an instruction to the hearer that the referent can be accessed and interpreted if the right spaces, elements, and connections are constructed.

The approach sketched here differs from other research into the definite article primarily because of its focus on the dynamic and creative aspects of definite article usage. Most theories of definiteness in the recent literature strongly emphasize the role of context in determining the appropriate use of the article, but the approach advocated here goes further. I pay close attention to new data, some of which involve rather unusual uses of definite articles. These data have rarely, if ever, been discussed in the literature and I advance a single explanation for both the unique identifiability uses and the less well-known uses (the latter are taken up in section 3). It often turns out — and I believe this to be the case here — that "unusual cases reveal the general nature of the operations at work, whereas the typical cases do not" (Fauconnier 1994: xix). Furthermore, my theory extends the notion of (low) accessibility to several types of discourse referent that would normally be analyzed as *new*, rather than *given*, because they are being introduced into the discourse for the first time. These referents may be construed as accessible, I claim, not because they are themselves already active to some degree in memory, but rather because some aspect of the particular context of utterance in which each occurs allows them to be linked to background knowledge that is itself accessible (i.e. currently available and therefore able to be activated). Moreover, speakers employ *the* to cue the hearer that these background assumptions *must* be accessed for the definite descriptions to be interpreted. The range of mental entities that may be considered accessible should therefore be expanded to include some types of entity which are being newly constructed in the discourse. And as Mira Ariel (personal communication) notes, it seems desirable to analyze these nonactive (new) discourse referents in the same way as already active (though not highly accessible) discourse referents, because languages consistently code these sorts of referent in the same formal fashion.

To summarize thus far, I am arguing that all occurrences of a definite article help nominals accomplish their grounding function by (explicitly) signaling to the hearer that the designated instance is accessible to a low degree. In addition, the nature of the grounding relation may be further specified (implicitly) in various ways, depending on the wider context in which the definite description appears. To take just one common example, if the designated instance has previously been mentioned, then the hearer may draw the more specific inference that the instance is uniquely identifiable. But the definite article may give rise to other sorts of inference, too, in different context types. We will examine these other grounding relationships in the next section.

3. Other uses of definite articles

Nominals with *the* do not introduce discourse referents in a neutral fashion. This section investigates some of the ways in which a speaker may set up a discourse referent the first time it is mentioned in the discourse. We will see that speakers construct discourse entities under various guises (i.e. possessing different characteristics and serving diverse functions), and that they attempt to persuade hearers to accept the referents into the discourse under these guises in order to achieve their communicative purposes. We will also see (in section 3.4) that the various functions of *the* are not mutually exclusive, i.e. a single article may simultaneously serve several functions.

3.1. Prominence

One type of grounding relationship specified by definite articles involves high prominence. The speaker may introduce an entity into the discourse for the first time by means of a definite description because she wishes the hearer to construe the entity as being especially important (highly prominent) in that context. The speaker may attribute the property of high prominence to an entity if that entity is (in the speaker's judgment) either highly topical or a particularly important member of a category. In these cases, the definite article primarily serves an expressive function (rather than a referential function), where expressivity is defined as "the foregrounding of a speaker's own involvement in an utterance, including subjective evaluation, special emphasis, surprise, admiration, etc." (Hanks 1992: 49–50).

A first reason for choosing a definite article is high topicality. Speakers sometimes employ definite descriptions to enter a new topic into the discourse, thereby foregrounding their own subjective evaluation of the entity as prominent with respect to the elements in the discourse context with which it co-occurs. The common literary strategy of introducing an important character at the start of a narrative with an initial definite mention nicely illustrates this use of the article (see Christophersen 1939: 29 for an example). But this strategy is not limited to either literary texts or the beginning of a discourse, as demonstrated by the use of *the* to introduce the notion of *jealousy* in (3). Another example is given in (4), where both *bitterness* and *depression* are introduced with definite descriptions. Each of these referents becomes a topic of discussion at some subsequent point in the text (*I was in a total depression*; *Bitter when his playing career came to a premature end*).

(4) He started around 8:30 A.M., shortly after his wife, Lana, left for work. For Curt Blefary, the drink of choice was whisky, a blend called Philadelphia. He took it with barely a splash of water and a handful of ice. By noon, he would have finished more than a quart.

With the drink came **the bitterness**, and with the bitterness, **the depression**. While he drank, Blefary read the sports sections, checking, enviously, on the progress of his former big league teammates and friends. Gene Michael was running the Yankees. Bob Watson was in Houston. Frank Robinson in Baltimore. He would see no-name players — guys who had less talent and less notoriety than he'd had — get hired as coaches or instructors.

And he would sit home, alone and unemployed, his left hip crumbling from a disease exacerbated by the alcohol, and wonder why it had never worked out for him.

"It was the same every day," Blefary said recently, sitting in the same easy chair where he used to pass his mornings. "I'd sit there drinking and drinking. I was in a total depression. I blamed everybody for my problems except myself."

...

Bitter when his playing career came to a premature end and his reputation as a drinker and carouser helped prevent him from getting a coaching job, Blefary continued to drink after he left the game. The years passed, and the drinking got worse. His kids visited more and more infrequently. He got laid off from a job driving a truck, then worked at a temporary agency for $4.25 an hour. He hated it, and he drank more. (*The New York Times*, 2/26/95, sec. 8, p. 2)

The writer of (4) employs the definite articles in *the bitterness* and *the depression* to prompt the reader to ascribe the property of high prominence to the representations of the referents set up by these nominals. The special prominence attributed to these discourse referents can be seen more clearly by comparing the interpretation of the nominals with *the* (*the bitterness* and *the depression*) with the interpretation that would arise if the articles were removed (*With the drink came **bitterness**, and with the bitterness, **depression***), an option which, though not taken in (4), would nonetheless have been grammatically possible. Without the articles, the interpretation is noticeably different. Now, the discourse status of these referents seems more neutral, in the sense that they attract no special attention and induce no special inferences (they are simply new information). In particular, we are not inclined to draw any inferences concerning the likelihood that these new referents will be mentioned again or not. To fully understand the expressive function of the definite article, it is quite useful to ask why speakers choose *the* when other articles (*a* or zero) are also possible.

The example in (5) is parallel to (3) and (4) in that *the abyss* establishes a new topic. This example also provides strong evidence that the new discourse entity set up by the definite description is not, in fact, uniquely identifiable. Notice that the second mention of the entity (*a twelve-hundred-foot drop straight down*) occurs with an indefinite article, which marks unidentifiable (inaccessible) referents. If the writer assumed that readers are unable to identify the entity on its second mention, then the same assumption must have held on its first mention as well.

(5) Most of the surface of this high mesa on which our man has disappeared is bare rock — there are few trails, and little sand or soft earth on which he might have left footprints. There are, however, many washes, giant potholes, basins, fissures and canyons in which a man could lose himself, or a body be hidden, for days or years.

There is also **the abyss**. A mile from where we stand is the mesa's edge and a twelve-hundred-foot drop straight down to what is called the White Rim Bench. From there the land falls away for another fifteen hundred feet or more to the Colorado River. (Abbey 1968: 209)

In general, the new discourse topics introduced by definite descriptions are neither uniquely identifiable nor familiar referents. They do not meet any of the criteria usually cited as justifying the occurrence of a definite article, i.e. anaphora, deixis, presence in the larger situation, or bridging (see section 2.1).

A second expressive use of the definite article involves the speaker's subjective evaluation that the referent is a highly prominent member of a category. In these cases, the referent is not unique in the relevant discourse domain, since it is being compared or contrasted with other instances of the same type. The article implies that, on a scale of importance, the referent in question surpasses all others in the contrast set. The nominal *the shot of the game* in (1a) exemplifies this usage, as does *the story* in (6). When the definite description is in predicate position (as in both 1a and 6), the nominal signals the prominence of the subject of the sentence.

(6) ... the rescuers, tantalized by competing offers from movie producers, formed two rival associations .... Each group had its own set of bylaws, with rules about what percentage of the vote was required to admit a new member, and what percentage of any eventual profits the various members would get. Each also had its own lawyer. And each agreed on three things: that it was a shame that they had to fight like this, that their group's story was *the* **story** and that they were interested only in the quality of the movie; it was the others, they said, who were interested only in the money. (*The New York Times* magazine, 7/23/95, p. 23; italics in the original)

This example is a good illustration of the subjective manner in which speakers employ the definite article to ground nominals. Objectively, there are two stories in this context, but the writer uses the article here to indicate that each group believes its story is more important than the other, i.e. each group wishes to attribute the property of high prominence to the referent.

The definite article often receives phonological stressing (or italics, in writing) when it is used to imply the importance of a referent within a category. However, special formal emphasis is not necessary to trigger this inference. Both examples in (1) lack italics, as does the one in (7). Like (1b), where the nominal *the plan to keep New York great* does not imply that this plan is the only one possessed by the mayoral candidates (instead, it suggests the superiority of that particular plan), in (7), the article in *the flaw* does not imply that this referent is the sole flaw in the system, but rather invites the reader to draw the conclusion that this is an especially critical flaw.

(7) Mr. Forbes' camp attributes its candidate's victory to the appeal of his flat-tax proposal and his message of "less government and more freedom." In fact, however, that is not the main reason he has been a factor in the campaign. His candidacy points out **the flaw** in a system where promiscuous spending can buy prominence that has not been

earned in either public service or through distinguished performance in the private sector. Mr. Forbes is where he is not because of accomplishments but because of his idiosyncratic willingness to spend lavishly his inherited fortune. (*The New York Times*, 2/29/96, p. A14)

Once again, to bring out the prominence reading in examples such as (1a) and (7) more explicitly, it is helpful to manipulate the data by substituting an indefinite article for the definite. Comparison of the two possibilities reveals that with the indefinite (*a plan*; *a flaw*), the importance of the entities is diminished because the indefinite article portrays a referent as inaccessible to the hearer, merely one arbitrary instance amongst many of the same type. Not surprisingly, the use of the definite article to convey prominence is common in political discourse, where *the* serves a clear strategic purpose by allowing speakers to subtly affirm the importance of certain entities.

It is worth mentioning that the definite article is also used to indicate prominence in other languages besides English. For instance, my own research has uncovered such usages in Old French and Kumeyaay (Yuman). To illustrate this, consider first the Old French example in (8) (for more examples, see Epstein 1995). The appearance of the definite article *la* on the initial mention of *la vïande* 'the food' is especially interesting because *vïande* is a mass noun and this particular mention of *la vïande* does not refer to any specific or individuated instance of food (in addition, note that in Modern French, a definite article would be ungrammatical in this sort of context, e.g. *courts de la viande, *courts des vivres 'short of the food'). However, the article occurs in (the initial mention of) *la vïande* because this nominal introduces a discourse entity that will be highly topical over the next portion of the narrative, as shown by the recurring mentions of *vïande* in the subsequent text.

(8) *Vos avez le plus grant afaire et le plus perillous entrepris que onques genz entrepreïssent: por ce si convendroit que on ovrast sagement. Sachiez, se nos alons a la terre ferme, la terre est granz et large; et nostre gent sont povre et diseteus de* **la vïande***: si s'espandront par la terre por querre la vïande; et il i a mult grant plenté de la gent el païs: si ne porriens tot garder que nos n'en perdissiens; et nos*

n'avons mestier de perdre, que mult avons poi de gent a ce que nos volons faire.

Il a isles ci prés, que vos poez veoir de ci, qui sont habitees de genz et laborees de blez et de vïandes et d'autres biens: alons iki prendre port, et recuillons les blés et les vïandes del païs; et quant nos avrons les vïandes recuillies, alomes devant la ville et fesons ce que Nostre Sires nos avra porveü. Quar plus seürement guerroie cil qui a la vïande que cil qui n'en a point. (Villehardouin [1938] 1972: §§ 130–131)

'You have undertaken the largest and most perilous enterprise ever attempted by men; you must therefore conduct yourselves wisely. Know that, if we go by land, the countryside is vast; and our men are poor and short of **(the) food**: thus we will spread out to look for the food; and there are many people in this country: so we will not be able to keep a close watch on everything without suffering losses; and we cannot afford losses, because we have very few men to accomplish what we want to do.

There are islands nearby, which you can see from here, and which are inhabited and provided with wheat and food and other resources: let us sail there, and gather the wheat and the food of the country; and after we have gathered the food, let us go before the city and do what our Lord would have us do. Because he who has food wages war better than he who has none.'

As for Kumeyaay[7] (not traditionally considered to possess articles), I have argued in other work that the nominal suffix *-pu* should in fact be classified as a definite article (Epstein 1993, 2000). And parallel to the definite articles in English and Old French, it can be employed to ground nominals whose referents are prominent. The passage in (9) shows that *-pu* can occur in a nominal introducing a new (not-yet-identifiable) referent into a story, if that referent is highly topical. The first half of the narrative from which (9) is drawn tells the story of why rocks have no eyes. Rocks are highly topical in this context, as reflected in the use of *-pu* when they are first entered into the discourse (9a). Overall, there are three overt mentions of *wii* 'rock' in the text, all with

-*pu* (the first two are shown in 9a and 9b), plus many implicit references to the rocks by means of zero anaphora.

(9)a. *Wii-pe-ch   ta-nyuwaay-ch   ma'ay   me-yak-x   w-i-chm*
     rock-PU-S AUX-be.located-SS where   2-lie-IR   3-say-DS

   me-yak-x   w-i-chm?
   2-lie-IR   3-say-DS

   'The rocks were there, and "Where will you lie down?" he [God] said. "Will you lie down?" he said.'

   b. *Wii-pu   ma'ay-ch   w-i-chm   may nemuuxay xmaaw*
      rock-PU what-SS   3-say-DS   NEG like   NEG

   ich   nyáama.
   say   really

   'The rock said something he didn't like.'

We have now seen that definite articles can serve the function of indicating that a discourse entity is highly prominent. The next question is: in what sense are these prominent entities accessible? In general, I claim that they should be considered accessible because hearers interpret them by attempting to link them to other accessible elements (some other retrievable knowledge structures) within the evolving discourse configuration. In the "important member of a category" uses of the definite article, the accessible information licensing the reading of prominence is supplied by knowledge of the category (of which the entity is a member) in the larger context. Once the category is retrieved from background knowledge, an access path can be established linking the entity to an important position therein, i.e. the entity is implicitly contrasted with, and interpreted as more important than, the other members of the category. This interpretation is conventionally associated with various formal signs co-occurring with the article, such as phonological stressing or italicization.

In the high topicality cases, the entity's accessibility depends on the hearer's ability to recognize that the entity will play an important part in the subsequent discourse (as a topic). Several other considerations, besides the presence of the definite article, may combine to facilitate the hearer's recognition of the entity's importance. First, these cases often involve referents that are, by their very nature, manifestly prominent. In other words, they are obviously interesting and/or unusual referents, which attract attention and naturally call for further elaboration: bitterness and depression in (4), an abyss in (5). If relatively more mundane referents are involved, certain formal indications of prominence may compensate for the lack of any obvious prominence. For example, the article may receive heavier stress than usual or it may occur in initial position in the text, a position that is inherently prominent (see Epstein, forthcoming, for illustrations of both of these possibilities). Finally, these prominent entities often appear in contexts that are conventionally associated with high topicality, e.g. at the start of a new paragraph or narrative episode (as in examples 3–5). Speakers count on the hearer's ability to mobilize diverse types of background knowledge, i.e. they assume that the hearer can and will access the lexical, grammatical, and pragmatic knowledge, knowledge of the conventions concerning each discourse genre, etc., necessary to infer the prominence of the referent. Background information of this sort must be available for the discourse prominence reading of a definite description to arise, and indeed, these uses of the definite article alert the hearer to access such information. Thus, highly topical referents can be considered accessible, not because their representations are stored in memory but because they must be linked to retrievable background information — i.e. some sort of knowledge structure that is itself available for activation — in order to be interpreted.

3.2. Roles

Another type of grounding relationship specified by definite articles involves *role* functions (*value-free interpretations* of nominals, in the terminology of Barwise and Perry 1983: 150–151). A nominal designating a role (e.g. *the President* in *The President is elected every four years*) picks out a fixed property (e.g. being the President), but the identity of the individual instantiating the role (the role's *value*) may vary (e.g. *Reagan, Bush, Clinton*, etc.; for details, see Fauconnier 1994: 39–51; Langacker 1991: 71–73).

On occasion, the roles introduced by definite descriptions are not uniquely identifiable. This usage is possible as long as the unidentifiable roles represent accessible entities (see example 2). More commonly, roles are identifiable by virtue of the fact that they fit into broader knowledge structures (such as frames) well known to everyone in the speech community. In fact, speakers frequently make use of definite articles to establish an entity in the discourse as an (accessible) role rather than as an (inaccessible) value; that is, speakers may introduce an entity into the discourse for the first time by means of a definite description, because they wish the hearer to construe the entity as a role in that context, not as an individual value of the role.

For instance, consider (10), in which the speaker selects *the* to trigger the role reading of the notions *broken home* and *alcoholic mother*. Under this reading, the nominals *the broken home* and *the alcoholic mother* do not refer to any specific individual broken home or alcoholic mother (this would be the value reading, but such a reading is unlikely in this context because these individuals are not accessible, not having been previously mentioned). Instead, the nominals refer to properties that are held constant across many different contexts. As a result, the speaker is able to imply that Clinton's background is similar to that of many blacks in the United States, i.e. poor people, just like Clinton, *typically* come from broken homes with alcoholic mothers. The roles *the broken home* and *the alcoholic mother* are accessible in this context because they are part of the background frame knowledge associated with poverty in the U.S.

(10) Then there is the color element. Mr. Clinton, according to Toni Morrison, the Nobel Prize-winning novelist, is our first black President, the first to come from **the broken home**, **the alcoholic mother**, the under-the-bridge shadows of our ranking systems. He is also the most relaxed and unaffected with black people, whose company and culture he clearly enjoys. (*The New York Times*, 10/15/98, p. A31)

Notice that the speaker could have chosen indefinite articles (*a broken home*, *an alcoholic mother*) to introduce these notions. In this case, the referents would have been entered into the discourse simply as inaccessible individual instances of the types *broken home* and *alcoholic mother*. No implication of typicality or common experience would have been invoked, then, and the link Morrison was attempting to draw between Clinton and blacks would therefore have been weakened or even eliminated entirely.

Speakers often have the choice of introducing a notion into the discourse as a role (with a definite article) or as a value (with an indefinite article). In (11), the speaker uses *the* to indicate that she expects a Coke machine to be present even in the middle of the desert, because the frame she associates with national parks contains a role for Coke machines. In her view, parks stereotypically have Coke machines.

(11) Labor Day. Flux and influx, the final visitation of the season, they come in herds, like buffalo, down from The City .... What can I tell them? Sealed in their metallic shells like molluscs on wheels, how can I pry the people free? The auto as tin can, the park ranger as opener. ...
 "Where's **the Coke machine**?"
 "Sorry lady, we have no Coke machine out here. Would you like a drink of water?" (She's not sure.) (Abbey 1968: 232–233)

The woman could have asked for *a Coke machine*, with an indefinite article (e.g. *Is there a Coke machine here?*), but by doing so, she would not have expressed her attitude and expectations about modern material comforts, which Abbey mocks, as explicitly as with the definite article.

The examples in (10)–(11) show that speakers use articles to attribute the characteristics of either role or value status to the entities they set up in the discourse. Even more interesting, the definite article can serve as a formal marker of the speaker's intention to bring a new role into existence. In (12), the article signals the creation, online, of a brand new role, solely for the purposes of the local discourse. This role, *the anti-Gump*, makes sense in the context of (12) because it arises via a metaphorical mapping from a source domain of religious discourse, which contains the familiar role *anti-Christ*, to a target domain involving movies such as *Forrest Gump* and *Pulp Fiction*.

(12) A vision like this elevates "Pulp Fiction" well above its own ebullient sense of fun, even establishing it as **the anti-"Gump."** Mr. Tarantino's film violently refutes the idea that drifting passively is a good way to fulfill one's destiny and get through life. It says, instead, that we make choices that can count. (*The New York Times*, 10/16/94, sec. 2, p. 13)

Before reading this passage, most readers had presumably never encountered the concept of *the anti-Gump*. Nevertheless, the definite article indicates that this novel role is accessible here, as long as the reader activates the relevant mental spaces from background knowledge (the religion frame and the movie frame) and then sets up the required connections (metaphorical mapping) between the relevant elements in those spaces.

The next piece of data, (13), provides another illustration of the complex conceptual work underlying some apparently simple definite nominals. The purpose of the definite article here (in *the parachute*) is to cue the hearer that the speaker intends the referent to be set up as a role that will be prominent in the frame serving as the source domain for a metaphor.

(13) Senator Arthur Vandenberg, the champion of postwar bipartisanship, once said Congress had to be in on the takeoffs if it was to be in on the crash landings. After his Vietnam experience, President Johnson commented ruefully to Eugene Rostow that he had

"failed to reckon with one thing: **the parachute**." He added, "I got them on the takeoff, but a lot of them bailed out before the end of the flight." (*The New York Times*, 9/17/94, p. 15)

First, Vandenberg evokes a "flight frame", with takeoffs and landings, as the source domain of a metaphor for bipartisan cooperation between Congress and the President (the target domain). President Johnson then extends Vandenberg's metaphor in a highly creative way. He talks about his own failed attempt at bipartisanship (with respect to the war in Vietnam) and brings in the notion of a parachute. Although the "flight frame" generally does include a slot for parachutes, this slot (role) was not present in Vandenberg's original metaphor, where bipartisanship meant that everyone had to crash together when things went bad. In effect, Johnson reframes the original situation evoked by Vandenberg: in Johnson's version of the metaphor, he alone stays until the end while everyone else bails out. Interestingly, Johnson uses the definite description *the parachute* to introduce a new role even before we have any way of knowing how this new role fits into the metaphorical political frame. As a result, after mentioning the parachute, Johnson has to explain exactly how he has extended Vandenberg's version of the metaphor (*I got them on the takeoff, but a lot of them bailed out before the end of the flight*). Without this explanation, it would be extremely difficult, if not impossible, to understand what Johnson meant by uttering *the parachute*, because the highly unconventional nature of the general metaphor being employed here obscures the parachute's place in it. In other words, Johnson's explanation provides the final link in the highly complex access path established by this definite description.

The last example in this section nicely demonstrates that speakers often have the choice of grounding entities under a variety of distinct guises, and that they utilize articles to make the guises they choose apparent to others. The writer of (14) selects an indefinite article to set up an instance of the type *rational attacker* as an arbitrary (thus, inaccessible) individual, but selects a definite article to set up the type *fanatic* as a role.

(14) The United States has no defense against an incoming ballistic missile. That's because we are frozen in a decade-old debate now devoid of meaning.

When President Reagan proposed a space-based defense in 1983, his plan was derided as "Star Wars," not only upsetting the theory of Mutual Assured Destruction (MAD), but technologically impossible — what system could stop thousands of incoming Soviet missiles?

Today, the threat is not from a superpower's thousands, but from a rogue state's handful; or from an accidental or misinformed launch ...; or from a group of terrorists who buy or steal one of Russia's 400 SS-25 mobile launchers and equip it with a nuclear or biological warhead.

We are using yesterday's strategic doctrine to fail to confront tomorrow's threat. Retaliation's fear stops **a rational attacker**; it does not deter **the fanatic**.

Consider the President who receives a nuclear missile threat from an Iraq or North Korea or Hezbollah. He could treat it as a bluff — at huge risk to an American city. He could counter-threaten to wipe the offending nation off the face of the earth — but suicidal fanatics don't care, and millions of Americans would not live to enjoy the terrible vengeance. (*The New York Times*, 5/9/96, p. A19)

Notice that, strictly in terms of their unique identifiability or familiarity, the rational attacker and the fanatic should be equivalent in (14): they are part of the same scenario and are mentioned for the first time in the discourse. In some objective sense, then, we might expect the choice of article to be parallel in the two nominals. Indeed, it would have been possible for both nominals to occur with either definite (*the rational attacker*; *the fanatic*) or indefinite articles (*a rational attacker*; *a fanatic*). The combination of articles actually used in (14), however, reflects the writer's subjective evaluation that her communicative purposes would be best served by construing these entities in distinct manners. Setting up the type *fanatic* as a salient role in the terrorism frame (as opposed to merely an arbitrary instance of the type, as *a fanatic* would have done) steers the reader's attention towards this entity, i.e. it implies that this entity is more highly accessible than the rational attacker, since it belongs to the terrorism frame, which is itself accessible. This greater degree of accessibility dovetails with the fact that *fanatics* is a topic in the following paragraph. The example spotlights, once again, the subjective nature of grounding predications, which do not simply mirror, in a passive fashion, the objective properties of entities in the world but instead furnish grammatical resources for speakers to actively shape, or even create, both the entities they talk about and the contexts in which they socially interact with other people (see also Laury, this volume).

3.3. Point of view

Another important aspect of the grounding relationship signaled by definite articles concerns the point of view from which a referent is construed (see Epstein 1996 for more details). In the default case, of course, any grammatical item is understood as reflecting the viewpoint of the speaker. But it is also possible for the article to reflect shifts to noncanonical viewpoints, for instance, that of a third person such as a fictive narrator or a discourse protagonist (Chafe 1994: 284 calls this *protagonist-oriented identifiability*).

The use of definite articles to mark a shift in viewpoint is well known amongst literary theorists, who analyze these articles as encouraging readers to empathize with, or adopt the point of view of, a narrator (Stanzel 1981: 11). However, definite articles are also used to help convey shifts to third-person points of view in nonliterary texts, as seen in (15). Here, the definite article in *the 45-minute jam-up* does not indicate that the sportswriter assumes readers already know about this referent, but rather that the referent is known (accessible) from the point of view of a third person, the big-market fan.

(15)　The big-market fan, forgotten consumer of the sports labor wars, pulled out a $20 bill the other night across the street from Madison Square Garden, but the parking attendant shook his head.
　　　"That's $23.75," the attendant growled.

The big-market fan fumbled with the buttons on his coat, while grumpy peers waited in line.

To begin with, the big-market fan was in one lousy mood. There was **the 45-minute jam-up** at the inbound Lincoln Tunnel. There was the usual eight-block bumper-car skirmish with Seventh Avenue cabbies. By the time the big-market fan reached the stuffed Park and Lock, $23.75 was worth park, no lock. (*The New York Times*, 12/23/94, p. B14)

This passage in general describes the mental experiences of the fan from the fan's point of view. The definite article in *the 45-minute jam-up* reflects the fact that this referent must be grounded with respect to the alternative ground provided by a conceptualizer who is not one of the speech act participants (a noncanonical point of view).

The data in (16) also illustrate a noncanonical perspective, though not that of a third person. This passage is told from the default point of view, that of the writer (who coincides with the first-person narrator), but the definite articles in the nominals *the threadbare couch* and *the cracks in the mirrored coffee table* indicate that these referents are presented to readers through the filter of the writer's consciousness, as she perceived them that day in her father's apartment (and not from the default perspective of the writer's present time).

(16)   My father died on Thanksgiving... My sister had helped my father move into his last apartment, on the Upper East Side of Manhattan, when his health began to fail; now, we agreed, I would move his possessions out... I wandered around my father's apartment, looking critically at things I hadn't really seen in years. I was shocked by the sparseness of the place, **the threadbare couch, the cracks in the mirrored coffee table**. I saw no vestiges of the well-appointed co-op on East End Avenue where he had lived with my mother, nor of the several penthouses where, divorced, he played as hard as he lived. Here, instead, were the trappings of old age and poor health — oxygen tank, wheelchair, portable toilet, walker, handrails. (*The New York Times*, 12/21/96, p. 25)

Though the referents are not uniquely identifiable to readers, they are known to the first-person narrator because they are part of her own experiences, as shown by expressions like *I wandered... looking* and *I saw*. They must therefore be accessed from the mental space that is set up to contain her perceptions from that day. Similarly, deictic expressions such as *here* in the last sentence of (16) are also anchored to this space.

The passage in (17) demonstrates the highly complex ways in which a point of view interacts with the background knowledge contained in frames. In this case, the writer employs definite articles (*the man on the bus*) to prompt readers to evoke the frame relating to bus rides in Los Angeles (one aspect of which is how disagreeable such experiences are). This knowledge is part of the cultural background shared by most readers of the *Los Angeles Times*. Notice, though, that the frame is evoked in a very indirect manner, through the use of an extremely detailed description of the man on the bus. All this detail, namely *wearing surgical slippers and asking if anyone can spare a couple of bucks for new shoes*, suggests, at first glance, that the writer is introducing a specific, identifiable man. However, this individual cannot be identifiable to readers; rather, the man can only be identifiable from the viewpoint of the third-person discourse protagonist, David Nathan.

(17) David Nathan has never gotten a parking ticket.
  That is one of the good things about not owning a car in Los Angeles. Among the bad is **the man on the bus** wearing surgical slippers and asking if anyone can spare a couple of bucks for new shoes.
  "There is a certain grimness on the bus," admits Nathan, who nevertheless eschews driving in favor of riding buses, taking cabs, relying on friends and walking. (*Los Angeles Times*, 4/11/94, p. B1)

Although the nominal *the man on the bus* appears to refer simply to a specific individual, notice that this definite description occurs in a clause whose main verb, *is*, is in the present tense. This usage provides a clue that the sentence should not be understood solely as a description of a specific event with a specific man, but also as a description of a stereotypical scene familiar to all residents of Los Angeles. In other words, this man represents a salient role within their bus frame. This complex, but very effective, strategy forces readers to vicariously ride the bus with Nathan by using definite articles to introduce a specific man accessible only in the mental space linked to Nathan's experiences. At the same time, the use of the present-tense main verb serves as a signal that this man symbolizes everything that is unpleasant about riding buses. Thus, the definite description introduces a value (an individual man) into the mental space associated with Nathan; the man also instantiates the role that is set up in the space associated with bus rides. This example, along with the others in this section, demonstrates that a crucial task accomplished by definite articles is the grounding of discourse referents from various points of view.

3.4. Further examples

Up to this point, we have seen that definite articles relate designated instances to the ground by indicating that those instances are accessible (to a low degree). Furthermore, the nature of the grounding relationship may be specified in greater detail — the speaker may intend the designated instance to have characteristics such as unique identifiability, high prominence, role, or value status. The instance may also be accessed from distinct points of view. However, these more specific details are not explicitly encoded by the article itself. Instead, they must be inferred by hearers on the basis of information from the broader context in which the definite nominal occurs. Several other issues arise in this respect that merit discussion.

First, it should be emphasized that the functions fulfilled by definite articles are not mutually exclusive. A single definite description may serve more than one of these functions at the same time. For instance, many uniquely identifiable referents are also discourse prominent (e.g. continuing, rather than new, topics); roles are frequently identifiable (see section 3.2); and a nominal with *the* referring to a discourse-prominent (or highly topical) entity may simultaneously indicate that the entity is being introduced into the discourse from a noncanonical point of view (see Epstein, forthcoming).[8] To take another example, in (18), the nominal *the discordant note* introduces a discourse referent that may be interpreted as a prominent individual, or as a role, or perhaps as both.

(18) But only a few days ago something happened which shook me out of my pleasant apathy.
 I was sitting out back on my 33,000-acre terrace, shoeless and shirtless, scratching my toes in the sand and sipping on a tall iced drink, watching the flow of evening over the desert. Prime time: the sun very low in the west, the birds coming back to life, the shadows rolling for miles over rock and sand to the very base of the brilliant mountains. I had a small fire going near the table .... Smiling, thoroughly at peace, I turned back to my drink, the little fire, the subtle transformations of the immense landscape before me. On the program: rise of the full moon.
 It was then I heard **the discordant note**, the snarling whine of a jeep in low range and four-wheel-drive, coming from an unexpected direction ... the jeep turned in at my driveway and came right up to the door of the trailer. It was a gray jeep with a U.S. Government decal on the side — Bureau of Public Roads — and covered with dust. Two empty water bags flapped at the bumper. Inside were three sunburned men in twill britches and engineering boots, and a pile of equipment: transit case, tripod, survey rod, bundles of wooden stakes. (*Oh no!*) (Abbey 1968: 42–43; italics in the original)

The prominence analysis is supported by the fact that *the discordant note* introduces an entity that is highly topical in the rest of the paragraph. At the same time, we could also analyze the nominal as introducing not an individual, but a role, in which case *the discordant note* is understood to be the negative element that inevitably arrives to disturb someone's existence in paradise. (Under the latter analysis, notice that the role should also be considered uniquely identifiable, since recognition of the paradise frame allows readers to infer, via bridging, the presence of a discordant note.) Which analysis is correct? I do not believe that any evidence can be found to allow us to decide this question. Nor do I see any reason to reject one of these analyses as "incorrect". Theoretically, it is plausible that two distinct sources of motivation may converge, in a single context, on the selection of the same morpheme (here, the definite article). Moreover, if it is true that "[l]anguage does not carry meaning, it guides it" (Fauconnier 1994: xxii), i.e. that the meanings of sentences are underspecified, then we should expect to find definite descriptions that prompt different people (or even a single individual) to draw distinct interpretations of the utterance in which the description occurs.

In (19), which is taken from the very beginning of a news item describing the legal problems of Aaron Spelling, the nominals *the bowling alley*, *the doll museum*, and *the gift-wrapping room* may be interpreted as individual entities accessible only from the mental space depicting Spelling's point of view. At this point in the text, Spelling, though not readers, can identify these particular referents, suggesting that the passage is told from his perspective. On the other hand, the nominals may be read as introducing roles. Under this interpretation, Spelling is portrayed as an ordinary homeowner because his house has the sorts of thing that are found in any typical home (the bowling alley, doll museum, and gift-wrapping room, like the kitchen, the bathroom, etc., are roles in the house frame). It is probably safe to assume that the writer intended the latter interpretation to be ironic.

(19)   When your attic has 20,000 square feet of floor space and 13-foot ceilings, you naturally don't want the roof to leak. After all, **the bowling alley, the doll museum**, and **the gift-wrapping room** might get wet. So what's a homeowner to do? Sue the contractor, of course.

But when the homeowner is Aaron Spelling, the creator of over-the-top television programs from "Fantasy Island" to "Beverly Hills 90210," and when the house is his 45-room, 56,500-square-foot mansion in the lush green enclave of Holmby Hills, the trial is no ordinary tale. (*The New York Times*, 7/3/97, p. A14)

As in (18), it also seems plausible to interpret the definite articles in (19) as simultaneously serving multiple functions; that is, they indicate both that the referents should be set up as roles and that the referents are accessible from a noncanonical third-person perspective.

Another issue that has not yet been discussed is the generic use of definite descriptions. It is well known that nominals with *the* potentially designate either an individual or an entire class of individuals (the generic interpretation).[9] For instance, the nominal *the computer* may designate a single computer or the class of computers in general. As usual, of course, the intended interpretation must be determined by contextual factors, such as the meaning of the verb. Thus, in *Turing repaired the computer*, the definite nominal designates an individual computer, while in *Turing invented the computer*, it designates the class of computers (these examples are taken from Ojeda 1991: 367). Generic definite descriptions represent accessible entities insofar as these entities belong to the background knowledge shared by all members of the speech community.

When it suits their communicative goals, speakers can take advantage of the fact that definite articles do not explicitly carry any meaning other than low accessibility, and that the precise interpretation of a definite nominal must be decided in context. Consider the striking example in (20). In this case, the writer knows that the most likely interpretation of the first mention of *the juniper tree* is generic. The reason is that the process of accessing discourse referents is guided by, amongst other things, the presumption of optimal relevance (in the sense of Sperber and Wilson 1986). Information is more easily accessed from short-term rather than long-term memory. Thus, accessing information from context types such as the immediately preceding utterances is relatively uncostly in terms of processing effort (Ariel 1990: 166; Kempson 1986: 214). But given that, here, no representation of the juniper tree can be retrieved from short-term memory (the juniper tree has not been previously mentioned in example 20), and given that the context is compatible with a generic interpretation of *the juniper tree*, many readers will access the representation of the type *juniper tree* which already exists in their long-term memory. However, the sentence following the first mention of the tree explicitly states that the generic reading is *not* the author's intended interpretation, and that the nominal does in fact refer to a single particular tree.

(20) Language makes a mighty loose net with which to go fishing for simple facts, when facts are infinite. If a man knew enough he could write a whole book about **the juniper tree**. Not juniper trees in general but that one particular juniper tree which grows from a ledge of naked sandstone near the old entrance to Arches National Monument. (Abbey 1968: xii)

In this unusual situation, it is possible that some readers will go back to the first occurrence of *the juniper tree* and reinterpret the nominal, substituting, post hoc, a "uniquely identifiable individual" interpretation for the original (mistaken) generic one. It is also possible that some readers will infer that in this context, the juniper is a prominent entity. And the tree does turn out to be prominent in the larger context of Abbey's book.[10] The inference that the tree is a prominent entity, however, will probably be the most difficult to draw (out of all possible interpretations of the definite article). Accessing prominent entities, especially new topics, exacts a high processing cost on hearers, because these entities must be held in short-term memory until an explanation of their prominence is supplied by the speaker. Nevertheless, the high processing costs are offset by the rich contextual inferences that are drawn concerning the entity and its relation to the context (because of its prominence), thereby assuring that optimal relevance still be achieved.

Once again, it may not be possible to decide which reading of (20) is "correct", or if indeed there can even be such a thing as a single correct reading (especially when dealing with a literary text). The examples in this section suggest that definite articles specify only certain aspects of the grounding relationship. The article explicitly signals the availability of an access path, but the exact nature of the path is underspecified. Consequently, any given definite description may be compatible with several distinct access paths, where each path corresponds to a distinct interpretation. The various paths arise because the article is able to trigger the construction of different mental space configurations (different combinations of mental spaces and trans-spatial connections), according to each hearer's background experiences and how the hearer reads the description in its context.

4. Discussion: Subjectivity and definiteness

In light of the evidence in section 3, showing that definite articles display a wide range of functions, the question arises: why has previous research on definiteness concentrated almost exclusively on the referential function (the unique identifiability/familiarity uses)? Some linguists have claimed that there is little more to definiteness than reference: "[unique identifiability] is both necessary and sufficient for appropriate use of the definite article *the*." (Gundel, Hedberg, and Zacharski 1993: 277) In this section, I will explore some of the possible causes of this referential bias in the literature on definiteness.

In a series of papers, Silverstein (1976, 1977, 1979, 1981, and elsewhere) argues that much work in linguistics pertains to reference because linguists and native speakers both tacitly accept a general referential folk model of language: "Reference, as Sapir noted, is the "official" use of speech in our own (and probably many other) societies; its privileged position comes from a metapragmatic awareness of the speakers constituted by overt, learned, metapragmatic norms: we use speech in order to represent things "out there"." (Silverstein 1977: 149) The referential model of language does not only predominate in our everyday intuitions about the function of language, but also in our theoretical conception of language: "this referential function of speech ... has formed the basis for linguistic theory and linguistic analysis in the Western tradition .... All of our analytic techniques and formal descriptive machinery have been designed for referential signs." (Silverstein 1976: 14–15) However, it must be recognized that this model, like all folk models, is not founded on the systematic study of empirical evidence. Rather, "[t]he priority of reference in establishing linguistic categories and structure rests squarely on the manipulability of this mode by the metalinguistic property. But reference itself is just one, perhaps actually a minor one, among the "performative" or "speech act" functions of speech." (Silverstein 1976: 18–19)

In a fascinating paper, Silverstein (1981) shows that speakers have relatively little conscious access to nonreferential (non-truth-conditional) meanings. The more *creative* or *performative* an indexical form is, the more likely its meaning will fall beyond the limits of native speakers' awareness. A relatively creative form, in Silverstein's sense, brings contextual features of meaning into existence which cannot be independently verified, i.e. it is essentially the sole signal of those features' existence (see Silverstein 1976: 34, 1981: 6–7). By way of illustration, Silverstein (1981: 8–10) describes the augmentative/diminutive forms of Wasco-Wishram Chinook, which are highly creative in that they index various speaker attitudes (e.g. positive affective evaluation) and which turn out to be quite difficult for native speakers to consciously manipulate. In addition, he notes that the nonreferential functions of language "are always being assimilated to reference in terms of native speaker awareness, and are in fact subject to conscious metapragmatic testimony only to the extent that they are assimilable to reference, or "ride along on" referential structure" (Silverstein 1981: 20).

Many definite article usages, such as the ones examined in this chapter, are also highly creative. For instance, the definite descriptions fulfilling an expressive function index the speaker's subjective attitudes, including the evaluations that an entity is discourse prominent (highly topical) or more important than other entities of the same type. In addition, being a role or a value is not an inherent or objective aspect of an entity — such features are assigned in accordance with the speaker's local discourse goals. As argued in section 3, the definite article is often the sole signal of the existence of these features. If the article is removed or replaced by another determiner, then features such as high topicality or role status disappear completely from the entity designated by the nominal. Even the attribution of features such as uniquely identifiability or familiarity is a relatively creative act: "a speaker's use of definiteness is not a merely automatic reaction to prior mention or to presence of a referent in the discourse situation. Speakers exert a considerable degree of control over their choice of alternatives. With the curiosity of the addressee in mind, the speaker makes judgments as to the salience of tracing an object's identity." (Du Bois 1980: 272) Nevertheless, identifiability is, in general, a less creative sort of feature than the others discussed here, because prior mention and deictic presence can be verified independently of the speaker's subjective judgments. As a result, we are apt to be consciously aware of just the referential function of the definite article. Worse yet, the heavy reliance, in most theorizing about definiteness, on a database of constructed sentences assures that referential uses of *the* will predominate (it is difficult to invent examples illustrating functions that one is not aware of), which in turn confirms, in circular fashion, the correctness of referential theories. The way to avoid this circularity is by analyzing a large number of article occurrences in naturally occurring discourse: "many crucial phenomena related to definiteness are either not found or not easily recognized within the domain of the one-sentence or two-sentence examples which are typically used." (Du Bois 1980: 204)

It is interesting to compare Silverstein's notion of creativity to Langacker's notion of subjectivity (see especially Langacker 1985, this volume a). For Langacker, an entity is construed subjectively "to the extent that it functions as the subject of conception but not as the object" (Langacker, this volume a: 17). A subjectively construed entity is not put onstage as a salient object of conception (it is not in the general locus of viewing attention); instead, it is offstage and nonsalient (which should not be taken to imply that it is somehow not relevant). Langacker (1991: 93) suggests that conceptualizers may not be consciously aware of entities that are construed in a highly subjective manner, since they are mostly absorbed in their conceptualization of more objective entities, which are the main focus of attention. As for definite articles, Langacker argues that one of the defining characteristics of grounding predications, such as articles, is that they do not profile the grounding relationship itself: "although they necessarily invoke the ground in some fashion, they construe the ground with the highest degree of subjectivity consistent with its inclusion in their scope." (Langacker, this volume a: 17) Thus, definite nominals profile the grounded entity but not the relationship between the entity and the ground. For example, a nominal such as *the book* profiles only an instance of the class of books, not the specific way in which this instance relates to the ground. The grounding relationship remains offstage (unprofiled), though it is of course still crucial for understanding the role of the entity in the broader discourse. And because it is offstage, we are unlikely to be consciously aware of the nature of the grounding relationship. This, too, may explain why it has proven so difficult to discern the diverse range of functions served by definite articles.

5. Conclusion

In this chapter, I have taken definite articles as the starting point for an examination of nominal grounding. I first proposed a unified explanation of the meaning of definite articles according to which all article occurrences explicitly signal that a referent is accessible to a low degree. However, I also argued that the article signals nothing more than the existence of an access path — it does not further specify what the exact interpretation of any nominal might be. Then, deploying evidence gathered from naturally occurring discourse, I showed some of the different ways in which definite articles interact with contextual factors to contribute extra nuances to nominal grounding. In addition to unique identifiability, articles may be used to imply high prominence, role/value status, and shifts to noncanonical points of view.

Langacker (this volume b: 33) portrays grounding and the use of grounding predications as part of the conceptualizer's effort to "gain control" over the picture of evolving reality that is constantly being constructed in discourse. This metaphor seems particularly appropriate in light of the data presented in this chapter, where I have emphasized the subjective elements guiding the speaker's choice of grounding predications (of definite articles, in particular). Speakers select definite articles to coordinate reference, certainly, and in this regard, they must take the hearer's needs into account, but at the same time, they also seek active control over the way discourse referents are constructed. The choice of determiner is one means by which speakers strive to oblige the hearer to accept referents into the discourse under the guise they desire and, more generally, to communicate their assessment of the overall status of what is being said.

Notes

1. I would like to thank Frank Brisard and René Dirven for their helpful comments on an earlier draft of this paper. I alone, however, am responsible for the errors that remain.
2. Other choices, e.g. a demonstrative, are possible, of course, but we cannot go into the differences between definite determiners in this chapter.
3. Thanks to Gilles Fauconnier for bringing this example to my attention.
4. See Epstein (1996, 1998, forthcoming) for further arguments and evidence against referential accounts of the meaning of the definite article in English.
5. I assume that the notion of accessibility is generally compatible with Langacker's notion of mental contact (see section 2). If an entity can be retrieved from memory (accessibility), then it can also be singled out for individual conscious awareness (mental contact). I prefer the term "accessibility" because it has been developed in much more detail than "mental contact", but either notion, in my view, can be taken to underlie the concept of definiteness.
6. De Mulder (2000) gives an analysis of the definite article in French that is highly compatible with the one I am proposing here. He argues that "the definite article never presents its referent as such, it always inserts it in a knowledge structure which is already set up in the context ... the definite article signals the accessibility of a discourse space" (De Mulder 2000: 4).
7. Kumeyaay is an Indian name for the speech varieties previously known to scholars as Diegueño. The Kumeyaay data are drawn from my own field notes. The following orthographic conventions are used in the transcriptions (based on the practical orthography developed for Kumeyaay by Margaret Langdon): ch=/č/; e=/ə/; x=/χ/; '=/ʔ/. Abbreviations used in the glosses are: 2=second person; 3=third person; AUX=auxiliary; DS=different subject; IR=irrealis; NEG=negative; S=subject; SS=same subject. The suffix -*pu* is phonologically reduced to -*pe* when it precedes other suffixes, such as the subject marker -*ch*-.
8. Generally speaking, prominence is closely related to point of view, since a discourse entity can only be construed as prominent from some conceptualizer's perspective.
9. And, of course, they can also designate roles, though this possibility has rarely been recognized in the literature. For the sake of clarity, it is worth pointing out that roles and generics are distinct sorts of interpretation and should not be confused (see Fauconnier 1994: 40).
10. It is mentioned a number of times later in the book. On several occasions, it is discussed at some length, for example: "My lone juniper stands half-alive, half-dead, the silvery wind-rubbed claw of wood projected stiffly at the sun. A single cloud floats in the sky .... Life has come to a standstill, at least for the hour. In this forgotten place the tree and I wait on the shore of time." (Abbey 1968: 135)

Sources of data

Abbey, Edward
    1968   *Desert Solitaire: A Season in the Wilderness.* New York: Simon & Schuster.

Villehardouin
    1972   *La conquête de Constantinople* [The Conquest of Constantinople], Volumes 1 and 2. Text and translation, edited by E. Faral. Paris: Société d'Edition "Les Belles Lettres". First published 1938.

References

Abbott, Barbara
    1999   Support for a unique theory of definiteness. In: Tanya Matthews and Devon Strolovitch (eds.), *Proceedings from Semantics and Linguistic Theory IX*, 1–15. Ithaca: Cornell University.

Ariel, Mira
    1988   Referring and accessibility. *Journal of Linguistics* 24: 65–87.
    1990   *Accessing Noun-Phrase Antecedents.* London: Routledge.

Barwise, Jon and Robin Cooper
    1981   Generalized quantifiers and natural language. *Linguistics and Philosophy* 4: 159–219.

Barwise, Jon and John Perry
    1983   *Situations and Attitudes.* Cambridge, MA: MIT Press.

Birner, Betty and Gregory Ward
    1994   Uniqueness, familiarity, and the definite article in English. In: Susanne Gahl, Andy Dolbey and Christopher Johnson (eds.), *Proceedings of the Twentieth Annual Meeting of the Berkeley Linguistics Society*, 93–102. Berkeley: Berkeley Linguistics Society.

Brisard, Frank
    this vol.   The English present.

Chafe, Wallace L.
    1976   Givenness, contrastiveness, definiteness, subjects, topics, and point of view. In: Charles N. Li (ed.), *Subject and Topic*, 25–55. New York: Academic.
    1994   *Discourse, Consciousness, and Time: The Flow and Displacement of Conscious Experience in Speaking and Writing.* Chicago: University of Chicago Press.

Chesterman, Andrew
    1991   *On Definiteness: A Study with Special Reference to English and Finnish.* Cambridge: Cambridge University Press.

Christophersen, Paul
1939   *The Articles: A Study of Their Theory and Use in English.* Copenhagen: Einar Munksgaard.
Clark, Herbert H. and Catherine R. Marshall
1981   Definite reference and mutual knowledge. In: Aravind K. Joshi, Bonnie L. Webber and Ivan A. Sag (eds.), *Elements of Discourse Understanding,* 10–63. Cambridge: Cambridge University Press.
Declerck, Renaat
1986   Two notes on the theory of definiteness. *Journal of Linguistics* 22: 25–39.
De Mulder, Walter
2000   Accessibility vs. presence: Demonstrative determiners, definite articles, and grounding. Paper presented at the 7th International Pragmatics Conference, Budapest.
Du Bois, John W.
1980   Beyond definiteness: The trace of identity in discourse. In: Wallace L. Chafe (ed.), *The Pear Stories: Cognitive, Cultural, and Linguistic Aspects of Narrative Production,* 203–274. Norwood: Ablex.
Epstein, Richard
1993   The definite article: Early stages of development. In: Jaap van Marle (ed.), *Historical Linguistics 1991: Papers from the 10th International Conference on Historical Linguistics,* 111-134. Amsterdam: John Benjamins.
1995   L'article défini en ancien français: L'expression de la subjectivité. *Langue française* 107: 58–71.
1996   Viewpoint and the definite article. In: Adele E. Goldberg (ed.), *Conceptual Structure, Discourse and Language,* 99–112. Stanford: Center for the Study of Language and Information.
1998   Reference and definite referring expressions. *Pragmatics and Cognition* 6: 189–207.
2000   A definite article in Kumeyaay. Unpublished manuscript.
forthcom. The definite article, accessibility, and the construction of discourse referents. *Cognitive Linguistics.*
Fauconnier, Gilles
1994   *Mental Spaces: Aspects of Meaning Construction in Natural Language.* Cambridge: Cambridge University Press.
1997   *Mappings in Thought and Language.* Cambridge: Cambridge University Press.
Givón, Talmy
1983   Topic continuity in discourse: An introduction. In: Talmy Givón (ed.), *Topic Continuity in Discourse: A Quantitative Cross-Language Study,* 5–41. Amsterdam: John Benjamins.

1984 *Syntax: A Functional-Typological Introduction*, Volume 1. Amsterdam: John Benjamins.
1992 The grammar of referential coherence as mental processing instructions. *Linguistics* 30: 5–55.

Gundel, Jeanette K., Nancy Hedberg and Ron Zacharski
1993 Cognitive status and the form of referring expressions in discourse. *Language* 69: 274–307.

Halliday, M.A.K. and Ruqaiya Hasan
1976 *Cohesion in English*. London: Longman.

Hanks, William F.
1992 The indexical ground of deictic reference. In: Alessandro Duranti and Charles Goodwin (eds.), *Rethinking Context*, 43–76. Cambridge: Cambridge University Press.

Hawkins, John A.
1978 *Definiteness and Indefiniteness: A Study in Reference and Grammaticality Prediction*. London: Croom Helm.
1991 On (in)definite articles: Implicatures and (un)grammaticality prediction. *Journal of Linguistics* 27: 405–442.

Heim, Irene R.
1982 The semantics of definite and indefinite noun phrases. Ph.D. dissertation, University of Massachusetts, Amherst.

Hintikka, Jaakko and Jack Kulas
1985 *Anaphora and Definite Descriptions: Two Applications of Game-Theoretical Semantics*. Dordrecht: Reidel.

Kadmon, Nirit
1990 Uniqueness. *Linguistics and Philosophy* 13: 273–324.

Kempson, Ruth
1986 Definite NPs and context dependence: A unified theory of anaphora. In: Terry Myers, Keith Brown and Brendan McGonigle (eds.), *Reasoning and Discourse Processes*, 209–239. London: Academic.

Kleiber, Georges
1992 Article défini, unicité et pertinence. *Revue Romane* 27: 61–89.

Lambrecht, Knud
1994 *Information Structure and Sentence Form: Topic, Focus, and the Mental Representations of Discourse Referents*. Cambridge: Cambridge University Press.

Langacker, Ronald W.
1985 Observations and speculations on subjectivity. In: John Haiman (ed.), *Iconicity in Syntax*, 109–150. Amsterdam: John Benjamins.
1991 *Foundations of Cognitive Grammar*, Volume 2: *Descriptive Application*. Stanford: Stanford University Press.
this vol. a Deixis and subjectivity.

this vol. b Remarks on the English grounding systems.
Laury, Ritva
 this vol. Interaction, grounding and third-person referential forms.
Löbner, Sebastian
 1985 Definites. *Journal of Semantics* 4: 279–326.
Lyons, Christopher
 1999 *Definiteness*. Cambridge: Cambridge University Press.
Nuyts, Jan
 this vol. Grounding and the system of epistemic expressions in Dutch: A cognitive-functional view.
Ojeda, Almerindo E.
 1991 Definite descriptions and definite generics. *Linguistics and Philosophy* 14: 367–397.
Prince, Ellen F.
 1981 Toward a taxonomy of given-new information. In: Peter Cole (ed.), *Radical Pragmatics*, 223–255. New York: Academic.
Russell, Bertrand
 1905 On denoting. *Mind* 14: 479–93.
Schnedecker, Catherine, Michel Charolles, Georges Kleiber and Jean David (eds.)
 1994 *L'anaphore associative: Aspects linguistiques, psycholinguistiques et automatiques*. Paris: Klincksieck.
Searle, John R.
 1969 *Speech Acts: An Essay in the Philosophy of Language*. Cambridge: Cambridge University Press.
Silverstein, Michael
 1976 Shifters, linguistic categories, and cultural description. In: Keith H. Basso and Henry A. Selby (eds.), *Meaning in Anthropology*, 11–55. Albuquerque: University of New Mexico Press.
 1977 Cultural prerequisites to grammatical analysis. In: Muriel Saville-Troika (ed.), *Georgetown University Round Table on Languages and Linguistics 1977: Linguistics and Anthropology*, 139–151. Washington, D.C.: Georgetown University Press.
 1979 Language structure and linguistic ideology. In: Paul R. Clyne, William F. Hanks and Carol L. Hofbauer (eds.), *The Elements: A Parasession on Linguistic Units and Levels*, 193–247. Chicago: Chicago Linguistic Society.
 1981 *The limits of awareness*. (Sociolinguistic working paper 84.) Austin: Southwest Educational Development Laboratory.
Sperber, Dan and Deirdre Wilson
 1986 *Relevance: Communication and Cognition*. Cambridge, MA: Harvard University Press.

Stanzel, Franz K.
    1981   Teller-characters and reflector-characters in narrative theory. *Poetics Today* 2: 5–15.

Interaction, grounding and third-person referential forms

Ritva Laury

1. Introduction[1]

This chapter deals with how the use of third-person forms, both pronouns and full nominals, is based on, and functions to organize, the ground in conversational discourse. I intend to show that the indexical ground (Hanks 1990, 1992), the contextual features relative to which reference in interaction is coded and interpreted and which are definable as "the speech event, its participants, and its immediate circumstances" (Langacker this volume b: 29), is not something that is given in advance to participants in a speech event, but rather something that they jointly create and modify in verbal interaction.

In itself, this claim is neither novel nor in principle contrary to the discussions of grounding in cognitive grammar. The point that the ground is dynamic and created through linguistic and nonlinguistic actions has been made previously by, *inter alia*, Goffman (1981), Goodwin (1981), Goodwin and Goodwin (1992), Hanks (1990), Ford and Fox (1996), Schegloff (1996), Laury (1997), Seppänen (1998), and Pekarek (1999, 2001). Likewise, discussions of grounding predications in terms of subjectivity and the need of speakers and hearers to establish perspective and to construe vantage points (Langacker this volume a: 19), do not exclude the possibility of the actual construction of the ground by the participants and in fact specifically define it as something distinct from the physical, "real-world" circumstances of the speech event.

However, my contribution does challenge the concept of grounding, as discussed by Langacker (this volume a,b), in two significant ways. In that work, in contrast to what I propose here, the ground is seen as inherently static and egocentric. Langacker (this volume a: 20) suggests that "maintaining a common deictic center, defined by the "here-and-now" of the speech event, is essential to the coherence of a complex sentence. Were the deictic center to shift on a clause-by-clause basis, always reflecting the vantage of the last conceptualizer introduced (or the one whose conception is being described), keeping things straight might be extremely difficult..." I will provide evidence from ordinary speech to show that the ground is not static, but rather dynamic and constantly shifting in interaction, as it is not only maintained but also created and modified by the participants. In addition, I view the ground as essentially sociocentric, something that is jointly shared by the participants, or something that is common to them, as suggested by the first part of Langacker's definition, rather than belonging to or created strictly from the viewpoint of a particular speaker or conceptualizer, as implied by the second part of his definition. Secondly, in the same vein as the paper by Nuyts (this volume), my paper seeks to expand the definition of grounding predications beyond the domain of grammatical devices. According to Langacker (this volume b: 29), "grounding predications constitute a small set of highly grammaticized elements, one of which has to be chosen as the final step in forming a full nominal or finite clause". I propose here that a wider range of resources, including full nominals, in addition to grammaticized elements such as pronouns and determiners, are used by speakers to construct, maintain, and modify the ground in interaction.

The chapter is organized as follows. After a brief description of the data, I will discuss the contribution that third-person forms which stand for participants in the speech event, make to the construction of the indexical ground, and especially to the participant framework (Goffman 1981), in conversation. The next section discusses the contribution of those third-person forms which do not stand for speech-act participants. The final section summarizes the discussion.

2. Data

The data for this paper come from ordinary conversations between friends, family, and coworkers in Finnish. Most of the data were audiotaped and transcribed by the author; some come from corpora collected at the University of Helsinki and the University of Turku (see Laury 1997 for details).

3. The use of third-person forms for participants in conversation

The observation that first- and second-person pronouns refer to speakers and addressees, and thus function to code and construct participant status in discourse, is obviously noncontroversial and probably also intuitively more believable than a similar claim about third-person referential forms. For example, Benveniste (1971: 196–201), in his well-known article on the nature of pronouns, discusses the connection of first- and second-person pronouns with the speech situation, and even goes as far as to claim that the third person is a nonperson, since the referents of third-person pronouns are not speech-act participants. Likewise, Jakobson (1990: 390) includes first- and second-person pronouns but omits third-person pronouns from his discussion of shifters, elements which become "full" or meaningful only on an occasion of use.

However, the two-participant model of conversation consisting only of the speaker and the addressee has been critiqued as too simplistic, first within sociology (Goffman 1981) and conversation analysis (Sacks 1992), and later also within linguistic pragmatics (Levinson 1988). Particularly important to subsequent work on conversational interaction are the analytical concepts developed by Goffman, in particular the participation framework, an account of the various roles that participants in conversation may take in the interaction, and footing, the alignment of a speaker toward her current utterance (for example, the speaker's epistemic stance), both of which are constantly shifting during interaction (Goffman 1981: 124–159). Further, Hanks (1990), Ford and Fox (1996), Schegloff (1996), Seppänen (1996, 1998), and Laitinen (1992), among others, have shown that third-person forms have much to do with the participation framework in a speech event, and can be used to refer to co-participants in conversation. Conversely, second-person pronouns do not automatically pick the current addressee as their referent, as shown by Lerner (1996).

In his foundational critique of the speaker/hearer model of conversational interaction, Goffman (1981: 129) suggests that dyadic conversation "is an arrangement for which the terms "speaker" and "hearer" fully and neatly apply — lay terms here being perfectly adequate for all technical needs". However, even in dyadic conversations, the addressee cannot always be taken for granted by the speaker, and third-person forms can function to refer to participants and construct and modify the ground. The following excerpt from a conversation between two sisters, ages 7 and 9, illustrates this. The girls are playing with a set of small dolls and their equipment, and are seated at a kitchen table across from each other. The talk revolves around inventorying and naming the toys, which the girls have just received as a gift, and deciding who is going to play with each particular doll. Several adults are present, coming in and out of the room and at times participating in the conversation, or carrying on conversations of their own, but the last seven turns on the tape involve the two children only, and the last exchange between the children and one of the adults is 41 turns back. Thus, while there have been some isolated turns produced by the adults which have been addressed to other adults during the last 41 turns, the two children have been speaking only to each other for quite some time. In such a situation one might assume that the participation framework (in this case, the reciprocal status of each girl as the addressee of the other girl) would be already established and would not require any extra work for the participants to maintain, but this assumption does not seem to be correct.

Example (1)

1 V *Tässon   iso[isä].*
    here-be.3sg grandfather
    'Here's grandpa.'

2 S　　　　　　　　[*Missä*]　*tän*　　　　*sauvatki*　　　*on.*
　　　　　　　　　WH-INE　this-GEN　pole-PL-CLTC　be-3sg
　　　　　　　　　'Where are this one's (ski)poles.'

3 V　... *Täällä.*
　　　　here
　　　　'Here.

4　　... *Tän*　　　　*pienen*　　<WH XXX WH>
　　　　this-GEN　small-GEN
　　　　This little one's' (inaudible)

5　　... (1.2)

6 S　**Veera.**
　　　'Veera.

7　　*Mitä*　　　*sä*　　*oikeen*　　*katselet.*
　　　WH-PRT　2sg　really　　look-2sg
　　　What are you looking at.

8　　... *Häiritset.*
　　　　disturb-2sg
　　　　You're bothering (me).

9　　... **Veera** *häiritsee.*
　　　　V.　　　disturb-3sg
　　　　Veera's bothering (me).'

10 V　... (.8) *Tässon,*
　　　　　　　here-be.3sg
　　　　　　　'Here's

11　　... *tän*　　　　*ison*　　　　*luis=timet.*
　　　　this-GEN　big-GEN　　skate-PL
　　　　this big one's skates.'

12 S ... <WH Tää   on   sinun. WH>
           this   be.3sg   2sg-GEN
        'This is yours.'

(playmobil)

In line 6, S uses a vocative third-person form, V's first name, in initial position just before she addresses V using a second-person pronoun in line 7. The fact that V's previous turn in lines 3 and 4 contains the second pair part of an adjacency pair initiated by S in line 2 (in other words, V has just answered a question posed by S), as well as the duration of the conversation's dyadic structure referred to above, might lead one to assume that at this point, S could count on V as a recipient for her talk. However, the vocative suggests that this may not be the case. It may not be possible, without a videotape[2] that would provide information about eye gaze direction, to determine with certainty exactly why S produces the vocative. However, S's turn involves a complaint about what V is looking at. Much work has shown that eye gaze is an important factor in turn taking (see, for example, Goodwin 1981; Ford and Fox 1996). Thus it is possible that at the point where S produces the vocative, V's gaze is directed at something other than S, and that S is using the vocative to regain V's attention, and thus (re)claim her as a recipient for her turn.

In addition, S's vocative-initial turn is preceded by a 1.2 second pause. Even a pause of that length may be sufficient for speakers to choose forms aimed at the reestablishment of the participant structure, that is, at establishing the ground. Further, since names are locally initial forms (Schegloff 1996; Downing 1996), the vocative may also be functioning as an index of a shift to a new type of activity, a complaint, and thus it may have a structuring function in terms of indicating discontinuity.

In line 9, lacking an uptake from V, S initiates a shift in footing (Goffman 1981), thus altering the ground. Although the form *Veera* is identical to the vocative in line 6, here it refers to, rather than summons, V, as shown by the third-person verb form which follows it. The turn in line 9 does the same complaining work that lines 7–8 did, only this time the intended recipient is someone other than V.

Thus, in this case, the locally initial form is not being used to initiate a new type of activity, but rather to initiate a change in the participant framework. S's attempt to gain an adult as a recipient for her turn appears to be unsuccessful, since there is no audible uptake from any of the adults, and V takes the next turn.

We have just seen that even in two-participant conversations, third-person forms can be used to alter the participant framework. Third-person forms can initiate a bid to reclaim an addressee's attention, or a shift to a new addressee. But in multi-party conversations, the role of the addressee can be even more complex. There can be many types of participant (Goffman 1981; Levinson 1988), and linguistic choices available to speakers are a resource which can be used to index the shifting roles and thus also to transform the ground. For example, Seppänen (1998) has shown that the Finnish demonstrative pronouns, which, unlike their counterparts in many European languages, can be used for human referents directly (not only as modifiers), are used for this purpose in an intricate and interesting way. Seppänen (1998: 9) shows, for example, that the demonstrative *tämä* 'this' is an index of the referent's status as a co-participant in the speech event. This makes it a very useful referential form when a speaker wants to say something about one of the participants to the other participants without excluding the person being talked about. Consider the following example,[3] which comes from an eight-party conversation. A group of women friends have gathered for dinner at the home of one of the participants. The women are eating mushroom pizza, and the segment opens with a brief conversation about where the hostess, M, has picked the mushrooms.

Example (2)

1 T *Nää   on   varmaa Hirvensalon,*
    this.PL be-3sg surely   H.-GEN

2   ... *sieniä.*
       mushroom-PL-PRT
       'These mushrooms must be from Hirvensalo.'

3 M .. *Mm.*
    PTCL
    'Mm.'

4 L ... *Vai onks Astan mökiltä .. osa.*
    or   be-Q A.-GEN cottage-ABL part
    'Or are some of them from Asta's cottage.'

5 M .. *No=,*
    PTCL
    'Well,

6 ... *mm=.*
    PTCL
    mm,

7 .. *ehkä,*
    maybe,

8 ... *en minä muista nyt.*
    NEG 1sg remember now
    I can't remember now.

9 ... *Mut enimmäkseen Hirvensalon,*
    but mostly H.-GEN
    But mostly from Hirvensalo,

10 .. *Ei oo paljon muissa käyty.*
    NEG be.3sg much other-PL-INE visit-P.PPLE
    (We/I) haven't gone to too many other places.

11 ... *Ellei sitte tuolta Velkuan,*
    if-NEG then that.LOC-ABL V.-GEN
    Unless (they come) from Velkua,

12 ... *Velkuan maalta.*
   V.-GEN land-ABL
   from around Velkua.'

13 A .. *Ku nää oli,*
   when this.PL be-PST
   'When they (lit., these) were,

14 .. *siel,*
   that.LOC-ADE
   there,

15 ... *siellä   meillä   ja.*
   that.LOC-ADE 1pl-ADE and
   at our place and,

16 ... *Marjatta löysi   hirveen hyvät*
   M.   find-PST terribly good-PL
   suppilovahverot   sieltä.
   funnel.chanterelle-PL that.LOC-ABL
   Marjatta found really good funnel chanterelles over there.'

17 M ... *Noist   jäi   pieniä.*
   that.PL-ELA remain-PST small-PL
   '(There were) small ones left behind from those.'

18 ... *Siel   oli   aika paljo tulossa.*
   that.LOC-ADE be-PST fairly much come-N-INE
   There were quite a few (of them) coming (up).'
   (*ompeluseura*)

In lines 1–2, T proffers a guess about the provenance of the mushrooms and receives a noncommittal response from the hostess, M. At that point, L, the sister of the hostess, suggests in line 4 that the mushrooms may come from the woods near the summer cottage of A, one of the other participants. In her turn in lines 5–12, M remains noncommittal about where she picked the mushrooms. However, since L has suggested that some of the mushrooms may come from near A's cottage, M is not in a position to entirely deny this, since picking mushrooms on another person's property is considered a privilege and needs to be acknowledged. After suggesting that most of the mushrooms come from the island of Hirvensalo, the location of her childhood home, M acknowledges that some of them may come from Velkua, where A's summer cottage is located.

At this point, A uses a token of *nää* 'these (people)', the plural form of *tämä* 'this', to refer to M and her (unspecified) family members, who accompanied her on her visit to A's cottage. As the gloss shows, the demonstrative is in some sense equivalent to English *this*. Traditional accounts consider *tämä* the proximal one in the three-member set of Finnish demonstratives, but investigations of its use in actual spoken discourse have shown that social accessibility rather than actual spatial proximity is the primary component of the meaning of this demonstrative. It stands for referents in the speaker's current attentional and social sphere. In other words, what affects the choice of the Finnish demonstrative forms is not the concrete spatial proximity or distance of referents, but rather questions of who is currently aware of them, socially responsible for them (e.g. in the sense of "belonging"), or attending to them in some sense (for details, see Laury 1997). In this case, for instance, the family members who accompanied M on the mushroom picking trip to A's cottage are not at home at the time this conversation is taking place, and thus they are not in any way proximal to the speaker, A. However, they are, in a social sense, part of the scene in which the talk is taking place, since it is their home. Another way to account for the use of this pronoun would be to consider M as a proxy for the entire group of people to whom the pronoun refers, due to the fact that they constitute, together with M, a socially defined group, viz. a family.

Given its interactional meaning, described by Seppänen and discussed above, *nää* is a particularly appropriate form for A to use at this point in the conversation, as she is about to tell the other participants something that is news to them, but known to M (and in fact *about* M). Accordingly, M is referred to in the third person. As Seppänen (1998) has shown, *tämä* is used in such circumstances to establish the referent as a co-participant in the speech event. Here, it allows A to speak about M to the other participants without excluding her as an addressee, which is an important concern at this juncture. This is because A's turn functions to make a compliment to M as a mushroom finder, at a point in the conversation where M has just run the risk of seeming ungrateful for the opportunity of being able to pick mushrooms at A's summer cottage. Since A is a guest and just eating the mushrooms M has picked, a move complimenting M's ability as a mushroom finder (she found those mushrooms, they were not given to her by A) functions to express her gratefulness and minimize M's social obligation to her. Thus the form is extremely felicitous in this context, since A's turn is addressed to M just as much as it is to the other participants. The analysis of the form as indexing participant status is confirmed by the fact that M takes the next turn, in which she builds on A's comment by explaining that she did not even exhaust the mushroom stand which she discovered near A's cottage. Here we can see that even pronominal third-person forms, when used to refer to current participants, can function to maintain, not just modify, the participant structure.

In addition to being used for co-participants in interaction, third-person forms can also be used by speakers to refer to themselves. The following example involves the use of a name and a kin term in quoted speech to index the age of the planned addressee. The excerpt comes from a conversation between a mother and her daughter. The daughter, R, is jokingly suggesting that the mother, E, call her one-year-old grandson to inquire about a lost item.

Example (3)

1 R *Pyydät tota,*
     ask-2sg that.PRT
     'You'll ask for,

2   ... *puhelimeen,*
     telephone-ILL
     to the telephone,

3   ... *tota   Lauria,*
     that-PRT   L.-PRT
     (that) Lauri, (i.e. you should ask Lauri to come to the telephone)

4   *ja   [ky]syt,*
     and   ask-2sg
     and (you'll) ask (him),'

5 E *[Joo.]*
     PTCL
     'Yeah.'

6 R *Mi[hin   Lauri on   laittanu,]*
     WH-ILL   L.   be-3sg   put.P.PPLE
     'Where has Lauri put/where Lauri has put,'

7 E *[Mihi   sä   panit,*
     WH-ILL   2sg   put-PST-2sg
     'Where did you put,

8   .. *mummon,]*
     grandma-GEN
     grandma's,

9   ... *Mihi   sä   panit   mummon   suolakiven.*
     WH-ILL   2sg   put-PST-2sg   grandma-GEN   salt.rock-ACC
     Where did you put grandma's salt rock.'

                                                    (*suolalohi*)

In quotations, as is well known (see, for example, Mayes 1990), the ground of deictic reference shifts from the current speech situation to the situation where the quoted speech took place, or is imagined or portrayed as taking place. In Goffman's (1981) terms, a transition from direct to quoted speech is a shift in footing, in that it accomplishes a shift in who is picked out as the recipient of the speech being produced, and thus involves a change in the alignment of the participants (speaker and addressee). In this case, the shift is shown clearly in the form *sä* 'you.sg' in line 7, which does not index E's current addressee, her daughter, but rather her addressee in the imaginary phone conversation, her grandson. The forms E is using to refer to herself within the quote, *mummon* 'grandma's' in lines 8 and 9, are referential indexes in that they refer to the current speaker in the imagined situation (who is also the speaker in the current situation, but note that the form used is irrelevant to that fact). In addition, as a kin term, the form is also a nonreferential index of the relationship between the speaker and the imagined addressee of the quote, and in terms of its form, also for the age of the recipient; as is well known, there is a cross-linguistic tendency to avoid the use of speech-act pronouns in caretaker speech with very young children.

In this sense, the form *Lauri*, the first name of E's grandson, produced by R in line 6, can also be analyzed as indexical for the recipient's age, in the same sense as the two tokens of *mummi* 'grandma' in lines 8 and 9 were. This utterance is intended as a quote as well; and although it is spoken by R, the intended or indexed speaker (the "principal", or the person whose position is expressed in the words chosen, in terms of Goffman 1981) is E, as can be seen in the second-person marker in the reporting phrase *kysyt* '(you'll) ask'. While the lexical and grammatical details visible on the transcript leave open the nature of the truncated clause in line 6 (as Finnish does not distinguish grammatically between direct and indirect questions), the prosody of the clause, clearly audible on the tape, indicates that even this clause was intended as a quote. The pronoun *mihin* 'where' in line 6 is stressed, indicating that it is not a relative pronoun, but rather an interrogative. This shows that even prosody plays a role in the construction of the ground.

Additionally, the footing shift, or transformation of the ground, cannot be attributed wholly to either one of the participants; rather, it is jointly achieved. The shift is initiated, or put in motion, in R's turn in lines 1–4, where she suggests that E call her grandson. E's response to her suggestion, *joo* 'yeah', overlaps with the reporting phrase produced by R, *kysyt* '(you'll) ask'. Almost immediately afterwards, only one syllable apart and overlapping, both E and R start their turns containing direct speech. At this point, the footing shift is already accomplished and indexed through the grounding predications used, the prosody and the form *Lauri* in R's turn in line 6, and the second-person pronoun and the kin terms in E's turn in line 7. In both simultaneously produced turns, the intended or imagined addressee (recipient) is Lauri, E's grandson, and the indexed speaker (principal) is E. This example, then, shows that shifts in the ground cannot always be attributed to shifts from the vantage point of any particular interactant to that of another, but rather that they are joint accomplishments that orient the use and interpretation of forms by the participants.

In this section we have seen how third-person forms, both full nominals such as names and kin terms as well as pronominal forms, all of which can be used to refer to participants in the current speech situation, function to maintain and construct the ground, which is constantly shifting in interaction. We have also seen that even prosody can be used to index and shift the ground. The next section discusses the way in which third-person forms which stand for referents that are not participants in the current situation also perform these types of function.

4. Third-person forms and reference to nonparticipants in conversation

It is well known that a major factor influencing the choice of referential forms in discourse has to do with the cognitive access that the speaker assumes the addressee has with respect to the referent (Chafe 1976, 1994; Ariel 1990; Givón 1979; Lambrecht 1994; and others).

Thus, for example, speakers use definite forms for referents which they assume their addressees can identify, and indefinite forms for referents they assume cannot be identified. They use pronouns and other minimal forms for referents they assume their addressees are fully aware of, usually because they have just been mentioned, and full lexical nominals for referents they assume their addressees are not currently actively aware of, because they have not been previously mentioned or otherwise evoked in the discourse. This is essentially the view of definiteness espoused in cognitive grammar as well. Langacker suggests that definiteness involves the coordination of reference in terms of establishing "mental contact"; for example, a speaker will choose a definite article if both speaker and hearer have achieved mental contact with the intended referent (Langacker this volume a: 7; see also Langacker 1991: 89–91).

However, the expression of definiteness has a range of more dynamic functions than the coordination of reference with respect to cognitive accessibility, as shown in the work by Epstein (1996, 1998, this volume) within the framework of cognitive grammar. Epstein shows that factors such as viewpoint, salience, and whether the definite nominal picks out a role or a value (in the sense of Fauconnier 1994) also motivate the expression of definiteness. While most of Epstein's data come from written language, the choice of referential form can become even more complicated and more dynamic in multi-party conversations, where different addressees have different states of knowledge and alternations of referential forms can also be manipulated at the speaker's will for various other kinds of contextual effect. For example, as briefly noted above, speakers can manipulate referential form in order to index (mark or create) episodic or actional structure (for more discussion, see, for example, Clancy 1980; Fox 1987; Pekarek Doehler 2001).

The choice of form used for referents under discussion can also affect the participation framework, and the expected succession of forms from initial indefinite forms to subsequent definite forms may be altered by interactional considerations (Ford and Fox 1996; Laury 2001, to appear). Consider example (4) below. This excerpt comes from a conversation between three young women friends. Two of them, AL and EL, are telling RV about the events of a recent evening the two of them had spent together at a restaurant. All three women have been actively participating in the discussion up to this. RV has been eliciting and responding to AL's and EL's narration of the evening's events with frequent questions and feedback tokens. However, the structure of the interaction changes with EL's turn in line 1 of example (4).

Example (4)

1 EL *Se   oli   hyvä kun ne   vanhat äijät*
      3sg be-PST   good when DET-PL old-PL man-PL
      'It was great when the old geezers

2   *meinas   tukehtuu   niihi   Paven   [juttuihi,]*
     mean-PST choke-1INF   DET-PL-ILL P.-GEN   story-PL-ILL
     almost choked over Pave's stories,'

3 AL   *[Jaa joo.]*
                                                 PTCL PTCL
                                                 'Oh yeah.'

4 EL *yhe- yhelt   pääsi   varman   kymmene*
     one- one-ABL   be.allowed-PST certainly ten
     lusikallist.
     spoonful-PRT
     'one let go of ten spoonfuls, I'm sure.

5 AL ((GIGGLES))

6   *Ne   oli   kyl   nii.*
     3PL be-PST   PTCL   so
     They were really something.

7 AL ((GIGGLES))

8   Paveli   selitti.
    P.   explain-PST
    Paveli was carrying on.'

9 AL *Niinku   Paveli   viäres   istu   ja,*
    so-as   P.-GEN   side-INE   sit-PST   and
    'See next to Paveli sat,

10 *istus   [jottai   semmosi,*
    sit-PST   some   such-PL-PRT
    sat like these,'

11 EL   *[semmosi   vanhoi   äijii   ne   oli,*
        such-PL-PRT   old-PRT man-PRT   3pl   be-PST
        'they were like these old geezers,

12 *va-   emmä   o ikinä semmosi   enne   siäl*
           NEG-1sg.   be ever such-PRT   before   that.LOC-ADE
    nähny.
    see.P.PPLE
    I've never seen such (people) there before.'

(*tutot*)

EL's mention of *ne vanhat äijät* 'the old geezers' in line 1 is the first mention of these referents in the conversation, but it is modified by the determiner *ne*, the plural form of *se*, an erstwhile demonstrative which is being grammaticized as a definite article in spoken Finnish (Laury 1997). The explicitly definite form indicates that EL considers the referent identifiable, but as we can see from line 12, she had first encountered the men during the evening she and AL are jointly telling RV about, and thus the referents are previously identifiable only to AL and EL herself, but not to RV. In other words, only AL, but not RV, is able to establish mental contact with the intended instance of old men. In lines 9–10, AL initiates a locative existential/introductory construction followed by the indefinite determiners *jotain* 'some' and *semmosi* 'such', which is overlapped by EL producing a formally indefinite nominal *semmosi vanhoi äijii* 'these old geezers' in line 11. My interpretation is that EL's earlier mention was in a turn addressed to AL only. This analysis is supported by the fact that only AL is providing feedback at this point in the conversation, in lines 3, 5, and 7. RV had been participating actively earlier, asking questions and providing feedback to the telling, but gives no feedback during this portion of the talk. AL's introductory existential construction and the indefinite nominal, jointly produced by AL and EL well after the initial definite introduction and subsequent mentions of the referents, function to expand the participation framework by being directed explicitly at RV and including her as an addressee.

Different forms can also be used for the same referent in conversation to express changes in footing other than changes in the participation framework. For example, referents well known to participants may be referred to by formally indefinite forms due to intentional vagueness (Du Bois 1980) or to indicate changes in footing of various types. The following excerpt comes from the same conversation as example (3). In this part of the conversation, the mother E and daughter R are concerned with the same topic they were discussing in that example, the unknown whereabouts of the rock, referred to by E as *suolakivi* 'salt rock' in example (3) above. E, the mother, has used this rock for many years to weigh down fresh salted salmon, a popular Finnish holiday dish.

Example (5)

1 R *Oisko*   **sitä**   *nyt   mihinkään   ^muuhun*
     be-COND-Q it-PRT now anything-ILL other-ILL
     tarvinnu   **joku**   *sitte.*
     need.P.PPLE someone   then
     'I wonder if anyone else might have needed it for something then.'

2 E ... *En*   ^*minä*   *en*   *oo tarvinnu*   *sitä,*
     NEG-1sg   1sg   NEG-1sg be need-P.PPLE it-PRT
     'Well I certainly haven't needed it,'

3 R ***Joku   ^muu   [on,***
    someone other   be.3sg
    'Someone else has,

4 E   *[On   voinu   @^tar=vita,]*
              be.3sg   be.able-P.PPLE   need-1INF
              'May have needed,

5 R   *tarvinnu.]*
                        need-P.PPLE
                        needed.'

6 E   *joo.]*
                        PTCL
                        yeah.'

7 R ***^Kysy   isältä,***
    ask.2sg.IMP father-ABL
    'Ask dad.'

8 E ... *E=I   ku   se,*
    NEG   because   3sg
    'No because he,

9   .. *ku   se   sanoo*
      because   3sg   say.3sg
      because he'll say,

10   *ettei   hän   ikinä   ^nähnykkää,*
    COMP-NEG   3sg   ever   see.P.PPLE-PTCL
    that he has never even seen,

11   .. ***sellasta kivee.***
      such   rock
      such a rock.'

                                          (*suolalohi*)

In this example, the first two forms used to refer to the rock, the continuing topic, in lines 1 and 2 are pronominal and definite, but the last mention in line 11, *sellasta kivee* 'such a rock', is indefinite (technically termed a late indefinite; Du Bois 1980). The indefinite form reflects the imagined speaker's (the principal in Goffman's 1981 terms) presumed epistemic attitude toward the rock; he is predicted to claim he has never even seen any rock like the one searched by his wife and daughter. Thus it is not only the current speaker's (who in this case is both an animator and an author, in Goffman's 1981 terms) footing toward a referent that can be responsible for referential form, but also stances attributed to reported speakers, even in indirect quotes.

The person to whom the imagined quote is attributed, E's husband and R's father, is referred to in four different ways in this excerpt, each one indexing a shift in footing. In line 1, R speculates that someone else may have needed (and presumably used, but not replaced) the rock. E denies that she has needed the rock, and in line 3, R reiterates the reference, this time adding and stressing the word *muu* 'other'. The humorous implicature that arises, due to the fact that E and her husband are the only two residents of their home, is that this minimal form refers to E's husband. This is confirmed by the laughter quality in E's voice as she overlaps with R and completes the utterance initiated by R, and also by the stress pattern in R's utterance in line 7. Here R makes the implicature explicit by using the form *isä* 'father' in such a way that the word *kysy* 'ask.2sg.IMP' receives primary stress, and the word *isä* 'father' is unstressed, since its referent is now presupposed. By producing this mention, R shifts from a humorous footing to a kin term which indexes her personal relationship with the referent. The two mentions of the same referent in E's turn in lines 8 and 9 are pronominal, as expected of a given mention. In line 10, however, the pronominal form changes. The pronoun *hän* 'she/he' has been described in traditional Finnish grammar as a specifically human third-person pronoun, but recent studies have shown that in most spoken forms of Finnish, the pronoun is logophoric. It refers to the speaker in indirect quotes (Laitinen 1992). Thus the form *hän* in line 10 accomplishes another shift in footing. It now indexes the referent's role as a participant in an imagined speech act.

In the previous discussion of the forms used to refer to the rock, we saw that shifts in the indexical ground can also be accomplished through lexical forms referring to nonhumans. Shifts of this type can also be managed through the use of demonstratives. The following example comes from a dinner-table conversation at a holiday meal.[4]

Example (6)

1 O *Simo ku sä olet siel se*
　　S. when 2sg be-2sg that.LOC-ADE DET
　　snapsin vartija,
　　schnapps-GEN guard
　　'Simo, since you're in charge of the schnapps over there,

2 　*ni tääl on näitä%* --
　　so this.LOC-ADE be.3sg this.PL-PRT
　　here are these,

3 　... *laseja [tyhjinä].*
　　glass-PL-PRT empty-PL-ESS
　　empty glasses.'

4 S 　*[Näitä] hörppä.*
　　this.PL-PRT gulp
　　'These gulp (ones).'

5 O *Siel on ... Martti ja on-* --
　　that.LOC-ADE be.3sg M. and be.3sg
　　'There's Martti and there's,

6 　... *Martilla ei o [enää] eikä,*
　　M.-ADEN EG be any.more NEG-and
　　Martti has no more and,'

7 S   *[Mhm]*.
      PTCL
      'I see.'

8 O .. *Eilalla.*
    E.-ADE
    '(neither does) Eila.'

                   (*snapsi*)

In this excerpt, the host, O, is asking his son, seated next to the bottle of schnapps, to fill the glasses of two of the guests. Observe the shifting uses of demonstratives, which do not index the concrete location but rather the social accessibility, here in terms of responsibility for, concrete objects without any actual movement of the speech participants or the objects in question. In line 1, O uses the demonstrative adverb *siel*, roughly 'there', to mention his son's current location. *Siel* is the specifically locative form of the demonstrative *se*, which is used by speakers of Finnish to establish and refer to the current addressee's attentional and social sphere (Laury 1997). In line 2, O uses the demonstrative adverb *tääl* 'here', the locative form of the demonstrative *tämä* 'this', for the location of the empty glasses. The reference to the glasses themselves is preceded by the plural form of *tämä*, *näitä*, which is functioning here as a determiner. As was mentioned before in the discussion of example (2) above, *tämä* is used for, and refers to, the current speaker's attentional and social sphere. In line 4, S, the son, clarifies which glasses his father meant, using a plural partitive form of *näitä* in his reference to the glasses. This use indicates that S considers the glasses to be in his sphere. In line 5, O uses the locative form *siel*, which he had used in line 1 for his son's location, but this time he describes the location of the guests whose glasses need filling. By using this demonstrative, O is shifting his footing; although neither the glasses, the guests, nor the two speakers have moved during this exchange, the ground has shifted in such a way that the glasses are now in S's sphere, and no longer in O's sphere, which was O's intention in directing his son to fill the glasses. The social responsibility for the glasses has shifted. Thus we can see that linguistically expressed footing shifts reflect and simultaneously accomplish shifts in the indexical ground.

5. Conclusion

Through an analysis of the use of third-person forms to refer both to participants in conversation, and to other referents which are not participants in the speech situation, I have proposed a revision of certain aspects of grounding theory. I have suggested that the indexical ground is not static, as implied by Langacker (this volume a), but rather dynamic and constantly shifting in interaction. I have also proposed that the ground is sociocentric in nature, jointly created and shared by the interactants, and not inherently related to the vantage point of a particular participant, as suggested by Langacker (this volume b). Further, I have suggested that the range of grounding predications be expanded beyond the strictly grammatical elements proposed by Langacker (this volume b), to include lexical elements as well.

The understanding of grounding presented here is in certain ways similar to what is proposed by several of the other authors in this volume. The treatment of definiteness by Epstein (this volume) proposes a view of the use of the definite article which is much more dynamic in nature than what has been previously proposed. De Mulder and Vetters (this volume) point out that the use of the *imparfait* in French frequently serves to shift the vantage point. The dynamic and sociocentric nature of the ground is also evident in the article by Brisard (this volume), who shows how the English present tense is used reflexively to construe and constitute the ground, and how the epistemic aspect of grammatically expressed temporality is related to a speaker's social relation to her words, i.e., footing, in terms of Goffman (1981). Finally, Nuyts (this volume) also suggests that lexical elements be included within the class of grounding predications. It is interesting to see that the last three articles mentioned, by De Mulder and Vetters, Brisard, and Nuyts, all deal with clausal rather than nominal grounding predications. It seems that the dynamic and sociocentric nature of the ground is reflected in the use of all grounding predications, and that the range of neither clausal nor nominal grounding predications is limited to grammaticalized elements.

Appendices

1. Morphological glosses

The nominative case, present tense, and active voice have been treated as unmarked and have not been indicated in the morphological glosses. Person and number in pronominal and verbal morphemes have been marked with a numeral and the customary abbreviations, for example, 1sg for first person singular, and so on.

1INF	first infinitive
ABL	ablative
ADE	adessive
ALL	allative
CLTC	clitic
COND	conditional
DET	determiner
ELA	elative
ESS	essive
GEN	genitive
ILL	illative
IMP	imperative
INE	inessive
LOC	locative
NEG	negation
NOM	nominative
PRT	partitive
PL	plural
PTCL	particle
P.PPLE	past participle
PST	past
WH	question word or relativizer
Q	interrogative clitic

2. Transcription symbols

The transcriptions have been done using a somewhat simplified version of the system described in Du Bois et al. (1993).

Intonation unit boundary	{carriage return}
Truncated intonation unit	--
Truncated word	-
Speech overlap	[word(s)]
Final intonation contour	.
Continuing intonation contour	,
Primary accent	^
Long pause (>.7 seconds)	... (number of seconds)
Medium pause (.3–.6 seconds)	...
Short pause (.2 seconds or less)	..
Glottalization	%
Laughter	@
Transcriber's comment	((COMMENT))

Notes

1. I thank Frank Brisard, René Dirven, and audiences at UC Santa Barbara and at the Fall 2001 meeting of the Finnish Cognitive Linguistics Association in Turku for their many helpful comments and suggestions. I am especially grateful to Marja-Liisa Helasvuo, Eeva-Leena Seppänen, and Sandy Thompson for much inspiration and encouragement. All omissions and mistakes remaining in this paper are, of course, mine.
2. In the course of several years of work on spoken language, I have become increasingly aware of the need for high-quality visual data for analysis. The contribution of gaze direction, posture, and gesture to reference and especially to its interactional features is undeniable. In this paper, I focus on linguistic choices only, but it is not my intention to deny that the analysis could be considerably enriched by access to visual aspects of the interaction.
3. This example, as well as example (6), were also analyzed in Laury (1997), although I have changed certain details of the analyses.
4. This excerpt has been simplified by removing an exchange between a toddler and his mother, who are also seated at the table.

References

Ariel, Mira
    1990   *Accessing Noun-Phrase Antecendents*. London: Routledge.

Benveniste, Emile
    1971   *Problems in General Linguistics*. Coral Gables: University of Miami Press.

Brisard, Frank
    this vol.   The English present.

Chafe, Wallace L.
    1976   Givenness, contrastiveness, definiteness, subjects, topics, and point of view. In: Charles N. Li (ed.), *Subject and Topic*, 27–55. New York: Academic.
    1994   *Discourse, Consciousness and Time: The Flow and Displacement of Conscious Experience in Speaking and Writing*. Chicago: University of Chicago Press.

Clancy, Patricia M.
    1980   Referential choice in English and Japanese narrative discourse. In: Wallace L. Chafe (ed.), *The Pear Stories: Cognitive, Cultural and Linguistic Aspects of Narrative Production*, 127–202. Norwood: Ablex.

De Mulder, Walter and Carl Vetters
    this vol.   The French *imparfait*, determiners and grounding.

Downing, Pamela
    1996   Proper names as a referential option in English conversation. In: Barbara A. Fox (ed.), *Studies in Anaphora*, 99–144. Amsterdam: John Benjamins.

Du Bois, John W.
    1980   Beyond definiteness: The trace of identity in discourse. In: Wallace L. Chafe (ed), *The Pear Stories: Cognitive, Cultural and Linguistic Aspects of Narrative Production*, 203–274. Norwood: Ablex.

Du Bois, John W., Stephan Schuetze-Coburn, Danae Paolino and Susanna Cumming
    1993   Outline of discourse transcription. In: Jane A. Edwards and Martin D. Lampert (eds.), *Talking Data: Transcription and Coding in Discourse Research*, 45–87. Hillsdale: Erlbaum.

Epstein, Richard
    1996   Viewpoint and the definite article. In: Adele E. Goldberg (ed.), *Conceptual Structure, Discourse and Language*, 99–112. Stanford: Center for the Study of Language and Information.
    1998   Reference and definite referring expressions. *Pragmatics and Cognition* 6: 189–207.

this vol. Grounding, subjectivity and definite descriptions.
Fauconnier, Gilles
1994 *Mental Spaces: Aspects of Meaning Construction in Natural Language.* Cambridge: Cambridge University Press.
Ford, Cecilia E. and Barbara A. Fox
1996 Interactional motivations for reference formulation: He had. This guy had, a beautiful, thirty-two O:lds. In: Barbara A. Fox (ed.), *Studies in Anaphora,* 145-168. Amsterdam: John Benjamins.
Fox, Barbara A.
1987 *Discourse Structure and Anaphora: Written and Conversational English.* Cambridge: Cambridge University Press.
Givón, Talmy
1979 *On Understanding Grammar.* New York: Academic.
Goffman, Erving
1981 *Forms of Talk.* Philadelphia: University of Pennsylvania Press.
Goodwin, Charles
1981 *Conversational Organization: Interaction between Speakers and Hearers.* New York: Academic.
Goodwin, Charles and Marjorie H. Goodwin
1992 Context, activity and participation. In: Peter Auer and Aldo di Luzio (eds.), *The Contextualization of Language,* 77-99. Amsterdam: John Benjamins.
Hanks, William F.
1990 *Referential Space: Language and Lived Space among the Maya.* Chicago: University of Chicago Press.
1992 The indexical ground of deictic reference. In Alessandro Duranti and Charles Goodwin (eds.), *Rethinking Context: Language as an Interactive Phenomenon,* 43-76. Cambridge: Cambridge University Press.
Jakobson, Roman
1990 Shifters and verbal categories. In: Linda R. Waugh and Monique Monville-Burston (eds.), *On Language: Roman Jakobson,* 386-392. Cambridge: Harvard University Press.
Laitinen, Lea
1992 *Välttämättömyys ja persoona: Suomen murteiden nesessiivisten rakenteiden semantiikkaa ja kielioppia [Necessity and person: Semantics and grammar of necessitative constructions in Finnish dialects].* Helsinki: Suomalaisen Kirjallisuuden Seura.
Lambrecht, Knud
1994 *Information Structure and Sentence Form.* Cambridge: Cambridge University Press.

Langacker, Ronald W.
   1991   *Foundations of Cognitive Grammar,* Volume 2: *Descriptive Application.* Stanford: Stanford University Press.
   this vol. a Deixis and subjectivity.
   this vol. b Remarks on the English grounding systems.

Laury, Ritva
   1997   *Demonstratives in Interaction: The Emergence of a Definite Article in Finnish.* Amsterdam: John Benjamins.
   2001   Definiteness and reflexivity: Indexing socially shared experience. *Pragmatics* 11: 401–420.
   to appear Second mention indefinites, accessibility and identifiability. Special issue of *Verbum,* edited by Denis Apothéloz and Simona Pekarek Doehler.

Lerner, Gene H.
   1996   On the place of linguistic resources in the organization of talk-in-interaction. *Pragmatics* 6: 281–294.

Levinson, Stephen C.
   1988   Putting linguistics on a proper footing: Explorations in Goffman's concepts of participation. In: Paul Drew and Anthony Wootton (eds.), *Erving Goffman: Exploring the Interaction Order,* 161–227. Cambridge: Polity.

Mayes, Patricia
   1990   Quotation in spoken English. *Studies in Language* 14: 325–363.

Nuyts, Jan
   this vol. Grounding and the system of epistemic expressions in Dutch: A cognitive-functional view.

Pekarek, Simona
   1999   Linguistic forms and social interaction: Why do we specify referents more than is necessary for their identification? In: Jef Verschueren (ed.), *Pragmatics in 1998,* 427–448. Antwerp: International Pragmatics Association.

Pekarek Doehler, Simona
   2001   Referential processes as situated cognition: Pronominal expressions and the social co-ordination of talk. In: Enikö Nemeth (ed.), *Cognition in Language Use: Selected Papers from the 7th International Pragmatics Conference.* Antwerp: International Pragmatics Association.

Sacks, Harvey
   1992   *Lectures on Conversation,* Volume 1. Edited by Gail Jefferson. Oxford: Blackwell.

Schegloff, Emanuel A.
1996   Some practices for referring to persons in talk-in-interaction: A partial sketch of a systematics. In: Barbara A. Fox (ed.), *Studies in Anaphora*, 437–488. Amsterdam: John Benjamins.

Seppänen, Eeva-Leena
1996   Ways of referring to a knowing co-participant in Finnish conversation. In: Timo Haukioja, Marja-Liisa Helasvuo and Elise Kärkkäinen (eds.), *SKY 1996: Yearbook of the Linguistic Association of Finland*, 135–176. Helsinki: Suomen kielitieteellinen yhdistys.
1998   *Läsnäolon pronominit: Tämä, tuo, se ja hän viittaamassa keskustelun osallistujaan [The pronouns of presence: Tämä, tuo, se, and hän in reference to participants in conversation]*. Helsinki: Suomalaisen Kirjallisuuden Seura.

The French *imparfait*, determiners and grounding

Walter De Mulder and Carl Vetters

0. Introduction

In French, the *imparfait* is traditionally considered one of two simple past tenses, the other being the *passé simple*. The difference between these two tenses has been analyzed in numerous works,[1] and definitions of the *imparfait* mostly refer, jointly or separately, to its past reference, its imperfectivity, or its anaphoricity. In this short contribution, we will first offer a "cognitive" definition of the *imparfait*, mainly based on work by Damourette and Pichon (1911–1936) and Doiz-Bienzobas (1995, this volume), and show that this definition allows us to explain the temporal as well as modal uses of the *imparfait*. This definition will then be used to analyze the other properties traditionally attributed to the *imparfait* and already mentioned above: its imperfective aspect and its anaphoric nature. With respect to these two characteristics, the *imparfait* will be shown to be comparable, respectively, to the partitive (*du, de la*) and the definite article (*le, la, les*) in French.

1. Past reference or "nonactual"?

The French *imparfait* has traditionally been defined as a past tense, situating the event expressed by the proposition in the past with respect to the speech time, as can be seen in (1):

(1) *Comme le soir **tombait**, l'homme sombre arriva.*
　'As the evening fell, the somber man arrived.'
　(Hugo, as cited by Grevisse 1986: 1290)

However, this definition of the *imparfait* as a past tense has been called into question in view of its "modal" uses.[2] These can be illustrated first of all by what has been called the "commercial" *imparfait* (*"imparfait commercial"* or *"forain"*), used by shopkeepers and tradespersons to speak to their clients. Berthonneau and Kleiber (1994: 63) and Wilmet (1997: 392) point out that this use of the *imparfait* typically requires a verb in the third person, an interrogative sentence, and some verb of desire (*vouloir, falloir, désirer*):[3]

(2) *Qu'est-ce qu'elle **voulait**, la petite dame?*
 'What did she want, the little lady?'
 (Berthonneau and Kleiber 1994: 60)

As has been pointed out by Berthonneau and Kleiber (1994: 76), this *imparfait* refers to a past situation — one where the client first intends to buy something —, but this past situation is considered to have present relevance. The same analysis can be applied to the so-called *imparfait* of "politeness", where the *imparfait* is used to attenuate queries and demands:

(3) a. *Je **voulais** vous demander d'intercéder en ma faveur.*
 'I wanted to ask you to intervene on my behalf.'
 b. *Je **venais** vous prier d'intercéder en ma faveur.*
 'I came to ask you to intervene on my behalf.'
 (*Grammaire du français contemporain*, as cited by Vetters 2000a: 182)

The verbs in these examples also refer to past situations, mostly past intentions or past movements that can be seen as current manifestations of those intentions (Berthonneau and Kleiber 1994: 83). In any case, the situation expressed by the *imparfait* still seems to be valid in the present, thus calling into question the characterization of the *imparfait* as a past tense. This is even more so in the following uses, where the sentences in the *imparfait* clearly refer to present situations.

- The *imparfait* expressing affection, when speaking to little children or animals in their presence, which is traditionally called the *imparfait "hypocoristique"*:[4]

(4)a. *Alors, on n'**était** pas sage? On **avait** faim?*
   'Well, haven't we been good? Were we hungry?'
   (Arrivé, Gadet, and Galmiche 1986, as cited by Vetters 2000a: 183)
 b. *Il **faisait** bon mon chien, auprès du feu?*
   'Was it nice, my dog, near the fire?'
   (Wilmet 1997: 384)

- The "pretend-game" *imparfait* ("*imparfait préludique*"), mainly used "in the negotiation of roles and settings that serves as a preface to children's make-believe games" (Fleischman 1995: 525):[5]

(5) *Moi, j'**étais** le gendarme et tu avais volé une voiture.*
   'Me, I was the cop, and you had stolen a car.'
   (Grevisse 1986: 1292)

And in the following usage types, the *imparfait* even refers to events situated in the future.

- The hypothetical *imparfait*, used in combination with conditional *si* 'if' to mark possibility (*potentialis*, 6a) or irreality (*irrealis*, 6b):[6]

(6)a. *Si par hasard il **venait**, vous lui diriez....*
   'If by chance he came, you would tell him....'
   (Simenon, *La fenêtre des Rouet*, as cited by Touratier 1996: 136)
 b. *Si vos parents **vivaient** encore, ils vous feraient de grands reproches et ils auraient raison.*
   'If your parents were still alive, they would criticize you and they would be right.'
   (Duhamel, *Cécile parmi nous*, as cited by Touratier 1996: 137)

- The *imparfait* expressing a desire or a wish:

(7) *Ah, si j'avais une fortune!*
  'Oh, if I only had a fortune!'
  (Arrivé, Gadet, and Galmiche 1986, as cited by Vetters 2000a: 183)

These uses can be likened to the *imparfait* of "thwarted imminence" (*"imminence contrecarrée"*), where the *imparfait* signals that a fact should have taken place, but finally did not. Thus, in the following example, when the young girl puts her hand on the latch, she is normally expected to leave, but the reaction of the second person shows that this has not yet happened, and that it is not even necessary that she will eventually leave:

(8) *Elle mit la main sur le loquet ... un pas de plus, elle était dans la rue.*
  - Sergeant, cria-t-il, ne voyez-vous pas que cette drôlesse s'en va?
  'She put her hand on the latch ... one step further, and she was on the street.
  - Sergeant, he shouted, don't you see that this hussy is leaving?'
  (Hugo, as cited by Vetters 2000a: 182)

It seems safe to conclude, then, that the *imparfait* does not necessarily locate a situation in the past, as can also be seen from its use in indirect speech:

(9) a. *Galilée soutint que la Terre **tournait** autour du soleil.*
  'Galilei held that the earth turned around the sun.'
  (Wilmet 1997: 384)

b. *Vous avez dit que j'**étais** là?*
'Did you say that I was here?'
(Courteline, *Coco, Coco et Toto*, "M. Félix", as cited by Damourette and Pichon 1911–1936: 176)

In (9a), the *imparfait* refers to a fact which is still supposed to be valid on the present day; in (9b), as pointed out by Damourette and Pichon (1911–1936: 176), the speaker is still at home when he addresses his maid, and M. Félix, the visitor to whom the maid has spoken, is still waiting in the next room. The same authors also show that in some cases, the *imparfait* in indirect discourse refers to future situations and can even be accompanied by the deictic adverb *demain* 'tomorrow':

(10) *Qu'est-ce qu'elle a dit qu'on **mangeait** demain, Jeanne?*
'What did Jeanne say that we would eat tomorrow?'
("M. P", 23 September 1929, as cited by Damourette and Pichon 1911–1936: 176)

Damourette and Pichon point out, however, that, even though the action of eating is to be situated in the future, the speaker can only know what he will eat through the indications given by Jeanne. The *imparfait* thus refers to a future event "through" or "via" a past one,[7] just like for the "commercial" *imparfait* and the *imparfait* of "politeness" in the analysis of Berthonneau and Kleiber presented above. Consequently, Damourette and Pichon (1911–1936: 177) propose that the *imparfait* is not first and foremost a past tense. Its function is to locate the situation expressed by the verb in an "actuality" other than that of the speaker at the moment of speaking. In other words, whereas the speaker most naturally construes the world and its events from an "egocentric" point of view, his own "here-and-now" (*moi-ici-maintenant*), the *imparfait* signals that the events are presented from a point of view different from the "here-and-now" of the speaker:[8]

> Ce qu'il faut retenir, parce que cela va être le caractère commun de tous les emplois du toncal pur, c'est que ce tiroir marque ici le placement du fait verbal dans une autre sphère d'action, une autre *actualité*, que celle où se trouve le locuteur au moment de la parole. La position naturelle et fondamentale de l'esprit, c'est de centrer le monde des phénomènes sur le locuteur se concevant lui-même dans l'instant présent: le "moi-ici-maintenant". Ce mode d'apercevance des phénomènes constitue l'actualité noncale. Toutes les fois, au contraire, que l'esprit fait l'effort de se reporter dans un monde phénoménal autrement centré, on est dans une actualité toncale, et il apparaît dans la phrase soit le saviez [l'imparfait], soit, selon les nuances nécessaires, le tiroir toncal approprié. (Damourette and Pichon 1911–1936: 177; emphasis in original)
> [What has to be remembered, because it will be the common element of all the uses of the pure *toncal*,[9] is that this tense here marks the location of the verbal fact in another sphere of action, another *actuality*, than the one where the speaker is at the moment of speaking. The natural and fundamental position of the mind is to center the world of phenomena around the speaker conceiving of herself in the present moment: the "here-and-now". This way of perceiving phenomena constitutes *noncal* actuality. In contrast, every time the speaker makes an effort to transfer herself into a world of phenomena centered in another way, one is in *toncal* actuality, and either the *saviez* [the *imparfait*] or another appropriate *toncal* tense appears.]

This definition allows Damourette and Pichon to explain the "modal" uses presented above. In its "hypocoristic" use, the *imparfait* signals that the speaker does not fully endorse her own words and adopts another point of view, for instance that of the children involved (Damourette and Pichon 1911–1936: 241); in its hypothetical uses, the *imparfait* presents the events as included in an actuality other than the one the speaker is engaged in and, thus, not real (Damourette and Pichon 1911–1936: 238). A similar explanation can of course be proposed for the "pretend-game" use and the use of the *imparfait* to express "thwarted imminence", where the *imparfait* can also be held to signal that the events or situations expressed are not part of the actual reality of the speaker, which is identified with reality as such.

It seems more difficult, however, to apply Damourette and Pichon's ideas to the uses of the *imparfait* to express politeness. Indeed, whereas it can be said that in its "commercial" use, the *imparfait* invites us to adopt the point of view of the "client", this is less evident for the "politeness" uses, where the verb is in the first person present and the pronoun thus refers to the speaker. The use of the *imparfait* can be justified, however, if one accepts, following Berthonneau and Kleiber (1994: 81–82), that the *imparfait* forms *je voulais* 'I wanted' and *je venais* 'I came' refer to a past situation of the speaker, when the signs of her desires were apparent even before she expressed them. This means, of course, that the idea that the *imparfait* situates the events in an actuality other than the speaker's current one, can receive two different interpretations: it can be interpreted in a chronological way, as meaning that the *imparfait* refers to a past situation, or it can be interpreted in a "modal" way, as referring to a possible or fictional situation, or one presented from the point of view of another participant than the speaker.[10] It also follows from Berthonneau and Kleiber's (1994) analysis that, when an event is situated in an actuality other than the speaker's, this does not imply that the situation expressed in the *imparfait* is cut off from the actual one, as has sometimes been suggested. On the contrary, in the "politeness" and "commercial" uses, the past situation must be accessible from the point of view of the present one: the salient or accessible situation for the "commercial" *imparfait* in (2) is one where the woman is waiting to buy something, not, for instance, one where she parks her car in front of the store (Berthonneau and Kleiber 1994: 78).

2. A cognitive interpretation of the *imparfait*

According to Damourette and Pichon (1911–1936: 216), the difference between the *imparfait* and the *passé simple* (simple past) is a "psychological" one, "a difference in the presentation of the facts". In cognitive terms, one could say that the difference between the *imparfait* and the *passé simple* is one of construal, defined as "our capacity for conceptualizing the same situation in alternate ways" (Langacker this volume a: 3). Damourette and Pichon (1911–1936: 219, 347, 363) thus hold that the *passé simple* — they use the term *priscal* — presents the events as "appearing" in the past, cut off from the present, and as "punctual", because they are presented in their totality. The *imparfait*, in contrast, presents the events as "actual", meaning that they are presented as "unfolding", as having an "actual", "vivid" duration, as seen from a "transferred" center, which is situated in the midst of the events.[11] The *imparfait* thus presupposes a center of "apperception" (*"apercevance"*, Damourette and Pichon 1911–1936: 177), which can sometimes be attributed to a "substance" or a "protagonist", as in indirect discourse, where this "protagonist" is frequently the subject of the main verb (Damourette and Pichon 1911–1936: 195).

The analysis of Damourette and Pichon (1911–1936) can be interpreted in terms of the cognitive notion of "viewing", as defined by Langacker (1995, 1999: 305) and Doiz-Bienzobas (1995: 42). Within a viewing situation, the viewer has a maximal field of vision, which contains a locus of attention called the viewing frame, comprising in its focus the event that is the target of perception. According to Langacker (1995, 1999), it is possible to conceive of conceptualization events as largely resembling this viewing situation: a conceptualizer conceives of the event as the target of conceptualization and the position of the "conceptualizer" functions as the viewpoint from which the event is conceptualized. Doiz-Bienzobas (1995) characterizes the difference between the Spanish preterit and imperfect partly in terms of this implied viewpoint. Whereas "the preterit involves

(i) a present viewpoint at speech time from where the situation is conceptualized;
(ii) the speaker's voice at speech time. Viewpoint and voice are the same"

(Doiz-Bienzobas 1995: 55), "the imperfect always involves

(i) a past viewpoint with respect to speech time. The exact location of the viewpoint in the past may vary and is determined by contextual elements, such as adverbs and other tense-aspect constructions in the sentence. ...
(ii) the voice of the speaker at speech time. The position of the speaker may be explicitly referred to when it acts as a reference point for the location of adverbs, determiners and other contextual elements. The viewpoint evoked by the imperfect

itself is past with respect to the speaker's position at speech time." (Doiz-Bienzobas 1995: 53)

The definition of the Spanish preterit can be used for the French *passé simple*, with one restriction, however: in French, the *passé simple* is explicitly opposed to the *passé composé* or present perfect. Whereas the *passé simple* presents the events as cut off from the present, as was pointed out by Damourette and Pichon, the *passé composé* presents the past events as having current relevance. This means that the reference point[12] for a situation expressed by a sentence in the *passé composé* can be considered to be the speech point, whereas this is not the case for the *passé simple*, where the reference point is in the past with respect to the speech point and coincides most frequently with another situation in the past.[13] As was already pointed out by Kamp and Rohrer (1983: 261), the events introduced into discourse by the French *passé simple*[14] are situated either after the last event already introduced in the discourse by a foregoing sentence in the *passé simple*, or as simultaneous with it. Thus the events in (11) are necessarily interpreted as following each other, whereas this is not the case in (12):

(11) *Pierre entra. Marie téléphona.*
'Peter came in. Mary was on the phone.'
(Kamp and Rohrer 1983: 253)
(12) *Marie chanta et Pierre l'accompagna.*
'Mary was singing and Peter was accompanying her.'
(Kamp and Rohrer 1983: 260)[15]

The need to identify a past reference point for the interpretation of the *passé simple* is not in contradiction with the definition of Doiz-Bienzobas, since a reference point "may or may not be the site for the viewpoint" (Doiz-Bienzobas 1995: 45). The viewpoint can be located at the speech point, since any text needs someone who produced it, a point raised by Genette (1983: 66–68) against Benveniste's ([1959] 1966: 241) idea that the events related in the *passé simple* do not suppose the intervention of an author.[16] As pointed out for Spanish by Doiz-Bienzobas (1995: 57), the fact that the viewpoint is at the speech point, and thus after the situation time of the predicate, "corresponds with native speaker's intuition that when the preterit [in French, the *passé simple*] is used, situation and speaker are detached, distant from one another".

As for the definition of the French *imparfait*, it seems to us that the associated viewpoint is not necessarily in the past, as is held by Doiz-Bienzobas with respect to the Spanish imperfect. In view of the "pretend-game" and "hypothetical" uses of the *imparfait* illustrated by the examples (5) and (6) above, we would rather propose that its viewpoint is to be situated either in the past or in the present. But the other elements of Doiz-Bienzobas' definition seem to capture in more cognitive terms the essence of the definition of the *imparfait* by Damourette and Pichon, as a tense which invites us to situate the event in an actuality other than the speaker's, where "actuality" is meant to refer to an "apperception", an experience of the events as they unfold themselves. Doiz-Bienzobas (this volume: 323), using notions of Fauconnier's (1984) theory of mental spaces, thus writes: "The role of the imperfect is to render accessible a space M different from the speaker's reality space R for the interpretation of the situation it designates." As is further pointed out by Doiz-Bienzobas (1995: 64, this volume), this means that the speech event does not invariably function as the ground, but that the ground can be shifted.[17]

The analysis of the meaning of the *imparfait* presented above makes it a "grounding predication" as defined by Langacker (1987a: 126–127, 1991: 53, this volume a,b). It specifies "the relationship between some facet of the ground and the entity profiled by the nominal or clause" (Langacker this volume a: 7; see also Langacker this volume b: 29), the ground being "the speech event, its participants, and its setting" (Langacker 1987a: 126). As is the case in the foregoing definition of the *imparfait*, grounding predications are basically "epistemic", and not purely temporal (Langacker 1991: 246). In the following, we will first explain why this is so, and show how the proposed definition can answer the problems traditionally raised against a nontemporal approach of the *imparfait*.

Langacker (1991: 241–242) holds that "a more adequate analysis of the grounding predications will have to be based on a clear understanding of their conceptual import. This in turns requires the description of certain idealized cognitive models, which function as the cognitive domains in terms of which these meanings are to be characterized." The models used for the analysis of the tenses are elaborations of the "basic epistemic model" described by Langacker (1991: 242–243; emphases omitted) and quoted here at length:

> Its essential notion is that certain situations (or "states of affairs") are accepted by a particular conceptualizer (C) as being real, whereas others are not. Collectively, the situations accorded that status constitute C's conception of known reality (which for now I will simply refer to as reality unless there is some need to make a distinction). Reality is neither simple nor static, but an ever-evolving entity whose evolution continuously augments the complexity of the structure already defined by its previous history; the cylinder depicting it should thus be imagined as "growing" along the axis indicated by the arrow. The leading edge of this expanding structure (i.e. the face of the cylinder) is termed immediate reality. It is from this vantage point — from reality at the latest stage of its evolution — that C views things, and he has direct perceptual access only to portions of this region. Irreality comprises everything other than (known) reality. It is important to bear in mind that a situation does not belong to reality or irreality on the basis of how the world has actually evolved, but depends instead on whether the conceptualizer knows and accepts it as part of that evolutionary sequence.

The "basic epistemic model" is elaborated into a "dynamic evolutionary model". This elaboration adds to the basic model the conception of the timeline, the axis along which reality evolves, and replaces the conceptualizer (as the vantage point from which things are seen — and conceived) by the ground, the speech event, comprising speaker and hearer and their conceptualizations, and its circumstances (Langacker 1991: 243). It also takes into account the force-dynamic aspects of the world's structure, which constrains and influences the events that unfold within it: "Part of what it means for the world to have a particular structure is that it is biased toward the occurrence of certain events and event sequences as opposed to others."

(Langacker 1991: 276) In other words, reality is in a sense always growing: there is always a "normal course of events", which can be projected from the present reality, comprising events that "are inherently disposed to occur whenever appropriate circumstances arise, and will do so unless energy is somehow exerted to counteract this tendency" (Langacker 1991: 276). Consequently, the past and the present tenses insert the situations into (known) reality, whereas the future modals *may* and *will* signal, respectively, that "nothing in the speaker's present conception of reality is seen as barring it from evolving along a path leading to the occurrence of that process" (Langacker 1991: 278), and that the event is placed in projected reality.

The opposition between reality and projected reality captures the widespread idea that the past and the present are part of our experience, whereas the future is not; future events are conceived of, in language, as "nonactual" because intended or scheduled (Benveniste [1968] 1974b: 132), and not as "actually unfolding".[18] It also allows the cognitive theory of tense to solve a problem raised by any analysis which holds that the *imparfait* is not basically a past tense, but that its interpretation as such is a contextual interpretation of a basically nontemporal meaning. Indeed, as pointed out recently by Gosselin (1999: 31–32), if the *imparfait* locates the situation in an actuality other than that of the speaker, why would this other "actuality", as presented in (13) for instance, have to be located in the past rather than the future?

(13) *Mardi, il pleuvait.*
      'On Wednesday, it was raining.'

According to Gosselin, this problem shows that the *imparfait* is really a past tense. However, Damourette and Pichon (1911–1936: 206) already suggested an answer to this problem:

> [L]e passé et l'avenir, au point de vue psychologique, ne sont nullement symétriques. Le passé a eu une vie. Il a laissé des traces. On peut par le souvenir se reporter à lui et en retrouver en quelque sorte la durée actuelle.

Dans l'avenir, au contraire, un pareil transport n'est possible que par l'imagination.
[The past and the future, from a psychological point of view, are by no means symmetrical. The past has had a life. It has left traces. One can transfer oneself to it through memory and recover, in a way, its actual duration. In the future, however, such a transfer is only possible by means of the imagination.]

In other words, the *imparfait* presents the events as actually unfolding ("*dans leur déroulement*" 'in the train of events', Damourette and Pichon 1911–1936: 208) before a perceiving mind, though not the speaker's actual one. But this is only possible if the events can be held to be (or have been) experienced, as is the case in the present or in the past but not in the future. Damourette and Pichon thus exploit the difference between the present and the past on the one hand and the future on the other, and associate the *imparfait* with (known) reality.[19]

This characterization of the *imparfait* as indicating a part of known reality could raise some problems, at least at first sight, since the *imparfait* also expresses potentiality and irreality. Langacker (1991: 245–246) points out, however, that the present and the past tenses do not present reality in the same way: in his view, the zero marking of the present iconically suggests that the event is presented as directly accessible or immediate to the speaker, whereas the overt marking of the past marks some kind of nonimmediacy or nonaccessibility. The application of these ideas to the *imparfait* can be interpreted as meaning that the *imparfait*, being overtly marked, locates the situation outside of the immediate reality accessible to the speaker and, thus, in an actuality other than the speaker's, confirming the analyses of Damourette and Pichon and Doiz-Bienzobas as presented above. This also has the consequence of presenting the morpheme marking the *imparfait* as one with an epistemic impact.

Nevertheless, one could still object that the most intuitive definition of the *imparfait* is in terms of a temporal distinction, the *imparfait* being a grammatical tense that situates events in the past with respect to the moment of utterance. Indeed, "from an utterance such as *Paul était intelligent* ['Paul was intelligent'], an interlocutor will normally infer that Paul is no longer intelligent, unless he has manifest reasons to believe the contrary" (Berthonneau and Kleiber 1994: 75).[20] As is already manifest from the last part of the quote, Berthonneau and Kleiber believe that the *imparfait* marks past reference "by default": it normally signals reference to a past event, unless there are indications to the contrary.[21] The same idea seems to be expressed by Langacker (1991: 244, 250), who distinguishes between the schematic characterization of the tenses with respect to the basic epistemic model and their prototypical value, which is defined with respect to the timeline model. Thus, the temporal value is defined as its prototypical one.

The modal uses, on the other hand, cannot simply be explained by a metaphoric transfer of the value of "nonimmediacy" of the *imparfait* to other domains than the temporal. Such an explanation has been proposed in French linguistics for the *imparfait* of politeness, where the distance implied by the *imparfait* would explain why the tense is felt to attenuate the reality of the present situation and to render the utterance more polite.[22] Berthonneau and Kleiber (1994: 67–70) list some problems posed by this kind of explanation. First, the nonimmediacy of the *imparfait* does not invariably suggest attenuation, as can be seen in the "commercial" uses of the type *Qu'est-ce qu'elle voulait, la petite dame* 'What did she want, the little lady?', where the intention of the shopkeeper is certainly not to attenuate his demand. Second, if the nonimmediacy of the *imparfait* explains the effect of attenuation, why is it impossible to use other verbs, such as *demander* 'ask' in *Je demandais...*, etc., to express politeness? And finally, if the idea of nonimmediacy as such explains the modal effects, and if this idea is linked to the past tense morphemes, then why is it impossible for the other French past tense, the *passé simple*, to have such modal interpretations?

These problems are not raised by a definition of the *imparfait* as implying a viewpoint other than the speaker's actual one. Such a definition is in fact compatible with the analyses proposed by Berthonneau and Kleiber (1994: 76, 82). The "commercial" *imparfait*, for instance, presents the situation from the viewpoint of the client, because the present situation is presented as the continuation of a past one, where the client was already manifesting her intentions (for instance, by looking around in the shop). The speaker thus, in a way, adopts her interlocutor's viewpoint, an observation which could explain the effect of politeness. In the case of the *imparfait* of "politeness", the speaker refers to a past situation where the signs of her intentions were already visible to the interlocutor. Thus, the interlocutor is presented as if she already knows which question will be asked, and the question itself seems to be less of a real question; it is as if the speaker responds to an implicit question concerning the reasons of her presence (Berthonneau and Kleiber 1994: 81–82).

3. Aspect

The difference between the *passé simple* and the *imparfait* in French has frequently been described in aspectual terms. In this conception, the *imparfait* expresses imperfective aspect, whereas the *passé simple* implies perfective aspect. In more explicit terms, this means that the *imparfait* presents the events from the inside, as ongoing, without their boundaries, whereas the *passé simple* presents them from the outside, including their boundaries, as a complete whole.[23] The imperfective aspect expressed by the *imparfait* is of course related to its characterization as expressing an actuality other than that of the speaker's "here-and-now", if one understands "actuality" as meaning that the event is presented as unfolding. This indeed implies that the event is presented from the inside, without any precision as to its boundaries.

Since the *imparfait* imposes a construal of the event as actual, implying an internal viewpoint, but does not give any indication with respect to the boundaries of the event, it is clear why this tense fits the expression of atelic events, such as states and activities, and why it imposes "contextual reinterpretations" of telic events, such as accomplishments and achievements, making them imperfective, as has been pointed out by Vet (1994) and de Swart (1995, 1998).[24] Such cases of "coercion" can be illustrated by the following examples from Vet (1994: 8):

(14) *Son arrivée* **surprenait** *Pierre.*
'His arrival surprised Peter.'
(15) *Marie* **atteignait** *le sommet.*
'Mary reached the top.'
(16) *Jean* **plantait** *un arbre.*
'John was planting a tree.'[25]

As pointed out by Vet (1994: 9), the achievement in (14) is reinterpreted as referring to the state resulting from the transition expressed by the verb, and the achievement in (15) as well as the accomplishment in (16) are reinterpreted as referring to the processes that take place before the transitions expressed by the predicates. This contextual reinterpretation is also known from the nominal domain, where count nouns can frequently be reinterpreted as mass nouns (17) and vice versa (18):[26]

(17) a. *Il y a beaucoup de pommes dans la salade.*
'There are many apples in the salad.'
b. *Il y a beaucoup de pomme dans la salade.*
'There is much apple in the salad.'

(18) a. *Il y avait beaucoup de bière sur la table.*
'There was much beer on the table.'
b. *Il y avait beaucoup de bières sur la table.*
'There were many beers on the table.'

These observations of course confirm the parallelism between the grounding relationships in the nominal and the clausal domains, already observed by Langacker (1987b), but they suggest moreover a parallelism between the states expressed by the *imparfait* and mass nouns. This parallelism is described in Vet (2000, 2001).[27] Mass nouns are characterized first and foremost by the homogeneity of their referents, a property that distinguishes them from count nouns, whose referents are nonhomogeneous. Vet (2000: 148) uses (19) to explain this difference:

(19) a. *Il y a un fromage dans la salade.*
 'There is a cheese in the salad.'
 b. *Il y a du fromage dans la salade.*
 'There is cheese in the salad.'

If one takes a piece of the cheese in (19b), it is still possible to use (19b) to speak of the rest of the cheese, but if one takes a piece of the cheese in (19a), one cannot continue to use (19a). This is so because all parts of cheese are still cheese, whereas the cheese of (19a) is seen as a whole such that, when one takes a (large enough) part of it, the rest can no longer be called 'a cheese'. As was already pointed out in a whole philosophical tradition from Aristotle to Quine (1960), the referents of mass nouns are characterized by their "cumulativity" and "divisibility", whereas the referents of count nouns such as *voiture* 'car' are neither divisible (a part of a car is not a car) nor "cumulative" (when one adds a car to another car, one has two cars, whereas when one adds beer to beer, one has more beer). Again, this does not mean that *voiture* cannot be reinterpreted as a mass noun; in fact, this is what sometimes happens when a count noun is determined by the partitive article *du*, as is illustrated in the following example cited by Vet (2000: 150):

(20) *Il y a de la voiture à perte de vue.*
 'There are cars (literally, 'there is car') as far as the eye can see.'
 (Galmiche 1989: 71)

In this example, there are so many cars that the individuality of each separate car is lost. Vet (2000: 152) shows that predicates can also differ with respect to divisibility. In *Mireille a couru (pour attraper son train)* 'Mireille has run (to catch her train)', the predicate *courir*, which denotes an activity, can be used to describe the activity that takes place in each subpart of the interval during which Mireille has run; but the predicate *manger (une tomate)*, denoting an accomplishment, cannot be used to describe the events that take place during a subpart of the interval designated by *Mireille a mangé une tomate*

'Mireille has eaten a tomato'. There is, thus, a parallelism between mass nouns and states, which has been shown by Hoepelman and Rohrer (1980) to extend to the *imparfait*. This extension can be justified by the difference in interpretation between (21a) and (21b):

(21) a. *Marie **mangea** une tomate.*
 'Mary ate a tomato.'
 b. *Marie **mangeait** une tomate.*
 'Mary was eating a tomato.'

As Vet (2000: 152) points out, the *passé simple* in (21a) presents the event as a whole and as finished, whereas the *imparfait* in (21b) presents the same event as an indeterminate quantity of eating a tomato.[28] Again, this illustrates the phenomenon of "coercion", or contextual reinterpretation, already observed in (15), (16), and (17), but (20) shows that the relevant parallelism is to be established between the *imparfait* and the partitive article *du*, rather than between the *imparfait* and states as such (Vet 2001: 169). And just as the partitive article expresses continuity, so does the *imparfait*: since it presents a situation as actually occurring, from the inside, no boundaries are imposed, and the situation can continue indefinitely, so to speak. This element of "continuity" inherent in the *imparfait* explains the difference between (22) and (23), as has been shown by Ducrot (1979: 77–78) and Anscombre (1992: 46):

(22) *Jean a-t-il vécu à Paris l'année dernière?*
 - Oui, en mai.
 - ??Non, seulement en mai.
 'Has John lived in Paris last year?
 - Yes, in May.
 - ??No, only in May.'

(23) *Jean vivait-il à Paris l'année dernière?*
 - ??Oui, en mai.
 - ?Non, seulement en mai.
 'Did John live in Paris last year?

- ??Yes, in May.
- ?No, only in May.'

The acceptability judgments of the answers to both questions show that the *passé composé* can be interpreted as concerning only part of the period evoked by *l'année dernière* 'last year', whereas the *imparfait* turns the question in (23) into one that concerns the entirety of last year, making an answer that does not concern the whole of last year unacceptable. Even if the events cannot objectively have occupied the period of time indicated, the *imparfait* suggests that this is the case. Thus, when one affirms (24),

(24) a. *L'année dernière à Paris, il faisait chaud.*
'Last year in Paris, it was warm.'

this does not mean that it was warm the whole of last year, but that last year can be characterized as globally warm. The warmth is presented as a global characteristic of last year in Paris, contrary to what is expressed when the *imparfait* is replaced by the *passé composé*:

b. *L'année dernière à Paris, il a fait chaud.*
'Last year in Paris, it has been warm.'

In that case, the sentence is interpreted as saying that it has been warm in Paris during some periods of last year. In terms of Ducrot (1979: 6), who proposes the foregoing analysis of (24a,b), the *imparfait* presents the situation as a property of the temporal theme *l'année dernière*.[29] Anscombre (1992: 46) expresses the same idea when he concludes from (22) and (23) that the *imparfait* presents the situation expressed in a homogeneous way: it is as if the predicates 'living in Paris' (23) and 'be warm' (24a) are true of every subinterval of 'last year'.[30]

These aspectual properties of the *imparfait* contribute to explaining some of its modal uses: since the event is presented as continuous, the *imparfait* in itself does not give any information about its boundaries. Thus, it is open-ended, as can be deduced from the fact that the event can be interrupted before it really reaches its end, which is very clearly shown in the following example of Leeman-Bouix (1994: 149–150):

(25) a. *Quand je suis arrivé, Paul **sortait** tout juste.*
'When I arrived, Paul was just leaving.'
b. *Paul **sortait** tout juste quand Marie le retint pour lui dire que ...*
'Paul was just leaving when Mary held him back to tell him that ...'

Paul's action is interrupted and does not reach its endpoint. The imperfective aspect can thus explain why the *imparfait* is used to express irreal or possible events: the endpoint is not specified, it is virtual (Mellet 1988).

However, in itself, the aspectual value of the *imparfait* is not capable of explaining all of its modal values. Mellet (1988: 10–11), for instance, explains the politeness effect of the *imparfait* through its "open-endedness": since the event is presented as open-ended, the speaker does not fully assert her intention but creates the impression that the interlocutor can still intervene. Berthonneau and Kleiber (1994: 71–72) list some problems with Mellet's explanation. First, if the imperfective aspectual nature of the *imparfait* also explains this modal value, then it must be explained why other tenses with the same aspectual value, such as the simple present, do not express the same modal values. Moreover, when the *imparfait* is used to express politeness, what is expressed in the *imparfait,* is not the fact of saying or asking something, but the fact of wanting or coming to say or ask something (*je voulais/venais vous dire/demander* 'I wanted/came to say/ask you'), and it seems rather difficult to interrupt intentions to say or ask something or the fact of 'coming' to say or ask something. Thus it seems that some modal uses of the *imparfait* cannot be directly derived from its aspectual value.[31] Their explanation is not problematic, however, if one accepts the characterization of the *imparfait* as necessitating the identification of a viewpoint other than the speaker's actual one, as we have already shown above (cf. section 2).

4. The anaphoric value of the *imparfait*

Several authors define the French *imparfait* as an anaphoric tense, meaning that it needs an element in the co(n)text which situates the expressed event in time and thus functions as its "reference point" in the sense of Langacker (1993).[32] Berthonneau and Kleiber (1993: 57–60) list three arguments frequently advanced in favor of an "anaphoric" analysis of the *imparfait*:
1) as observed by Ducrot (1979: 7), a sentence such as *La France s'appelait la Gaule* 'France was called Gaul' cannot be used in the beginning of a story if the context does not allow the audience to find a past moment which justifies the *imparfait*;
2) the absence of a past interval makes (26a), but not (26b), incomplete:

(26) a. *Jean mangeait de la choucroute.*
      'John ate sauerkraut.'
   b. *Jean a mangé de la choucroute.*
      'John has eaten sauerkraut.'

3) as pointed out by Tasmowski-de Ryck (1985: 69), a question which combines the *imparfait* with *quand* 'when', such as *Quand Jean épousait-il Marie?* 'When did John marry Mary?', seems rather strange out of the blue, since the moment which can serve as the antecedent is by definition not known by the speaker.

In our view, this property of the *imparfait* follows from the definition presented above. If the *imparfait* presents an event as an actuality seen from a center or viewpoint other than the "here-and-now" of the speaker, the question is how this center or viewpoint is to be situated with respect to "(known) reality" as part of the "dynamic evolutionary model". In other words, one needs a "reference point" in order to identify the viewpoint from which the situation is conceptualized.[33] However, as has been pointed out by Kleiber (1993), Berthonneau and Kleiber (1993, 1994, 1998), and Irandoust (1998a,b), the relation between the "reference point" and the situations presented by the sentences in the *imparfait* are not to be described in purely temporal terms, but are at least partly of a conceptual nature. Examples like (24a,b) suggested to Ducrot (1979) that the situation expressed by the sentence in the *imparfait* describes a property that characterizes a temporal theme, but Irandoust (1998a: 73, 1998b: 313) objects that (27) is far less acceptable than (24a):

(27) *Pendant toute l'année, Jean travaillait à la Poste.
'The whole year, John worked at the post office.'

Berthonneau and Kleiber (1993: 63) also point out that temporal adverbs such as *pendant* and *durant*, meaning 'during', are not compatible with the *imparfait*:

(28) *Pendant deux ans / durant deux ans / pendant toute l'année / toute l'année, Paul vivait à Paris.
'For two years / during the whole year / last year, Paul lived in Paris.'

This can be explained if one accepts, contrary to Ducrot (1979) and others, that the reference point of the situation expressed by the sentence in the *imparfait* is not a temporal point, but a situation, as is also suggested by the following example of Molendijk (1993: 174):

(29) Jean se mit en route dans sa nouvelle Mercedes. Il attrapa une contravention. Il **roulait** trop vite.
'John drove off in his new Mercedes. He was fined. He was driving too fast.'

According to Molendijk (1993: 173–174), (29) shows that the rule for the *imparfait* proposed by Kamp and Rohrer (1983: 253), stating that the *imparfait* introduces into discourse a new state *s* which "contains the last event *e* introduced by a sentence in the *passé simple*", cannot be upheld as such. Indeed, the last sentence in the *passé simple* in (29) is *il attrapa une contravention* 'he was fined', but the situation in the *imparfait, il roulait trop vite* 'he was driving too fast', cannot be interpreted as simultaneous with it. Thus, in order to maintain that the *imparfait* expresses simultaneity with the moment introduced by the last sentence in the *passé simple*, Molendijk (1993: 179) proposes to consider the situation expressed by the sentence in the *imparfait* as simultaneous with the implication of *Jean se mit en route dans sa nouvelle Mercedes* 'John drove off in his new Mercedes', which is *Jean se déplacer dans un véhicule* 'John move around in a vehicle'. The problem with this analysis, as pointed out by Berthonneau and Kleiber (1993: 69), is that in the interpretation of (29), it is natural to establish a relation between 'be fined' and 'drive too fast', but not between 'John move around in a vehicle' and 'John be fined'. The relevance of this relation is shown, e.g., by the less acceptable status of (30):

(30) *Jean se mit en route dans sa nouvelle Mercedes. Il attrapa une contravention. ?Il **roulait** avec plaisir.*
'John drove off in his new Mercedes. He was fined. He enjoyed driving.'

The conclusion to be drawn from these and other arguments given by Berthonneau and Kleiber (1993, 1994, 1998) and Irandoust (1998a,b), is that a sentence in the *imparfait* is only acceptable if it can be related to some foregoing situation that is accessible in conceptual rather than purely temporal terms. In this sense, the *imparfait* can be compared to the definite article, which also signals the accessibility of its referent (Epstein 1999). More specifically, its use can be likened to the so-called "associative" use of the definite article (Kleiber 2001), which can be illustrated by (31):

(31) *Nous entrâmes dans un village. L'église était située sur une hauteur.*
'We entered a village. The church was on a rise.'

In any case, it seems better to compare the anaphoric function of the *imparfait* to the definite article, rather than to that of the pronoun *il*, since this pronoun normally expresses co-reference, whereas the sentence in the *imparfait* always introduces a new situation. Moreover, just as is the case with the "associative" uses of the definite article, the antecedent or reference point of the situation expressed by the sentence in the *imparfait* is only accessible if there is some kind of conceptual link between the reference point and that situation. Berthonneau and Kleiber (1998: 61) even suggest that the temporal value of simultaneity does not determine the choice of the reference point, thus criticizing Molendijk's attempt to explain the difference between (29) and (30).

Maintaining that the antecedent of the *imparfait* must be a simultaneous situation, Molendijk (1996: 115) proposes that the antecedent situation must be related to that in the *imparfait* by a relation of textual coherence that respects the temporal simultaneity value of the *imparfait*. This is the case in (29): the antecedent of the *imparfait* is the situation implicated by the first sentence, 'John drive in his new Mercedes', since this situation is simultaneous with the situation expressed by the sentence in the *imparfait*, and since there is, moreover, a coherence relation, that of manner/precision, which links the two situations. Molendijk (1996: 115–116) can even explain the relation of cause/effect between 'getting fined' and 'driving too fast': it is established by a general principle of coherence, requiring that two subsequent sentences in discourse be related to one another by some coherence relation. In (30), however, the situation in the *imparfait*, 'enjoy driving', cannot be related to 'getting fined', and the coherence requirement is not satisfied.

In fact, it seems that Molendijk still considers the temporal relation of simultaneity to be the crucial element in the search for an antecedent or reference point, adding coherence relations to filter out the cases where the simultaneity requirement is satisfied but the *imparfait* is not acceptable. However, Berthonneau and Kleiber (1998: 61) show that even his enriched theory cannot rule out (32):

(32) Jean se mit en route dans sa vieille Fiat. ?*Il **roulait** trop vite.*
 'John drove off in his old Fiat. ?He was driving too fast.'

Indeed, the *imparfait* can be said to express simultaneity with the implied situation 'John drive in his old Fiat', and the two situations can be said to be linked by a coherence relation of the type manner/precision. Nevertheless, the *imparfait* is unacceptable, suggesting that the temporal idea of simultaneity does not determine the selection of the reference point.

This discussion, presented in more detail in De Mulder and Vetters (1999), Vetters and De Mulder (2000), and Vet (1999), shows in any case that the identification of the "reference point" of the *imparfait* is subject to conceptual restrictions. Berthonneau and Kleiber (1998: 55–56) thus propose that the *imparfait* demands the construction of a larger situation, something like *Jean qui attrape une contravention* 'John who gets fined' in the case of (29), and that the situation in the *imparfait* presents an ingredient of this larger situation. In terms of Irandoust's (1998a: 70–71) analysis, the *imparfait* can be said to be anaphoric, not because it requires a temporal reference point, but because it must be possible to integrate the situation expressed by the sentence in the *imparfait* into an accessible frame. This is illustrated in the following example by Ducrot (1979: 2, 9):

(33) *Les Iraniens s'en prennent maintenant aux intérêts américains. Hier deux banques américaines étaient saccagées (prononcée par un speaker de la télévision).*
 'The Iranians now attack American interests. Yesterday two American banks were sacked (said by a speaker on television).'

Contrary to Ducrot (1979), both Berthonneau and Kleiber (1993: 69) and Irandoust (1998a: 74) hold that the antecedent of the *imparfait* is not *hier* 'yesterday', but the situation, or "reference frame" in Irandoust's terms, made accessible by the first sentence, 'The Iranians attack American interests'. The sentence in the *imparfait* expresses a situation which verifies the state of affairs set up by the first sentence and which is one of the ingredients of this wider situation, just like the definite article in an "associative" use such as (31) specifies an element already contained within its antecedent.[34]

5. Conclusions

The *imparfait* can be defined cognitively as implying a particular way of construing the situation referred to. It signals that this situation is to be conceived as an "actuality" viewed from a center other than that of the speaker and, thus, other than her "here-and-now". We have tried to show that this cognitive definition of the *imparfait*, which we developed on the basis of the work by Damourette and Pichon (1911–1936) on the French *imparfait* and by Doiz-Bienzobas (1995, this volume) on the Spanish imperfect,[35] can explain the modal uses of the *imparfait*, as well as the aspectual and anaphoric properties it is usually held to manifest. With respect to the theory of grounding, our definition of the *imparfait* implies that the speech point or moment of utterance is not always the viewpoint from which a scene is conceptualized, but that this viewpoint ultimately has to be identified via accessible contextual clues. We suggested, with Berthonneau and Kleiber and others, that the accessibility relation involved can be likened, in some respects, to that expressed by the definite article, whereas the aspectual value of the *imparfait* should rather be compared to the continuity expressed by the partitive article in the nominal domain. The accessibility relation involved in the use of the *imparfait* needs more refining, however. It remains to be seen, also, how the basic meaning of the *imparfait* as sketched here can explain its use in habitual and generic sentences, and how it functions in contexts of indirect discourse.[36]

Notes

1. For a survey, see e.g. Touratier (1996: 107–141), Vetters (1996: 107–164), and Wilmet (1997: 384–402).
2. We will enumerate these modal uses according to Vetters (2000a: 182–183); for other lists of such uses, see e.g. Berthonneau and Kleiber (1994: 89–90)

and Wilmet (1997: 384). Doiz-Bienzobas (1995: 3, 12–13) gives corresponding Spanish examples and Cutrer (1994: 4) gives English examples of the simple past.
3. According to Wilmet (1997: 392), this use of the *imparfait* was first registered by Cohen (1963).
4. Wilmet (1997: 394) signals that this use of the *imparfait* was already noted by Buffin (1925), and that Tesnière (1926) suggested the term "*hypocoristique*". Damourette and Pichon (1911–1936: 241), however, attribute the term to Brun-Laloire (1929). This use has also been studied by Sletsjoë (1963, 1964).
5. This use of the *imparfait* is frequent in Belgium, but has recently also been observed in France (Grevisse 1986: 1292; Wilmet 1997: 391). In France, however, the most common way to express this meaning is the *conditionnel*: *Moi, je serais le gendarme...* 'Me, I would be the cop'. According to Wilmet (1997: 391), this conditional suggests the need for approval, whereas the *imparfait* assigns the roles with more authority. See also Henry (1954), Warnant (1966), and Pohl (1972). Doiz-Bienzobas (this volume) contains an analysis of this use of the imperfect in Spanish.
6. See also Wilmet (1976, 1983). Some authors prefer to refer to both uses as "fictional". In their view, French only marks an opposition between two hypothetical modes: the "real" and the "fictional" (Sechehaye 1906; Wagner 1939; Bonnard 1981; Cappello 1986; Vetters 2000a).
7. This point is also made by Doiz-Bienzobas (this volume: 310–311) with respect to her example (20). As she rightly points out, the viewpoint in these cases is in the past, away from the ground.
8. Comparable analyses of the *imparfait* have been developed in Cornu (1953), Coseriu (1980), Le Goffic (1986, 1995), Herslund (1987), and Touratier (1996, 1998).
9. Damourette and Pichon use the term *toncal* (cf. Latin *tunc* 'then') to refer to the *imparfait* and other tenses that are centered around an actuality other than the "here-and-now", as opposed to *noncal* (cf. *nunc* 'now').
10. Damourette and Pichon (1911–1936) use the term *protagoniste* ('protagonist') to refer to such other participants.
11. Cf. the following citation: "Dans l'actualité toncale, on se transporte avec suffisamment de vivacité en dehors du présent pour ressentir en quelque sorte la durée vécue d'un laps de temps." [In toncal actuality, one is transferred with sufficient vivacity out off the present, in order to sense in a way the lived duration of a span of time.] (Damourette and Pichon 1911–1936: 198)
12. A reference point is a salient entity used to locate another, less noticeable entity in relation to it (Langacker 1993).
13. Doiz-Bienzobas (this volume) mentions that, for the Spanish preterit in direct speech time, the reference point is the ground. This would distinguish the French *passé simple* and the Spanish preterit.

14. According to Kamp and Rohrer (1983), the situations introduced by the *imparfait* are states.
15. As has been pointed out by many authors, a causal interpretation, which can be found in English (*John fell. Max pushed him.*), cannot be expressed by the French equivalent in the *passé simple*. For more details, see e.g. Lascarides and Asher (1993), Caenepeel (1995), Vet (1995, 1996), de Saussure (1998, 2000), De Mulder (2000), and Vetters and De Mulder (2000).
16. For a more detailed discussion of this question, see, e.g., Vetters (1996: 168–180), Caenepeel (1995), and De Mulder (2000).
17. This explains why the *imparfait* can be used to express shifts of point of view in fiction, as was already observed by Fleischman (1990), Sthioul (1998), and Sthioul and de Saussure (1999: 179).
18. See also Benveniste ([1965] 1974a: 76) and the opposition between "certain" and "forthcoming" (*certain/à venir*) in the work of Fuchs and Léonard (1979), Desclés (1994), and Le Goffic (1986), and that between fact and prediction in Cutrer (1994). For other references and an extended discussion, see Brisard (1999).
19. Vetters (2000a: 186, 2000b: 45) suggests that the "nonactual" value of the *imparfait* is to be subordinated to its "nonulterior" value. It is not clear, however, whether this "nonulterior" value can be identified with what could be called "nonprojected" in Langacker's model: Vetters (2000a: 186) defines "nonulterior" as "excluded from the actuality of the moment of utterance", and thus either "in the past with respect to the moment of utterance" or "in the nonulterior part — and thus present or past — of a universe other than the one including the moment of utterance".
20. "... d'un énoncé tel que *Paul était intelligent*, un interlocuteur inférera normalement que Paul n'est plus intelligent, à moins d'avoir des raisons manifestes de penser le contraire." (Berthonneau and Kleiber 1994: 75) One could of course also conclude that Paul is dead by now, as one of our readers has pointed out to us.
21. Berthonneau and Kleiber (1994) refer to Martin's analysis of *Il travaillait chez Renault* 'He worked for Renault'. According to this author, "cette phrase laisse entendre ou bien qu'il ne travaille plus chez Renault ou bien que j'ignore s'il y travaille encore" [this sentence says either that he does not work for Renault anymore, or that I do not know whether he still works there] (Martin 1987: 132). The last part of the quote confirms the epistemic interpretation of the *imparfait*.
22. Several authors (a.o. Imbs 1960 and Fleischman 1989) have suggested that the temporal distance marked by the *imparfait* is used as a metaphor for distance in other domains. Doiz-Bienzobas (1995: 238) proposes a comparable analysis for the use of the Spanish imperfect to express *irrealis*. For a discussion of

the French *imparfait* in this respect, see also Cutrer (1994: 184–185); for a more general discussion, see Brisard (1999).
23. This definition is not to be confused with the one proposed by Langacker (1991: 21), which concerns the process expressed by the verb and, thus, what is traditionally called *Aktionsart* or lexical aspect.
24. In this respect, there seems to be a difference between the French *imparfait* and the Spanish imperfect, since Doiz-Bienzobas (1995: 32) claims that the viewing arrangement of the Spanish imperfect does not interact with the boundedness of the situations referred to. She also mentions, though, that the imperfective best combines with atelic situations, that in some cases there is interaction (cf. note 22 on the same page), and that the choice between the two tenses can be meaningful, with the imperfective mostly suggesting the presence of a viewpoint (Doiz-Bienzobas 1995: 92–98).
25. In fact, to appreciate the awkwardness of the *imparfait* in some of these sentences, it would probably be better to translate it systematically by the past progressive in English.
26. These examples are from de Swart (1995: 93).
27. For the parallelism between mass nouns, states, and the *imparfait*, see also Mourelatos (1978), Hoepelman and Rohrer (1980), Carlson (1981), Ter Meulen (1984), Bach (1986), Krifka (1987), Borillo (1987), Langacker (1987b), and Filip (2001). For an analysis of French mass nouns, see Van de Velde (1995).
28. See also Vet (1994, 2001: 167–170) and de Swart (1995, 1998).
29. The capacity of the *imparfait* to express a property can serve as a basis to explain its uses in habitual and generic sentences. Doiz-Bienzobas (1995: 105, this volume) links this capacity, in the case of the Spanish imperfect, to the idea that it does not necessarily provide a temporal specification of the situation, as opposed to the preterit. Thus, the imperfect may state that the situation expressed belongs to the structural or the actuality plane, in Langacker's (1997) terms (Doiz-Bienzobas 1995: 127, this volume). We do not analyze the generic and habitual uses of the *imparfait* in this article.
30. This also explains why Jayez (1998: 142) holds that the *imparfait* can only be used if the event expressed has parts and if it is possible to transmit the type of the total event to each subpart.
31. One could also object that the *imparfait* is not always imperfective; this thesis is sometimes defended with respect to the *imparfait narratif* ("narrative imperfect"). However, in Vetters and De Mulder (to appear), we have tried to show that even in these uses, the *imparfait* still has its imperfective aspectual value. See also Vetters and De Mulder (2000: 26–30).
32. Most authors defending the anaphoric nature of the *imparfait* use the traditional term "antecedent". However, van Hoek (1997) shows that Langacker's

notion of "reference point" can also replace the idea of an "antecedent" in the analysis of (pro-)nominal anaphora.
33. Jayez (1998: 151) affirms the anaphoric nature of the *imparfait* on the basis of its "homogeneous" nature: "D'une manière générale, la sélection de l'intérieur d'un événement n'est pas naturelle, sauf si l'on veut indiquer un repère précis. En effet, quelle raison aurait-on de mentionner l'intérieur d'une entité plutôt que l'entité elle-même si ce n'est d'utiliser le type (descriptif) de l'entité pour caractériser un repère?" [In general, the selection of the interior of an event is not natural, except if one wants to indicate an exact point of reference. Indeed, which reason would one have to mention only the interior part of an entity rather than the entity itself, if not in order to use the (descriptive) type of the entity to characterize a point of reference?] From this point of view, the *imparfait* could again be compared to mass nouns.
34. One could also say that the definite noun phrase in (31) expresses a slot in the frame activated by *village* or a role in a "mental model". In terms of Langacker (1993) and van Hoek (1997), the referent is accessed through a reference point, because it is situated in its dominion.
35. Doiz-Bienzobas (1995: 1) suggests that the French *imparfait* is in many ways comparable to the Spanish imperfect.
36. Doiz-Bienzobas (1995) and Cutrer (1994) already offer an analysis of these points.

References

Anscombre, Jean-Claude
    1992   Imparfait et passé composé: Des forts en thème/propos. *L'information grammaticale* 55: 43–53.
Arrivé, Michel, Françoise Gadet and Michel Galmiche
    1986   *La grammaire d'aujourd'hui*. Paris: Flammarion.
Bach, Emmon
    1986   The algebra of events. *Linguistics and Philosophy* 9: 5–16.
Benveniste, Émile
    1966   Les relations de temps dans le verbe français. In: *Problèmes de linguistique générale*, Volume 1, 237–250. Paris: Gallimard. First published *Bulletin de la Société de Linguistique* 54: fasc. 1 [1959].
    1974a   Le langage et l'expérience humaine. In: *Problèmes de linguistique générale*, Volume 2, 67–78. Paris: Gallimard. First published *Diogène* 51: 1–13 [1965].

1974b Les transformations des catégories linguistiques. In: *Problèmes de linguistique générale*, Volume 2, 126–136. Paris: Gallimard. First published in: *Directions for Historical Linguistics*, 85–94. Austin: University of Texas Press [1968].

Berthonneau, Anne-Marie and Georges Kleiber
1993 Pour une nouvelle approche de l'imparfait: L'imparfait, un temps anaphorique méronomique. *Langages* 112: 55–73.
1994 Imparfaits de politesse: Rupture ou cohésion? *Travaux de linguistique* 29: 59–92.
1998 Imparfait, anaphore, et inférences. In: Andrée Borillo, Carl Vetters and Marcel Vuillaume (eds.), *Variations sur la référence verbale*, 35–65. (Cahiers Chronos 3.) Amsterdam: Rodopi.

Bonnard, Henri
1981 *Code du français courant*. Paris: Magnard.

Borillo, Andrée
1987 Notions de "massif" et "comptable" dans la mesure temporelle. In: Jean David and Georges Kleiber (eds.), *Termes massifs et termes comptables*, 215–237. Paris: Klincksieck.

Brisard, Frank
1999 A critique of localism in and about tense theory. Ph.D. dissertation, University of Antwerp.

Brun-Laloire, L.
1929 L'imparfait de l'indicatif est-il un temps? *Revue de Philologie française* 40: 56–86.

Buffin, Jules-Marc
1925 *Remarques sur les moyens d'expression de la durée et du temps en français*. Paris: Presses Universitaires de France.

Caenepeel, Mimo
1995 Aspect and text structure. *Linguistics* 33: 213–253.

Cappello, Sergio
1986 L'imparfait de fiction. In: Pierre Le Goffic (ed.), *Points de vue sur l'imparfait*, 31–41. Caen: Presses Universitaires de Caen.

Carlson, Lauri
1981 Aspect and quantification. In: Philip Tedeschi and Annie Zaenen (eds.), *Tense and Aspect*, 31–64. (Syntax and Semantics 14.) New York: Academic.

Cohen, Marcel
1963 *Nouveaux regards sur la langue française*. Paris: Éditions sociales.

Cornu, M.
1953 *Les formes surcomposées du français*. Bern: Francke.

Coseriu, Eugenio
   1980   Aspect verbal ou aspects verbaux? Quelques questions de théorie et de méthode. In: Jean David and Robert Martin (eds.), *La notion d'aspect*, 13–25. Paris: Klincksieck.

Cutrer, Michelle
   1994   Time and tense in narrative and everyday language. Ph.D. dissertation, University of California, San Diego.

Damourette, Jacques and Édouard Pichon
   1911–1936   *Des mots à la pensée: Essai de grammaire de la langue française*, Volume 5. Paris: d'Artrey.

De Mulder, Walter
   2000   Retour à Benveniste? Quelques réflexions préliminaires sur la valeur textuelle du passé simple et du passé composé. In: Martine Coene, Walter De Mulder, Patrick Dendale and Yves D'Hulst (eds.), *Traiani Augusti Vestigia Pressa Sequamur: Studia Linguistica in Honorem Lilianae Tasmowski*, 393–410. Padova: Unipress.

De Mulder, Walter and Carl Vetters
   1999   Temps verbaux, anaphores (pro)nominales et relations discursives. *Travaux de linguistique* 39: 37–58.

de Saussure, Louis
   1998   L'encapsulation des événements: L'exemple du passé simple. In: Jacques Moeschler (ed.), *Le temps des événements: Pragmatique de la référence temporelle*, 245–270. Paris: Kimé.
   2000   Quand le temps ne progresse pas avec le passé simple. In: Anne Carlier, Véronique Lagae and Céline Benninger (eds.), *Passé et parfait*, 37–48. (Cahiers Chronos 6.) Amsterdam: Rodopi.

de Swart, Henriette
   1995   Contraintes aspectuelles et réinterprétation contextuelle. *Sémiotiques* 9: 89–116.
   1998   Aspect shift and coercion. *Natural Language and Linguistic Theory* 16: 347–385.

Desclés, Jean-Pierre
   1994   Quelques concepts relatifs au temps et à l'aspect pour l'analyse des textes. *Études cognitives* 1: 57–88.

Doiz-Bienzobas, Aintzane
   1995   The preterit and imperfect in Spanish: Past situation vs. past viewpoint. Ph.D. dissertation, University of California, San Diego.
   this vol.   The preterit and the imperfect as grounding predications.

Ducrot, Oswald
   1979   L'imparfait en français. *Linguistische Berichte* 69: 1–23.

Epstein, Richard
    1999   Roles, frames, and definiteness. In Karen van Hoek, Andrej Kibrik and Leo Noorman (eds.), *Discourse Studies in Cognitive Linguistics*, 53–74. Amsterdam: John Benjamins.
Fauconnier, Gilles
    1984   *Espaces mentaux: Aspects de la construction du sens dans les langues naturelles*. Paris: Minuit.
Filip, Hana
    2001   Nominal and verbal semantic structure: Analogies and interactions. *Language Sciences* 23: 453–501.
Fleischman, Suzanne
    1989   Temporal distance: A basic linguistic metaphor. *Studies in Language* 13: 1–50.
    1990   *Tense and Narrativity: The Present Tense from Medieval Performance to Modern Fiction*. Austin: University of Texas Press.
    1995   Imperfective and irrealis. In: Joan Bybee and Suzanne Fleischman (eds.), *Modality in Grammar and Discourse*, 519–551. Amsterdam: John Benjamins.
Fuchs, Catherine and Anne-Marie Léonard
    1979   *Vers une théorie des aspects*. Paris: Mouton.
Galmiche, Michel
    1989   Massif/comptable: De l'un à l'autre et inversement. In: Jean David and Georges Kleiber (eds.), *Termes massifs et termes comptables*, 63–77. Paris: Klincksieck.
Genette, Gérard
    1983   *Nouveau discours du récit*. Paris: Seuil.
Gosselin, Laurent
    1999   Les valeurs de l'imparfait et du conditionnel dans les systèmes hypothétiques. In: Svetlana Vogeleer, Andrée Borillo, Marcel Vuillaume and Carl Vetters (eds.), *La modalité sous tous ses aspects*, 29–51. (Cahiers Chronos 4.) Amsterdam: Rodopi.
Grevisse, Maurice
    1986   *Le bon usage: Grammaire française*. Paris: Duculot. 12th edition, revised by André Goosse.
Henry, Albert
    1954   L'imparfait est-il un temps? In: *Mélanges Charles Bruneau*, 11–17. Geneva: Droz.
Herslund, Michael
    1987   Catégories grammaticales et linguistique textuelle: La catégorie du temps en français. *Copenhagen Studies in Language, CEBAL* 10: 89–108.

Hoepelman, Jaap and Christian Rohrer
    1980   On the mass-count distinction and the French imparfait and passé simple. In: Christian Rohrer (ed.), *Time, Tense, and Quantifiers*, 85–112. Tübingen: Niemeyer.

Imbs, Paul
    1960   *L'emploi des temps verbaux en français moderne*. Paris: Klincksieck.

Irandoust, Hengameh
    1998a   Épisodes, cadres de référence et interprétation temporelle: Application à l'imparfait. In: Andrée Borillo, Carl Vetters and Marcel Vuillaume (eds.), *Variations sur la référence verbale*, 67–89. Amsterdam: Rodopi.
    1998b   Reference frames: An application to imparfait. In: Jean-Pierre Koenig (ed.), *Discourse and Cognition: Bridging the Gap*, 309–322. Stanford: Center for the Study of Language and Information.

Jayez, Jacques
    1998   DRT et imparfait: Un exemple de traitement formel du temps. In: Jacques Moeschler (ed.), *Le temps des événements: Pragmatique de la référence temporelle*, 123–154. Paris: Kimé.

Kamp, Hans and Christian Rohrer
    1983   Tense in texts. In: Rainer Bäuerle, Christoph Schwarze and Arnim von Stechow (eds.), *Meaning, Use and Interpretation of Language*, 250–269. Berlin: de Gruyter.

Kleiber, Georges
    1993   Lorsque l'anaphore se lie aux temps verbaux. In: Carl Vetters (ed.), *Le temps: De la phrase au texte*, 117–166. Villeneuve d'Ascq: Presses Universitaires de Lille.
    2001   *L'anaphore associative*. Paris: Presses Universitaires de France.

Klum, Arne
    1961   *Verbe et adverbe*. Uppsala: Almqvist & Wicksell.

Krifka, Manfred
    1987   *Nominalreferenz und Zeitkonstitution: Zur Semantik von Massentermen, Pluraltermen und Aspektklassen*. Munich: Fink.

Langacker, Ronald W.
    1987a   *Foundations of Cognitive Grammar*, Volume 1: *Theoretical Prerequisites*. Stanford: Stanford University Press.
    1987b   Nouns and verbs. *Language* 63: 53–94.
    1991   *Foundations of Cognitive Grammar*, Volume 2: *Descriptive application*. Stanford: Stanford University Press.
    1993   Reference-point constructions. *Cognitive Linguistics* 4: 1–38.
    1995   Viewing in language and cognition. In: Philip Davis (ed.), *Alternative Linguistics: Descriptions and Theoretical Modes*, 153–212. Amsterdam: John Benjamins.

1997   Generics and habituals. In: Angeliki Athanasiadou and René Dirven (eds.), *On Conditionals Again*, 191–222. Amsterdam: John Benjamins.
1999   *Grammar and Conceptualization*. Berlin: Mouton de Gruyter.
this vol. a   Deixis and subjectivity.
this vol. b   Remarks on the English grounding systems.

Lascarides, Alex and Nicholas Asher
1993   Temporal interpretation, discourse relations, and commonsense entailment. *Linguistics and Philosophy* 16: 437–493.

Le Goffic, Pierre
1986   Que l'imparfait n'est pas un temps du passé. In: Pierre Le Goffic (ed.), *Points de vue sur l'imparfait*, 55–69. Caen: Centre de Publications de l'Université.
1995   La double incomplétude de l'imparfait. *Modèles linguistiques* 16: 133–148.

Leeman-Bouix, Danielle
1994   *Grammaire du verbe français: Des formes au sens*. Paris: Nathan.

Martin, Robert
1987   *Langage et croyance: Les "univers de croyance" dans la théorie sémantique*. Brussels: Mardaga.

Mellet, Sylvie
1988   *L'imparfait de l'indicatif en latin classique: Temps, aspect, modalité*. Leuven: Peeters.

Molendijk, Arie
1993   Présuppositions, implications, structure temporelle. In: Carl Vetters (ed.), *Le temps: De la phrase au texte*, 167–191. Villeneuve d'Ascq: Presses Universitaires de Lille.
1996   Anaphore et imparfait: La référence globale à des situations présupposées ou impliquées. In: Walter De Mulder, Liliane Tasmowski-de Ryck and Carl Vetters (eds.), *Anaphores temporelles et (in-)cohérence*, 109–123. Amsterdam: Rodopi.

Mourelatos, Alexander
1978   Events, processes and states. *Linguistics and Philosophy* 2: 415–434.

Pohl, Jacques
1966   *Symboles et langage*. Paris: Sodi.

Quine, Willard V. O.
1960   *Word and Object*. Cambridge, MA: MIT Press.

Sechehaye, Albert
1906   L'imparfait du subjonctif et ses concurrents dans les hypothétiques normales en français. *Romanische Forschungen* 19: 321–406.

Sletsjoë, L.
1963 L'imparfait dit hypocoristique: Y a-t-il en français un emploi plus général ("d'emphase") de cet imparfait ? *Le français moderne* 31: 241–261.
1964 L'imparfait dit hypocoristique (suite). *Le français moderne* 32: 27–44.

Sthioul, Bertrand
1998 Temps verbaux et point de vue. In: Jacques Moeschler (ed.), *Le temps des événements: Pragmatique des temps verbaux*, 197–220. Paris: Kimé.

Sthioul, Bertrand and Louis de Saussure
1999 L'imparfait narratif: Point de vue (et images du monde). *Cahiers de praxématique* 32: 167–188.

Tasmowski-de Ryck, Liliane
1985 L'imparfait avec et sans rupture. *Langue française* 67: 59–77.

Ter Meulen, Alice
1984 Events, quantities and individuals. In: Fred Landman and Frank Veltman (eds.), *Varieties of Formal Semantics*, 259–279. Dordrecht: Foris.

Tesnière, Lucien
1926 L'emploi des temps en français. *Bulletin de la Faculté des Lettres de Strasbourg*, numéro hors série, cours de vacances 1926–1927: 39–60.

Touratier, Christian
1996 *Le système verbal français*. Paris: Colin.
1998 L'imparfait, temps du passé non marqué. In: Andrée Borillo, Carl Vetters and Marcel Vuillaume (eds.), *Regards sur l'aspect*, 21–28. (Cahiers Chronos 2.) Amsterdam: Rodopi.

Van de Velde, Danièle
1995 *Le spectre nominal: Des noms de matières aux noms d'abstractions*. Leuven: Peeters.

van Hoek, Karen
1997 *Anaphora and Conceptual Structure*. Chicago: University of Chicago Press.

Vet, Co
1994 Petite grammaire de l'Aktionsart et de l'aspect. *Cahiers de grammaire* 19: 1–17.
1995 Anaphore et déixis dans le domaine temporel. In: Walter De Mulder, Liliane Tasmowski-de Ryck and Carl Vetters (eds.), *Anaphores temporelles et (in-)cohérence*, 147–163. (Cahiers Chronos 1.) Amsterdam: Rodopi.
1996 Aspect, anaphore, et interprétation du discours. *Hermès* 16: 93–106.

1999	Les temps verbaux comme expressions anaphoriques: Chronique de la recherche. *Travaux de linguistique* 39: 113–130.
2000	Référence temporelle, aspect verbal et les dichotomies massif/comptable et connu/nouveau. In: Jacques Moeschler and Marie-José Reichler-Béguelin (eds.), *Référence temporelle et nominale*, 145–166. Bern: Lang.
2001	Les temps verbaux comme déterminants de la phrase. In: Dany Amiot, Walter De Mulder and Nelly Flaux (eds.), *Le syntagme nominal: Syntaxe et sémantique*, 161–177. Arras: Artois Presses Université.

Vetters, Carl
1996	*Temps, aspect et narration*. Amsterdam: Rodopi.
2000a	Le conditionnel: Ultérieur du non-actuel. In: Patrick Dendale and Liliane Tasmowski (eds.), *Le conditionnel en français*, 169–207. Metz: Université de Metz.
2000b	Réflexions sur la référence temporelle. Habilitation, Université de Nice-Antipolis.

Vetters, Carl and Walter De Mulder
2000	Passé simple et imparfait: Contenus conceptuel et procédural. In: Anne Carlier, Véronique Lagae and Céline Benninger (eds.), *Passé et parfait*, 13–36. (Cahiers Chronos 6.) Amsterdam: Rodopi.
to appear	Sur la narrativité de l'imparfait. In: *Hommages Theo Venckeleer*.

Wagner, Robert-Léon
1939	*Les phrases hypothétiques commençant par "si" dans la langue française des origines à la fin du XVIe siècle*. Paris: Droz.

Warnant, Louis
1966	"Moi, j'étais le papa...": L'imparfait préludique et quelques remarques relatives à la recherche grammaticale. In: *Mélanges Maurice Grevisse*, 346–366. Gembloux: Duculot.

Wilmet, Marc
1976	*Études de morpho-syntaxe verbale*. Paris: Klincksieck.
1983	L'imparfait forain. *Romanica Gandensia (Mélanges Louis Mourin)* 20: 159–167.
1997	*Grammaire critique du français*. Paris: Duculot.

Deictic principles of pronominals, demonstratives, and tenses

Theo A. J. M. Janssen

1. Introduction[1]

Personal pronouns, demonstratives, and tenses are generally seen as deictic elements.[2] This suggests that they share some important semantic characteristics. This possibly common set of characteristics asks for an explanation of both their cognitive functionality and the way speakers and addressees construe the situation for which deictics are applied. Therefore, I will explore the cognitive structuring of the framework of the speech situation. With regard to the use of deictics, I will suggest that the speaker and, in her wake, the addressee discern a specific structuring of the cognitive framework of the speech situation. The main characteristics of this framework are, first, the speaker's vantage point, second, her mental field of vision, and, third, the division of the speaker's mental field of vision into a number of deictic dimensions, each of which is divided into at least two distinct regions or zones. The entities referred to by means of deictic expressions are conceived of as each occupying a different region of the speaker's mental field of vision.

The terminology (*field of vision*, *deictic dimension*, *region*, and *zone*) might suggest that my approach to deixis is based on a localist assumption. However, I will argue that deictics such as demonstratives cannot be adequately characterized on the basis of spatial notions. I will describe demonstratives — and tenses — in a way similar to personal pronouns, namely by means of a nonlocalist analysis. The semantic interconnectedness of personal pronouns (which is reflected morphologically in some languages, as I will show) appears to be closely related to the internal interconnectedness of demonstratives with regard to both their semantic and — in some languages — their morphological structure.

In section 2, I will concentrate on the cognitive structuring of the framework of the speech situation when personal pronouns are used. In section 3, I will elaborate the description of the framework of the speech situation by considering demonstratives. In section 4, I will draw tenses into the framework of the speech situation. In section 5, I will briefly compare my approach to deixis with the analysis of Reichenbach (1947).

2. The framework of the speech situation

Deixis, including grounding,[3] is the linguistic procedure by means of which a speaker relates an entity to the current speech situation in such a way that the addressee gains cognitive access to or mental contact with the entity concerned (Hanks 1989, 1990; Langacker 1987: 126, 1991: 91). The main issue of the deictic procedure, then, is: how can the addressee succeed in gaining cognitive access to an entity when it is related by the speaker to the current speech situation? In order to deal with this general question, we need to begin with more specific issues such as: what is the current speech situation? What are the prerequisites of any speech situation? How is the speech situation construed cognitively? How, then, does the speaker relate an entity to the current speech situation?

Let us first consider these preliminary questions about the inventory and the structure of the speech situation. I assume that the core elements of a speech situation are a speaker and her addressee (cf. Langacker 1987: 127), each of them with possibly one or more associates. The speaker plays the central role in this configuration (Langacker 1997: 244); she is the one who chooses the addressee, irrespective of whether it is a real person, possibly herself, or a fictive person. When the speaker starts to talk, the person who is the addressee might not know that she actually is the addressee. It is probably just from the course of the current act of speech that it emerges whom the speaker is addressing. In the case of face-to-face interaction, the person whom the speaker is looking at is most probably the addressee. But speaker and addressee do not need to look at each other in their conversation, as is apparent from telephone conversations.

When a person is on the verge of addressing somebody, the main prerequisite for a speech situation is present. As soon as a person addresses another person and the latter starts to understand that she is being addressed, the two share a speech situation, albeit that they have different roles in it, since one of them is the speaker and the other the addressee. Establishing and maintaining a speech situation is, in Cornish' (1999: 150) phrasing, "fundamentally a joint undertaking, involving an interaction between the speech participants in play". For both the speaker and the addressee (possibly with their associates) the speech situation serves as the primordial framework for the ongoing conversation. This framework is a dynamic entity. In Hanks' (1989: 108) words, when "interactants move through space, shift topics, exchange information, coordinate their respective orientations, and establish common grounds as well as non-commonalities, the indexical framework of reference changes". This flexible, socio-centric (Jones 1995: 47), cognitive framework of the speech situation, in which the interactants harmonize their orientation, is crucial for how the speaker can indicate entities in the ongoing conversation. It is highly decisive for the question of whether or not the speaker can use a definite description.

A definite description can consist of, for instance, a nominal introduced by a definite article, demonstrative, or possessive. Furthermore, a definite description can consist of a proper noun or a personal pronoun. The question we have to ask now is: is there any relationship between a definite description and the framework of the speech situation, and, if so, what kind of relationship is it? Let us start with the speaker in an arbitrary speech situation.

Whatever the circumstances may be, a speaker can assume that in her own and her addressee's view some entities have a special status in the cognitive framework of the speech situation; good examples are the discourse roles of the speaker and the addressee. The parties fulfilling these discourse roles form a set of two. Therefore, none of them is unique in the framework of the speech situation. It is only in one of the two discourse roles that one of the parties is unique. Thus, each of both parties is unique in a different discourse role. This uniqueness allows the speaker to refer to herself by using the (definite) pronoun *I*, and it allows her to refer to the addressee by using the (definite) pronoun *you*.

The configuration of the discourse roles of the first and second person can be seen as one of the dimensions[4] of the dynamic cognitive framework of the speech situation. In this view, each dimension is divided into at least two distinct regions or zones.[5] The dimension of the first- and second-person discourse roles consists of a region of the speaker's discourse role and a region of the addressee's discourse role, so that each of both regions is filled by a party which is unique in one of the regions.

This type of analysis of the cognitive framework of a speech situation requires a number of tools for characterizing its structure. These tools are provisionally defined in Table 1.

Table 1. The basic structure of a speech situation

The speaker and the addressee assume that
a. the current speech situation is a cognitive framework which they observe from their vantage points, or possibly from their common vantage point;
b. the cognitive framework of the current speech situation has several dimensions;
c. each dimension is divided into at least two separate regions;
d. each region can be occupied by an entity which is unique in it;
e. one dimension is the dimension of the discourse roles;
f. one region is occupied by an entity in the discourse role of the speaker, another by an entity in the discourse role of the addressee.

The entity which occupies the speaker's region of the discourse-role dimension can be referred to by means of the definite description *I*. The entity which occupies the addressee's region of the discourse-role dimension can be referred to by means of the definite description *you*. The structure of this speech situation is shown in Figure 1. The discourse-role dimension consisting of the speaker's and the addressee's regions is represented by the upper oblong viewed from the speaker's vantage point; it visualizes the speaker's mental field of vision in the speech situation. In the phrasing of Hanks (1990:

142), "the speaker projects himself as a "figure", a protagonist in a scene, story ... the individual acting as a speaker, the one who performs the current act of reference, constitutes himself or herself as an object of description, as well as an actor engaged in executing a speech act."[6]

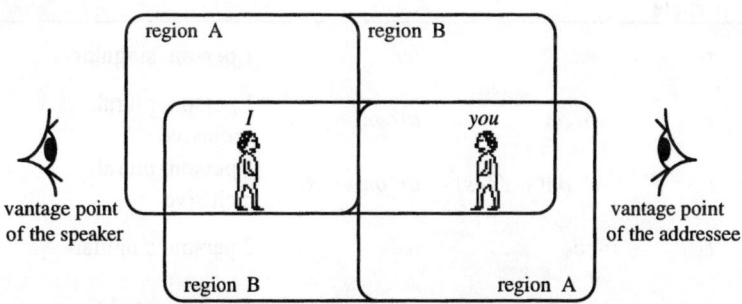

Figure 1. The cognitive frame of reference of the speech situation in which *I* and *you* are used

In my view, region A of the discourse-role dimension in the speaker's mental field of vision is the frame of reference to which the party referred to by means of *I* can be considered as uniquely related. Region B of the discourse-role dimension in the speaker's mental field of vision is the frame of reference to which the party referred to by means of *you* can be considered as uniquely related.

Both Table 1 and Figure 1 deal with the first- and second-person discourse roles only. How is the third-person discourse role related to the dimension of the first- and second-person discourse roles? Do we have to conceptualize the discourse-role dimension as consisting of three regions, or is another analysis more insightful? In English the first-, second-, and third-person pronouns do not feature any internal morphological structure. However, a language such as Maya, spoken in Yucatán, shows a morphology which relates the first- to the second-person pronouns but distinguishes them from the third-person pronouns or pronominals. Table 2 shows that the Maya lexical personal pronouns consist of two sets. The set of the first- and second-person pronouns has the relational particle *t-* as its base; the set of the third-person pronouns uses the complex form *le ti?*, in which *le* is comparable to a definite article.

Table 2. Lexical personal pronouns in Yucatec Maya (cf. Hanks 1990: 155–162)

Definite article	Relational particle	Suffix	Personal pronoun	
	t-	*-en*	*ten*	1.person, singular
	t-	*-ó?on*	*tó?on*	1.person, plural, exclusive
	t-	*-ó?on(+-é?eš)*	*tó?on(é?eš)*	1.person, plural, inclusive
	t-	*-eč*	*teč*	2.person, singular
	t-	*-é?eš*	*té?eš*	2.person, plural
le	*ti?*		*le ti?*	3.person, singular
le	*ti?*	*-ó?ob'*	*le ti?ó?ob', le ó?ob ti?'*	3.person, plural

The pronominal formation *tó?oné?eš*, indicating the first person inclusive, consists of the pronoun indicating the first person plural exclusive and the suffix of the pronoun indicating the second person plural. The first- and second-person pronouns, which lack the formative *le*, indicate the "core participants" in the situation of speech (cp. Hanks 1990: 141); these two parties constitute the current conversation. Alongside the morphological characteristics in Table 2, the grammatical status of the category of core participants is encoded in various ways. First- and second-person pronouns differ from third-person pronouns in some of their syntactic and morphological applications, as shown by the structures in (1) and (2).

```
        a.          b.          c.
(1) Yàan (ti?-)X    ¢iímin.     X: a personal pronoun of 1. or
                                   2.PERS
    exist DAT-X     (a) horse(s) 'I (etc.) have (a) horse(s).'
```

(2) *Yàan ȼiímin   ti ?(-X).*   X: a personal pronoun of 3.PERS
    exist (a) horse(s) DAT-X   'He (etc.) has (a) horse(s).'

In these two structures, Hanks (1990: 164–166) observes three grammatical differences between personal pronouns in Yucatec Maya. First, in the case of the first- and second-person pronouns, the relational particle *ti?*, which serves as a dative prefix, can be omitted, as shown in the b-constituent of structure (1). Second, the third-person pronoun can be omitted, as shown in the c-constituent of structure (2). Third, the position of the first- and second-person pronouns in structure (1) differs from that of the third-person pronoun in structure (2). Thus, the b- and c-constituents of structures (1) and (2) show a permutation.

Additionally, a morphological difference can be mentioned. It is only in the case of the third-person pronoun that the plural suffix *ó?ob'* is the same as the optional plural marker of common nouns, as shown in (3) and (4).

(3) *le ti?ó?ob'*   'they'
(4) *le maákó?ob'* 'the men'

The third-person "pronouns" in Maya are grammatically related to other types of third-person definite description, as shown in Table 3, which presents the third-person "pronouns" together with some other definite descriptions of the third person. The article *le* in Table 3 marks all third-person descriptions as definite. This implies that all formations introduced by *le* constitute a natural coherent class. The forms *a?* and *o?* in Table 3, in combination with the article *le*, serve as demonstratives. Thus, nominals with the terminal deictic element of a demonstrative can be considered to form a specific subclass of the definite descriptions introduced by the article *le*.

What can the twofold formal differentiation in the Maya data of Table 2 tell us about the structure of the framework of the speech situation? I interpret the distinction as dividing the domain of the discourse roles into two dimensions, as is suggested for the personal pronouns in Japanese by Tamba (1992: 191).

Table 3. Third-person definite descriptions in Yucatec Maya (Hanks 1990: 18–20, 156)

Initial deictic	Terminal deictic	Definite description	
le		le ti⁷	'he, she, it, the one'
le		le ti⁷ó⁷ob', le ó⁷ob' ti⁷	'they, the ones'
le		le maák	'the man'
le		le maákó⁷ob'	'the men'
le	a⁷	le maák a⁷	'this man'
le	o⁷	le maákó⁷ob'a⁷	'these men'
le	o⁷	le maák o⁷	'that man'
le	o⁷	le maákó⁷ob'o⁷	'those men'

The twofold discourse-role structure of the lexical personal pronouns in Maya can then be conceived of as shown in Diagram 1.

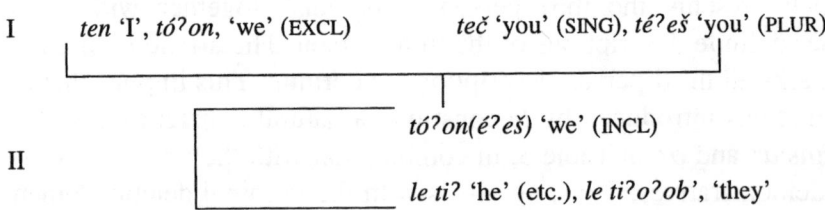

Diagram 1. The discourse-role structure of the lexical personal pronouns in Yucatec Maya

System I consists of the first- and second-person discourse-role dimension. The first-person discourse role of system I is fulfilled by the speaker, possibly with one or more associates differing from the addressee. In the case of one or more associates, the first-person discourse role can be said to be fulfilled by exclusive 'we'. The second-person discourse role of system I is fulfilled by the addressee, possibly with one or more associates different from the speaker.

System II consists of the first- and third-person discourse-role dimension. In this case the first-person discourse role is fulfilled by a party consisting of both the speaker and the addressee, possibly with one or more of their associates. Thus, in the second system the first-person discourse role can be said to be fulfilled by inclusive 'we'.

Whoever the speaker's possible associate(s) may be, the discourse role of the speaker is primordial or central in both systems. This can be expressed in the naming of both systems. Thus, I term the first discourse-role dimension the 1/2-perspective, and the second discourse-role dimension the 1/3-perspective. The two perspectives are connected by the presence of the speaker as at least a member of the first party. The interconnectedness of both perspectives is shown in Figure 2.

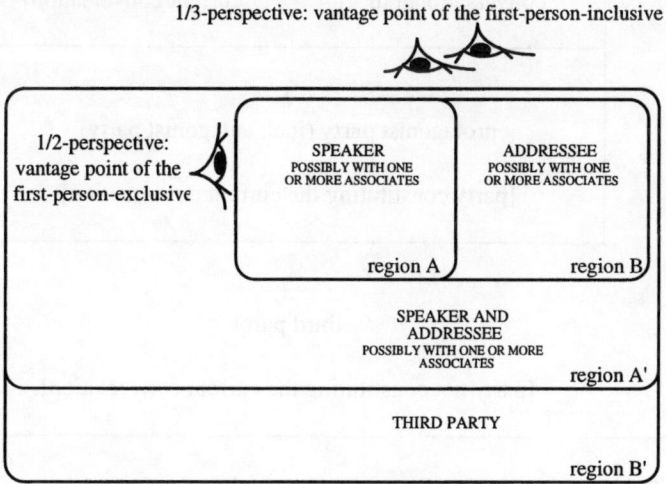

Figure 2. The framework of the speech situation with two discourse-role perspectives

Figure 2 shows that the framework of the speech situation is divided into an inner dimension forming the 1/2-perspective, and an outer dimension forming the 1/3-perspective. Each of both dimensions consists of two regions. In the inner dimension, the speaker (the first-person-exclusive) sees herself as being located in region A and the addressee as being located in region B; in the outer dimension, both speaker and addressee (the first-person-inclusive) are seen by the speaker as being located in region A' and the third party as being located in region B'. These two perspectives of the discourse roles in the speech situation, which can switch[7] very flexibly, are further elucidated in Figure 3.[8]

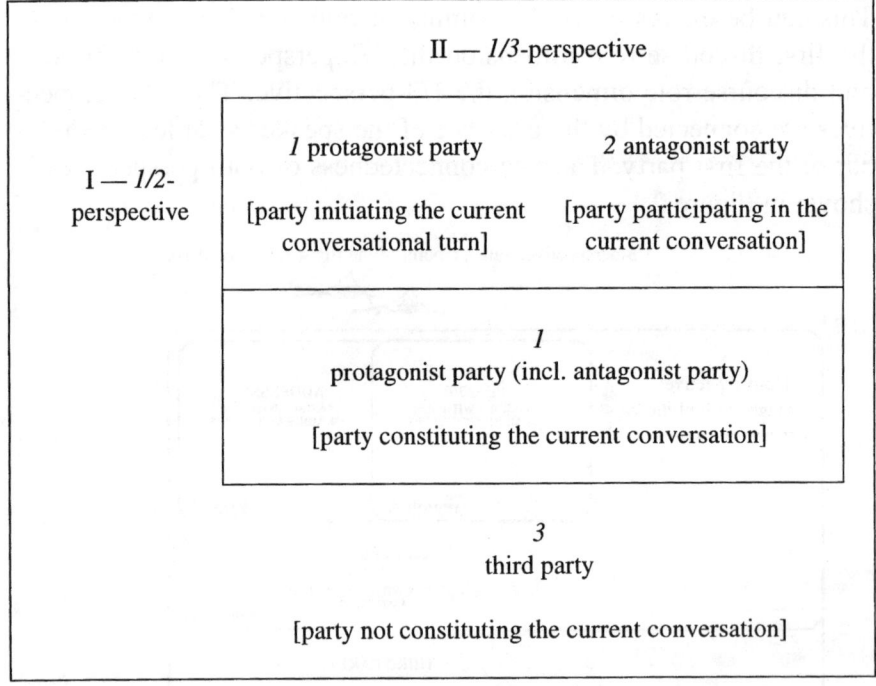

Figure 3. Double interactive perspective of the roles in the speech situation

Figure 3 contains a double dotted box. Its upper part represents the protagonist party and the antagonist party as seen from the 1/2-perspective. The referents of the protagonist and antagonist parties in the upper part are the same as those of the protagonist party of the lower part when seen as related to the third party from the 1/3-perspective.

What kinds of linguistic element can serve as the third party? Table 3 showed various Maya third-person forms which feature the definite article *le*. This indicates that all these nominals can be seen as belonging to the third party category. In Diyari third-person pronouns, determiners, and local adverbs form a morphologically related group, as apparent from the data in Table 4 (Austin 1982: 274, 281).

Table 4. Morphologically related third-person forms in Diyari

Base	Suffix			
	PROXIMAL	PROXIMAL VISIBLE	DISTAL INVISIBLE	
	-rda	-ya	-wa	
Pronoun				
nhani	nhanirda	nhaniya	nhaniwa	personal pronoun, determiner
Locative				
nhingki	nhingkirda	nhingkiya	nhingkiwa	local adverb

The third-person system of Wolof is even more extensive, as shown in Table 5 (Wills 1990; Sauvageot 1992). Table 5 shows two types of definite article concurring with two types of gestural and two types of "plain" demonstrative, while the latter two types share a pronominal use. The system of local adverbs also shares the same structure. All forms have the proximal suffix -*i* and the distal suffix -*a* (allomorph -*e*), with corresponding extensions. The twofold applicability of the suffix system in Table 5 does not only suggest that categories 1–3 and 4–6 are natural classes, but also that these categories together form a natural class in Wolof.

Table 5. Third-person forms in Wolof

Base		Suffix				
CLASSIFIER	PROXIMAL		DISTAL			
	-i	*bi*	*-a*	*ba*	1.	definite article
C-	*-ii*	*bii*	*-ee*	*bee*	2.	demonstrative (+gesture)
C-	*-ile*	*bile*	*-ale*	*bale*	3a.	demonstrative
C-†	*-ile*	*kile*	*-ale*	*kale*	3b.	pronominal
f-	*-i*	*fi*	*-a*	*fa*	4.	nondemonstrative local adverb
f-	*-ii*	*fii*	*-ee*	*fee*	5.	demonstrative (+gesture) local adverb
f-	*-ile*	*file*	*-ale*	*fale*	6.	demonstrative local adverb
C-:	{*b-, m-, j-, s-, w-, g-, l-, k-*}SING, {*ñ-, y-*}PLUR					
C-†:	{*k-*}SING.HUM					

This suggests that entities referred to by means of local adverbs can also be considered third-party entities. Alongside the deictic domains shown in Table 5, Wolof also has forms for time, manner, and degree, featuring a similar morphology (Wills 1990: 198–199).[9]

3. Recursion in the framework of the speech situation

Many languages feature an overtly morphological relation between definite articles and demonstratives (adnominal, pronominal, and local), and also between categories such as third-person pronouns and nondemonstrative local adverbs. In order to explain such interwoven systems, I assume a cognitive recursion of one basic deictic schema (Janssen 1995b). I will now consider some morphologically interconnected deictics.

In sundry languages the category of deictic forms applicable to third-party entities can be divided into a great variety of subcategories. For instance, a regular morphological system of deictic distinctions (with the exception of the form *asoko*) can be found in Japanese, as shown in Table 6 (Coulmas 1982; Tamba 1992).

Table 6. Deictic dimensions in Japanese

	Base			Suffix	
	ko-	so-	a-		
1.	kono	sono	ano	-no	determiner
	'this'	'that'	'that'		
2.	kore	sore	are	-re(ra)	pronominal
	'this one'	'that one'	'that one'		inanimate
3.	koitsu	soitsu	aitsu	-tsu(ra)	pronominal
	'this one, it'	'that one, it'	'that one, it'		(in)animate

Each of the rows 1–3 in Table 6 presents a deictic dimension with three regions (or zones; cf. Hanks 1990: 67–68, 77–78) signaled by the bases *ko-* (the region closely related to the speaker), *so-* (the region closely related to the addressee), and *a-* (the region not closely related to either speaker or addressee). Each region is instrumental to the addressee in gaining access to the entity referred to.

The threefold structure of the deictic dimensions presented in Table 6 is described by Tamba (1992: 191) as "un double système binaire, à quatre valeurs définies par le jeu de deux couplages: celui des formes en KO et A d'une part; et des formes en KO et SO d'autre part" [a double, binary system, with four values defined by the interplay between two links: that of forms with *ko-* and *a-* on the one hand; and of forms with *ko-* and *so-* on the other]. Thus, the structure can be conceived of as determined by two discourse-role perspectives, as shown in Figure 4 (Janssen 1995b), pace Aoyama (1995), who argues for one linear high versus low dimension of deixis.

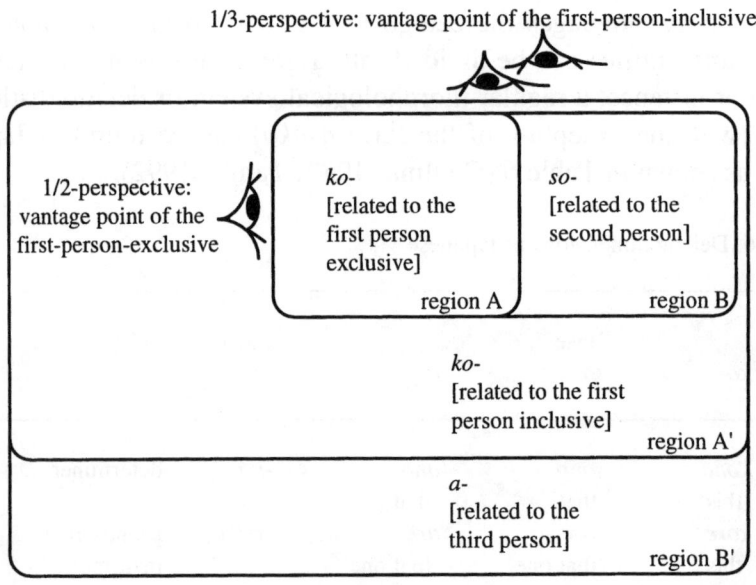

Figure 4. The threefold deictic dimension of Japanese demonstratives

Apart from Japanese, a number of languages (e.g. classical Greek, Latin, Italian, Spanish, and Vietnamese — see Nguyên 1992; Anderson and Keenan 1985: 282–285) share an overtly morphological system of three demonstratives which can be considered as determined by the double perspective shown in Figure 4. Both perspectives can be applied to a single utterance, as in sentence (5), where the a-constituent is a form of the 1/2-perspective and the b-constituent is a form of the 1/3-perspective (Nguyên 1992: 180).

(5)a.   b.
   đấy   là bà   A.;   kia   là bà B.

   'there   be Mrs. A.   there   be Mrs. B.'
   (near you)   (not near me & you)

Let us return to the Maya forms in Table 3. When looking at the different third-person forms, one may wonder how the referents of these forms in concrete usages can be seen as uniquely related to region B', as shown in Figure 2. Of course, it is necessary for the referent involved to be seen as the only one that is qualified or, rather, that region B' in a dimension of the speaker's mental field of vision has such a shape that the referent can be considered the only one that is qualified in it. Thus, in each of the formations *le ti?* 'he, she, it, the one', *le ti?o?ob'* 'they, the ones', and *le maák* 'the man', the referent has to be the only person or group of persons eligible in region B' of the 1/3-perspective.

In the case of the demonstrative formations *le maák a?* 'this man' and *le maák o?* 'that man', there is an interesting complication. The presence of the definite article *le* in these demonstrative formations suggests that they basically have to be analyzed in a way comparable to the previous third-person formations, namely as fundamentally connected with region B' of the 1/3-perspective. How can we explain the obviously more specific function of the demonstrative elements *a?* and *o?*?

Let us assume that it is the function of the demonstrative elements to individuate the referents within the region of the third party. In the case of the formations *le maák a?* 'this man' and *le maák o?* 'that man', the referents are not distinguished from each other by means of different descriptive markings, such as different nouns or adjectives, but by the different deictic markers *a?* and *o?*. These markers indicate, in my view, a deictic dimension within region B' of the dimension of the 1/3-perspective. Before looking at the deictic structure of the Maya demonstratives, let us consider the systems of demonstratives in Tahitian and Palauan, which both have a structure with two dimensions.

Diagram 2, which is based on data provided by Lazard and Peltzer (1992: 210–211), shows the twofold system of demonstratives in Tahitian within the system of third-person forms.

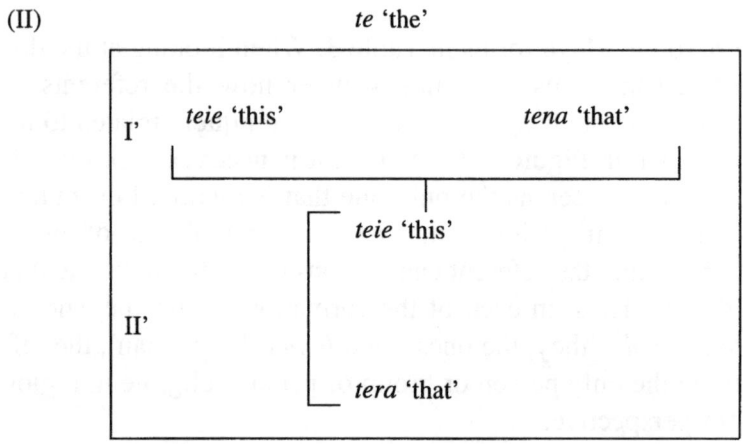

Diagram 2. Tahitian system of demonstratives within the system of the third-person forms

The definite article in Tahitian is *te* 'the'; the demonstratives are all based on this element. The form *teie* 'this' can be compared with the first-person pronouns, exclusive or inclusive. The form *tena* 'that' is comparable with the second-person pronoun, whereas the form *tera* 'that' is comparable with the third-person pronoun. Thus, we can consider the forms in the box of Diagram 2 to consist of an elaboration of the third-party region in Figure 2. The content of Diagram 2 has the same structure as the overall schema for subsystems I and II; subsystems I' and II' show the demonstratives in the 1/2- and 1/3-perspectives, respectively.

Important evidence for the idea that all subsystems I' and II' can be conceived of as recursive applications of a single basic cognitive schema is found in, for instance, Palauan. This language has a demonstrative system with distinct morphological suffixes for all of its functions. Thus, Palauan has different forms for demonstratives comparable with the first-person pronoun exclusive, demonstratives comparable with the second-person pronoun, demonstratives comparable with the first-person pronoun inclusive, and for demonstratives comparable with the third-person pronoun. The data are shown in Table 7 (Josephs 1978: 344, 360); both the subject and nonsubject forms are third-person forms.

Table 7. Palauan third-person forms

Base			Suffix				
SUBJ	NONSUBJ				DEM		
			1 EXCL	2	1 INCL	3	
			-ile	-ilecha	-(i)ka	-(i)ke	
ng	ng	ngii	ngile	ngilecha	ng(i)ka	ng(i)ke	SING.HUM
t(ir)	te	tir	tirile	tirilecha	tirka	tirke	PLUR.HUM

The box of Diagram 3, where only the singular forms are considered, shows that Palauan demonstratives can be divided into two subsystems, comparable to the two discourse-role perspectives of the personal pronouns. The suffixes of subsystem I' share the string *-ile-*, and those of subsystem II' share *-(i)k-*. If these strings are considered to have morphological status, then the morphology of each subsystem is marked in a distinctive way (Janssen, in press).

If the systems of demonstratives in Tahitian and Palauan can be seen as part of the third-person region in the dimension of the 1/3-perspective, and if in both languages the structure of this system is comparable to the twofold perspectival system of the discourse roles, we can assume a recursive cognitive schema in the deictic system of the personal pronouns and in that of the demonstratives.

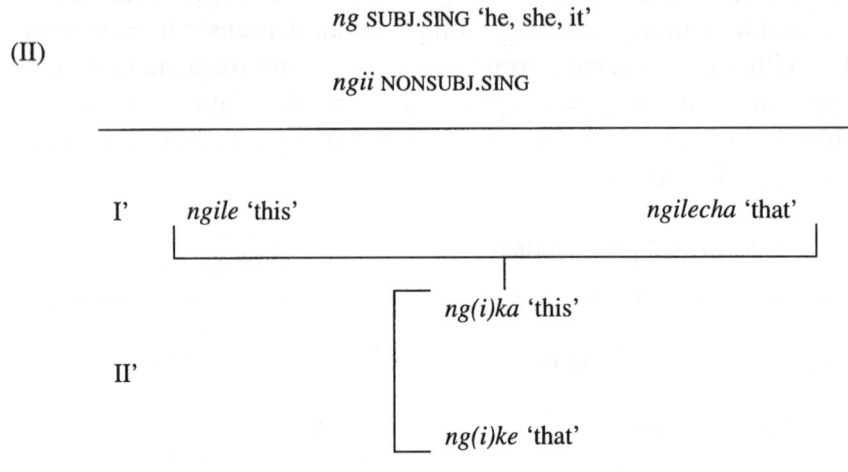

Diagram 3. Palauan third-person forms

The system of Diagram 3 is an extension of the third party category in Figure 2. The recursion hypothesis explains why a number of languages have an overtly morphological relation between definite articles and demonstratives (adnominal, pronominal, and local), and also between categories like the third-person pronouns and non-demonstrative local adverbs, as shown in Tables 3–7. It is entirely in accordance with this view that the Maya system of discourse roles shown in Diagram 1 can be extended to the multiply recursive system in Diagram 4. The extension is located in the smaller inner box. Its content has the same structure as the overall schema for subsystems I and II. Subsystems I' and II' show the uses of the demonstratives in the 1/2- and 1/3-perspectives, respectively. The boxes of Diagram 4 contain a variety of forms, all of them featuring the (p)article *le*.

Let us briefly return to the Palauan constellation of subsystems, as shown in Diagram 3. The strongest evidence for the idea that the subsystems in this diagram are recursive applications of one basic cognitive schema can be found in a language such as Palauan. As we have seen, this language has a twofold third-person system with distinct morphological suffixes for each function, i.e. for both the demonstrative related to the addressee and for the demonstrative related to the speaker and addressee with their possible associate(s).

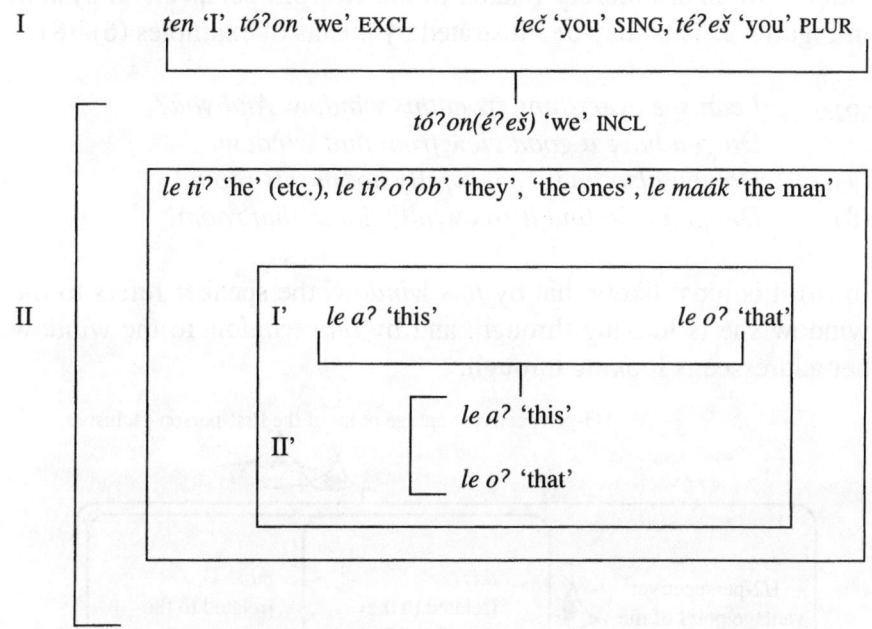

Diagram 4. The Maya discourse-role system with a recursive extension

Fourfold demonstrative systems are generally described as constituting one linear dimension with a range of regions progressively distant from the speaker (exclusive and inclusive, if applicable) and the addressee. Further research is required to determine whether distance can have a cognitive effect as a result of more basic relations, such as those represented by the systems based on the 1/2- and 1/3-perspectives (cf. Anderson and Keenan 1985: 282–285). In any case, the feature of distance relative to the speaker seems to be required for deictic dimensions with more than three or four distinct forms (Anderson and Keenan 1985: 292–295), as in Malagasy.

One can ask if each of the two perspectival subsystems can be considered an instantiation of a single cognitive schema (Janssen

1995b). We can find evidence for this idea in languages such as English, which has a system with only two "adjectival" demonstratives.

In English the demonstratives *this* and *that* can have two interpretations which are closely related to the twofold perspectival system in Figures 2. This may be illustrated by means of examples (6)–(8).

(6)   *I can see everything from this window. And you?*
       Do you have a good view from that window?
(7)   *Do you also find it so awfully hot in this room?*
(8)   *Did you also find it so awfully hot in that room?*

In (6) it is most likely that by *this window*, the speaker refers to the window she is looking through, and by *that window* to the window her addressee is looking through.

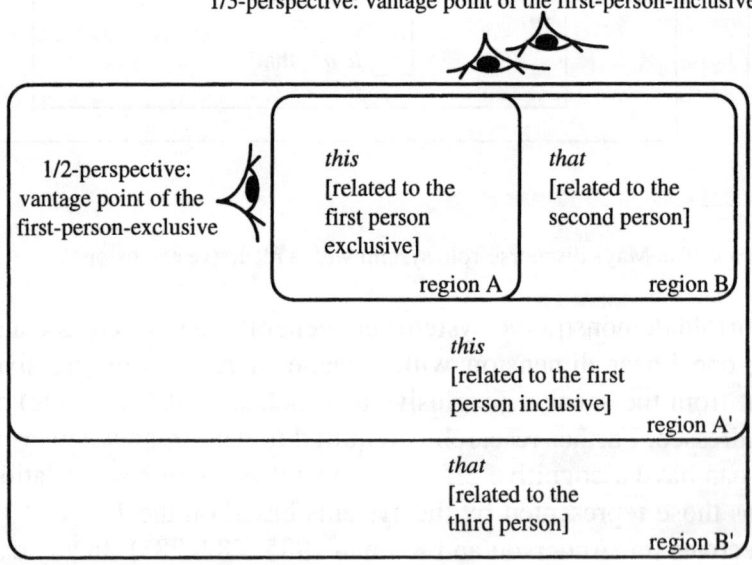

Figure 5. Two interpretations of English demonstratives

In this interpretation, the use of *this* and *that* is determined by the 1/2-perspective. In (7) and (8) the speaker and her addressee may be in the same place. According to this interpretation, the speaker's use of *this* in (7) is positively related to the position shared by her addressee, whereas her use of *that* in (8) is negatively related to their current positions. Thus, in (7) and (8) both *this* and *that* are based on the 1/3-perspective. These observations on examples (6)–(8) imply that both *this* and *that* can have two interpretations, one determined by the 1/2-, and the other by the 1/3-perspective. The twofold perspectival interpretations are shown in Figure 5. When comparing *this* and *that* with the demonstratives of Tahitian and Palauan, we may draw the following conclusion. The twofold interpretability of both *this* and *that* implies that these demonstratives have a more abstract meaning than the demonstratives of Tahitian and Palauan. This is shown by Table 8, which also contains the two Maya demonstratives. Roughly speaking, the meanings of English *this*, Maya *le a?*, and Tahitian *teie* cover those of Palauan *ngile* and *ng(i)ka*. The meanings of English *that* and Maya *le o?* cover those of Tahitian *tena* and *tera* and of Palauan *ngilecha* and *ng(i)ke*. The fact that, for instance, both *this* and *that* can be related to the 1/2- and the 1/3-perspectives as well suggests that the structures of these perspectives can be viewed as highly comparable.

Table 8. Semantic relationships between demonstratives of four languages

RELATED TO	FIRST-PERSON EXCL	SECOND PERSON	FIRST-PERSON INCL	THIRD PERSON
English	*this*	*that*	*this*	*that*
Maya	*le a?*	*le o?*	*le a?*	*le o?*
Tahitian	*teie*	*tena*	*teie*	*tera*
Palauan	*ngile*	*ngilecha*	*ng(i)ka*	*ng(i)ke*

Now, the question arises: how do both perspectives of demonstratives correspond to each other? And, if we include the analogy between personal pronouns and demonstratives: how do the dimensions of the demonstratives correspond to those of the personal pronouns? Obviously, the central question is: if all of the perspectival dimensions under scrutiny are divided into two regions, what, then, is the cognitive relationship between both regions? In other words, in what way does the A-type region differ from the B-type region in the dimensions of the various deictic domains? One might suggest that the dichotomy "proximal" versus "distal" is the core opposition in all the dimensions. But this distinction does not suffice in cases where *this* and *that* are used in a seemingly spatial opposition, as can be seen in (9) (Kirsner 1979, 1993; Janssen 1991, 1993, 1995a,b).

(9) a. Doctor: *Is this where it hurts?*
    b. Patient: *Yes, that is where it hurts.*

If a doctor is palpating a patient, she may utter the a-sentence; the patient might answer with the b-sentence. The patient's answer shows that the semantic difference between *this* and *that* cannot simply be characterized in terms such as "in the vicinity of the speaker" and "not in the vicinity of the speaker", because the spot indicated by the patient is in her immediate vicinity.[10] Lyons (1999: 18; emphases in original) comments on this issue: "*This* and *that* are often termed *proximal* and *distal* demonstratives, respectively. But it is possible to relate this distance contrast to the category of person. *This* is used to refer to some entity which is close to or associated in some way with the speaker; so *this article* could be 'the article which I am reading', 'the article which you and I are discussing', or 'the article which you and I are interested in', among other possibilities. ... *That* is used where the referent is associated with a set including hearer but not speaker ... or a set including neither speaker nor hearer."

How can we interpret example (9)? When using the deictic *this*, the doctor observes the spot at issue through her palpating hand. The functional position of her hand must be seen as determining her vantage point. Through her hand the doctor sees herself fully faced with the spot being palpated; it is at the center of her mental field of vision, and this enables the doctor to refer to the spot as her high-focal concern in a discourse-organizational respect. This is illustrated by Figure 6.

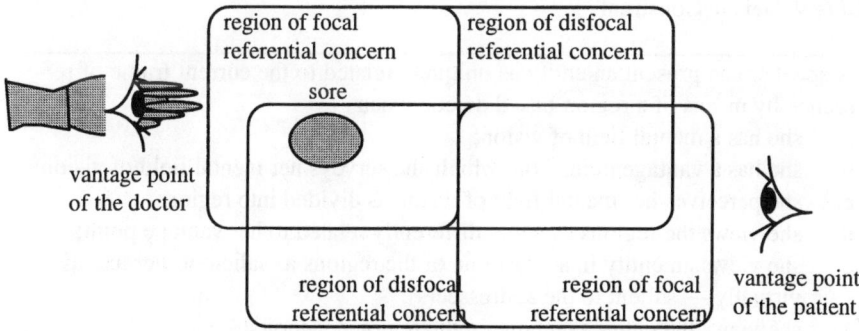

Figure 6. The division of a deictic dimension into two regions seen from two vantage points

By using *that*, the patient signals that she does not share the doctor's vantage point. At the same time she is signaling that the spot being palpated is in her mental field of vision, and that she views the spot as lying outside of the center of her mental field of vision. Apparently, the patient regards the functional relation which the doctor has with the region of the palpated spot of greater importance for distinguishing the spot and for referring to it than the intrinsic physical relation she herself has with it. It must be due to such a construal of the circumstances at issue that the patient indicates the spot as being in a region which is of disfocal concern to her.

It is very difficult to characterize the semantic difference between *this* and *that*. When using both *this* and *that*, the speaker sees the spot as salient and as virtually salient to her addressee. What distinguishes *this* from *that* in a referential sense is how the entity concerns the speaker at the current stage of the discourse.[11] The determinant factor is whether she sees the entity in the region of her focal (high-focal or central) or disfocal (low-focal or noncentral) referential concern at the current stage of the discourse.

These observations on the demonstratives enable us to characterize the deictic procedure in more detail by assuming the tools listed in Table 9.

Table 9. Deictic Construal

A speaker can present an entity as uniquely related to the current frame of reference by means of a region-based deictic when
a. she has a mental field of vision;
b. she has a vantage point from which she surveys her mental field of vision;
c. she perceives her mental field of vision as divided into regions;
d. she views the regions as being differently related to her vantage point;
e. she views an entity in at least one of the regions as salient to her and as — virtually — salient to the addressee(s);
f. she views the entity as unique in the region concerned;
g. there is a linguistic element by which she cannot only indicate that an entity is related to a region as unique in it, but also to which particular region it is related, i.e. the region of focal or that of disfocal referential concern.

Thus, by using a region-based deictic, the speaker refers to an entity uniquely related to one of the regions into which she perceives her field of vision to be divided.

A few remarks on Table 9 may be useful for the following discussion. I will sometimes use the terms *focal* and *disfocal* region, instead of the more precise but rather wordy *region of focal* and *region of disfocal referential concern to the speaker*. Perhaps, I should substitute the terms *high-focal* and *low-focal* for *focal* and *disfocal*. This would be in accordance with Hanks (1990: 22) stating: "All *a?* constructions signal perceptual, spatial, or temporal immediacy or anticipation of a referent. They are associated with high-focus gestures (presenting in hand, touching, pointing to the referent) referring to unique objects (as opposed to classes or vaguely known ones), with new (as opposed to already shared) information. *o?* [formations] convey ... less immediate spatial, perceptual, or temporal access, accompanied by less exacting gestures (point, wave, glance), maintenance of shared information (anaphora, reference to prior talk), or shared background knowledge." Hanks' characterization of both demonstrative types is highly comparable to the distinction between high and low deixis made by Kirsner (1979, 1993) for demonstratives. Anyhow, I will preserve the notion of "concern", which I will discuss at the end of section 5.

4. Tense in the framework of the speech situation

Now I will address the functions of the present and the preterit in English and Dutch by relating them to some functions of demonstratives. The semantic parallelism between the present and preterit tense morphemes and demonstratives[12] such as *this* and *that* implies, in the analysis I will propose, that a sentence such as *Romeo loves Juliet* is conceived of as 'Romeo love-in-this-context-of-situation Juliet', and a sentence such as *Romeo loved Juliet* is conceived of as 'Romeo love-in-that-context-of-situation Juliet'.[13]

(10) a. *Romeo loves Juliet.*   'Romeo love-in-this-context-of-situation Juliet.'
b. *Romeo loved Juliet.*   'Romeo love-in-that-context-of-situation Juliet.'

This analysis hinges on two ideas. First, tense morphemes are analyzed as adjectival demonstratives, related to the current frame of reference.[14] Second, tense morphemes are not analyzed as related to, or as specifying, a particular time but as related to the current context of situation, i.e. the current frame of reference.

If tenses are indexical, the semantic similarities between tenses and other indexicals must be analyzed. Therefore, I will examine the following issues. First, does considering tenses to be semantically on a par with adjectival demonstratives imply that tenses constitute definite descriptions in which the entities described are situations (Janssen 1991, 1993)? Second, does analyzing a tensed clause as a definite description imply that the tense involved serves to locate the situation concerned at a particular time (Janssen 1991)?

Let us consider some semantic similarities between tenses and demonstratives. Adjectival demonstratives do not refer to entities (things or situations), nor do tense morphemes. But since a speaker can refer to an entity as uniquely related to the current frame of reference by using a nominal introduced by an adjectival demonstrative, it is not surprising that she can refer, by means of a tensed clause, to a situation as uniquely related to her current frame of reference.

Before going into the relationship of adjectival demonstratives and tenses, I have to discuss the distinction between deixis and anaphora. Formulating a clear-cut and generally accepted distinction between deictic and anaphoric uses of indexical elements seems to be a source of everlasting discussions between linguists. In my view, there is no fundamental difference between the two. I will take the distinction into consideration in order to prevent the reproach of having overlooked an interesting point.

I define the deictic (exophoric or situational) and anaphoric (endophoric or cotextual) uses of tenses and demonstratives as in (11) and (12).[15]

(11) *Deictic use of an indexical element:*
An indexical element is used deictically if it is referentially related to information derivable from the current situational frame of reference, which is cognitively accessible to a basically constant set of speaker(s) and addressee(s).

(12) *Anaphoric use of an indexical element:*
An indexical element is used anaphorically if it is referentially related to information derivable from the current text-based frame of reference, which is cognitively accessible to a basically constant set of speaker(s) and addressee(s).

However, the distinction between deictic and anaphoric uses of indexical elements is inadequate. In the case of deictic uses, the current situational frame of reference is often constituted by the utterance containing the indexical; the utterance itself can contribute greatly to determining the reference concerned. Conversely, in the case of anaphoric uses, the reference concerned must often be inferred from scant or highly implicit or indirect linguistic information, on the basis of which a situation has to be construed or assumed into which the intended reference fits. Furthermore, sometimes an indexical can be conceived of as being used in such a way that it is impossible to distinguish between a deictic and an anaphoric interpretation.

Let us have a look at example (13) and compare the deictic use of the present tense with that of the demonstrative *this*.

(13) *So she began: "O Mouse, do you know the way out of this pool? I am very tired of swimming about here, O Mouse!"*
(Carroll 1990: 26)

Prior to the situation presented in (13), Alice and the Mouse did not verbally interact. Therefore, in the first sentence, the Mouse does not only have to determine the relevance, but also the reference, of the present form *do* on the basis of the situation that has arisen through Alice's question. The same can be said with regard to *this pool*. Thus, the use of both *do* and *this* can be interpreted as deictic.

In the second sentence of (13) we notice the present *am* and the demonstrative *here*. According to definition (12), *am* has to be interpreted as anaphoric, since the Mouse can referentially relate the situation described by *am* to that of the previous sentence. It has to infer that Alice is asking the question because she is very tired of swimming in the pool. The same goes for *here*.[16] However, one could call the anaphoric nature of both *am* and *here* into question, since the interpretation would have been very similar if the first sentence had been missing or if it had followed. This definitional dilemma is caused by the fact that the situation relevant to determine what is referred to by the second sentence does not hinge on any textual introduction since, due to its factual presence, the relevant situation is cognitively accessible to both the speaker (Alice) and the addressee (the Mouse).

Let us now turn to the deictic and anaphoric uses of the preterit and comparable uses of demonstratives. Example (14) gives some fine instances. The preceding passage tells us how Alice was locked up in the Rabbit's house. Now the Rabbit and his companions try to dispel her, and Alice hears "the sound of a good many voices all talking together".

(14) *"Here, Bill! Catch hold of this rope — Will the roof bear? — Mind that loose slate — Oh, it's coming down! Heads below!" (a loud crash) — "Now, who did that? — It was Bill, I fancy — Who's to go down the chimney?"* (Carroll 1990: 48)

The preterit in the clause *who did that* can be interpreted as both deictic and anaphoric. As an onlooker, the character uttering this sentence can relate it directly to what happened. Here, the preterit can be seen as deictic. However, it is also possible that the situation has to be related to what is presented by the sentence *Oh, it's coming down*, which leads to an anaphoric reading.

A comparable observation can be made with regard to *that* in the sentence *who did that*. If *that* is interpreted as what caused the crash, it allows for a deictic reading. But if *that* is seen as directly related to what is presented by *it's coming down*, the anaphoric reading has to be preferred. Things are different in the case of the nominal *that loose slate*. Here, *that* is unambiguously deictic. Admittedly, there is a relationship between the slate at issue and the roof mentioned previously, but the slate is presented as an entity that is independent of the roof. It is the demonstrative *that*, the description (*loose slate*), and the current circumstances which enable the addressee(s) to determine what has to be seen as the reference of the nominal *that loose slate*. Such indications also enable the addressee to determine what is referred to by means of a tensed clause.

A tense example which has to be interpreted unambiguously as deictic is presented in the sentence *How was it, old fellow* in (15). When she felt threatened by the Lizard Bill, who had to go down the chimney, Alice gave it "one sharp kick, and waited to see what would happen next".

(15) *The first thing she heard was a general chorus of "There goes Bill!" then the Rabbit's voice alone — "Catch him, you by the hedge!" then silence, and then another confusion of voices — "Hold up his head — Brandy now — Don't choke him — How was it, old fellow? What happened to you? Tell us all about it!"* (Carroll 1990: 48–50)

The question *How was it, old fellow* relates to the flight the Lizard made following Alice's kick. Since the Lizard and its companions had not interchanged any word about the flight before, the preterit *was* can be interpreted as deictic. The preterit in *What happened to you*, however, can be seen as both deictic and anaphoric because this question is directly related to the flight the Lizard made, but also to what is presented by the preceding question *How was it, old fellow*.

The following phenomenon shows that both the present tense and the demonstrative *this* can be used in an apparently wrong context. See, for instance, example (16). Urged by its companions' questions and request *How was it, old fellow? What happened to you? Tell us all about it!*, the Lizard finally reports on its experience by using the so-called historical present.

(16) *Last came a little feeble, squeaking voice ("That's Bill," thought Alice), "Well, I hardly know — No more, thank ye; I'm better now — but I'm a deal too flustered to tell you — all I know is, something comes at me like a Jack-in-the-box, and up I goes [sic] like a sky-rocket!"* (Carroll 1990: 50)

By using the present tense in *comes* and *goes*, the Lizard tells its story with great empathy.[17] This may remind us of the use of *this* or *now* in references to past moments, as in (17) and (18). Consider the use of the adverbial *just at this moment* in (17), and of the adverb *now* in (18).

(17) *"They must go by the carrier," she thought; "and how funny it'll seem, sending presents to one's own feet! And how odd the*

directions will look! ..." Just at this moment her head struck against the roof of the hall .... (Carroll 1990: 20–21)
(18) *And so it was indeed: she was now only ten inches high, and her face was now the right size for going through the little door into that lovely garden.* (Carroll 1990: 15)

We can explain the use of *this* and *now* in these examples by assuming an empathetic perspective on the part of the storyteller.

The last similarity to be discussed between the uses of tenses and of demonstratives pertains to the reference of both verbs and demonstratives which are projected into the future. Consider first example (19).

(19) *"— but I shall have to ask them what the name of the country is, you know. Please Ma'am, is this New Zealand? Or Australia?"* (Carroll 1990: 11)

Assuming that she is falling "right *through* the earth", Alice wonders what she will ask when she surfaces at the other side. By means of the indirect and direct questions *what the name of the country is* and *is this New Zealand,* Alice refers to situations at the moment of her arrival. Similarly, by using *this,* Alice refers to the country where she will surface. Thus, in order to determine these references, one has to share Alice's vantage point, which is the time and place of her arrival at the other side of the earth.[18]

Sentences (20) and (21) show that both the preterit and the demonstrative have to be interpreted as related to the time at which the question will be asked.

(20) *Jack will tell you a joke and he will ask later: Did you know that one?*
(21) *Jack will tell you a joke and he will ask later whether you knew that one.*

In these sentences the preterit *did* and the demonstrative *that* have to be interpreted referentially from the vantage point defined by Jack's asking the question. According to definitions (11) and (12), *did* and *that* in sentence (20) are used deictically, and *knew* and *that* in sentence (21) are used anaphorically.

Examples (13)–(21) may have shown that the distinction between deictic and anaphoric uses is merely a matter of interpretation, which does not constitute a sound reason to distinguish linguistically between deictic and anaphoric *forms*. If, in view of the examples above, one subscribes to the idea that the present and preterit tenses are comparable to demonstratives such as *this* and *that*, one will be ready to subscribe to the idea that all uses of the present and preterit — and, of course, all uses of *this* and *that* as well — call for a principled, uniform analysis which can account for their great variety.

What are the basic properties of indexicals such as demonstratives and tenses? I assume that both types of indexical share the set of properties listed in Table 9. By using a region-based deictic, the speaker refers to an entity uniquely related to one of the regions into which she perceives her field of vision to be divided. These properties are visualized by Figure 7.

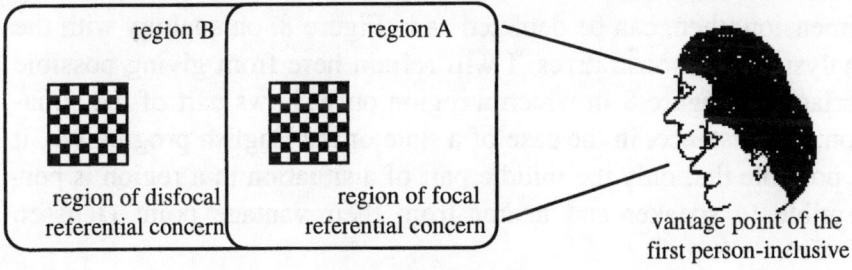

Figure 7. The deictic dimension

When using a demonstrative, the speaker has a vantage point in mind from which she and possibly the addressee survey a mental field of vision. The field that they survey from their vantage point is displayed in Figure 7 as the encompassing oblong; speaker and hearer conceive of the field as being divided into distinct parts, indicated here as regions A and B. From their vantage point they see an entity of type C in region A and another in region B. They envisage the entity in region A as uniquely related to region A. Likewise, they envisage the entity in region B as uniquely related to region B. From their vantage point speaker and hearer consider themselves to have a relationship R_A with the entity in region A, and a relationship R_B with the entity in region B. If the words *this* and *that* can be used to indicate these two relationships, and if the word *chessboard* can be used to name an entity of the kind C, then the speaker can refer uniquely to the entity in region A with the nominal *this chessboard*, and to the entity in region B with the nominal *that chessboard*.

Thus, when a speaker refers to an entity with the help of a demonstrative, she signals that she is referentially concerned with the entity given the situation obtaining at the current stage in the discourse.

Now, let us turn to tense. How can we understand the present-tense and past-tense forms as expressing the concepts of focal and disfocal referential concern? In my view, the speaker signals with the present that the situation referred to is of focal referential concern to her and the addressee. She signals with the preterit that the situation at issue is of disfocal referential concern to them. The tense dimension, then, can be depicted as in Figure 8, on analogy with the analysis of demonstratives. I will refrain here from giving possible variants of Figure 8 in which a region only shows part of the situation. For instance, in the case of a state or the English progressive, it is possible that only the middle part of a situation in a region is perceptible to speaker and hearer from their vantage point (Janssen 1995c).

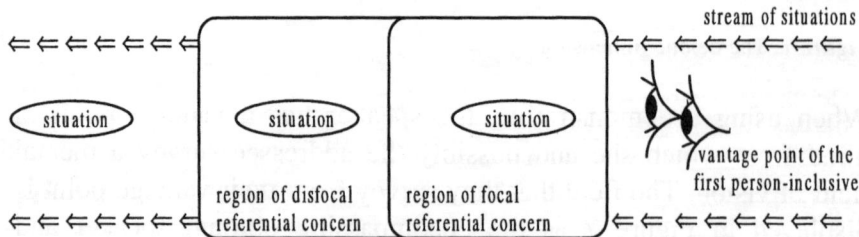

Figure 8. Deictic dimension of tenses (a review of situations in a temporal sequence)

5. Final remarks

My analysis of indexicals characterized by means of the Deictic Construal in Table 9 owes a number of insights to Bühler ([1934] 1982a), Reichenbach (1947), Kirsner (1979, 1993, 1996), Langacker (1991, this volume b), Hanks (1989, 1990), and many others I referred to. I will briefly consider the influence of Bühler's central ideas, and I will present a brief comparison between Reichenbach's and my own approach to deixis.

The notion of a mental field of vision comes from Bühler. The notion of the speaker's vantage point can also be traced back to Bühler, because in his view the *origo* is not only the central position of the deictic coordinate system, but also "the starting point of the coordinates of the directions of gaze" (Bühler 1982b: 25).[19] Bühler's notion of an *origo* inextricably unites the most central region in the speaker's mental field of vision and the starting point for the coordinates of directions of gaze. In my approach, those two aspects are differentiated into the notions of the speaker's vantage point, and of the most central region in the speaker's mental field of vision (i.e. the region of focal referential concern).

The idea for distinguishing the starting point of Bühler's coordinate system from the most central region in the speaker's mental field of vision goes back to Reichenbach's (1947) analysis of tenses. Consider the leftmost parts of Tables 10 and 11. Reichenbach assumes three basic notions, namely the point of speech, the point of reference, and the point of the event. The point of reference coincides with the point of speech in the case of the present tense, whereas it precedes the point of speech in the case of the preterit. Reichenbach's point of speech and point of reference can coincide, whereas in my view the speaker's vantage point and the regions of focal and disfocal referential concern are strictly separated.

The point of the event can coincide with the point of reference in the case of the present tense and the preterit, but can differ from it for certain compound "tenses". Since there are good reasons to consider the simple tenses to be the only grammatical tenses in English and Dutch, I will confine the following comparison to the present tense and the preterit. Consider Table 10.

Table 10. Concepts for the analysis of tenses and demonstratives

Concepts for the analysis of tenses (Reichenbach)		Concepts for the analysis of tenses and demonstratives (Janssen)	
The point of speech:	S	The speaker's (and hearer's) vantage point:	V
The point of reference:	R	A region in the speaker's (and hearer's) mental field of vision:	R
The point of the event:	E	The entity referred to:	E

On the basis of Table 10, we can compare Reichenbach's notions for analyzing tenses with the tools of my approach, which apply more generally to indexicals such as tenses and demonstratives.

Table 11. Two analyses of the tenses present and preterit

	Reichenbach	Janssen
PRESENT	E is simultaneous with R	E is in R
	R is simultaneous with S	R is focal to V
PRETERIT	E is simultaneous with R	E is in R
	R is anterior to S	R is disfocal to V

Table 11 shows that Reichenbach's point of the event is comparable with the salient entity viewed by the speaker in relation to a region in her mental field of vision, as a unique entity in that particular region. Reichenbach's point of reference is comparable with one of the regions in the speaker's mental field of vision. And Reichenbach's point of speech is comparable with the vantage point from which the speaker surveys her mental field of vision, as defined in the Deictic Construal.

The relationship seen by Reichenbach between the points of speech and of reference is comparable with the relationship between the speaker's vantage point and one of the regions in the speaker's mental field of vision. In Reichenbach's theory, the point of reference need not be simultaneous with the point of speech; it can also precede or succeed it. I only allow for a relationship of the speaker's vantage point with the regions of focal and disfocal referential concern. In Reichenbach's theory, in turn, the point of the event can be simultaneous with the point of reference, as well as lie before or after it.[20] I only allow for one type of relationship between the salient entity and a focal or disfocal region.

When attempting to adjust Reichenbach's point of reference in order to handle demonstratives, one needs to take into account that they constitute definite descriptions. If tenses are also definite, we have to look for a frame of reference to which the entity at issue can be related as unique in it. One has to assume a frame of reference for the entity at issue, and the entity must be conceivable as uniquely related to that frame of reference (Hawkins 1984). This means that the entity cannot be outside of the frame of reference.

My approach to deictic elements using the notion of "referential *concern*" leaves room for an explanation of various attitudinal uses of tenses, such as the so-called historical present and the modal uses of the preterit (see, e.g., Lakoff 1970; Bazanella 1990), as well as the attitudinal uses of demonstratives (see, e.g., Lakoff 1974; Kirsner 1979). The incorporation of attitudinal uses into the present "referential-concern" approach can be assumed to imply that all of the deictics dealt with in this chapter are to be seen as epistemic means.

I hope that my generalizing approach to deictic (and grounding) phenomena points to some aspects of the human organization of experience and elucidates some properties of the human information processing system.

Abbreviations

DAT	dative
DEM	demonstrative
EXCL	exclusive
HUM	human
INCL	inclusive
NONSUBJ	nonsubject

PERS	person
PLUR	plural
SING	singular
SUBJ	subject

Notes

1. I would like to thank Frank Brisard, René Dirven, Bob Kirsner, and Kevin Moore for their valuable comments on an earlier draft.
2. See, e.g., Janssen (1991, 1993) and Langacker (1991, this volume a,b). In Langacker's view a full nominal designates a grounded instance of a thing type, and a finite clause a grounded instance of a process type.
3. In Langacker's view (this volume a,b), grounding predications are needed to form full nominals or finite clauses. I refer to Nuyts (this volume), who considers grounding as a primarily conceptual phenomenon, rather than as a primarily linguistic one.
4. Hanks (1990: 67–68) mentions "at least seven deictic dimensions for Maya: Participants, Perception, Spatial, Temporal, Attention focus, Discourse, and Background knowledge".
5. Hanks (1990: 77–78) defines the term *zone* as follows: "We will use the word "zone" to designate any portion of the deictic field that is centered on a single participant or configuration of participants, distinguishing, for instance, the "proximal zone" from the "distal zone" and the "speaker zone" from the "addressee zone"."
6. Following Goffman ([1979] 1981: 147).
7. As shown in Janssen (1995a: 141–143), both perspectives can be relevant in the same sentence, as in:
   (i) *My wife and I convinced ourselves of Tom's recovery.*
   (ii) *Did you and Jim convince yourselves of Tom's recovery?*
   In sentence (i) the referents of *I* and *ourselves* are presented as being seen from the vantage point of the first-person-exclusive, whereas the referent of *my wife* is presented from the vantage point of the first-person-inclusive (nevertheless, my wife is also included in the group referred to by means of *ourselves*). In sentence (ii) the referents of *you* and *yourselves* are presented from the vantage point of the first-person-exclusive, whereas the referent of *Jim* is presented from the vantage point of the first-person-inclusive. In both sentences the referents of *Tom* and *Tom's recovery* are presented from the vantage point of the first-person-inclusive.
8. In accordance with their grammatical features, the lexical personal pronouns in Maya can be analyzed in terms of their discourse-role system as shown in

Figure 3. For different but related analyses, see e.g. Frei (1944), Benveniste (1956), Kurylowicz (1972), Zwicky (1977), Bátori (1982), Beifuss et al. (1985), Hanks (1989), Nguyên (1992), Smith (1992).
9. See Janssen (in press) for some references to related data in other languages.
10. One could consider the use of *that* to be due to an anaphoric relationship with *this*, as used by the doctor. However, the doctor can ask *Tell me when it hurts*, and when she touches the sore, the patient can also react with (9b). For the quasi-grammatical distinction between deixis and anaphora, see section 4 and Kleiber (1992) and Cornish (1999).
11. I assume any distinction between stages in written and spoken discourse to be grammatically irrelevant and cognitively epiphenomenal. See also section 4 and, e.g., Kleiber (1992).
12. Compare Gildea (1993), Langacker (this volume b), and Stassen (1997: 76–91), who presents various copulas with a pronominal or demonstrative origin. Peter Trudgill inquired about the presumably pronominal origin of an Arabic copula on the "lingtyp" list (lingtyp@listserv.linguistlist.org, Febr. 3, 2002). Several languages were reported to show diachronic relationships between pronouns and copulas. Lucyna Gebert pointed out: "Also Slavic languages use a pronoun (a demonstrative) as a copula. Polish:
Jan to moj dobry przyjaciel.
Jan DEM my good friend ('Jan is a good friend of mine.')
Ten czlowiek to potwor.
this man DEM monster ('This man is a monster.')
The same construction is used in Russian." (Febr. 4, 2002)
13. This section relies on Janssen (1996).
14. The two tense morphemes can be used both deictically (related to information derivable from the current situational frame of reference) and anaphorically (related to information derivable from the current textual frame of reference). This double applicability underscores the assumption that the distinction between deixis and anaphora is epiphenominal.
15. Vetters (1993) and Kleiber (1993) present recent overviews of various approaches to defining tense deixis and tense anaphora.
16. Langacker (1987: 127) analyzes expressions such as *here* and *now* in their adverbial functions as deictic, and not as grounding, because he assumes that they participate in a relational predication.
17. For the so-called historical present, see, e.g., Janssen (1993), Tyler and Evans (2001), and Brisard (this volume: 287–288). In line with the empathy suggested by the present tense, the third person indicated by *goes* seems to suggest that the Lizard sees itself as an "objectified" subject with no will of its own.
18. See Janssen (1991: 169) for the relation between cataphoric *this* and the present tense referring to the future.

19. In this respect, Bühler uses also the term *zero-point*, possibly introduced by Jespersen (1924: 259).
20. For an overview of cognitive-linguistic (and related) approaches to tense with and without Reichenbach's point of reference, see Boogaart and Janssen (to appear).

References

Anderson, Stephen R. and Edward L. Keenan
    1985   Deixis. In: Timothy Shopen (ed.), *Language Typology and Syntactic Description*, Volume 3: *Grammatical Categories and the Lexicon*, 259–308. Cambridge: Cambridge University Press.

Aoyama, Takashi
    1995   Deixis and value: A semantic analysis of the Japanese demonstratives. In: Ellen Contini-Morava and Barbara Sussman Goldberg (eds.), *Meaning as Explanation: Advances in Linguistic Sign Theory*, 289–320. Edited with the assistance of Robert S. Kirsner. Berlin: Mouton de Gruyter.

Austin, Peter
    1982   The deictic system of Diyari. In: Jürgen Weissenborn and Wolfgang Klein (eds.), *Here and There: Crosslinguistic Studies on Deixis and Demonstration*, 273–284. Amsterdam: Benjamins.

Bátori, István
    1982   On verb deixis in Hungarian. In: Jürgen Weissenborn and Wolfgang Klein (eds.), *Here and There: Crosslinguistic Studies on Deixis and Demonstration*, 155–165. Amsterdam: Benjamins.

Bazanella, Carla
    1990   'Modal' uses of the Italian *indicativo imperfetto* in a pragmatic perspective. *Journal of Pragmatics* 14: 439–457.

Beifuss, Karin, Hartmut Czepluch, Joachim Tuschinsky and Wolfgang P. Schmid
    1985   Zur Klassifikation pragmatischer Elemente in der grammatischen Beschreibung. *Sprachwissenschaft* 10: 81–106.

Benveniste, Émile
    1956   La nature des pronoms. In: Morris Halle, Horace G. Lunt, Hugh McLean and Cornelis H. van Schooneveld (eds.), *For Roman Jakobson: Essays on the Occasion of his Sixtieth Birthday, 11 October 1956*, 34–37. The Hague: Mouton.

Boogaart, Ronny and Theo A.J.M. Janssen
    to appear   Tense and aspect. In: Hubert Cuyckens and Dirk Geeraerts (eds.), *Handbook of Cognitive Linguistics*. Oxford: Oxford University Press.

Brisard, Frank
   this vol.   The English present.
Bühler, Karl
   1982a   *Sprachtheorie: Die Darstellungsfunktion der Sprache.* Stuttgart: Fischer. First published Jena [1934].
   1982b   The deictic field of language and deictic words. In: Robert J. Jarvella and Wolfgang Klein, (eds.), *Speech, Place and Action: Studies in Deixis and Related Topics,* 9–30. Chichester: Wiley.
Cornish, Francis
   1999   *Anaphora, Discourse, and Understanding: Evidence from English and French.* Oxford: Clarendon.
Coulmas, Florian
   1982   Some remarks on Japanese deictics. In: Jürgen Weissenborn and Wolfgang Klein (eds.), *Here and There: Crosslinguistic Studies on Deixis and Demonstration,* 209–221. Amsterdam: Benjamins.
Frei, Henri
   1944   Systèmes de déictiques. *Acta Linguistica* 4: 111–129.
Gildea, Spike
   1993   The development of tense markers from demonstrative pronouns in Panare (Cariban). *Studies in Language* 17: 53–73.
Goffman, Erving
   1981   Footing. In: Erving Goffman, *Forms of Talk,* 124–159. Philadelphia: University of Pennsylvania Press. First published in *Semiotica* 25: 1–29 [1979].
Hanks, William F.
   1989   The indexical ground of deictic reference. In: Bradley Music, Randolph Graczyk and Caroline Wiltshire (eds.), *Papers from the 25th Annual Regional Meeting of the Chicago Linguistic Society, Part 2: Parasession on Language in Context,* 104–122. Chicago: Chicago Linguistic Society.
   1990   *Referential Practice: Language and Lived Space among the Maya.* Chicago: University of Chicago Press.
Hawkins, John A.
   1984   A note on referent identifiability and co-presence. *Journal of Pragmatics* 8: 649–659.
Janssen, Theo A.J.M.
   1991   Preterit as definite description. In: Jadranka Gvozdanovic and Theo A.J.M. Janssen (eds.), *The Function of Tense in Texts,* 157–181. Amsterdam: North-Holland.

1993 Tenses and demonstratives: Conspecific categories. In: Richard A. Geiger and Brygida Rudzka-Ostyn (eds.), *Conceptualisations and Mental Processing in Language*, 741–783. Berlin: Mouton de Gruyter.

1995a Cognitive semantics of region-based deixis. In: Richard A. Geiger (ed.), *Reference in Multidisciplinary Perspective: Philosophical Object, Cognitive Subject, Intersubjective Process*, 141–165. Hildesheim: Olms.

1995b Deixis from a cognitive point of view. In: Ellen Contini-Morava and Barbara Sussman Goldberg (eds.), *Meaning as Explanation: Advances in Linguistic Sign Theory*, 245–270. Edited with the assistance of Robert S. Kirsner. Berlin: Mouton de Gruyter.

1995c The preterit enabled by the pluperfect. In: Pier Marco Bertinetto, Valentina Bianchi, Östen Dahl and Mario Squartini (eds.), *Temporal Reference, Aspect and Actionality*, Volume 2: *Typological Perspectives*, 239–254. Torino: Rosenberg & Sellier.

1996 Deictic and anaphoric referencing of tenses. In: Walter De Mulder, Liliane Tasmowski-De Ryck and Carl Vetters (eds.), *Anaphores temporelles et (in)cohérence*, 79–107. Amsterdam: Rodopi.

in press Deixis and reference. In: Geert Booij, Christian Lehmann and Joachim Mugdan (eds.), *Morphology: A Handbook on Inflection and Word Formation* [Handbuch zur Sprache und Kommunikation]. Berlin: Mouton de Gruyter.

Jespersen, Otto
1924 *The Philosophy of Grammar*. London: Allen & Unwin.

Jones, Peter
1995 Philosophical and theoretical issues in the study of deixis: A critique of the standard account. In: Keith Green (ed.), *New Essays in Deixis*, 27–48. Amsterdam: Rodopi.

Josephs, Lewis S.
1978 Anaphora in Palauan. In: John Hinds (ed.), *Anaphora in Discourse*, 339–375. Edmonton: Linguistic Research.

Kirsner, Robert S.
1979 Deixis in discourse: An explanatory quantitative study of the modern Dutch demonstrative adjectives. In: Talmy Givón (ed.), *Syntax and Semantics*, Volume 12: *Discourse and Syntax*, 355–375. New York: Academic.

1993 From meaning to message in two theories: Cognitive and Saussurean views of the modern Dutch demonstratives. In: Richard A. Geiger and Brygida Rudzka-Ostyn (eds.), *Conceptualisations and Mental Processing in Language*, 83–114. Berlin: Mouton de Gruyter.

1996   The human factor and the insufficiency of invariant meanings. In: Edna Andrews and Yishai Tobin (eds.), *Toward a Calculus of Meaning: Studies in Markedness, Distinctive Features and Deixis*, 83–106. Amsterdam: Benjamins.

Kleiber, Georges
1992   Anaphore-déixis: Deux approches concurrentes. In: Mary-Annick Morel and Laurent Danon-Boileau (eds.), *La Déixis: Colloque en Sorbonne (8–9 juin 1990)*, 613–626. Paris: Presses Universitaires de France.
1993   Lorsque l'anaphore se lie aux temps grammaticaux. In: Carl Vetters (ed.), *Le temps: De la phrase au texte*, 117–166. Lille: Presses Universitaires de Lille.

Kuryłowicz, Jerzy
1972   The role of deictic elements in linguistic evolution. *Semiotica* 5: 174–83.

Lakoff, Robin
1970   Tense and its relation to participants. *Language* 46: 838–849.
1974   Remarks on *this* and *that*. In: Michael W. LaGaly, Robert A. Fox and Anthony Bruck (eds.), *Papers from the Tenth Regional Meeting of the Chicago Linguistic Society*, 345–356. Chicago: Chicago Linguistic Society.

Langacker, Ronald W.
1987   *Foundations of Cognitive Grammar, Volume 1: Theoretical Prerequisites*. Stanford: Stanford University Press.
1991   *Foundations of Cognitive Grammar, Volume 2: Descriptive Application*. Stanford: Stanford University Press.
1997   The contextual basis of cognitive semantics. In: Jan Nuyts and Eric Pederson (eds.), *Language and Conceptualization*, 229–252. Cambridge: Cambridge University Press.
this vol. a   Deixis and subjectivity.
this vol. b   Remarks on the English grounding systems.

Lazard, Gilbert and Louise Pelzer
1992   La déixis en tahitien. In: Mary-Annick Morel and Laurent Danon-Boileau (eds.), *La Déixis: Colloque en Sorbonne (8–9 juin 1990)*, 209–219. Paris: Presses Universitaires de France.

Lyons, Christopher
1999   *Definiteness*. Cambridge: Cambridge University Press.

Nguyên, Phu Phong
1992   La déixis en vietnamien. In: Mary-Annick Morel and Laurent Danon-Boileau (eds.), *La Déixis: Colloque en Sorbonne (8–9 juin 1990)*, 177–186. Paris: Presses Universitaires de France.

Nuyts, Jan
   this vol. Grounding and the system of epistemic expressions in Dutch: A cognitive-functional view.

Reichenbach, Hans
   1947 *Elements of Symbolic Logic*. New York: The Free Press.

Sauvageot, Serge
   1992 De l'expression de la déixis dans quelques langues du groupe ouest-atlantique (Afrique Noire). In: Mary-Annick Morel and Laurent Danon-Boileau (eds.), *La Déixis: Colloque en Sorbonne (8–9 juin 1990)*, 151–155. Paris: Presses Universitaires de France.

Smith, John Ch.
   1992 Traits, marques et sous-spécification: Application à la déixis. In: Mary-Annick Morel and Laurent Danon-Boileau (eds.), *La Déixis: Colloque en Sorbonne (8–9 juin 1990)*, 257–264. Paris: Presses Universitaires de France.

Stassen, Leon M.H.
   1997 *Intransitive Predication*. Oxford: Clarendon.

Tamba, Irène
   1992 Démonstratifs et personnels en japonais: Déixis et double structuration de l'espace discursif. In: Mary-Annick Morel and Laurent Danon-Boileau (eds.), *La Déixis: Colloque en Sorbonne (8–9 juin 1990)*, 187–195. Paris: Presses Universitaires de France.

Tyler, Andrea and Vyvyan Evans
   2001 The relation between experience, conceptual structure and meaning: Non-temporal uses of tense and language teaching. In: Martin Pütz, Susanne Niemeier and René Dirven (eds.), *Applied Cognitive Linguistics*, Volume 1: *Theory and Language Acquisition*, 63–105. Berlin: Mouton de Gruyter.

Vetters, Carl
   1993 Temps et déixis. In: Carl Vetters (ed.), *Le temps: De la phrase au texte*, 85–115. Lille: Presses Universitaires de Lille.

Wills, Dorothy D.
   1990 Indexifiers in Wolof. *Semiotica* 78: 193–218.

Zwicky, Arnold M.
   1977 Hierarchies of person. In: Woodford A. Beach, Samuel E. Fox and Shulamith Philosoph (eds.), *Papers from the Thirteenth Regional Meeting of the Chicago Linguistic Society*, 714–733. Chicago: Chicago Linguistic Society.

Source

Carroll, Lewis
   1990   *Alice's Adventures in Wonderland and Through the Looking-Glass and What Alice Found There.* Edited by Peter Newell as *More Annotated Alice.* New York: Random House.

Part II
Clausal grounding

The meaning and distribution of French mood inflections

Michel Achard

1. Introduction

In Cognitive Grammar (CG), grounding predications specify the relation that exists between a conceptualized entity and the speech situation or ground, namely the speech act participants (speaker and hearer), and the immediate circumstances of the utterance. In the case of a clause, these predications evaluate the epistemic status of the event the clause designates.

In French, the grammatical tools that allow conceptualizers to address the epistemic status of events include markers of person, tense, and mood, often grouped together into a single verbal ending. The goal of this paper is to investigate the meaning and distribution of the indicative, subjunctive, and conditional inflections.[1] Mood selection is determined by the evaluation of the status of the conceptualized event with respect to reality. The presence of the indicative inflection indicates that the event is reported as a proposition, that is to say that it includes a putative address in reality. The conditional inflection indicates that the event is construed as an alternative to reality. Finally, the subjunctive inflection indicates that the conceptualized event is not considered with respect to reality, but to a specific, more local mental space.

The paper is organized in the following fashion. Section two introduces the basic notions about grounding that will be required throughout the analysis. Section three describes the French mood system. Section four presents the semantic import of the indicative, conditional, and subjunctive inflections. Section five examines the distribution of these inflections in the context of the negative propositional attitude verb *penser* 'think'. Section six summarizes the results and concludes the paper.

2. Grounding

Grounding represents the final layer of semantic functions, the whole range of which is reflected in the progressive elaboration of the clause from a bare verb stem to a finite clause (Langacker 1991: 33).

The conceptual core of a clause is the verb stem, whose semantic function is to present a process type. A verb like *courir* 'run' presents a certain activity type. It can be recognized and differentiated from other related activities such as walking or sprinting, but it is not instantiated, that is to say anchored to a specific time, place, and participants. If the type level is the level at which different activities are kept separate, the instance level is the level at which different realizations of the same activity type are differentiated. Because a type is instantiated when it is considered with respect to its domain of instantiation (time for verbs), two different instances of the same type have two different temporal addresses (Langacker 1987, 1991). For example, Mary's running at 10:00 a.m. and 6:00 p.m. represent two instances of the running type. At the instance level, the process evoked by the verb is also tied to specific participants. Consequently, two running episodes by John and Mary may count as two separate instances of the running type, even though they occur at the same time.

Any instance of a process type can be quantified. For verbs, the nonfinite markers provide the quantification. In French, nonfinite markers that can be added onto a verb stem are the aspectual and voice markers. As it applies to verbs, quantification can be understood as providing information relative to the internal structure of the process. Aspectual markers code information relative to "the internal temporal consistency of a situation" (Comrie 1976: 3). The passive marker provides information concerning the specific coding of the participants in the process. More precisely, it "overrides the content verb with respect to one dimension of imagery, namely which processual participant assumes the status of trajector" (Langacker 1991: 197). The sentences in (1) and (2) illustrate the notion of quantification as applied to verbs:

(1) *Je voudrais être revenu à sept heures.*
     'I would like to have returned by seven o'clock.'

(2) *Jean doit avoir été élu president.*
     'John must have been elected president.'

Both (1) and (2) represent instances of a process type. In (1), the returning event type is anchored in a specific time (before seven) and participant (*je*). In (2), the election event type is predicated of a specific person (*Jean*), and the election has its own address in time, even though this remains implicit. Both instances are also quantified, because the perfect and voice markers contribute information relative to the internal structure of the processes they attach to. In (1), the return must be completed before seven o'clock. In (2), the perfect marker codes the completion of the election process at the time of the utterance, and the passive marker shows that the grammatical subject is not the agent of the profiled relation.

When an instance of a process type is quantified, it can be grounded. Grounding predications presuppose that an instance has been established, and they situate it with respect to the speech act participants (most importantly, the speaker and hearer). In a French clause, a single verb ending combines information pertaining to the mood, tense, and person of the considered process. For example, the -*ons* ending of *nous parlons* 'we speak' indicates that the conceptualized process is presented in the indicative mood, the present tense, and the first person plural. Both mood and tense categories should be considered separate grounding predications because they can occur independently of each other. We will see in sections 4.5 and 4.7 that the subjunctive and conditional inflections do not incorporate tense predications. The status of the person category is less clear-cut because it never occurs in the absence of mood (and sometimes tense) markers. Following the position expressed in Achard (1998), I will treat it as a grounding predication because its semantic function is to relate information pertaining to the main participant in the conceptualized event. This role is expressed by Moignet (1981: 91) in the following way: "La déclinaison en personne établit un rapport entre l'être concerné par l'évènement dit dans l'énoncé et l'être qui conduit l'évènement qu'est l'énoncé, le locuteur." [Person marking establishes a connection between the entity involved in the event which is being reported, and the entity which does the reporting event, the speaker.][2]

In terms of their semantic function, different clause types provide different levels of grounding. An indicative clause represents the highest possible level of elaboration of a process, namely a fully grounded instance of a process type. The notion of full grounding means that the conceptualized process is not only evaluated with respect to reality, but that its putative location within reality is also specified. This location is provided by the tense predications that necessarily occur with the indicative mood.[3] Conditional and subjunctive markers are also grounding predications because they address the epistemic status of the conceptualized process, but since they situate this process outside of reality (to be specified further in the following sections), they do not include tense predications. The grounding they provide is therefore less specific.

3. Mood distribution in French

This section provides a quick overview of the distribution of the indicative, conditional, and subjunctive moods across different grammatical constructions.[4]

3.1. The indicative

The indicative mood is found in most independent or main clauses, as illustrated in (3):

(3) a. *Les enfants ne vont pas à l'école aujourd'hui.*
'The children are not going to school today.'
b. *Il pleut beaucoup en été au Texas.*
'It rains a lot in Texas in the summer.'

In subordinate clauses, the indicative follows verbs of perception (4a) and declaration (4b). With verbs of propositional attitude, the indicative is most often present in the positive form (4c), but it competes with the subjunctive in the negative and interrogative forms (4d and e):

(4) a. *J'ai vu qu'il y avait beaucoup de monde.*
'I saw that there were a lot of people.'
b. *Il a dit qu'il venait.*
'He said that he was coming.'
c. *Je crois qu'elle a acheté une voiture.*
'I think that she bought a car.'
d. *La police ne pense pas qu'il reviendra(IND)/revienne(SUBJ) sur les lieux du crime.*
'The police do not think that he will return to the crime scene.'
e. *Crois-tu qu'elle a(IND)/ait(SUBJ) compris?*
'Do you think that she understood?'

The indicative also follows adverbial clauses introduced by temporal adverbs such as *quand* and *lorsque* 'when', *depuis* 'since', or *dès que* 'as soon as'. This is illustrated in (5):

(5) a. *Elle emménagera dès qu'elle aura trouvé une maison.*
'She will move in as soon as she finds a house.'
b. *Il parle anglais depuis qu'il habite aux Etats Unis.*
'He has been speaking English since he arrived in the States.'

Finally, the indicative mood is found in relative clauses, as illustrated in (6):

(6)a. *J'ai vu un écureuil qui grimpait dans l'arbre.*
'I saw a squirrel climbing up a tree.'
b. *J'aime les voitures qui ne consomment pas trop.*
'I like cars that have good gas mileage.'

3.2. The subjunctive

The subjunctive can be found in independent clauses. Its use, however, is restricted to the kind of optative illustrated in (7):

(7)a. *Qu'il sorte, s'il y tient tant que ça.*
'Let him go out if he wants it so badly.'
b. *Qu'il l'achète, s'il peut trouver l'argent.*
'Let him buy it, if he can find the money.'

The subjunctive is most frequently found in subordinate clauses following verbs of volition (8a) and emotional reaction (8b). As indicated earlier, the subjunctive competes with the indicative following the interrogative and negative forms of propositional attitude verbs:

(8)a. *Le patron veut que vous reveniez tout de suite.*
'The boss wants you to come back right away.'
b. *Je suis heureux que vous soyez sorti de ce piège.*
'I am happy that you got out of that trap.'

Adverbials such as *jusqu'à ce que* 'until', *avant que* 'before', and *pour que* 'so that' are also followed by the subjunctive:

(9)a. *Je serai parti avant qu'il revienne.*
'I will have left before he returns.'
b. *Je reviendrai avec toi pour que tu ne sois pas seul.*
'I will come back with you, so that you are not alone.'

The subjunctive also occurs in specific relative clause constructions, where it competes with the indicative and the conditional. These constructions are illustrated in (10):

(10) a. *Je voudrais travailler avec quelqu'un qui me comprenne*(SUBJ)/*comprend*(IND)/*comprendrait*(COND).
'I would like to work with someone who understood me.'
b. *Je cherche un secrétaire qui sache*(SUBJ) / *sait*(IND) / *saurait*(COND) *parler chinois*.
'I am looking for a secretary who could speak Chinese.'

Finally, the subjunctive inflection follows superlative and restrictive expressions, as shown in (11). In these cases, it also competes with the indicative:

(11) a. *C'est le meilleur joueur que j'aie*(SUBJ)/*j'ai*(IND) *jamais vu*.
'He is the best player I have ever seen.'
b. *Jean est le seul qui ait*(SUBJ)/*a*(IND) *compris quelque chose*.
'John is the only one who understood anything.'

3.3. The conditional

From a morphological standpoint, the conditional represents the combination of a future stem and imperfect endings. This form occurs in independent or main clauses, as illustrated in (12):

(12) a. *On dirait un vieux bateau.*
'It looks like an old boat.'
b. *On croirait qu'il n'a jamais quitté le pays.*
'One would think that he never left the country.'

Very often, the use of the conditional in independent clauses has an attenuating effect:

(13) *Je voudrais du pain s'il vous plait.*
'I would like some bread please.'

(14) *Je vous demanderais un peu de silence.*
'I would ask you to be quiet.'

The utterance in (13) is more polite than its indicative counterpart *Je veux du pain* 'I want some bread'. In (14), the presence of the conditional attenuates the illocutionary force of the indicative *Je vous demande* 'I ask you'.

The conditional also occurs in subordinate clauses, where it competes with the indicative:

(15) a. *Je croyais qu'il viendrait*(COND)/*venait*(IND).
'I thought that he would come.'
b. *Je pense qu'il comprendrait*(COND)/*comprenait*(IND).
'I think that he would understand.'

In hypotheticals and counterfactuals, the conditional occurs if the protasis is in the imperfect or pluperfect, as illustrated in (16):

(16) a. *Si je la connaissais, j'irais lui parler tout de suite.*
'If I knew her, I would go and talk to her right away.'
b. *Si j'y avais pensé, je ne serais pas venu.*
'If I had thought about it, I would not have come.'

3.4. Conditional: Tense or mood? Preliminary issues

The analysis of the conditional as a specific mood will become clear in section 4.7, but this section introduces some preliminary considerations. In a language such as French, where conjugated verbs combine the categories of mood, tense, and (sometimes) aspect into one single form, it is not always easy to precisely determine what a "tense" means. Most grammatical manuals propose a radical solution. Each verbal paradigm constitutes a specific tense. Under this familiar view, the future (*je reviendrai* 'I will come back') and future anterior (*je serai revenu* 'I will have come back') represent separate tenses. Linguists, however, have rejected this position. They prefer to recognize one future tense, available in both the future and future perfect, and analyze the difference between the two in terms of aspect. It is therefore clear that because they are so intertwined, the best way to characterize the notions of mood, tense, and aspect is to rely on precise definitions formulated within well-articulated theoretical models. This, of course, raises its own questions. The classification of a form as a tense or a mood can be influenced by system-internal considerations. The only comfort in this position is that such a classification merely holds heuristic value. The most important aspect of any analysis is the descriptive accuracy of the forms under consideration, not the label under which they are categorized.

This issue is particularly important with respect to the analysis of the French conditional, alternatively described in the literature as a separate mood, or as a tense of the indicative. Following Guillaume's principle that "[l]a grammaire est essentiellement la science des formes linguistiques" [grammar is primarily the science of linguistic forms] (Guillaume 1929: 56), the position that the conditional is a tense of the indicative rests firmly on morphological (formal) grounds. Wilmet (1997: 289) writes:

> Quant au "conditionnel", marcherais, marcherais, marcherait, marcherions, marcheriez, marcheraient, l'indice -r- du futur (marcherai, marcheras, marchera, marcherons, marcherez, marcheront) et la désinence -ais, -ais, -ait, -ions, -iez, -aient de "l'imparfait" (marchais, marchais, marchait, marchions, marchiez, marchaient) le rattachent sans l'ombre d'une indication à l'indicatif.
>
> [As to the "conditional" *marcherais, marcherais, marcherait, marcherions, marcheriez, marcheraient*, the *-r-* future marker (*marcherai, marcheras, marchera, marcherons, marcherez, marcheront*) and the "imperfect" endings *-ais, -ais, -ait, -ions, -iez, -aient* (*marchais, marchais, marchait, marchions, marchiez, marchaient*) connect it to the indicative without the shadow of a doubt.]

Outside of the formal domain, however, the picture is not so clear, because the conditional unquestionably possesses both temporal and modal aspects. Describing its appearance in Roman between the seventh and ninth centuries, Brunot (1905: 195) writes: "En outre il est né: a) un temps-mode, le conditionnel présent qui en qualité de temps sert de futur dans le passé, *portereie*; b) un conditionnel passé *aureie portet*." [Besides were born: a) a tense-mood, the conditional present, which as a tense is used as a future of the past, *portereie*; b) a past conditional *aureie portet*.] Even the strongest advocates of the temporal value of the conditional for formal (systemic) reasons provide a meaning that seems to lack the precise characteristics of a tense. For example, Guillaume (1929: 48) describes it as "un futur particulièrement hypothétique" [a particularly hypothetical future], which seems to indicate a primarily modal meaning.

I believe that the formal side of the conditional story is rather overstated. The emergence of the conditional as a blend of two indicative forms does not per se yield any clue as to its semantic function. It is perfectly natural for the meaning of the forms from which it was created to extend toward an area where it is most accurately described as a mood. Morphological origin cannot therefore constitute the final argument in the characterization of the conditional as a tense. Section 4.7 argues that the conditional is best described as a mood, and that its temporal value of "Future in the Past" merely represents an extension of its modal sense.[5]

4. Semantic characterization of mood inflections

It has already been mentioned that grounding predications evaluate the position of the conceptualized event with respect to reality. In order to precisely determine the conceptual import of the indicative, subjunctive, and conditional inflections, we therefore need to consider the different cognitive models that articulate our conception of reality, as well as the processes that enable a given conceptualizer to include certain selected facts in her own conception of reality.

4.1. Two levels of reality

Our conception of reality is so complex that the presentation of an inclusive model is well beyond the scope of this paper. This section merely introduces the elements that most directly pertain to our current concerns.

In our idealized view, reality is an objective entity, independent from all conceptualizers, of which we all have a limited and fragmentary knowledge. We know certain things and we ignore others, and we are aware that our knowledge of some facts is incomplete or perhaps false. We also know that other people may have a different set of elements they consider true, and thus have a different view of the world. Despite reality's abstract objectivity and independence, each individual is only aware of the subpart that constitutes her own conception of reality. Within her own conception, a given conceptualizer apprehends the events that occur in the world at different levels, and these levels reflect different conceptualizations. Two of those levels, basic and elaborated reality, are particularly relevant to the semantic characterization of the mood markers.

At the most basic level, reality represents the history of what happened. This includes the events (in the broad sense which incorporates states) which are currently in progress or have actually occurred, the ones which we see (or think we see) happening, and those which have (or we think have) happened. This conception of reality is inherent in Langacker's basic epistemic model, illustrated in Figure 1.

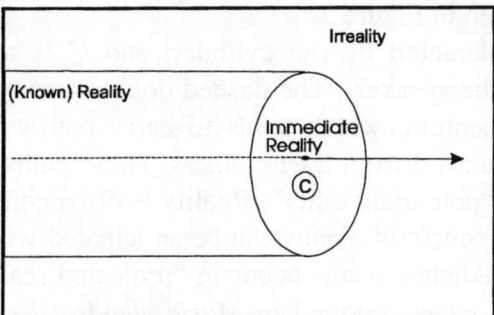

Figure 1. Basic epistemic model (Langacker 1991: 242)

Basic reality represents the level at which events are directly apprehended, that is to say observed, dreaded, dreamed, imagined, ... At this level, events are recorded, but their epistemic status is not questioned or assessed.

Our knowledge of reality cannot, however, be restricted to the direct apprehension of events but must also include our capacity to evaluate the position of those events with respect to reality. This epistemic evaluation is rendered possible by the dynamic nature of reality. Langacker (1991: 242) talks about reality being perceived as an "ever evolving entity whose evolution continuously augments the complexity of the structure already defined by its previous history". Its evolution along the time axis yields a force-dynamic dimension to our conception of reality that constrains and influences the elements that unfold within it (Langacker 1991: 276). This "evolutionary momentum" allows the future course of events to be predictable to some extent. Some elements are seen as likely, while others are definitely excluded from the possible turn of events. Part of our conception of reality therefore includes the understanding that the way it has already evolved leaves the potential for further development in constrained directions. The possibility of predicting with reasonable confidence which among those directions will actually be realized is by itself a reflection on the way reality has evolved so far. In this sense, it is part of reality. It represents, however, a more abstract and inclusive level than basic reality, and will be referred to as elaborated reality. Elaborated reality is reflected in Langacker's dynamic evolutionary model, given in Figure 2.

Reality is depicted by the cylinder, and C is a conceptualizer (identified as the speaker). The dashed double arrow represents evolutionary momentum, which tends to carry reality along a certain path and precludes it from taking others. Those paths that are not excluded define "potential reality". Reality is often constrained enough that the future course of events can be anticipated with relative accuracy. These predicted events occur in "projected reality". For example, the future event reported in *Marie viendra demain* 'Mary will come tomorrow' is viewed as an element of projected reality. Her knowledge of Marie's current circumstances allows the speaker to expect reality to evolve in such a way as to include the profiled event in the future.

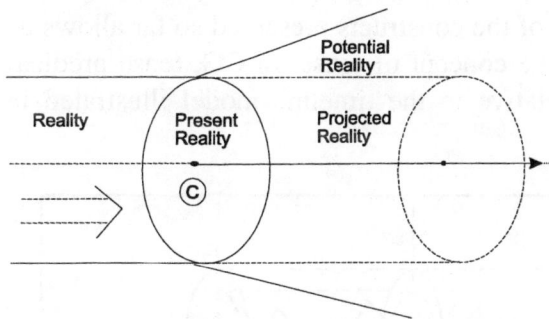

Figure 2. Dynamic evolutionary model (Langacker 1991: 277)

Elaborated reality represents the level at which the precise location of events with respect to reality must be determined. Consequently, the elements of elaborated reality need to include a putative address in reality. Tense predications provide that address by placing the conceptualized element in a specific area of reality (to be explained in further detail in the next section). Because they include tense predications, the elements that compose elaborated reality are called "propositions" (Langacker 1991: 551). As basic reality is the level of events, elaborated reality is the level of propositions.

The difference between these two conceptions of reality deserves to be restated. Basic reality is the level at which events are observed; elaborated reality is the level at which their epistemic status is determined. Because this determination requires a putative address in reality, the propositions that make up elaborated reality include tense predications. Under this view, elaborated reality is the level at which events are reported or communicated. For example, if *Jean* witnesses *Marie*'s arrival at 5 o'clock, that event is part of his conception of basic reality. When he reports the event as *Marie est arrivée à 5 heures* 'Mary arrived at 5 o'clock', it is reported as accomplished at the time of speech, and therefore as part of (past) reality. The event is thus described as a proposition, that is to say with respect to its location in elaborated reality.

4.2. A note on tense

The two models of reality introduced in the preceding section are exclusively epistemic. None of the constructs presented so far allows us to precisely characterize the concept of tense. In CG, tense predications are characterized relative to the timeline model illustrated in Figure 3.

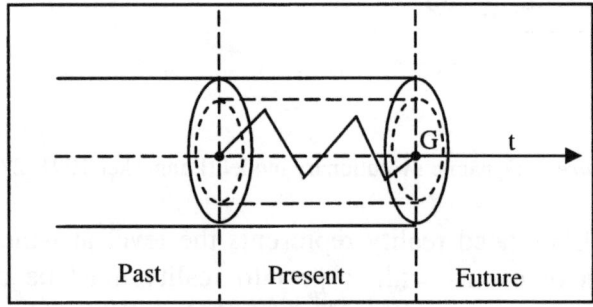

Figure 3. Timeline model (Langacker 1991: 244)

The time line model elaborates the basic epistemic model in two important ways. The first one is time, i.e. the axis along which reality evolves. The second one is the ground (G), or in other words the locus of the speech event. The ground is situated at the moment of speech (immediate reality), and it constitutes the vantage point from which the speaker and hearer conceptualize an expression's meaning. Because a speech event has a significant duration in real time, both the ground and the portion of immediate reality associated with it also have some duration in real time. On the basis of that duration, time can be divided into present, past, and future (see also Guillaume 1929).

The three models presented in this section constitute the conceptual base relative to which the meaning of the French moods and tenses gets characterized. To give just one example that prefaces the analysis provided in sections 4.3 and 4.5, the distinction between basic and elaborated reality subtends the contrast between the subjunctive and the indicative moods. The meaning of the subjunctive mood needs to be characterized at the level of basic reality, where its presence indicates that the mere occurrence of the conceptualized event is being considered. Conversely, the indicative is characterized with respect to elaborated reality because it provides the conceptualized event with a putative address in the present, past, or future.

These models also clearly show how the notions of mood and tense are related yet separate. The grounding system is inherently epistemic. Time considerations emerge from the superimposition of the timeline model onto the dynamic evolutionary model. This accomplishes two results. First, it explains why the indicative is the only mood that includes tense predications. Secondly, it affords a simple way of characterizing the import of tense predications. In French, these predications situate the profiled process in one of the three regions of elaborated reality. The present locates it in immediate reality, the future in projected reality. Both the simple past (*passé simple*) and the imperfect (*imparfait*) locate the proposition in (past) reality, the difference between them being one of aspect.[6]

4.3. Meaning of the indicative: Epistemic control of a proposition

In order to characterize the meaning of the indicative inflection, we need to examine in closer detail the processes by which a conceptualizer comes to consider a given proposition true. It is important to note that the inclusion of a proposition in someone's conception of elaborated reality indicates some measure of conceptual control over that proposition (Langacker 1991, 2001). Conceptual control is expressed by the possible manipulation of these abstract objects. Like concrete objects, the propositions considered true can be arranged, exchanged, sold, or borrowed, etc. A parallel can therefore be drawn between conceptual control and concrete possession. Just like the set of objects a person owns defines her dominion (Langacker 1991, 1993, 2001), the set of propositions she considers true (i.e. her conception of elaborated reality) represents a person's conceptual dominion.[7]

The inclusion of a proposition in a conceptualizer's dominion represents the result of a complicated process by which control is gradually and progressively asserted. Langacker (2001) follows Sumnicht (2001) in proposing the following "mental control cycle" that leads to inclusion.

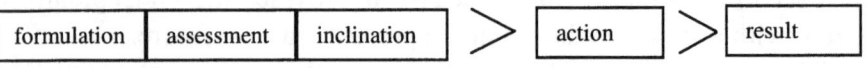

Figure 4. Mental control cycle (Langacker 2001)

The different stages of the cycle are illustrated in (17) with verbs of propositional attitude:

(17) a. *Je considère la possibilité qu'elle ne viendra pas.* (formulation)
'I consider the possibility that she won't come.'
b. *Je me demande si elle est venue.* (assessment)
'I wonder if she came.'
c. *Je crois qu'elle est venue.* (inclination)
'I think she came.'
d. *J'ai décidé qu'elle venait.* (action)
'I decided that she would come.'
e. *Je sais qu'elle est venue.* (result)
'I know that she came.'

This scale indicates the different levels of conceptual effort by which the status of a proposition with respect to reality can be determined. It therefore allows us to formulate a definition of the indicative inflection. I suggest that the indicative codes the epistemic effort required to establish the conceptualized event's putative location in elaborated reality. To put it differently, the indicative codes the conceptualized event as a proposition.[8] Importantly, this definition applies to any kind of epistemic effort that aims to establish control over the proposition, or in other words, to every stage of the mental control cycle.[9]

4.4. Indicative uses

This definition of the indicative clause naturally accounts for the uses described in section 3. The production of any sentence has to be understood against the background of a model of communication. Communication can be thought of as the sharing of information. Part of what we do when we share information is address the status of what is being said with respect to elaborated reality. Consider the independent clause previously given in (3) and repeated here for convenience:

(3)a. *Les enfants ne vont pas à l'école aujourd'hui.*
'The children are not going to school today.'
b. *Il pleut beaucoup en été au Texas.*
'It rains a lot in Texas in the summer.'

The examples in (3) present independent clauses. In each instance, the speaker is the conceptualizer of the sentence. Each independent clause represents a proposition. The tense predications define the precise location of the proposition in a specific area of elaborated reality. In (3a) for example, the present tense provides the proposition's putative address in immediate reality. There is no obvious way of knowing if the speaker considers the proposition true, or if she is deliberately lying. In both cases, however, the propositions expressed in the independent clauses are presented with respect to elaborated reality, justifying the indicative inflection.

Independent clauses in the indicative can anchor the conceptualized proposition in different areas of reality, as illustrated in (18):

(18) a. *Les enfants n'iront pas à l'école demain.*
'The children will not go to school tomorrow.'
b. *Il pleuvait beaucoup cet été au Texas.*
'It was raining a lot in Texas this summer.'

In (18a), the future grounding predication potentially locates the proposition in projected reality, while in (18b), the past predication places it in established reality.

The distribution of the indicative inflection in subordinate clauses is analyzed in detail in Achard (1998: chapter 6), so it will not be repeated here. It will simply be noted that the subordinate verb is in the indicative mood if the semantics of the main verb are compatible with the construal of the event in the complement as a proposition. Verbs of propositional attitude (in the positive form) have already been considered in this respect. Verbs of perception indicate the precise manner in which the proposition comes to be included in the conceptualizer's dominion. Verbs of declaration communicate a proposition to another person. In order to be communicated, that proposition first needs to be considered with respect to reality. The situations where the indicative competes with the subjunctive or the conditional will be considered after the meaning of these inflections has been presented. The distribution of the three moods following verbs of propositional attitude in the negative form will be presented in section 5.

4.5. Meaning of the subjunctive inflection

As indicated earlier, the subjunctive needs to be characterized at the level of basic reality, because it primarily codes the possible occurrence of events rather than their location in reality. Consequently, the subjunctive does not include tense predications. This focus on the occurrence of events directly accounts for the use of the subjunctive in the independent sentences presented in (7) and repeated here:

(7)a. *Qu'il sorte, s'il y tient tant que ça.*
 'Let him go out if he wants it so badly.'
 b. *Qu'il l'achète, s'il peut trouver l'argent.*
 'Let him buy it, if he can find the money.'

The examples in (7) do not describe specific facets of reality. Rather, they indicate the conditions under which the events coded in the complement clause might take place. The speaker is resigning her power to obstruct them, therefore allowing their occurrence.

In complement clauses, the mood distribution depends on whether the complement content is construed as an event or as a proposition. Achard (1998) argues that the meaning of volition verbs is incompatible with the meaning of an indicative clause, because those verbs do not allow the event expressed in the complement to be construed as a proposition. Volition verbs only present the desire of their subjects, not their assessment of the way things are. Consequently, these verbs offer no basis for the evaluation of their complement content with respect to reality. The presence of the subjunctive inflection reflects the fact that the event in the complement is not considered with respect to reality, but to the more specific and local mental space of the subject's desires (Achard 1998).

Verbs of emotional reaction are not incompatible with the meaning of an indicative clause, but the construal of the complement scene as a proposition (although possible) is not directly relevant to their meaning. The presence of the subjunctive inflection indicates that those verbs primarily present their subject's reaction to the event in the complement. The notion of direct relevance can be illustrated by the contrast between (19) and (20):

(19) *Je sais qu'elle a échoué.*
      'I know that she failed.'

(20) *Je suis désolé qu'elle ait échoué.*
      'I am sorry that she failed.'

In (19), the communicative purpose of the sentence is to establish (or confirm) a particular facet of elaborated reality. The construal of the complement content as a proposition is thus directly relevant to the meaning of the main verb. In (20) by contrast, the presence of the complement content in reality is not asserted but presupposed. The purpose of the sentence is to present the speaker's reaction to the failing event, not to report that event with respect to reality.[10]

4.6. The subjunctive and the indicative in contrast

We can now consider the cases where the indicative and the subjunctive are in competition, namely following adverbials and in relative clauses. The situation in relative clauses is clear. Consider the pair in (21):

(21) a. *Je voudrais travailler avec quelqu'un qui me comprend* (IND).
'I would like to work with someone who understands me.'
b. *Je voudrais travailler avec quelqu'un qui me comprenne* (SUBJ).
'I would like to work with someone who would understand me.'

The semantic structure of the examples where the indicative and subjunctive are in competition is remarkably similar. The speaker is attempting to locate a certain entity that possesses the property described in the relative clause. The general intuition is that the mood of the relative verb determines the speaker's confidence in locating that entity. The presence of the indicative reflects greater confidence than that of the subjunctive. This intuition is readily explained by the analysis presented here. Using (21) as an example, the existence of *quelqu'un* 'someone' is directly inferred from the presentation of *quelqu'un qui me comprend* 'someone who understands me' as a possible facet of elaborated reality. Note that the proposition's address in immediate reality is not per se sufficient to establish the pronoun's referent, but at the very least, it indicates a strong belief in its existence. The inference of the existence of the antecedent of the relative pronoun is not so easily available when the relative verb is in the subjunctive, as in (21b). In this case, the relative clause is construed as an event that may or may not occur. The use of the subjunctive in such cases is reminiscent of the situation with verbs of volition or desire. The event of finding someone with a capacity to understand is confined to the space of the conceptualizer's wishes. The event's remoteness from reality makes it more difficult to infer the existence of its main participant in reality.

The subjunctive/indicative contrast following superlative and restrictive relative clauses can be treated in a similar way. Consider the pair in (22):

(22) a. *Jean est le seul qui a compris quelque chose.*
'John is the only one who understood anything.'
b. *Jean est le seul qui ait compris quelque chose.*
'John is the only one who understood anything.'

The cases presented in (22) are obviously different from the ones in (21) because the pronoun's referent is clearly identified as John. The main difference between (22a) and (22b) is that the presence of the subjunctive in (22b) increases the dramatic aspect of John's uniqueness. This is consistent with the analysis proposed here. The example in (22a) presents a statement of fact, a facet of reality. The one in (22b) does a bit more. By construing the complement content outside of reality, the presence of the subjunctive allows the inference that John is the only one with the predicated qualities in all possible imagined worlds.

These constructions are problematic because it is difficult to isolate specific semantic effects consistently associated with the presence of the indicative or subjunctive inflections. Consider for example the contrast in (23):

(23) a. *C'est le seul qui peut vous satisfaire.*
'He is the only one who can satisfy you.'

b. *C'est le seul qui puisse vous satisfaire.*
'He is the only one who could satisfy you.'

The indicative in (23a) indicates that the proposition *qui peut vous satisfaire* 'who can satisfy you' is considered with respect to elaborated reality. In (23b), it is merely presented as an event that might or might not happen. The combination of the restrictive and the subjunctive allows us to infer that the request might have been unreasonable in the first place. This nuance does not exist with the indicative in (23a). The exact nature of the semantic effects produced by the presence of the subjunctive inflection depends on the context, however, and cannot be predicted with precision.

The situation is also straightforward with adverbial phrases. The conjunctions followed by the indicative, namely temporal *quand* 'when', *dès que* 'as soon as', *après que* 'after', or causal *parce que* 'because' all introduce a state of the world that can be directly observed before the process in the main clause occurs. In most cases, the event in the adverbial clause must occur first for the main event to occur as well. This is particularly true when the presence of a perfect marker in the adverbial clause indicates that the process it codes must be accomplished. This is the case in the example presented in (5a) and repeated here:

(5)a. *Elle emménagera dès qu'elle aura trouvé une maison.*
    'She will move in as soon as she finds a house.'

The presence of the indicative is clear. The event coded in the adverbial clause will be firmly established in reality by the time the main event occurs. Its coding in the indicative reflects its construal as a proposition.

Conversely, the conjunctions followed by the subjunctive present events that will not have occurred when the main event is performed. This includes among others the temporal *avant que* 'before', and the purposive *pour que* and *afin que* 'so that'. Consider the example presented in (9a) and repeated here:

(9)a. *Je serai parti avant qu'il revienne.*
    'I will have left before he returns.'

In (9a), the process coded in the main clause will be accomplished before the event in the adverbial clause occurs. By the time the main clause event (*partir*) occurs, the *revenir* event will not be established in reality. Consequently, its representation as a proposition does not constitute the preferred choice. Its subjunctive marking reflects its construal as an event that has yet to occur. The distribution of the indicative and the subjunctive moods in adverbial clauses therefore mirrors the internal organization of the main and subordinate clauses. If, at the time of occurrence of the main event, the event coded in the adverbial clause has occurred, it tends to be construed as a proposition and marked by the indicative. If it has not occurred, it is usually not construed as a proposition and is consequently marked by the subjunctive.[11]

The situation is not, however, always so clear-cut. Compare for example the contrast illustrated in (24) and (25):

(24) *Je partirai dès qu'il reviendra.*
 'I will leave as soon as he comes back.'

(25) *Je resterai jusqu'à ce qu'il revienne.*
 'I will stay until he comes back.'

The mood contrast between (24) and (25) cannot be explained by the temporal organization of the sentences. In both cases, the event in the subordinate clause occurs prior to the one in the main clause. Consequently, given temporal considerations alone, the subordinate event in (25) could be construed as a proposition just like the one in (24). The difference between the two, I believe, comes from more subtle semantic considerations. The communicative purpose of (25) is to present the temporal limit of the main clause process. That limit is provided by the occurrence of the subordinate event. I suggest that in such cases, the presence of the subjunctive is motivated by the greater relevance of the occurrence of the subordinate event (as a trigger to the main event) than its possible construal as a proposition.[12]

4.7. Meaning of the conditional

It is now time to investigate the semantic import of the conditional inflection. As was already indicated, the conditional is analyzed as a specific mood rather than a tense of the indicative. The reasons for this position should now be clear. The information the inflection provides is not primarily temporal. More specifically, it does not provide an address that reliably allows the hearer to place the conceptualized event in the past, present, or future. Compare the future sentence in (26a) to the conditional one in (26b):

(26) a. *Je crois qu'il viendra.*
'I think that he will come.'
b. *Je crois qu'il viendrait (s'il avait une voiture).*
'I think that he would come (if he had a car).'

In (26a), the presence of the future indicates that the speaker places the proposition *il viendra* 'he will come' in projected reality. The time of (predicted) occurrence is unambiguously the future. In (26b), by comparison, the possible time of occurrence could be the present (or habitual), or the future. This indeterminacy seems to be an important aspect of the meaning of the conditional. It is well captured by Guillaume (1929: 57), who writes: "Le conditionnel reste ainsi indéfiniment dans une époque qui n'est ni un présent proprement dit ni un futur, mais une indivision de ces deux temps infiniment extensible et non achevable." [The conditional thus remains indefinitely in a period that is neither properly speaking a present nor a future, but a union of these two times, of infinite extension and interminable.] This temporal indeterminacy of the conditional prevents us from following Guillaume in analyzing it as a hypothetical future tense. Rather, the account proposed here focuses on its modal value. I propose that the conditional inflection marks the conceptualized event as an alternative to reality, an alternative that can only be realized if specific conditions are met. Because the notion of alternative to reality is modal rather than temporal in character, the conditional will be considered a separate mood.

The notion of alternative to reality is firmly rooted in reality. Evolutionary momentum does not only allow us to predict the natural outcome of events, but by providing the world with a structure, it also allows us to envisage different outcomes depending on the occurrence of specific events. These outcomes might never materialize because the conditions are not favorable, but they are rightfully considered alternatives to reality because their conception results from our knowledge of the structure of reality. They could be figuratively described as the paths that reality did not take. In that sense, the knowledge of what could happen, or have happened, is based on reality. It is considered an alternative to reality (as opposed to being totally disconnected from it) because its inner structure is based on the same evolutionary momentum. Just like the future, the conditional therefore codes the speaker's predictive effort.

The difference between projected and alternative reality is clearly illustrated by the contrast between (26a) and (26b). In (26a) the course of events is expected to naturally evolve in a manner so as to include the proposition *il viendra* 'he will come'. In (26b) on the other hand, the upcoming event can only occur if the condition of having a car is met. Because its existence is constrained by the presence of prerequisite conditions, the event is presented as an alternative to reality, and thus marked by the conditional inflection. In (26b), the conditions that restrict the occurrence of the main process are specified in a hypothetical clause.[13] Even in the absence of such a clause, however, a process in the conditional is nonetheless subject to unspecified conditions. Because it represents an alternative to reality, the conditional inherently contains the idea that the occurrence of this alternative path depends on certain conditions, even though they may not be explicitly mentioned. The reminder of this section argues in favor of the proposal that the presence of the conditional inflection presents the conceptualized event as an alternative to reality. The analysis is restricted to hypothetical (*si*) constructions. I first concentrate on counterfactual cases, before turning to the conditional's predictive value.

Si clauses often participate in counterfactual constructions, where the main clause presents an event that did not take place. This is illustrated in (27). The examples in this section are taken from articles from the news agency *Agence France Presse* (AFP). The relevant verbs are indicated in bold print:

(27) *Devant plus de 500.000 spectateurs, le souriant Villeneuve a eu une pensée pour son père, Gilles, ancien pilote de la Formule 1 qui a trouvé la mort en 1982 lors des essais du Grand Prix de Belgique. "Je sais que s'il **était** là, il **serait** très fier de moi."*
'In front of over 500,000 spectators, the smiling Villeneuve had a thought for his father Gilles, a former Formula 1 driver who died in 1982 during the time trails of the Belgian grand prix. "I know that if he were here, he would be very proud of me."'

The counterfactual nature of (27) makes it clear that the main clause event is not presented as a facet of reality, but as an alternative to reality. Rather than what is, the main verb describes an event that would have taken place if the conditions expressed in the protasis had obtained. This alternative event is marked by the conditional.

The conditional inflection retains the same semantic function when the hypothetical construction is not counterfactual, even though that function might not be as obvious as in the counterfactual cases. Consider the example in (28):

(28) *Comme Bruno Martini, il se garde bien de déclencher une polémique qui n'a pour l'instant pas lieu d'être. Mais il admet cependant que "si Joël Bats **prenait** sa retraite, il y **aurait** une place à prendre".*
'Like Bruno Martini, he is very careful not to start a controversy that has no reason of being at the moment. He admits, however, that "if Joël Bats were to retire, the position would be up for grabs".'

In (28), despite the fact that nobody knows whether Joël Bats will retire or not, I would like to argue that the conditional nonetheless presents the retiring process as an alternative to reality. In order for the argument to be convincing, we need to investigate the predictive value of hypothetical constructions, as well as the role of the imperfect that follows *si* in those constructions.

The predictive value of hypothetical constructions is largely independent of their counterfactual status. Regardless of the mood of the main verb, these constructions describe how the world might, may, or will develop given the presence of specific conditions. The main verb is often in the future, as illustrated in (29):

(29) *Si demain des manifestants **envahissent** le plateau de "Sacrée soirée", je ne me **battrai** pas. Je leur **tendrai** le micro pour qu'ils puissent s'exprimer.*
'If tomorrow some demonstrators break into the studio during a shoot of "Sacrée soirée", I will not fight. I will hand them the microphone so that they can express themselves.'

The example in (29) presents the speaker's prediction about a potential future event. His experience of his own reactions to similar situations leads him to believe that a world that includes the proposition *Des manifestants envahissent le plateau de "Sacrée soirée"* 'Some demonstrators break into the studio during a "Sacrée soirée" shoot', also includes *Je ne me battrai pas* 'I will not fight' and *Je leur tendrai le micro pour qu'ils puissent s'exprimer* 'I will hand them the microphone so that they can express themselves'. The *si* clause represents the restriction on the occurrence of the main events. The indicative in the apodosis illustrates the speaker's confidence in the effect the event in the protasis will have on the course of reality, and therefore highlights her predictive effort. If hypothetical constructions are predictive regardless of the mood of the main verb, how can we characterize the meaning differences between the present/future combination illustrated in (29), and the imperfect/conditional pair presented in (28)?

When the protasis is in the present, the communicative focus of the utterance is on the inescapable quality of the main event. The subordinate event is accepted as given (even if only for the sake of discussion) with the sole purpose of identifying the logical conclusion of the chain of events it triggers. This construction is particularly favored when the event in the *si* clause is firmly established in reality as it describes an ongoing situation. This is illustrated in (30):

(30) *Ennemi juré du chauvinisme, le prophétique Camil Petrescu écrivait déjà, en 1940: "Si les Roumains **tolèrent** encore longtemps la bêtise, leur pays **finira** par tomber sous la tyrannie d'un cordonnier."*
'A sworn enemy of chauvinism, the prophetic Camil Petrescu already wrote in 1940: "If Romanians tolerate stupidity much longer, their country will end up under the tyranny of a shoemaker."'

The protasis in (30) describes what the author perceives as the current situation in Romania. The location of the tolerating event in reality is therefore not questioned. The restriction that *si* introduces concerns its prolonged duration. The future in the main clause expresses the result that cannot fail to obtain given the path reality has been following.

The present/future construction also frequently describes the quasi-automatic occurrence of the main event, given the situation expressed in the *si* clause. This is illustrated in (31):

(31) *Si notre motion l'emporte — c'est-à-dire si elle fait plus de voix que toutes les autres motions — que se passera-t-il? — Comme Mr Chirac est un démocrate, si notre motion **l'emporte**, eh bien, il lui **appartiendra** d'assumer la transformation du mouvement.*
'If our motion wins — that is to say if it gets more votes than all the other motions — what will happen? — Since M. Chirac is a democrat, if our motion wins, well, it will be up to him to initiate some changes in the party.'

Part of being a democrat entails yielding to the will of the majority. Therefore M. Chirac has no choice but to act in a predictable fashion. The presence of the future in the main clause indicates the speaker's confidence that his reaction can indeed be anticipated. The important trait which the examples in (30) and (31) share is that the presence in reality of the event in the protasis is not questioned but accepted as given in order to illustrate the predictability of the ensuing outcome.[14]

When the event in the protasis is in the imperfect, it is not accepted as given but merely presented as a possible option, one of the many paths reality might take.[15] The speaker's predictive effort involves the consideration of the event in the *si* clause, as well as its logical consequences. Expectedly, these constructions are favored when the event in the protasis clearly represents one among several (at least two) paths reality might adopt, as illustrated in (32):

(32) *"Le franc se tient bien, et il gardera sa parité avec le mark", a déclaré le ministre de l'économie, Mr Bérégovoy, le 5 janvier sur Antenne 2. Depuis un an, le ministre s'en tient à ce credo. Si le mark devait être réévalué, le franc suivrait.*
'"The franc is holding on well, and it will keep on a par with the mark", the Secretary of Economic Affairs, M. Bérégovoy, declared to Antenne 2 on January 5th. For a year now the secretary has been holding on to this credo. If the mark had to be readjusted, the franc would follow.'

It is clear in (32) that the need to readjust the franc is not currently part of reality. The paragraph presents a contingency, that is to say an event that might become real, as well as the expected response it would trigger. Because the event in the protasis is not accepted as given, it is presented as a plausible occurrence and marked in the imperfect. In a way consistent with the definition proposed earlier, the conditional in the main clause indicates that the resulting event represents an alternative to reality, an expected response that would necessarily follow the occurrence of the event in the protasis.

This analysis is congruent with the often-made observation that the construction with a present in the *si* clause and a conditional in the main clause represents a stronger prediction than its counterpart in the imperfect and conditional (see Dancygier 1993 for English). This situation obtains because the event in the protasis in a "*si* + imperfect" clause is coded as a possible path reality might take, rather than the one currently accepted (posited as real) in a protasis in the present. Similarly, the conditional in the main clause presents the apodosis as the alternative state of reality that would result from the occurrence of the process in the protasis. The weakness of the prediction can be directly imputed to the presentation of the event in the protasis as an alternative to projected reality. This semantic trait of the imperfect/conditional construction is important because it is frequently used to express the speaker's degree of confidence in the occurrence of the event in the protasis. Consider for example the paragraph in (33):

(33) *La Bundesbank se refuse à faire des propositions monétaires à la RDA: "La RDA doit d'abord dire ce qu'elle envisage de faire et ce qu'elle souhaite". Selon Mr Poehl, le gouvernement issu des élections libres du 6 mai prochain devrait prendre toute une série de mesures (sur les prix, la propriété...) qui lui permettront de parvenir à une convertibilité de leur monnaie. Celle-ci pourrait s'arrimer au DM. Si les bonnes décisions **étaient prises**, "la RDA **aurait** de bonnes chances de parvenir à un niveau de vie occidental". Dans le cas contraire, a conclu Mr Poehl, "si les capitaux ne vont pas aux gens, les gens iront aux capitaux", faisant ainsi référence à l'exode qui se poursuit de la RDA vers le RFA.*
'The Bundesbank refuses to make financial propositions to the GDR: "The GDR must first say what they are planning to do and what they want". According to M. Poehl, the government elected upon the free elections of May 6 should take a whole series of measures (concerning prices, property...) that will allow them to convert their currency, which could link itself to the mark. If the right measures were taken, "the GDR would have a good chance to reach a Western lifestyle". In the opposite case, M. Poehl concluded, "if the money does not go to the people, the people will go to the money", a reference to the continuing exodus from the GDR towards West-Germany.'

It is clear from the paragraph in (33) that the Bundesbank is not ready to do business with the GDR before knowing what kind of reforms its new leadership will put forward. It is also clear that only certain measures will be considered appropriate. Two separate paths, each resulting from a specific set of measures, are carefully outlined. The imperfect marker in the protasis indicates that taking the right measures is merely a possibility, not an accepted state of events. The imperfect/conditional construction fits very well with the overall tone of the passage, which exudes only a moderate confidence in the GDR's chances of adopting a Western lifestyle.[16]

This function of marking an alternative path reality might take (have taken), accounts for the polite uses of the conditional, where its presence attenuates the illocutionary force of the request. Let us take the polite formula *Je voudrais du pain s'il vous plait* 'I would like some bread (if you) please' not as a set expression, but as a regular instance of the imperfect/conditional construction. The main clause presents the request as an alternative to reality. The function of the protasis is to show that the occurrence of the main process (the request itself) is subject to the hearer's agreement (the person to whom the request is made). The hearer's participation in the way in which the request is carried out considerably reduces its illocutionary force. Even without the protasis, as for example in *Je vous demanderais un peu de silence* 'I would request a moment of silence', the illocutionary force of *demander* 'request' is attenuated by the consideration of the process as one among other possible alternatives.

4.7.1. The "Future in the Past"

When the conditional in the subordinate clause follows a main verb in the imperfect, it is sometimes called a "Future in the Past".[17] In this use, it is often considered a mere structural reflex, a result of the necessary sequence of tenses. This section argues that this use of the conditional is not only meaningful, but that its meaning is directly related to the one it exhibits in the hypothetical constructions presented in the previous section. As a preface to the investigation of mood distribution in complement clauses in section 5, consider the example in (34):

(34) *En septembre 1985, Luis Ocana, Francis Castaing et Alain Bondue signèrent des contrats. Tout le monde **croyait** dur comme fer que le sponsor **serait** la chaine de télévision américaine ABC. Pure invention, évidemment.*
'In September 1985, Luis Ocana, Francis Castaing, and Alain Bondue signed the contracts. Everybody strongly believed that the American TV network ABC would be the sponsor. An obvious fabrication.'

The text in (34) describes a scam, a situation where the victims' expectations were markedly different from the eventual turn of events. The clause in the conditional presents the prediction about reality the victims made when they signed the contracts. The conditional codes that prediction as an alternative to reality. The difference between the victims' prediction and the actual outcome is made specific by the phrase *Pure invention, évidemment* 'An obvious fabrication'.

It is crucial to note that the conceptualizer's prediction is coded in the conditional, even when it is confirmed by reality. For example, an alternative to (34) could be *Tout le monde savait que le sponsor serait ABC* 'Everybody knew that ABC would be the sponsor'. I suggest that in such cases, the conditional codes the conceptualizer's prediction rather than the corresponding facet of reality (even though the two coincide), and that it treats this prediction as an alternative to reality. The treatment of the conceptualizer's prediction as an alternative to reality is motivated by the necessary separation that exists between predicting and observing the prediction's eventual outcome. These two activities constitute two different cognitive routines performed at different times, even when the observation of reality confirms the prediction.

5. Distribution of indicative, conditional, and subjunctive inflections

One of the most basic tenets of a CG analysis is that the meaning of an expression should allow us to predict (at least partially) its distribution in discourse. This section shows that the meaning of the indicative, subjunctive, and conditional inflections, as they were presented in section 4, allows us to account for their distribution. The investigation is conducted within the context of the sentential complement construction following the negative form of *penser* 'think', because all three inflections frequently occur in the subordinate clause in this context. The data for this section consists of 142 examples from AFP articles.

Verbs of propositional attitude code the conceptualizer's various degrees of confidence toward the presence in reality of the event in the complement. *Penser* illustrates the inclination stage of the control cycle (see section 4.3), where the conceptualizer's opinion about the presence of the proposition in reality is beginning to take shape. In the positive form, the proposition is viewed as a likely candidate for insertion into reality (Achard 1998: chapter 6). The indicative constitutes the only possible choice because the proposition needs a putative address in reality in order to be located there. The negative form indicates that the conceptualizer is leaning toward a rejection of the conceptualized event as part of reality. The mood on the subordinate verb reflects alternative ways of expressing her denial. The presence of the indicative inflection conforms to the analysis presented in section 4. Because the conceptualizer produces some epistemic effort to assess the reality of the complement process, the latter can be construed as a proposition, even though it is eventually rejected. The two other moods signal competing construals. The subjunctive indicates that the conceptualizer treats the complement process as an event that may or will probably not occur. This is reminiscent of the situation with volition verbs.[18] Finally, the complement content can be considered as an alternative to reality, in which case the conditional represents the preferred choice.[19]

In the contexts where these three construals are possible, all three inflections can occur on the subordinate verb, as illustrated in (35):

(35) *Le chef de la diplomatie égyptienne Amr Moussa a estimé vendredi à Londres que "Israël et les pays arabes étaient sur une voie solide" en saluant le "pas historique vers un nouveau Proche Orient" accompli avec les récents accords palestino-israéliens. "C'est une voie à sens unique et je ne **pense** pas que l'on **puisse** [pourrait/pourra] revenir sur ce qui a été accompli", a-t-il dit à l'Institut royal des affaires internationals...*
'In London, the leader of Egyptian diplomacy Amr Moussa said on Friday that "Israel and the Arab countries were on a promising path" when he saluted the "historical step toward a new Middle East" taken through the recent agreements between Palestine and Israel. "It is a one-way street and I do not think that we could come back on what has been accomplished", he said at the Royal Institute for International Affairs.'

In (35), in addition to the attested subjunctive (in bold), a conditional (*pourrait*), or a future (*pourra*) would be felicitous. Such examples should serve to outline the necessarily limited scope of our investigation. Mood selection is first and foremost a matter of construal, and its ultimate motivation is simply speaker's choice. The parameters of that choice are particularly difficult to pin down accurately because it is impossible to conceive of all the reasons that might factor in the selection of a particular inflection. Fortunately, however, mood selection is not random. The observation of the data reveals regular patterns where specific contexts tend to favor consistent mood choices. Because these contexts match up well with the meaning of the inflections presented in section 4, these patterns provide useful insights into some of the conditions that favor specific construals. For expository purposes, these conditions are grouped into three broad categories. It should be noted, however, that inflectional choice often partakes of a more general communicative strategy that can only be made explicit with the presentation of sufficient context. The examples in this section are therefore somewhat longer than the norm.

5.1. Reality is known

The indicative mood is expectedly favored when the communicative purpose of the complement clause is to describe a known facet of reality. This is clearly the case when the subordinate process occurred or is scheduled to occur at a particular point in time. There are nine such cases attested in the corpus.[20] This is illustrated in (36) and (37):

(36) *L'annulation d'une visite de l'empereur japonais Akihito au mémorial de Pearl Harbor (Hawaï) pendant son voyage en juin aux Etats-Unis provoque des réactions houleuses au Japon, certains n'hésitant pas à critiquer ce qu'ils considèrent comme une embarassante gaffe diplomatique. Ni le ministère des Affaires étrangères, ni la maison impériale n'ont confirmé cette annulation, mais la presse japonaise avait largement fait état jeudi d'une décision qui résulterait des nombreuses critiques sur le bien-fondé d'un tel déplacement de la part de celui qui reste le symbole du Japon. "Pour commencer, je ne **pense** pas que l'empereur **devait** visiter (Pearl Harbor). Mais une fois la décision prise de réaliser cette visite, elles (les autorités japonaises) auraient dû aller jusqu'au bout", a commenté vendredi Osamu Kuno, un philosophe et critique du militarisme japonais.*

'The cancellation of a visit by the Japanese Emperor Akihito to the Pearl Harbor Memorial (Hawaii) during his June trip to the United States provoked a stormy reaction in Japan, where some people were highly critical of what they consider an embarrassing diplomatic faux-pas. Neither the Foreign Affairs Department nor the Imperial House have confirmed the cancellation, but the Japanese press published numerous comments about the decision that triggered widespread criticism about the felicity of such a visit by the person who remains the symbol of Japan. "To start with, I do not think that the Emperor had to visit (Pearl Harbor). But once the decision was made, they (the Japanese authorities) should have gone ahead with the visit", said Osamu Kuno, a philosopher and opponent to Japanese militarism, on Friday.'

(37) *La Russie a récemment fortement relevé ses droits de douane pour les produits estoniens, alors que les discussions entre les deux pays sur le retrait des troupes russes sont dans l'impasse. M. Kozyrev a déclaré que les russophones ne devaient pas s'attendre à un soutien financier de la Russie "qui a assez de problèmes" et les a exhortés à privatiser leurs appartements et les entreprises. Il a écouté les griefs des anciens combattants, dont l'un, invalide de guerre, s'est plaint de ne pas bénéficier des avantages, notamment médicaux, dont jouissent les vétérans en Russie. Après avoir écouté les explications de "Andreï Vladimirovitch" la plupart des participants exprimaient une certaine déception. "Je ne **pense** pas que Moscou nous **aidera**, mais il est bien que la question de la minorité russe soit sur l'agenda des conférences internationales", a estimé Boris, ex-officier de 66 ans qui s'est refusé à donner son nom de famille.*
'Recently Russia strongly increased its custom taxes on Estonian products, at a time when the discussions between the two countries about the withdrawal of the Russian troops have reached an impasse. Mr. Kozyrev declared that the Russian minority should not expect any financial help from Russia, "which has enough problems", and incited them to privatize their apartments and companies. He listened to the woes of the veterans, including a war invalid who complained that he did not benefit from the same advantages that other veterans enjoyed in Russia, especially in the medical domain. After listening to "Andreï Vladimirovitch's" explanations, most of the participants were rather disappointed. "I do not think that Russia will help us, but it is positive for the question of the Russian minority to be debated at international conferences", said Boris, a 66-year-old former officer who declined to give his last name.'

In (36), the indicative is preferred because the tense predications it contains indicate that the specific instance of the process under discussion (the emperor's visit to Pearl Harbor) occurred at a precise moment in the past. The use of the subjunctive (*doive*) would yield a general statement that could not be directly related to the recent visit. The presence of the conditional (*devrait*) would indicate that, although a visit has been planned, it has not taken place yet. The indicative is clearly the only possible choice to indicate that reality includes a specific proposition which the speaker disagrees with. In such cases, the meaning of *Je ne pense pas* 'I do not think' is close to that of 'I do not agree'.

The same kind of analysis accounts for the example in (37). Kozyrev's speech allows the audience to predict Russia's forthcoming attitude toward them. The expected help clearly belongs in the future. Here again, only the indicative is capable of locating the proposition in the complement clause in projected reality. The presence of the subjunctive would create two ambiguous readings. In the first (closest to the attested one), the speaker expresses doubts towards the future occurrence of the helping event. In the second one, he questions Russian assistance in general, including possible current help. The use of the conditional would indicate that the aid is subject to unspecified conditions.

In a different, though related, type of situation (five cases in the corpus), the speaker expresses her reaction (or the lack thereof) to an event that occurred in the past. Even though this event did take place, the speaker failed to recognize its reality at the time. The construction provides a commentary after the fact, where unfolding events force the speaker to reconsider the position she held at a previous point in time. These cases are illustrated in (38) and (39):

(38) *Un collègue de l'auteur présumé des coups de feu tirés samedi contre la Maison Blanche a affirmé mardi dans une interview à une agence de presse américaine que Francisco Duran lui avait confié qu'il avait un plan pour assassiner le président Bill Clinton. "Il venait fréquemment chez moi et il me racontait comment il pensait avoir été floué par le gouvernement et par-*

*lait d'assassiner le président. Je ne **pensais** pas qu'il **était** sérieux"*, *a ajouté David Millis, 20 ans, dans un entretien réalisé dans le Colorado où Duran travaillait.*

'During an interview with an American press agency on Tuesday, a colleague of the person who allegedly fired shots at the White House on Saturday claimed that Francisco Duran told him he had a plan to assassinate President Bill Clinton. "He often came to my house, and he told me how he was cheated by the government, and was talking about assassinating the president. I did not think he was serious", David Mills, 20, added in an interview he gave in Colorado, where Duran worked.'

(39) *"Samedi on s'est laissé surprendre, il y avait des tireurs partout, sur les toits, dans les maison, ça tirait de toutes parts et on ne savait pas où riposter", explique Aslambeg, la trentaine. "Je ne **pensais** pas que Doudaïev **avait** tant de monde, il nous faut absolument plus de forces, plus d'armes."*

'"On Saturday, they caught us by surprise, there were snipers everywhere, on the roofs, in the houses, there was shooting everywhere and we did not know where to fire back", explained Aslambeg, approximately thirty years old. "I did not think that Doudaïev had so many people, we absolutely need more firepower, more weapons."'

In the examples in (38) and (39), the meaning of *je ne pensais pas* 'I did not think' could be paraphrased as 'I did not realize'. The speakers are confronted with moments of past reality they held false beliefs about. These errors in judgment were revealed when unexpected events directly contradicted their beliefs. The speakers reexamine their past beliefs in the new light of unforeseen developments. The indicative mood obviously represents the preferred choice to code the event in the complement, because the occurrence of that event is by now well attested.

The examples in (38) and (39) can be compared to other situations that describe erroneous predictions made in the past. In those cases, the conditional represents the only possible choice. This is illustrated in (40):

(40) *Parisien d'origine, cet agriculteur qui exporte ses géraniums vers la France et l'Allemagne vit, avec la visite du chef de l'OLP dans la bande de Gaza, "les jours les plus tristes et les plus humiliants" de son existence. Il s'est imposé un choix difficile: finir ses jours à Ganei Tal ou regagner la diaspora. "Je ne **pensais** pas que nous **serions** un jour contraints de vivre à nouveau dans un ghetto."*
'With the PLO leader's visit to the Gaza strip, this farmer, who is originally from Paris and exports geraniums to France and Germany, is living "the saddest and most humiliating days" of his life. His self-imposed choice is a difficult one: finish his days in Ganei Tal or rejoin the Diaspora. "I did not think that we would have to live in a ghetto again one day."'

The case in (40) is similar to the one presented in (34). Some time ago, the speaker made a prediction concerning his future life that has now been proven wrong. The presence of the conditional indicates that the complement content is presented as his prediction, and hence as an alternative to reality. The fact that this failed prediction now matches (an element of) reality emphasizes the surprising aspect of the conceptualized situation. The use of the subjunctive (*soyons*) would be possible, because it could indicate his disbelief in an event that should not have occurred, but it would not evoke the speaker's predictive effort.[21]

5.2. *Reality is interpreted*

The indicative mood is also favored when the speaker reacts to some conception of reality, although that conception is not established beyond controversy (six cases). The examples in (41) and (42) illustrate cases where speakers disagree with the interpretation of reality they are presented with. In these examples, the meaning of *penser* is close to that of *croire* 'believe':

(41) *Le président Bill Clinton a applaudi vendredi "l'action rapide et déterminée" du président Jean Bertrand Aristide après l'assassinat mardi d'une opposante haïtienne, affirmant qu'il fallait attendre les résultats de l'enquête avant d'accuser qui que ce soit. Pour sa part, M. Aristide a répété qu'il ne **pensait** pas que son ministre de l'Intérieur Mondésir Beaubrun **était** impliqué dans l'assassinat de cette opposante, Me Mireille Durocher-Bertin.*
'On Friday, President Bill Clinton praised "the fast and determined action" of President Jean Bertrand Aristide following the assassination on Tuesday of a Haitian opponent, saying that we should wait for the results of the investigation before accusing anyone. For his part, Mr. Aristide repeated that he did not think that his Secretary of Internal Affairs Mondésir Beaubrun was implicated in the assassination of this opponent, Ms Mireille Durocher-Bertin.'

(42) *Le président croate Franjo Tudjman en sort militairement et politiquement renforcé. La "capitale" des Serbes sécessionnistes de Krajina, Knin, est à sa portée, quatre ans après le soulèvement serbe qui a débouché sur la guerre et la proclamation unilatérale d'une "république serbe de Krajina" ("RSK"), sur environ 25% du territoire de la Croatie. Proportion ramenée aujourd'hui à 20% après plusieurs actions "éclairs" de l'armée croate. Contrairement à l'ONU à Sarajevo, les commentateurs militaires à Posuje ne **pensent** pas que M. Tudjman **marchera** directement sur Knin, qui coupe le principal axe routier et ferroviaire nord-sud, entre Zagreb et la côte dalmate.*
'The Croatian president Franjo Tudjman's position is strengthened from a military and political standpoint. The "capital" of the Krajina separatist Serbs, Knin, is within his reach, four years after the Serb uprising that led to war and the unilateral

proclamation of a "Serb Republic of Krajina" ("KSR") on approximately 25% of Croatian territory. This proportion was reduced to 20% after several "special operations" by the Croatian army. Unlike the UN in Sarajevo, military commentators in Posuje do not think that M. Tudjman will march on Knin directly, despite its position on the North-South main road and rail axis between Zagreb and the Dalmatian coast.'

In examples such as (41) and (42), the way in which events have unfolded allowed some observers to present specific facts as real (the Ministry of the Interior is responsible for murder; M. Tudjman will invade Knin). The speaker expresses her disagreement with this interpretation of reality. The indicative represents the preferred choice, because the speaker reacts to the model of reality currently under discussion. Her denial directly addresses specific aspects of that model that are presented as such. The communicative purpose of the utterances is not so much to present the speakers' versions of the facts, but to record their reaction to the interpretation that is presented to them.

In other cases (four instances in the corpus), the subordinate event makes reference to a carefully arranged sequence of events such as a schedule or an agenda, respectively illustrated in (43) and (44):

(43) *Américains et Japonais se retrouveront samedi pour la troisième journée consécutive afin de tenter de trouver les moyens de réamorcer leurs négociations commerciales suspendues depuis février dernier. Après un peu moins de trois heures de discussions vendredi, M. Bowman Cutter, conseiller du président Clinton pour la politique économique, a déclaré à la presse: "nous nous rencontrerons encore demain matin." ... Selon le conseiller de M. Clinton, les discussions qui avaient débuté jeudi matin étaient terminées pour la journée de vendredi. "Je ne **pense** pas que nous nous **rencontrerons** de nouveau aujourd'hui", a dit M. Cutter.*
'Americans and Japanese will meet on Saturday for the third day in a row to attempt to find the means to reopen their trade

talks interrupted since February. After a little less than three hours of talks on Friday, Mr. Bowman Cutter, an economic policy adviser to President Clinton, told the press: "we will meet again tomorrow morning." ... According to Mr. Clinton's advisor, the discussions that had started on Thursday morning were finished for Friday. "I do not think that we will meet again today", Mr. Cutter said.'

(44) *Une réunion au niveau ministériel de la quadrilatérale (Etats-Unis, Japon, Canada, Union européenne) aura lieu en septembre à Los Angeles (Etats-Unis), a indiqué mardi un porte-parole de la Commission. La date définitive n'a pas encore été fixée, a-t-on précisé de même source. ... L'ordre du jour de la réunion n'a pas encore été définitivement arrêté mais les grands thèmes seront l'état des ratifications de l'Uruguay Round par les membres du Gatt, les questions laissées en suspens lors de la conclusion de cet accord (services, transports maritimes, aéronautique) et l'accession de la Chine au Gatt, a-t-on précisé de même source. ... Le porte-parole de la Commission a indiqué qu'il ne **pensait** pas que ce point **figurait** à l'ordre du jour de la réunion mais que chaque pays participant pouvait y évoquer des sujets particuliers.*

'A meeting of the Secretaries of State of the four countries (United States, Japan, Canada, European Union) will take place in September in Los Angeles (United States), a spokesperson for the commission announced on Tuesday. The date has not yet been set, said the same source. ... The agenda for the meeting is not finalized, but the main themes will be the state of the ratification of the Uruguay Round by the Gatt members, the issues tabled when this agreement was signed (services, transport by sea, airline industries) and China's membership to the Gatt, the same source said. The commission's spokesperson indicated that he did not think that this point was on the agenda for the meeting, but that each participant could bring up specific issues.'

The meetings discussed in (43) and (44) have been carefully planned. The organizational tools that structure them (schedule or agenda) constitute a specific interpretation of their reality. Consequently, the preferred way of describing any aspect of that organization is to construe the relevant event as a proposition, that is to say an element of that organized reality. It is also noteworthy that in such official contexts, the invocation of upcoming events as part of a well-established schedule constitutes a way for the speaker to avoid any personal interpretation of the events. Because schedules and agendas are usually established jointly by all the participants, any reference to their structure cannot be perceived as the speaker's own view of reality.

Finally, the indicative is obviously favored when the speaker wants to present her own views as part of reality, even though their status may be controversial. These cases (five in the corpus) are illustrated in (45) and (46):

(45) *Le Premier ministre d'Australie Paul Keating, quelques heures avant son départ pour l'Europe où il doit assister aux cérémonies du Débarquement, a créé l'émotion au Parlement de Canberra jeudi en déclarant à nouveau que l'Union Jack britannique devrait être retiré du drapeau australien. ... "Je ne **pense** pas que les symboles et représentations de la souveraineté de la nation australienne **pourront** jamais être entiers tant que nous aurons le drapeau d'un autre pays dans le coin de notre drapeau" a répondu le Premier ministre.*
'The Australian Prime Minister Paul Keating triggered an emotional response at the Canberra Parliament, a few hours before his departure to Europe where he will be attending the D-day ceremonies, when he declared again that the British Union Jack had to be removed from the Australian flag. ... "I do not think that the symbols and representations of the sovereignty of the Australian nation will ever be complete as long as we have another country's flag in the corner of our flag" the Prime Minister answered.'

(46) *John Holum, directeur de l'Agence américaine de désarmement et de contrôle des armements, a de son côté rappelé que pour les Etats-Unis, il était inconcevable d'imposer une date à Israël, tant que le principal allié américain dans la région "reste entouré d'un certain nombre de pays qui ne **pensent** pas qu'Israël a le droit d'exister".*
'John Holum, the director of the American Agency for the disarmament and the control of weapons, stated that for the United States, it was inconceivable to impose a date on Israel as long as the Americans' main ally in the region "remains surrounded by a certain number of countries that do not think Israel has the right to exist".'

The speakers in (45) and (46) are emotionally committed to the reality of the event in the complement. The presence of the indicative on the subordinate verb represents a way of strengthening their positions. In (45), the Prime Minister's strategy is to state that a favorable outcome cannot be reached as long as the Australian flag is not changed. By establishing the least favorable outcome as part of predicted reality until the change is made, he underlines the necessity for change. In (46), the American position clearly favors Israel, as evidenced by the use of the phrase *le principal allié américain dans la région* 'the main American ally in the region'. The American world view therefore obviously contains the proposition *Israel a le droit d'exister* 'Israel has the right to exist'. The use of the indicative in the complement clause represents an additional way of making this position explicit.[22]

5.3. Characteristics of the immediate context

In addition to the cases where reality is well established or presented as such, some semantic characteristics of the subordinate clause also motivate the choice of mood inflection. This section presents three such cases.

The subjunctive is strongly favored when the complement clause has a generic value (five instances in the corpus). In some cases, this value is enhanced by the presence of an indefinite subject as shown in (47):

(47) *"Nous avons commémoré en couverture chaque anniversaire du Débarquement depuis 1949", explique Daniel Okrent, rédacteur en chef du magazine. "Je ne **pense** pas que qui que ce soit **ait** quelque chose de neuf à dire par rapport à nous", ajoute-t-il.*
'"We have celebrated each anniversary of D-day on our front page since 1949", Daniel Okrent, the editor of the magazine, explained. "I do not think that anyone has anything new to say compared to us", he added.'

The presence of the subjunctive in (42) is congruent with its semantic function. It was pointed out in section 4 that the indicative inflection presents a fully grounded instance of a process type. It is uniquely identifiable, in a way similar to a definite nominal (Langacker 1991). A subjunctive clause is not uniquely identifiable because it does not have a putative address in reality. In Achard (1998), I argue that the subjunctive designates an arbitrary instance of a process type conjured up to fulfill a specific purpose. The subjunctive inflection therefore performs a semantic function similar to the indefinite article in predicate nominal constructions (*John is a doctor*), generic uses (*A cat is a mammal*), or the nonreferential reading in opaque contexts (*John wants to marry a blonde*) (Langacker 1991). The use of the subjunctive in (47) is clearly consistent with its semantic function. The communicative purpose of the clause is not to locate a specific proposition that describes the event in the complement, but to deny the possible existence of such proposition. The strategy used to achieve that goal matches up an indefinite subject with a virtual instance of the type *quelque chose de neuf à dire* 'something new to say', to show that the complement content cannot possibly be located in reality.

The examples in (48) and (49) also emphasize the generic value of the complement clause:

(48) *Le nouveau président noir sud-africain Nelson Mandela restera "au moins cinq ans au pouvoir", mais ensuite "je ne **pense** pas que ce **soit** raisonnable, pour un homme de 80 ans, de continuer à exercer un mandat politique", a-t-il affirmé dans un entretien.*
'The black South-African president Nelson Mandela will remain "at least five years in power", but then "I do not think that it is reasonable for an 80-year-old man to continue to hold political office", he declared in an interview.'

(49) *La proclamation de l'état d'urgence par Emile Jonassaint, le président provisoire d'Haïti (non reconnu par la communauté internationale), n'aura aucun effet selon William Gray, conseiller spécial de la Maison Blanche pour Haïti ... "Je ne **pense** pas qu'un discours prononcé à deux heures du matin par un gouvernement fantoche **ait** une signification quelconque surtout quand les deux tiers du pays ont voté pour le président Aristide", a ajouté M. Gray.*
'The declaration of a state of emergency by Emile Jonassaint, Haiti's temporary president (not recognized by the international community), will have no effect according to William Gray, special advisor to the White House for Haiti ... "I do not think that a speech made at 2 a.m. by a government no one recognizes has any significance especially when two thirds of the country voted for President Aristide", M. Gray added.'

In both (48) and (49), the situation presented in the subordinate clause is specific. In (48), it refers to Mandela himself staying in power. In (49), the speech in question is clearly Jonassaint's. However, both situations are presented with a broader meaning. The statement in (48) is presented as true for all 80-year-old men, and the one in (49) applies to all similar instances of political discourse. The statements thus have a generic value. That generic value combined with the negative form of the main verb provides strong motivation for the subjunctive inflection. Since no instance of the type considered could be part of reality, the specific situation under consideration cannot possibly be real.

Interestingly, note that when a specific instance deviates from the expected norm, the indicative inflection is often preferred, as illustrated in (50):

(50) *Quant à Alexander Muller, il est libre pour l'instant. Mais son cas sera soumis au procureur de l'Etat. "Dans l'absolu, un tel délit peut entraîner un maximum de 15 ans de prison. Mais je ne **pense** pas que ce **sera** le cas", a déclaré le sergent Holloway.*
'As to Alexander Muller, he is free for the moment, but his file will be forwarded to the state's Attorney General. "In theory, such a crime carries a maximum sentence of 15 years. But I do not think it will be the case with him", Sergeant Holloway declared.'

The preceding context provides a long description of the specifics of Muller's case. This helps the reader to distinguish between his situation and similar instances of the same type. The presence of the indicative indicates that the circumstances of the case allow the police sergeant to predict the future with confidence. This obviously helps set the case apart from other similar ones.

Finally, in six instances, the presence of the future auxiliary *aller* 'go' in the complement clause correlates with the presence of the indicative. This is illustrated in (51):

(51) *Abbas Kiarostami ne **pense** pas que leur passage devant la caméra **va** troubler leur vie: "ils sont tellement loin du monde du cinéma, de tout ça", dit-il en montrant la Croisette "que ça ne va pas les perturber."*
'Abbas Kiarostami does not think that their appearance in front of the camera will disrupt their life: "they are so far removed

from the world of the movies, from all this", he said, pointing at the Croisette "that it will not disturb them."'

Because the future modal value of *aller* 'go' directly conflicts with the meaning of the other inflections, it can obviously only be observed in the indicative. The presence of a subjunctive or conditional would yield a nonmodal, directional sense. Note that this distribution is clearly imputable to the nature of *aller*'s modal value, and not simply to the presence of a modal, because other nontemporal modals such as *pouvoir* 'can' are perfectly acceptable in the subjunctive or the conditional, as the example in (35) attests.

The different patterns isolated in this section provide evidence that mood selection is indeed determined by the construal of the conceptualized scene. The only chance of evaluating construal lies in the careful investigation of the immediate context of mood selection. We can therefore assume that consistent contexts reflect consistent construals. The key point for the purposes of this paper is that the situations in which specific moods are systematically selected are highly consistent (although more specific), with their meaning presented in section 4. These contexts therefore also provide evidence for the validity of those meanings. They clearly establish them among the panoply of tools speakers use to express their communicative strategies. These strategies include a careful selection of lexical items and constructions, among which mood inflections find their rightful place.

6. Recapitulation and conclusion

The goal of this paper was to investigate the meaning and distribution of the indicative, conditional, and subjunctive inflections in French. These three grounding predications were shown to allow the speaker and hearer to assess the epistemic status of an event coded in a clause.

An indicative clause indicates that the conceptualized event is reported as a proposition. As such, it codes the epistemic effort required to establish the event's putative location in elaborated reality. The tense predications provide that location. When the verb is marked in the subjunctive, the conceptualized event is viewed at the level of basic reality. The occurrence of the event is considered with respect to a specific mental space separate from reality. The presence of the conditional inflection establishes the conceptualized event as an alternative to reality.

The meaning of the three inflections has also been shown to account for their distribution in discourse. The patterns of regularity observed in the data clearly show that construal is not random, and that even though it may not be fully predictive, it can nonetheless be valuably invoked to describe the distribution of mood inflections.

Notes

1. The reasons for the analysis of the conditional as a specific mood rather than a tense of the indicative will be explained in sections 3.4 and 4.7.
2. Because the meaning of the person category is not primarily epistemic, an alternative analysis could treat it, not as a grounding predication per se, but as parasitic on mood (and possibly tense) predications. The analysis of mood markers presented in this paper is, however, largely independent from a specific account of person, and I will leave the matter for future research.
3. Tense predications also often carry aspectual values (Wilmet 1997). This issue is, however, beyond the scope of this paper.
4. In addition to these three personal moods, French also has two impersonal moods. Because the infinitive and participial moods do not include grounding predications, they will not be considered here.
5. The fact that upon its emergence in Roman the conditional gradually took over a significant number of the functions previously covered by the subjunctive (Brunot 1936) also argues in favor of its analysis as a mood.
6. This statement is not intended as an exhaustive description of these two tenses. For a thorough description of the different senses of the *imparfait*, see De Mulder and Vetters (this volume).
7. In this case, conceptual control can be viewed as a specific case of abstract possession. The relation that exists between concrete and abstract possession can be analyzed in several compatible ways. Some researchers invoke the metaphor of "knowing is owning" (Reddy 1979; Lakoff and Johnson 1980; Lakoff 1987). In Langacker (2001), both concrete and abstract possession rep-

resent specific implementations of a very general and ubiquitous cognitive model called the "mental control cycle". Both analyses are compatible with the solution proposed in this paper.

8. A confirmation that the presence of the indicative inflection is motivated by the conceptualizer's epistemic effort is provided by the cases where this effort is absent. Consider the following examples:
   (i) *Il se peut/Il arrive/Il est possible qu'il soit malade* (SUBJ).
   'It is possible/it happens that he is sick.'
   The examples in (i) differ from the ones in (17) because they merely present the knowledge that an event might occur, rather than the effort to ascertain its epistemic status. The presence of the subjunctive reflects this absence of effort.

9. This definition represents a refinement over the one I proposed in Achard (1998), but it is perfectly compatible with it. In particular, it attempts to clarify the importance of the notion of dominion while removing some of the regrettable confusion the (1998) formulation might have produced. In Achard (1998) I claim that the presence of the indicative inflection indicates that the conceptualized event is part of a conceptualizer's dominion, that is to say considered with respect to elaborated reality. In this paper, the term dominion is reserved for a conceptualizer's conception of elaborated reality. The two uses of the terms are not, however, incompatible. One can legitimately consider the set of propositions that a person attempts to evaluate with respect to reality (at every stage of the cycle) as a higher-level dominion. It is in this sense that the term is used in the (1998) analysis.

10. This mixed status of emotional reaction verbs is reflected both diachronically and cross-linguistically. In Old French, the indicative was possible following verbs of emotional reaction. In Spanish and Romanian, the subjunctive and indicative moods are in competition in this context.

11. This parallel is corroborated by the placement of the perfect marker in the main and adverbial clause in (5a) and (9a), respectively. It is located in the adverbial clause in (5a), whereas it is in the main clause in (9a).

12. It is important to bear in mind that the choice of grammatical constructions is greatly a matter of social conventions. For example, it is perfectly possible to construe the subordinate event as a proposition in (9), because the dynamic structure of reality allows us to predict future events with reasonable confidence. For example, the English translation 'I will leave before he comes back' presents 'he comes back' as a proposition. However, in the global French ecology that includes the subjunctive inflection, that construal is not favored.

13. James (1986: 479) points out the restrictive nature of English *if* clauses in the following way: "The subordinate conjunction "if" in conditional sentences can be described semantically as an instruction to let the apodosis stand under

the right circumstances, which are when the conditions contained in the protasis are met."
14. In some limiting cases, the protasis is treated as a mere afterthought. The communicative purpose of the utterance rests solely on the expected outcome. This is illustrated in (i):
(i) *L'Américain Pete Sampras a été gâté. Opposé d'entrée à un qualifié, le Numéro 1 mondial, s'il s'impose, rencontrera le vainqueur d'une rencontre entre deux qualifiés.*
'The American Pete Sampras was lucky. The world's Number 1 will play a qualifier in the first round and take on, if he wins, the winner of a match between two qualifiers.'
The communicative goal of the passage is to present an overview of the player's trajectory in the initial stages of the tournament. The event in the *si* clause is not viewed as an obstacle to overcome. Sampras is clearly expected to win. *S'il s'impose* 'if he wins' is presented as a mere technicality that reminds the reader of the conditions necessary for players to advance in the draw.
15. The use of the *imparfait* to describe a possible path of reality is fully consistent with the other modal senses of this tense. In particular, it seems very close to the "suggestive" meaning illustrated in *Et si on allait au cinéma?* 'What if we went to the movies?'. For an analysis that reconciles the modal and temporal (past referential) senses of the *imparfait*, see De Mulder and Vetters (this volume).
16. The presence of the present/future construction would also be possible. Its use would indicate greater optimism on the speaker's part that the right measures will indeed be taken.
17. The term is found in several grammars. For a useful discussion of its meaning in Guillaume's "Psychomechanics" model, see Hewson (1997: 107–110).
18. The close relation that exists between the subjunctive and negation is insightfully discussed in Wierzbicka (1988).
19. Unlike the subjunctive, the conditional is also felicitous following *penser* in the positive form, as in *Je pense qu'il viendrait (s'il avait une voiture)* 'I think he would come (if he had a car)'. The analysis presented in section 4.7 accounts for those cases.
20. The numbers given in this section do not claim to provide any real statistical value. They simply show that the described situations do constitute consistent semantic islands where construal is systematic. Importantly, only one mood is attested within each pattern.
21. Note that the *imparfait* is infelicitous in this context. This is due to the presence of *un jour* 'one day', which enforces a dissociation between the time of the prediction and that of the unfortunate outcome.

22. The fact that the original quote is most likely a translation is not problematic for the analysis presented here. Obviously, the speaker is not responsible for this mood choice, since English does not present the same alternatives. However, the translator's choice is equally interesting, and it is her decision that is evaluated here.

References

Achard, Michel
    1998   *Representation of Cognitive Structures: Syntax and Semantics of French Complements*. Berlin: Mouton de Gruyter.

Brunot, Ferdinand
    1905   *Histoire de la langue française des origines à 1900*, Volume 1. Paris: Colin.
    1936   *La pensée et la langue*. Paris: Masson.

Comrie, Bernard
    1976   *Aspect*. Cambridge: Cambridge University Press.

Dancygier, Barbara
    1993   Interpreting conditionals: Time, knowledge, and causation. *Journal of Pragmatics* 19: 403–434.

De Mulder, Walter and Carl Vetters
    this vol.   The French *imparfait*, determiners and grounding.

Guillaume, Gustave
    1929   *Temps et verbe*. Paris: Champion.

Hewson, John
    1997   *The Cognitive System of the French Verb*. Amsterdam: John Benjamins.

James, Francis
    1986   Semantics and pragmatics of the word *if*. *Journal of Pragmatics* 10: 453–480.

Lakoff, George
    1987   *Women, Fire, and Dangerous Things: What Categories Reveal about the Mind*. Chicago: University of Chicago Press.

Lakoff, George and Mark Johnson
    1980   *Metaphors We Live By*. Chicago: University of Chicago Press.

Langacker, Ronald W.
    1987   *Foundations of Cognitive Grammar*, Volume 1: *Theoretical Prerequisites*. Stanford: Stanford University Press.
    1991   *Foundations of Cognitive Grammar*, Volume 2: *Descriptive Application*. Stanford: Stanford University Press.

1993   Reference-point constructions. *Cognitive Linguistics* 4: 1–38.
2001   The control cycle: Why grammar is a matter of life and death. Manuscript.

Moignet, Gérard
1981   *Systématique de la langue française*. Paris: Klincksieck.

Reddy, Michael
1979   The conduit metaphor: A case of frame conflict in our language about language. In: Andrew Ortony (ed.), *Metaphor and Thought*, 284–324. Cambridge, MA: Cambridge University Press.

Sumnicht, Anne
2001   A cognitive perspective on negative raising. Manuscript.

Wilmet, Marc
1997   *Grammaire critique du français*. Louvain-la-Neuve: Duculot.

Wierzbicka, Anna
1988   *The Semantics of Grammar*. Amsterdam: John Benjamins.

The English present

Frank Brisard

1. Introduction[1]

English[2] presents a peculiar case, particularly in comparison with some of its closer siblings in the Germanic family, when it comes to the formation of present-time expressions at the verb level, or rather to the way in which these expressions divide the labor of referring to states of affairs that are simultaneous with the time of speaking. It makes use of two distinct morphological paradigms, either of which is common enough, typologically speaking, in its own right and serves semantic functions that can be found throughout the world's languages. The so-called simple present (henceforth indicated as "present tense") constitutes one of the two (inflectional) tenses that characterize the verb paradigm in English and that roughly contrast with each other in terms of "coincidence with" vs. "anteriority to" the time of speaking. The progressive variant is a periphrastic form that may occur in all three of the time frames — past, present, and (the *shall/will*) future — and generally denotes the ongoingness or continued duration of a state of affairs. However, it is the distribution of these two constructions within the context of referring to the present that generates a number of more idiosyncratic properties. Crucially, these properties cannot be studied in isolation for each of both constructions but need to be seen in relation to one another, with one construction clearly marking the semantic boundaries of the other.

In languages like Dutch and German, the present progressive, which is relatively isomorphic in structure to its counterpart in English, comes across as a rather marked way of locating states of affairs in the present, because it almost always implies a very strong sense of duration. In contrast, this aspectual component need not always be present in English, notably in instances where a certain class of verbs takes the present progressive by default, i.e., because using these verbs in the present tense would, barring a restricted number of special contexts, make them hard or even impossible to interpret. This extremely sharp fissure is thus not a matter of free variation or stylistic preference but defines the very grammaticality of sentences that incorporate a reference to the present moment. It seems, then, that *perfective* verbs like *learn/write/study/recite/copy* obligatorily take the present progressive as a default form and that, when they do, no intimation of any type of temporal progression is necessarily being conveyed. This is not the case for *imperfective* verbs like *know/like/understand/see/have*, which are typically set in the present tense and have the possibility of using the progressive construction if a durational, repetitive, etc. meaning needs to be explicitly indicated.

Langacker (1991: 262–269) proposes a "naïve" and minimal picture of the meaning of the present tense, in which the notion of (full) coincidence with the time of speaking constitutes the sole defining feature. More specifically, according to this purely temporal characterization the present tense in English is seen as consistently indicating *the occurrence of a full instantiation of the profiled process that precisely coincides with the time of speaking*. At first blush, this definition appears to stay within the boundaries of more traditional conceptions of the present tense (and of tense in general), which treat tense predications as grammatical markers of temporal locations and posit one-to-one correspondences between the tenses' basic meanings and the temporal frames that their nomenclatures betray — "present" for the present tense, "past" for the past tense, etc. (for a classic example of this "localist" approach to tense, see Comrie 1985). However, the emphasis in Cognitive Grammar on a strict correlation between the beginning and end of a profiled process and the boundaries of the speech event in which this process is expressed, substantially transforms the temporal basis of such an approach. In fact, it suggests a view of tense meaning that can readily be integrated into an "elaborated epistemic model" of tense and modality (Langacker 1991: 240–249). Langacker uses the definition of the present tense to explain why an imperfective verb can always occur in the present tense whereas a perfective one, at least if it is to express the mere "presentness" of a process, cannot. To motivate this distributional fact, the property of (im)perfectivity is directly related to the objective scene or *immediate scope* of a predication, which, in the case of the present tense, is restricted to that portion of reality whose temporal profile coincides with the speech event (the ground). In contexts where a speaker wishes to say something about a current state of affairs, an imperfective verb like *know* can always take the present tense because any instance of 'knowing' represents a full instantiation of the process type designated by that verb. Consequently, the requirement that a full instantiation coincide exactly with the boundaries of the speech event is clearly met in the case of imperfectives. With a perfective verb like *learn*, on the other hand, the bounded process that constitutes its semantic pole should be taken in its entirety and be made to coincide exactly with the speech event, such that the resulting configuration yields the "one instance right now" interpretation said to typify the present tense. Mostly for pragmatic reasons, this interpretation generally does not come about (Langacker 1991: 251). More recently, Langacker (1999c, 1999d, 2001, 2002) has radicalized his earlier ideas on the temporal basis for a unified characterization of the semantics of the present tense. In these publications, Langacker is examining the consequences of maintaining his view against the backdrop of the blatant observation that time (i.c., the "present") cannot uniquely and exhaustively be called in to cover the whole meaning range of that tense in English. The problem of perfectivity in relation to the present tense is more explicitly cut up into a "durational" (temporal) and an "epistemic" component. In Langacker (2001), the situation for perfective verbs that are to be located in the present is described in terms of a "pragmatic unlikelihood": on the temporal side, there exists no intrinsic connection between the length of the profiled process and that of the speech event, while an epistemic perspective reveals that a speaker cannot generally both observe and identify/describe an event at the very same time.

Although the epistemic problem of naming an unfolding event *in situ* is obviously associated with certain temporal restrictions, no explicit attempt is made to conceive of these two aspects as manifestations of a common underlying principle, which, if formulated in a more abstract way, might succeed in reading the temporal constraint as one (and only one) of its realizations. Instead, the stringent temporal criterion of exact coincidence is exploited further to account for uses of the present tense where a designated process, whether perfectively or imperfectively construed, is not located in the present at all. Cases of "futurate" uses of the present tense (referring to scheduled activities in the future), as well as stage directions, photo captions, and generic utterances are all treated as invoking the conception of a *virtual plane* onto which representations of events that are not (yet) actualized in reality (more specifically, in the present itself) are projected. It is these (fictive/mental) representations that are said to coincide exactly with the time of speaking, allowing the straightforward application of the temporal constraint that holds for clear-cut present-time uses of the present tense. Now, while this analysis manages to capture all of the possible usage contexts in which the present tense occurs, I suggest that its heavy emphasis on temporal constructs slightly obscures the fundamental contribution of modal values to that tense's meaning. The epistemic hallmark of the present tense, for one, which almost invariably reveals a high degree of *certainty*, is neither motivated nor acknowledged as one of its structural semantic qualities (but see the final note in Langacker 2001).

In what follows, I will momentarily suspend the function of "temporal coincidence" as a notion that is needed to arrive at a satisfactory account of the use of the present tense in English, in order to concentrate more on its modal foundations. This move necessitates a "resistance" to make use of certain constructs advanced in the Cognitive Grammar analysis of the present tense, even if it does not imply an outright rejection of that analysis. I agree with Langacker's proposals insofar as they illustrate the various detailed mental operations that need to be assumed for a sense of "epistemic certainty" to arise in the first place. Nevertheless, I do not want to start from the strictly temporal premises that are proposed for prototypical, present-time uses of the present tense, because I would like to show that an epistemic approach yields more schematic and ultimately more basic analytical constructs while still managing to cover the whole range of usage types for the present tense. So the analysis will have to start from scratch, as it were, and not assume the type of "one instance right now" meaning that Cognitive Grammar adopts, if only to attempt to close the circle and exclusively work with nontemporal concepts. This also means that, at least for the sake of argumentation, I cannot accept certain implications that would follow from Langacker's own discussion of noncanonical usage types (e.g., that the epistemic judgment that is identified for those uses, including the context of virtual occurrences, is necessarily coincident with the time of speaking). Within the general category of tense predication, epistemic meanings will thus be identified as the basic schematic frames to which all (temporal, modal, and other) usages must conform. For the present tense, this entails that the idea of *immediate apprehension* provides the analytical starting point for a truly epistemic approach that is both comprehensive and unified and that ultimately respects Cognitive Grammar's commitment to the epistemic nature of grounding. In the end, both Langacker's and my own approach offer some attempts, if formulated from diverging angles, to explicate the various ways in which nonpresent occurrences can nonetheless be available for immediate apprehension, and in that sense they are clearly complementary.

2. A temporal perspective

2.1. (Im)perfectivity

Consider the following examples:[3]

(1) *Fran is getting up right now.*
(2) **Fran gets up right now.*
(3) *Fran gets up at 8 o'clock.*
(4) *Fran is never getting up on time (lately).*

The process designated by *get up* can be characterized, in the terminology of Cognitive Grammar, as perfective, which means that it profiles a bounded process that can be punctual or of limited duration.[4] A perfective verb usually features a dynamic, as opposed to static, state of affairs whose beginning and end are by necessity included within the profile determining the verb's semantics. (Typically, these two extremities limiting the temporal contour of a perfective verb also remain fairly contiguous in "real" time.) If the bold section of the timeline in Figure 1 represents the time of speaking, a perfective verb may only select the present tense if its own profile (the bold wavy line) coincides *exactly* with the profiled interval of the timeline. In real-life situations involving *actual* occurrences of states of affairs, this rarely happens, since we must generally first observe what is happening before we can describe it. Thus, I must first see and interpret a singular, nonrepetitive instance of Fran's getting up — including the beginning and end of that action — before I can utter (1) (but not 2). The difference, then, between the simple and the progressive variant of the present tense is not only aspectual, with the first situation being viewed as incomplete and the second as complete. It is also directly related to the meaning of this tense. While it may not discriminate by itself between verbs with differing *Aktionsart* (perfective vs. imperfective), the complete coincidence of a verb's profile and that of the speech situation is generally reserved for imperfective processes, due to largely pragmatic effects of how the world is conceptually organized and how this organization can be brought to bear on its linguistic expression.

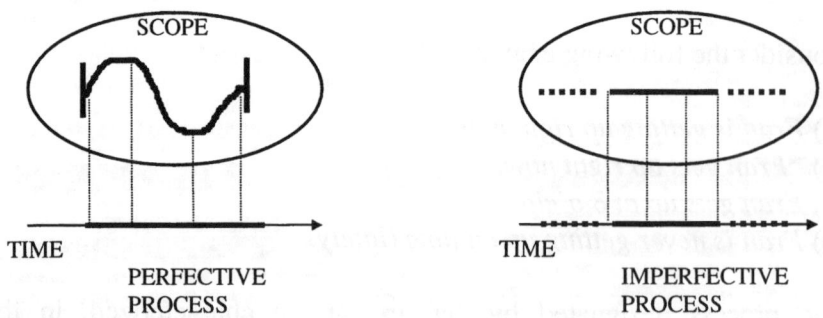

Figure 1. Perfective and imperfective construal (Langacker 1987: 261)

In English, perfective processes take the progressive form when the speaker wants to express that the activity in question is to be interpreted as more or less coinciding with the time of speaking (hence, the adverb *now* in example 1). For imperfective verbs, the opposite generally holds. They take the present tense when a state of affairs (prototypically, a state) is expressed that coincides with the time of speaking. Moreover, again with respect to perfective processes, *habitual* construals of a state of affairs may license the use of the present tense, as exemplified in sentence (3). Yet this is not a matter that can reliably be attributed to the effects of a type of sentence "operator", as a similar habitual context, with or without a temporal adverb limiting the relevant time stretch in which the process is to hold (cf. sentence 4), may sanction the progressive form as well. In this case, the additional qualification is one of temporary validity, if the temporal profile of the process in question is the focus of attention, or, in contexts where a strong emotional investment is indicated, of irritation or some other negative emotion. (The same connotations are also relevant, by the way, for imperfective verbs that may occur in the progressive form.)

This explanation of the correlation between predication type (perfective/imperfective) and aspectual form (progressive vs. simple) is colored by the theoretical orientation adopted in Cognitive Grammar with respect to tense. The semantics of the present-tense morpheme is characterized as follows: "PRES indicates the occurrence of a full instantiation of the profiled process that precisely coincides with the time of speaking" (Langacker 1991: 250). From the argumentation put forward here, we should then conclude that it is the requirement that a "full instantiation", as opposed to any partial one, is to coincide with the present which is the crucial element in this definition. This is precisely the reason why perfective processes, which are of limited duration but whose occurrence can almost never be taken to coincide exactly with the time of speaking, do not sanction the present tense under normal circumstances, whereas imperfective processes, for which the same requirement holds, can bypass this condition, so to speak, by relying upon the property of contractibility (cf. Langacker 1991: 251–252). In other words, the motivation for sanctioning a simple or progressive form in the present is *deictic* in origin, in the sense of taking the ground or time of speaking (the deictic *origo*) as the absolute basis for deciding which form to select. Nevertheless, based on the behavior of habituals in the present (more specifically, of those marked by the present tense, as in 3), it might be argued that more is at issue than the purely deictic concern with exact coincidence. The distinction between tense and aspect cannot exclusively relate to the superimposition of a processual profile onto the time of speaking. For habituals, the function of the present tense is clearly not just a deictic one. Instead, when the present tense is used to denote a habit, matters of temporal location (situating a state of affairs as simultaneous with the present) seem to be combined with aspectual concerns of iteration. When both functions of a tense are taken into account, as I will attempt here, the result does not have to be a hybrid explanatory model in which, depending on context, deictic and aspectual meanings are more or less arbitrarily distributed over the progressive and the simple form. In fact, such an account might well yield a picture in which both the present-tense morpheme and that of the progressive contribute their own specific, altogether rather fixed, schematic meanings to the constructions in which they figure as a whole.

2.2. "One instance right now"

Let us accept Langacker's characterization of why perfective verbs cannot occur in the present tense without engendering some "special" reading, while imperfective verbs can, and use it as an analytical starting point. Generalizing the "one instance right now" explanation (Langacker 1991: 252), we can examine why it is that only imperfective verbs, at least under normal conditions, seem to satisfy this stringent criterion. In Figure 2, "OS" indicates the *objective scene* or immediate scope of a verb predication. It includes the (temporal) region that constitutes the focus of a predication's meaning as its unique profile.

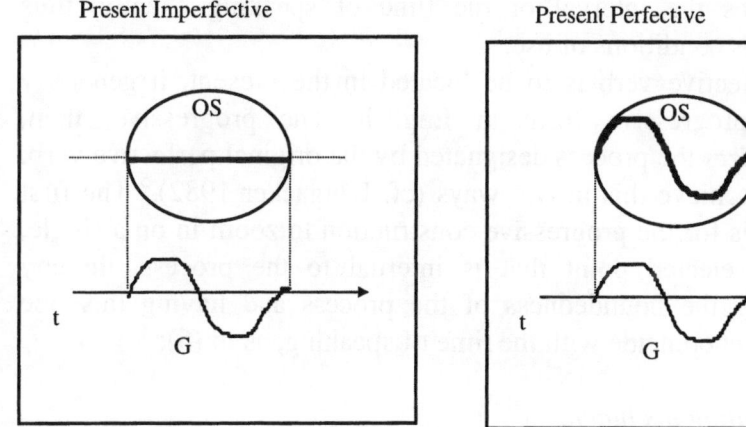

Figure 2. The present tense (Langacker 1991: 251)

A profile is that part of a predication's configuration that is actually designated. For perfective verbs like *get up*, the OS is constituted by all of the phases which, taken together, form the process of 'getting up', i.e., including the very start of the act up to what is considered its terminal point, the point beyond which one can no longer speak of 'getting up'. It is also the totality of these phases, viewed as taking place in immediate reality ("now"), that needs to coincide exactly with the speech event if a present tense is to be used. The ground ("G") stands for the speech event and occupies a limited interval in time, which is precisely why it generally precludes present-tense instances of perfective verbs: "The duration of an event is seldom equal to that of an utterance describing it, and perfectives lack the property of contractibility (hence the entire event — including its endpoints — must be profiled for it to count as a full instantiation of the process type)." (Langacker 1991: 251–252) For imperfectives, the precise coincidence of a verb's profile and the time of speaking is not a problem, since any component state that happens to coincide with the ground will do as a full instantiation of the process in its entirety. For instance, as each interval of knowing counts as a full-fledged instance of the process (type) 'know', the present tense selects one that matches the interval of the time of speaking exactly, thus satisfying its conditions of use.

If a perfective verb is to be located in the present, it generally adopts a progressive form in English. The progressive, then, *imperfectivizes* the process designated by the original perfective verb, and it can achieve this in two ways (cf. Langacker 1982).[5] The first possibility is for the progressive construction to zoom in on a single, arbitrarily selected point that is internal to the process, thereby disregarding the boundedness of the process and having this one focused point coincide with the time of speaking, as in (5):

(5) *Joe is eating his lunch.*
(6) *Sally's blinking.*

In this case, the imperfectivization involved simply narrows the focus of attention (or takes an internal perspective on a homogeneously construed process), up to the point where the boundaries of the originally perfective process become locally irrelevant, i.e., they are no longer in focus. Alternatively, for an expression like (6), the punctual character of the described process practically precludes this first option. The imperfectivizing construal involved in (6) is different, insofar as the progressive form now indicates quick repetitions of the same event. This replication, in turn, allows an internal perspective like the one adopted for nonpunctual perfectives and thus also has the process coincide exactly with the time of speaking. It is understood that the replication of perfective processes in the course of imperfectivization generates a *higher-order temporal relationship* (i.e., for the purpose of expressing the "present" location of a perfective, the indefinite replication of that bounded process constitutes a unit in its own right). In both cases, Cognitive Grammar posits the *derivation* of an imperfective process from a perfective one, as signaled by the progressive form.

Finally, this account of the differential effect which the progressive form has on imperfective and perfective processes needs to be complemented with one that centers on the notion of *structured-world knowledge* (Langacker 1991: 263–266), as an analytical tool for dealing with the interpretation of perfective verbs in the present tense. If perfective verbs do not take the present tense because the full coincidence of a designated process and the time of speaking is a matter of fairly exceptional circumstances, then an additional mechanism must be assumed which would warrant the use of the present tense for such verbs in *general-validity* contexts. This mechanism, then, is motivated by Goldsmith & Woisetschlaeger's (1982) discussion of *structural* and *phenomenal* knowledge types, an epistemological distinction which differentiates between structural (substantial) and incidental (accidental) properties of the world and of events happening in it. Two rather different types of knowledge about the world are distinguished according to which level of a description is focused upon: "One may describe the world in either of two ways: by describing what things happen in the world, or by describing how the world is made that such things may happen in it." (Goldsmith & Woisetschlaeger 1982: 80) In this light, Cognitive Grammar claims that habitual constructions such as illustrated in example (3), though formally marked by the present tense, actually express another higher-order, imperfective process, any instantiation of which is regarded as representing the process as a whole — a derivation which makes a seemingly perfective verb eligible for a present-tense construal.[6] This would then sanction the occurrence of such a perfective verb in the present tense without abandoning a definition of the present tense that hinges on the crucially temporal notion of "full coincidence". In general, the interpretation of this "derived" verb, designating an imperfective process, focuses on "the continuation through time of the stable situation in which the process type in question is part of the world's structure" (Langacker 1991: 265). It is to be read concretely as rendering someone's habit, a generic property of the physical world (as in scientific, law-like statements), or even more abstract postulates regarding the type of universe we claim to inhabit (e.g., in mathematical or logical expressions using the so-called timeless present). We will see in section 3.2 that this analysis underwent a few changes that have slightly shifted the focus from these original derivational mechanisms to the postulation of multiple planes of representation.

3. An epistemic stance

While the gist of the argumentation presented above is certainly one I would agree with, certain qualifications can still be made. For one, Cognitive Grammar's postulation of an imperfective process (whether obtained through zero derivation or through projection onto a virtual plane) for general-validity expressions in fact equates the structural force of such statements with the notion of "imperfectivity". But the same work could be done by having a truly perfective process adopt a present-tense meaning that readily accommodates interpretations of general validity directly, i.e., by locating the habitual or generic meaning in the interaction between an original verb form and a (nontemporal) tense meaning. In reserving the term "structural" for the meaning of the tense proper, instead of using it only for the kinds of generalization involved in generics and habituals in particular, I am in effect broadening its range of application. I suggest, in this respect, that the concern with "structuration", as a manifestation of the category of structural knowledge, is qualitatively distinct from (yet obviously compatible with) the type of "generalization" that is relevant to general-validity statements, and that it is only the first phenomenon that can arguably be assumed to function as the basic meaning of a tense predication.

For a simple illustration, consider the following examples, taken from Langacker (2002):

(7) *The triathletes ran along the coast for several miles.*
(7') *The triathletes run along the coast for several miles.*
(8) *These mountains run along the coast for several miles.*

In (7), involving a past context, an individual dynamic process is being presented that is objectively construed in the sense of being wholly onstage. Interestingly, the same sentence cannot take the present tense if the state of affairs is construed as coinciding with the time of speaking. Instead, the progressive is called for then, as in *The triathletes are running along the coast (for several miles)*. A present-tense variant on this same example (7') would have to be interpreted as conveying something like the planned route that the triathletes are supposed to take, which is not conceivable as involving one specific (physical) event in time. It is, rather, a more or less stable situation that somehow indicates what is perceived as a piece of structural knowledge (at a very local level, of course), just like in example (8), where the position of the mountain range vis-à-vis the coastline is pretty much treated as a (noncontingent) given, too. Therefore, if we attribute a semantics to the tense predication per se that might account for the emergence of aspects of stability and structure in the meanings of these constructions, then the *interpretation* of "general validity" comes from the interaction between the construal of a perfective process and the structural quality of the present tense itself. This approach should unify the analysis of present-tense perfectives and imperfectives as it proposes that the present tense *directly* conveys a structuring quality, but at the same time it leaves room for subtle differences in how this interpretation comes about for both predication types. In the case of a present-tense perfective, there is little else than general validity that the structural construal of a perfective process can evoke, whereas present-tense imperfectives, by virtue of their intrinsically stable profile, may lead to any level of structural interpretation (from extremely local to general), depending on their contextually defined scope (see section 3.2). And so *run*, a perfective verb in the context of (7), acquires a more stable, less "objective" meaning in (7') because of what the present tense does. I am not denying the imperfective character of that same verb in (8), but there the imperfectivity is lexically, rather than grammatically, motivated and is not called in just to deal with the effects of one grammatical predication (tense) on the construction of the scene as a whole.

Instead of emphasizing the purely temporal functions of the present tense, I will rather propose that it is primarily concerned with a degree of *immediate* ("present") *givenness* that warrants the attribution of epistemic certainty to a state of affairs. As a phenomenological category, such immediate certainty, it might be argued, can only be observed in two cases. When an event is expressed that is to be seen as present, either the speaker reports on what is directly perceived by her and thus automatically assumed to be wholly given, or she relies upon her knowledge of the structure of the world and divides statements into those which are in full accordance with it and those which are not (i.e., only partially so, or only inferentially so, etc.). Clearly, the first category (of direct perception) is of little use by itself for any concrete analysis of the English present tense, for both perfective and imperfective processes can be directly perceived while still receiving a differentiated treatment in terms of their tense assignment. Therefore, what is needed for those cases where something is directly reported is an additional condition which states that the process in question must also, at least if the present tense is selected, meet the demands imposed by one's knowledge of the world's structure (what is given, presumably — or ideally — for both speaker and hearer). These terms, "givenness" and "immediacy/presence", will thus provide the basis for an epistemic account of tense meaning in English, and in particular of the meaning of the present tense. It should be capable of explaining those prototypical (present-time) uses of the present tense that traditional temporal analyses of this category are able to explain. In addition, however, it should account for the (many) uses that fall outside such a temporal scope, either because they are typically described as secondary "connotations" (Comrie 1985) that do not instantiate the "true" meaning of the present tense and thus need to be derived in some way or other, or because they are simply discarded as relevant objects of study, as in the case of (many varieties of) tense logic and a host of other, semi-logical treatments (e.g., Allen 1966).

3.1. Immediate certainty

I want to arrive at a characterization of the English present tense which combines the epistemic status of knowledge coming from perception (the only possible source for the acquisition of experience and, for that matter, one that is to be exclusively located in the present) and the type of generic knowledge which is generally formulated in terms of timeless, gnomic statements. I will suggest that the present tense typically calls upon these two modes of experience (perception and generality) and that, accordingly, it accommodates two basic types of meaning. Immediate certainty is attained in cases where a state of affairs is either directly present (in time) or just always present (out of time, as a structural part of our model of reality).

The link with the present tense's primary function, as the most *unmediated* way of referring to the ground, is straightforward in this respect. The ground (and thus any reference to it) constitutes, in a phenomenological sense (Husserl 1970; see also Habermas 1998), the background of our thematic knowledge and is therefore always, if implicitly, present at a pre-reflective stage. This implies that the ground does not merely consist of the spatio-temporal (empirically verified) relations holding at the time of speaking, but that it must also include those elements of our rational conception of reality which are held to be generally valid, or given. In this sense, the present tense's dual function reflects the privileged status of the ground as both the locus of direct experience and the container of general knowledge, which will evolve with us through time as a continually updated and always negotiable repertoire of known or anticipated information. Experientially, the ground keeps the contingency in check of new input coming in (through perception) at any moment in time, and it does so through proximity to experience.[7] Using certainties that we obtain from personal experience or through the cultural transmission of knowledge, the ground erects a firewall against *surprises* (Peirce 1934), critical experiences that could render the background character of the ground problematic. This is why surprises (i.e., experiences that cannot directly be anticipated on the basis of what we know about reality) are not expressed by using the present tense, which focuses on those statements whose epistemic status is essentially compatible with the background character of the ground. Instead, such surprises, which we constantly encounter in our dealings with reality and which are thus not so rare as the dramatic epithet bestowed upon them would suggest, will be indicated, in English, by the progressive form of the present. The present progressive is concerned with contingent states of affairs that may not fundamentally alter our model of the world but do not exactly follow from it in a predictable way either. Compared with the background status of present-tense meanings, then, the present progressive typically presents a state of affairs that is the object of direct perception (i.e., located in the present and therefore potentially perceivable by an observer — not necessarily the speaker, though — at the time of speaking) as relatively *foregrounded* precisely by virtue of its incidental status with respect to the ground as an epistemic background. What belongs to the ground, in other words, is unmarked (the *simple* present), and what does not belong there is marked, also morphologically (the progressive). The latter category comprises events that just happen to occur at some present time but could not actually have been foreseen, which represents an overwhelming majority of events that are actualized in reality. At any given moment, surprises are thus momentarily included in the ground but do not constitute it.

Let us approach the problem of temporality from another angle, i.e., in terms of the conceptualization work needed to arrive at a phenomenology of temporal categories or frames. If the meaning of the present itself, as an experiential category, had to be put in terms of the notions of "givenness" and "immediacy", the question would need to focus on what the combination of these two factors yields that the past, which is to be considered as comprising some type of givenness as well, does not. A preliminary answer could be formulated as follows. Knowledge is construed as immediately given either through direct perception or through some less direct mode of knowledge acquisition (e.g., cultural transmission, logical deduction, etc.) that is nonetheless construed as generating equally strong and warrantable epistemic judgments. When we produce or interpret a predication expressing an immediately given process, as the present tense seems to do in English, this mode of knowledge effectively attributes to the expression in question the status of a structural statement, i.e., one which is not essentially contingent or dependent on contextual factors. Thus, the present tense, expressing the immediately given by virtue of its association with the experiential present as a temporal category, imposes an additional constraint (i.e., on top of mere temporal location) upon its conditions of use, specifying that a designated event needs to be construed as *justifiably* belonging to the present. Here, the present is not just another temporal moment, but it is construed as that critical point in time, concurrent with the perspective of the ground, up to which all previous events (the past) are expected to lead on the basis of some (mostly unspecified or vague) general model of the world. Expressions that take the present tense must be constituted by this, and only this, particular conception of the present. It is, in other words, not enough that the states of affairs they refer to simply coincide with the time of speaking.

In order to schematize the relation between grammatical form (i.e., tense) and the conceptual category that the form is referring to (i.e., time), we might take recourse to the following formulations:

PRESENT TIME: "present" (or "immediate"), "given"
PRESENT TENSE: "given", "necessary" (i.e., "necessarily now" or noncontingent)

The present tense, then, borrows from its notional counterpart, the temporal frame of the present, the fundamental idea of "immediate givenness". Based on the facts of present-tense usage in English, this notion is interpreted in a fairly specific way, viz., as selecting only that type of information which can reasonably be construed as conforming to the speaker's (or rather, a speech community's) view of the essential properties of the world. Thus, states of affairs that are objectively situated in the present (as a very short interval in which a clause or utterance can be produced) correspond to such a characterization, provided that they also exhibit the quality of being constitutive of the world at that time. Conversely, expressions of states of affairs that are not part of the present may yet take the present tense, but only if their conceptual representation co-constitutes the ground, even if, referentially speaking, they belong to the past or even the future. (It is not so hard to see how, in cognitive terms, the future can be *constitutive* of a present state of mind, or of a conception of the present world's structure. The case of scheduled future activities, whose scheduling has necessarily taken place before the moment of their actualization, illustrates convincingly how real such representations can be in the mind of a present speaker and how they could, accordingly, influence the structure of a world that exists before they do, thus conforming to the constraint given here for the use of the present tense. See also section 3.3, as well as Kochańska, this volume.)

What is traditionally regarded as the prototypical use of the present tense (its designation of states of affairs occurring in the present) can now be revealed for what it really is, i.e., one manifestation, among many others, of the schematic characterization provided above. At the same time, we manage to include a notion of necessity into the description of tense usage, resuscitating the old idea that tense semantics might have something to do with modality after all. In line with this modal orientation in the analysis of tense meaning, the notion of immediacy can be slightly reinterpreted as well. While it retains the idea of proximity that is certainly at work in cutting up the conceptual space reserved for tense (with the past tense indicating a departure from the ground, or "distance"), the analysis does not essentially hinge on the spatial metaphor that is lying behind the use of these terms. Rather, "immediacy" refers primarily to the unmediated character of the knowledge that is expressed when using the present tense. Again, temporal proximity is one obvious correlate of this category, but not the only one.

3.2. Scope building

The first problem we have to tackle in advancing an epistemic account of tense meaning in Cognitive Grammar can be illustrated in a straightforward way. Let us look at example (9):

(9) *Your keys are on the table.*

Given this example, we should ask what is *structural* about it. Apparently, it makes no claims of "structural knowledge" that go beyond the very local context in which such an utterance might be produced. The answer to this problem is much less straightforward.

First of all, we are of course dealing with an imperfective process here. This implies that we need not worry about imperfectivizing procedures at this point. An intrinsically imperfective process, such as indicated by the verb *be*, is stable in its own right. And it is therefore directly compatible with at least one aspect of the meaning of the present tense, specifying that a designated process is seen as more or less constant through time. But the use of the present tense also requires that the process be seen as part of the ground, i.e., as representing a structural aspect of reality. This is much harder to imagine for an expression like (9). What we need in addition to the specified tense meaning, then, is a pool of devices that allows the language user to indicate or reconstruct the particular *scope* in which a (tensed) statement is taken to hold. Scope is a technical term in Cognitive Grammar and refers to the "stage" or general locus of attention in a predication. As a matter of definition, a (lexical) predication's profile is onstage and objectively construed as the primary focus of attention within that expression's immediate scope (see also Langacker 1999a). By contrast, the ground and the grounding relation are offstage and construed subjectively. The grounding relation represents a certain way of "viewing" the focused entity onstage (i.e., within the immediate scope). The specific nature of that viewing constitutes the grounding relation, which is what distinguishes one grounding predication from another (Langacker 1999c).

Let us now assume that the immediate scope for the present tense is defined in an epistemic, not a temporal, domain, and that this scope can be "built" in a variety of ways, involving both its reduction and its extension, possibly into infinity. The viewing relation involved specifies an epistemic assessment of the content verb's profile, viz., one of immediate certainty, as well as its range of application, as indicated by the tense's scope. As to the concrete interpretation of this mechanism, we might state that the tense predication consistently profiles the process designated by the content verb but offers varying ways of construing the (maximal or minimal) ground to which this profile is related. What seems to happen in example (9) is that the tense predication's immediate scope gets restricted to the actual profile of the grounded process and thus coincides with it. The absolute validity of the present state of affairs in (9), in terms of its immediate givenness, is indeed asserted but does not transcend the local speech situation in which that sentence is uttered. This is what one might expect from a present-tense construal of at least some imperfective processes, which come in many varieties, including instances that designate very local or temporary processes. Imperfectivity is therefore not simply synonymous with something like "timeless stability" but is rather a matter of construing a process, whether point-like or eternal, in a certain way. Besides, the idea that imperfectivity involves more, or other, factors than the mere homogeneity and temporal stability of a process can also be inferred from observing the semantics of truly imperfective processes that are "imperfectivized" by means of the progressive construction. In those cases, the local character of the scope imposed by the present tense is retained for the auxiliary, but the *-ing* form adds a connotation of nontypicality (always in relation to the ground). To be sure, this is difficult to realize for sentences like (9), because there it would be hard to grasp how a typical state of 'being on the table' might differ from a nontypical one, as far as keys are concerned.[8] But consider sentence (10), involving the attribution of a property to an animate (human) subject:

(10) *You're being silly.*

Here, the imperfectivization effected by the *-ing* form is not simply redundant, which it would be if that process were exclusively defined in terms of temporal unboundedness.[9] It suggests, for one, that the behavior predicated of the subject is not what one would expect, given what is known about the subject, but that it constitutes something of a surprise. We will see, furthermore, that this line of reasoning can be made analogous to what happens with a perfective verb in the progressive. Note that expressions of a specific subclass of the type "*be*+adjective", despite their implication of a certain measure of volitional control (typical of perfectives), are still treated as real imperfectives in the present description, because the intended interpretation actually generalizes over any kind of processual predication that might figure in the construction, not just these "pseudo-imperfectives".[10] In short, if perfective verbs that take the progressive form convey a meaning of contingency, i.e., the direct opposite of the stable, structuring relations reserved for the present tense, so do imperfective ones in the present progressive.

For a sentence like (11) below, which might be uttered in the context of a paranormal experiment, Langacker (2001) argues that the originally perfective verb *move* is imperfectivized by means of the participial -*ing* form attached to it. That is how perfective verbs designating an actual state of affairs in the present are generally treated, and their derived imperfective status then allows a portion of the resulting process to coincide exactly with the time of speaking, as required in Cognitive Grammar. Yet the actual construal involved in the "present" participle, one might argue, is, again, not so much of a temporal but of an epistemic nature. Thus, for all tense purposes, the imperfective auxiliary *be* behaves just like in example (9) and it has the same restriction of scope that is typical of such momentary events as 'being on the table' or '(being) moving'. It is the participial verb form, in contrast with its bare infinitive and finite counterparts, that takes care of the epistemic modulation characterizing the English progressive construction as a whole. Because it seems that in English "progressive" is once more something of a misnomer for a marker that, in many of its uses, refers rather to notions like contingency and incompleteness, which are decidedly more epistemic in nature than the mere absence of temporal bounding, or than the temporal quality of "ongoingness" traditionally ascribed to this form (Goossens 1994). Thus, only insofar as the idea of imperfectivity is compatible with such epistemic qualifications can the perfective stem of a progressive form be said to really imperfectivize. Imperfectivization then implies that the process at issue is construed as *nonconstitutive* of the ground, a description which would at least fit prototypical progressive forms of perfective verbs, where often (observations of) very transitory events are described that are unpredictable from the "timeless" perspective of the ground — surprises, as in (11):

(11) *Your keys are moving on the table.*
(12) *Sally is tall.*
(13) *The Earth is round.*

Thus, while the expression of perfective processes located in the present seems to favor the progressive construction (as an indication of their generally ephemeral nature), English treats imperfective processes that might be as momentarily or contingently belonging to the present differently, with the present tense attributing a structural quality to them that holds within a limited scope (as in 9). The reason for this distinct treatment probably lies in the realization that imperfectives, as a verb class, tend to profile more stable qualities, which is a matter of construal, and some aspect of this property is bound to be retained in their tense-related behavior. Notice now that, if the present tense were used in example (11), the sentence would have to be interpreted in a subtly different way. We can imagine a situation where the speaker is supremely confident in the reality of paranormal phenomena and is merely waiting for a confirmation of her beliefs, which constitute the local ground for her. In that sense, a present-tense use would not function as a description of whatever happens to "impress" the speaker at the time of speaking, but rather as an affirmation of what she already knows to be the case, even if what is the case has not yet been actualized: *See? Your keys move on the table. I told you they would...* This use of the present tense would thus call for an analysis that pays more attention to how the speaker presents a situation (i.e., as a surprise or a given). We will see in section 3.4 that the speaker's *attitude* towards (the epistemic status of) a description determines many of the nontemporal uses of the present tense.

The situations in (9–11) represent a limiting case of present-tense construal. (At this point, I'm including 10 and 11 only with respect to the tensed auxiliary figuring in these statements.) Many other imperfective verbs, however, may lead to statements whose validity does transcend the situation of speech, as in (12). The relevant cues triggering a widening of the tense's scope will be mainly lexical and contextual (taking into account the information that is contained in the whole of the clause, and not just in the verb form), and of course they are hard to formalize. Now, to obtain a clearer view of how scope building may work, let us examine a sentence like *During an interview she is quite relaxed*, describing a structural property of the subject that may not hold in every conceivable situation ('she' can be quite nervous on other occasions). Here, the scope builder is explicitly mentioned, such that the validity of this statement is lexically indicated as being limited to those portions of reality that may count as 'an interview'. Notice, in this respect, that such slices of reality need not be temporally continuous or contiguous at all. Similarly, if I say that *She keeps calm under pressure*, the prepositional phrase that functions as a scope builder indicates some more or less clearly defined region in semantic space, consisting of situation types which share a fairly abstract property that can be described as "causing stress in a person". If seen from a temporal perspective only, however, the actual situations instantiating this type would be randomly and unevenly distributed over time and, in analytical terms, they would not make up much of a scope to work with. Scope is therefore not an essentially temporal notion as far as tense meaning is concerned.

Next, a limiting case at the other extremity of the scale of epistemic validity is illustrated in (13). Here, the immediate scope is widened to include all of reality/time, and thus by definition also the ground. This present-tense use, then, is motivated by the same epistemic characteristics of the profiled process (i.e., immediate givenness), not because that process is (locally) construed to coincide with the ground, but because it is always coincident with it. The utterer of (13) does not need to perceive the situation she describes, because she naturally assumes that it holds at the time of speaking as a matter of culturally transmitted knowledge. Thus, in examples (9–13), an imperfective process, including the auxiliary *be*, directly sanctions the use of the present tense because it conforms with that tense's two conditions of use: givenness (i.e., its construal in terms of "reality") and immediacy, or the unmediated access to its epistemic status.

As noted previously, general-validity statements, including habituals and generic[11] sentences, make use of the same principles of construal and respect the semantic character of the present tense that is being presented here. But of course they come in two varieties: with imperfective verbs, as in (13), or with perfective ones, as in (14):[12]

(14) *John drinks heavily.*

Perfective generics and habituals receive a special treatment in Langacker's (2001) account of the present tense. There are some difficulties involved in this, though. First of all, it is unclear to me whether such present-tense perfectives are imperfectivized (through zero derivation), as was still claimed in Langacker (1991: 264). It seems that imperfectivization is no longer essential in current Cognitive Grammar accounts of general-validity statements in the present tense, but at least such a process would not go against the spirit of the new explanation in terms of "virtual entities", as diagrammed in Figure 3. When projected onto a virtual plane, 'John's drinking' may in fact be represented as a type that belongs to the structure of the world, in which case it might as well retain its perfective construal, or as a series of 'drinking' events whose very persistence through time may indicate their structural nature.[13] In the latter scenario, there is room for imperfectivization in the standard Cognitive Grammar sense. Next, regardless of whether or not the perfective process in (14) undergoes imperfectivization, the process in question is projected onto a plane representing structural aspects of the world, where it becomes a virtual (i.e., nonactual) entity. This should reflect the intuition that general-validity statements are not about individuated events but rather about generalizations pertaining to a number of similar events. This virtual entity thus effectively transforms the perfective process 'drink', which in other contexts refers to singular instances, into a specification "capturing what is common to an open-ended set of instantiations in actuality" (Langacker 1999d: 96).[14]

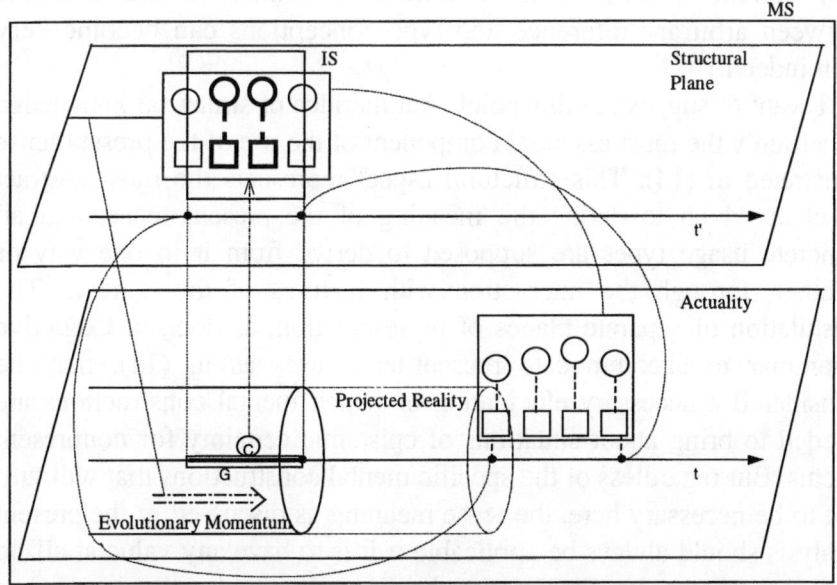

Figure 3. Virtual projection (C=conceptualizer; G=ground; t=conceived time in actuality; t'=conceived time in virtuality; IS=immediate scope; MS=maximal scope; adapted from Kochańska, this volume)

So, at least this type of virtual plane, a notion that Cognitive Grammar proposes to deal with other uses of the present tense (cf. section 3.2), may actually be said to comprise entities at a *type* level, which would represent one case where a grounding predication (i.e., the present tense) is interpreted as designating types instead of instances: if the immediate scope for a statement like (14) is seen as extending indefinitely (which would be another way of representing structural knowledge), then the process profiled in the statement will be *interpreted* as designating a type, because a type is what all instances of a given kind have in common within a set scope. Elsewhere, Langacker (2002) appears to redress this implication by suggesting that the fictive entities concerned are "arbitrary" instances of such (structural) types, and that the designation involved in the general-validity use of the present tense therefore still pertains to instances rather than types. (This line of reasoning follows some of the argumentation laid out for the analysis of the indefinite article and certain quantifiers in Cognitive Grammar, where the line between arbitrary reference and type conceptions can become very thin indeed.)[15]

I want to suggest, at this point, that the idea of structural knowledge is certainly the most essential component of the use of the present tense illustrated in (14). This structural aspect represents the most abstract level at which to define the meaning of the present tense, and all concrete usage types are supposed to derive from it in one way or another, through the interaction with features of the context. The postulation of separate planes of representation, as done in Cognitive Grammar to accommodate present-tense uses as in (14), may be considered a necessary elucidation of which mental constructions are needed to bring about situations of epistemic certainty for nonpresent events. But regardless of the specific mental constructions that will turn out to be necessary here, the tense meaning as discussed in the present analysis should always be applicable if it is to have any value at all. In addition, whether we characterize the representation involved in (14) as an arbitrary instance or as a true type, in the end both versions of the analysis will need to find a way of having that representation satisfy the epistemic criteria for using the present tense, since the generalization it expresses is always "now in force" or immediately given. Consequently, we might talk of this and similar uses of the present tense as not being referential at all. If a present-tense statement does not refer to any *actual* instance, the tense marker might still be said instead to project its usual epistemic qualification onto the process in question, only without triggering the search for a corresponding entity in (present) reality. It is in this sense that I would propose that these usage types (e.g., general-validity statements) are *extremely subjectified* (Langacker 2002), in any case more so than their straightforwardly referential present-time counterparts.

Extreme subjectification, in my eyes, does consist in the loss of an objectively construed entity (in time), i.e., it eliminates any direct concern with the occurrence of actual events. It could be said to happen as soon as the local scope of the speech event is even slightly transcended, including statements like (12). Yet it need not be assumed for each and every context that this loss of objectivity should be analytically recovered by multiplying (levels of) representations "outside time" or "within the conceptualizer", as it were. What seems to be common about most "nonprototypical", non-present-time uses of the present tense is that the semantic entity they conjure up inheres solely in the conceptualizing activity itself and thus no longer depends on any objective (let alone temporally coincident) "input" from the outside world. This *conceptual occurrence* of a state of affairs at the time of speaking does suffice to motivate the use of the present tense, and of course any piece of structural knowledge can be evoked at any given time by definition. However, once we establish the analytical relevance of such a conceptual occurrence, it is not the temporal unfolding of the "occurring" event that seems to matter, as a kind of mirror image of what may be happening (or the case), but the very fact that it can be evoked, i.e., its occurrence as a sign of its given epistemic status. The latter is an act of interpretation or categorization, not necessarily tied to any referential concerns and in particular not easily amenable to a kind of "internal perception/observation" of the mental event that would be "going on" at the time of speaking.

The usefulness of positing such internal perception is obvious in a model which stresses the strictly temporal conditions for using the present tense but disappears when we view the tense's meaning as essentially epistemic in nature. Concretely, in a generic utterance like *The Earth is round* (example 13), I find it intuitively strange to hold that the judgment of this utterance should occur "in the present". Rather, the judgment involved is a culturally transferred one that does not need to be replicated, as it were, every time a speaker decides to use that phrase (it is "given" in this sense). The judgment in this type of generic, and in other usage types like in (14), can be one that has been made in the past by some authority, possibly the speaker herself, and that is simply adopted without necessarily being "performed" over and over again. For other usage types (the more temporally oriented ones), it is undoubtedly true that some kind of epistemic judgment is necessarily linked to the time of speaking, but this does not automatically hold for every use of the present tense. And if the whole range of usage types is to be covered (if only schematically), something else is needed by way of analysis than the mere assumption of a temporal coincidence between the speech event and a profiled (objective or subjective) process. Even terms like "present" or "immediate", as defined in the present account, are not so much temporal notions as they point to the direct accessibility of the given status of a state of affairs within the ground, as opposed to a kind of mediated accessibility of its givenness (e.g., in the case of the past tense). Crucially, I do not discuss terms like givenness or immediacy in processing terms, and this may be the main difference with the standard account of the present tense in Cognitive Grammar.

Given the focus in this section on matters of scope (reduction or extension) to explain various uses of the present tense, I feel that the type/instance distinction informing grounding theory in Cognitive Grammar can be construed as epiphenomenal for a number of such predications, including certain uses of the present tense. What is perceived by the analyst as a type or instance specification of a state of affairs is ultimately a function of scope. In one limiting case (examples 9 through 11), the scope of the present tense marker actually coincides with the profile of the grounded process, which is then interpreted as indicating a state of affairs whose epistemic validity does not transcend the situation of speech. This represents what we might call an "instance". At the other extremity (examples 13–14), the scope coincides with reality and there is thus no one actual event that is focused upon. The representation involved in this kind of construal might be called a "type". This is not to say that the type quality is part of the meaning of the present tense, but that in certain general-validity contexts, for instance, it follows quite naturally from that meaning in combination with a perfective construal of the verb process. In instances where general-validity statements take the past tense or the (*shall/will*) future, the meaning is exactly one of "generality" without implying the kind of ground-constituting (or simply "grounding") force that typifies present-tense uses. The latter types of statement express a notion of general validity that is not, however, essentially tied to the speaker's conception of the ground; general validity in itself expresses more of an aspectual concern that has something to do with construing different instances over time and is thus by itself not conducive to any kind of structural interpretation (in the sense employed here). The conception of a type, I would say, emerges from the interaction between generalization (aspect) and structuration (tense) that is typical of some perfective present-tense uses, since in those cases they are not really "about" specific (actual or even virtual) instances of some process. This does not appear to pose much of a threat to the overall idea that grounding is about instantiating type conceptions, since the type interpretation that is at stake here emerges from an interaction and is therefore pragmatic, not part of the meaning of the present tense.

3.3. Space building

In discussing virtual planes, Langacker often refers to Fauconnier's (1994, 1997) "Mental Spaces" account of such phenomena as nonspecific reference in indefinite nominals, as in *I want to marry a princess who speaks five languages* (where 'the princess' at issue might not even exist). Here, *a princess* indicates a referent that is conjured up in a local context only, more specifically one that is constructed by the mental predication *want*. The main verb in that sentence can thus be considered a *space builder*, because it establishes a new space (not necessarily in reality), with new elements within them and relations holding between these elements. Insofar as this space is perceived as somehow removed from "reality", the process of space building differs from that of scope building. However, the principles involved, specifically in regard to tense meaning, remain the same.

If a statement is made that is not taken to hold in what the speech participants at one point interpret as reality, the process of scope reduction/extension will not suffice as a tool of analysis. Such statements can also take the present tense, and if we want to pursue a truly integrated analysis of this tense, it is mandatory that similar semantic and pragmatic mechanisms can be shown to be at work in these nonreal spaces, too, which may present their own grounds. Let us therefore look at some of the possible usage types that might call for an analysis in terms of space building:[16]

(15) *If the blood test is positive, he won't get a life insurance.*
(16) *(In this picture) Nixon says farewell from the steps of his helicopter.*
(17) *Tomorrow I take you to the zoo.*

The most clear-cut case is, of course, the conditional use of the present tense (15). When the present tense is used in a conditional subclause (the protasis), givenness is presented as a concept that can be interpreted relative to the internal structure of the hypothetical space that is created by the conditional context. The conditional construction as a whole should hence be seen as building this hypothetical space, in which a differentiation is made between protasis (setting up the premises for a type of inferential reasoning) and apodosis (presenting the conclusions drawn from these — and other, implicit — premises). In the protasis, then, the present tense indicates the conditional premises, which are given in a hypothetical context, i.e., the information in the subclause belongs to a hypothetical reality with respect to which information presented in the main clause is inferred and thus nongiven (hence, the "future" *will* form; cf. Brisard 1997). The epistemic status of the information expressed in the conditional is crucial for the characterization of the present tense appearing in it. A tense's referential value, as an indicator of temporal positioning, is of secondary or no importance for conditionals. But what matters most in our present discussion is the observation that the hypothetical space created by the conditional accommodates the epistemic status of the information presented therein, which will be construed as supplying a given background. In a way, the protasis creates the ground for the hypothetical space while it describes it, and any processual predication that figures in that ground (and thus constitutes it) will consequently take the present tense. (With past-tense or past-perfect protases, we might still describe the subclause as presenting a "ground" for the subsequent reasoning, but there additional qualifications need to be made — concerning the clause's epistemic status — which are linguistically expressed through the relevant morphological markings.)

Sentence (16) might have been a photo caption in a seventies newspaper. If the adverbial, *in this picture*, is explicitly added to it, it is this phrase which will function as a space builder, indicating the "world" in which an event is described as if it is taking place. So, although the event lies in the past with respect to the picture's time of publication, it sanctions the use of a present marker. Not just any marker, though, because in contrast with the expression of (perfective) events taking place now, the use of the present progressive would sound a bit odd in the context of a photo caption. The combinability of a perfective verb and the present tense thus suggests that the world described is not the actual one (though there is no doubt about its objectivity in the real past, of course), but one that subtly differs from it. A photo is an icon of past reality, a sort of lagged mirror, which thus inhabits its own space. In such contexts, the explicit marking of the space as separate from reality is not necessary, because the photo frame offers its own context and is thus in itself a kind of "builder", at a nonlinguistic yet decidedly semiotic level. With or without the prepositional phrase, sentence (16) therefore functions in the same way with respect to its use of the present tense. What this function ultimately comes down to, remains an issue to be discussed in the context of "current report" uses of the present tense (cf. section 3.4). Let me simply note at this point that it is precisely the framed character of the photographic world that is being negated through this tense use. We will therefore first need the presupposition of a separate space that is built for purposes of describing a photograph, in order to establish how the present tense comes to negate this very frame.

Finally, the futurate use of the present tense, as in (17), can, but need not, be explicitly signaled by a temporal adverb. This adverb builds the space of a "reality" that is, from an objective point of view, potential or projected,[17] but certainly not given as yet. Nevertheless, the use of the present tense suggests its givenness in a way that resembles what happens in the context of a paranormal "believer" (cf. the discussion of example 12) construing the givenness of a situation with respect to her own local (and perhaps idiosyncratic) expectations. The mere fact that the speaker selects the present tense in (17) indicates her absolute confidence or certainty. Symbolically, the event is treated as given and wholly constitutive of the ground, even though it has not taken, or will indeed never take, place. The notion of a fixed plan or schedule expresses this very attitude, whereby the future is not construed as uncertain and, instead of a prediction, a matter of fact is being stated. Other present forms, notably the progressive and *be going to* (Brisard 2001), may be used to refer to the future as well, though not quite in the futurate sense that is reserved for the present tense. In the case of the progressive, for instance, the *-ing* form indicates a degree of contingency in the projected state of affairs, and the prediction should thus be that the use of the progressive in future contexts will signal a lower degree of epistemic certainty (and, conversely, that the construction behaves more liberally with respect to temporally unqualified or less specific predictions; cf. note 17). I believe this prediction is confirmed by English usage conventions. Remark that, due to the strictly nonactualized character of a future state of affairs, we might still talk of a separate space being built (as the future, *qua* temporal category, is not seen as part of the ground), but the distinctions between "reality" and what is expected to become real in the (near) future are progressively blurred in these futurate contexts. At some point in the analysis, we will probably have to concede that scope and space building are an analyst's way of making sense of the attitudes that can be displayed in the process of "world making", and that the specific metaphysics involved in these analytical choices are not necessarily those of the language users exploiting this process.

3.4. Footing in "special" uses

The one unambiguous case where a present-tense perfective might actually be said to refer *directly* to an actual state of affairs that literally coincides with the time of speaking, is the performative use of certain (institutionally sanctioned) verbs. Interestingly, this very same case also represents the most clearly definable "horizon" (as a limiting notion) against which other usage types can be marked out.

In that sense, performative uses of the present tense should actually be considered central in the analysis, instead of being marginalized, as the tradition goes, because of their weak link with more canonical "descriptions" of reality. Let us then examine what happens in the following example:

(18) *I hereby pronounce you husband and wife.*

I would like to discuss this and other examples, including some that were introduced above, in terms of Goffman's (1974, 1979) notion of "frame analysis", focusing on the exploitation of participation statuses, or the social relation of a "member" vis-à-vis her utterance, and in particular on the alignment of *footing*. Indeed, the problem of performativity seems to call for such a reflexive turn in the analysis. Footing, in this context, is understood to be a procedure through which a speaker chooses to put herself onstage, so to speak, and presents that "figure" — a figure in a statement — as performing a certain role in the world that is spoken about. Such a description may be taken as building upon Langacker's (2001) observations regarding the "special" viewing arrangement that is involved here. Indeed, there is something distinctive about performative uses in the way of relating subjective and objective levels of conceptualization, which might be seen as a manifestation of the process of extreme subjectification that is posited for uses of the present tense that go beyond the mere location of a state of affairs in the present. I would also like to suggest at this point that something in the nature of managing "production formats", omnipresent and unavoidable, is probably going on in many, if not all, of the usage types that can be distinguished for the present tense.

In (18), the speaker might be seen to function objectively as a "principal", in a legalistic sense, i.e., "someone whose position is established by the words that are spoken, ... someone who has committed himself to what the words say" (Goffman 1979: 17). In the case of (18), it is obvious that by uttering the sentence the speaker is simultaneously claiming a particular social identity which sanctions the use of these particular words in a specific institutional setting. This is an essentially reflexive mechanism that has little to do with matters of temporal alignment at the level of semantic representation. That is to say that the reflexivity implied in this type of performative use "solves" the *epistemic* problems noted in Cognitive Grammar with respect to the use of the present tense for perfectives. Thus, the speaker of (18) is effectively transforming the world while uttering the sentence, and she can do so by adopting a certain stance in which the givenness of the situation described is actually created on the spot. A performative use of the present tense constitutes the ground as a matter of definition, and the resulting identity of the speech event and the profiled process gets rid of the canonical differentiation between the observation and identification of a state of affairs. In analytical terms, a performative use blurs any distinctions in the objective/subjective status of linguistic representations, because it is the subject of conceptualization (i.e., the speaker as a principal) that effects or produces the objective categories being described. In this case, a (local) ground is linguistically shaped that was not there before, a process which seems to transcend previously discussed levels of transformation affecting the ground. But, of course, once again the contrast between extending/reducing scope, building nonreal spaces, and creating a new ("real") ground is far from absolute. If anything, that contrast would serve more as an analytical shortcut for distinguishing between tense uses that really form a continuum, as they are all about construing and manipulating (aspects of) the ground.

As a result of a performative's radical independence from what is perceived as objectively real, the speaker can also be described as *controlling* the content and construal of her statement in an absolute fashion. That is, she knows that her statement is epistemically valid (that it constitutes the ground), exactly because she presents it as such. Another way of describing this would be to say that the speaker is aware of existing presuppositions regarding the use of the present tense. These presuppositions[18] can then be exploited as readily as in other realms of lexicon and grammar, where processes of "accommodation" (Lewis 1979) abound. So if a present tense is used in a context where it is clear, from the audience's point of view, that the state of affairs in question could not in any objective sense already constitute the ground ("reflection"), then the next interpretive move, i.e., to read the utterance in a subjectified frame ("creation"), presents itself naturally. And this principle is exactly what performative usage types share with many other noncanonical uses of the present tense. In this and similar cases, the mode that the speaker finds herself in is not a descriptive but a creative one, and such acts of creation, which are presumably correlated with the construction of virtual entities in Cognitive Grammar, can be found all over the place in language use. For instance, if we consider the futurate use of the present tense, as in example (17), we might reinterpret the space building that was shown to go on there as a case of extreme accommodation, whereby the speaker presents a future state of affairs as given even though (she knows that) her addressees contextually assume that it is not. The only way to interpret such "violations" is by attributing to the speaker a high degree of certainty with respect to the predicated state of affairs, i.e., by considering the knowledge state that the speaker must be in at the time of speaking, which is what the present tense seems to convey anyway, and concluding that the speaker creates the givenness of that future state as a matter of fact. In this case, as in all others, the present tense means exactly what it should mean, viz., that some state of affairs necessarily belongs to the ground. It is reality itself that sometimes lags behind.

Performative, or futurate, uses of the present tense represent a kind of *instruction* to the hearer to just assume (perhaps contrary to objective evidence) that the predicated state of affairs is really given in the ways specified above. Here are some other examples of the same mechanism:

(19) *Hamlet moves to center stage.*
(20) *You head north on highway 107.*
(21) *"The rest of the carcass goes into sausages and rolls."* [a butcher teaching tricks of the trade to an apprentice]

One way of explaining these uses is by pointing out the space-building characteristics of each of them. The sentences all *describe* situations that are not real at the time of speaking/writing, but that are portrayed as such in the world that seems to be at issue then (respectively, the "world" of an actual theatrical performance, an actual drive, and the actual production of "meat").[19] For one, this descriptive illusion allows the speaker to issue directions in a less face-threatening way, for these present tenses are modal statements disguised as reports.[20] Moreover, they offer descriptions of what "should" happen (within the world at issue) that do not essentially rely on the speaker's individual claim to authority, which is another way of reducing possible threats to the hearer's face. In fact, the reason why the present tense can be used in this way at all is precisely because of its intimation of necessity within the ground, which is not a matter of any individual's authority but rather of the structure of the world as such. Here, too, the speaker has control over what happens just by saying that it is "the case", yet it is a type of control that is highly subjectified and is therefore several steps removed from more objective formulations, where the mood or modal "force" involved would be presented onstage.

None of these "descriptions" is essentially about temporal duration or location. They are concerned with presenting a state of affairs *as if* it necessarily held in reality (or, as holding in some version of reality), regardless of how it relates to a specific temporal interval. What is part of their present-tense meaning, then, is that they should hold at any time t — that is what makes them structural. Thus, in any actual stage performance of *Hamlet*, the directive in (19) is taken to hold as a description of what should happen at a given moment in that performance, even if it is not in reality acted upon. In this light, and as a final point of contention, I would like to present some examples brought up by Langacker (2001) to defend the position that the idea of a speaker "controlling" events set in the present is necessarily linked up with the intrinsic *duration* of these events:

(22) *Now I raise my hand. And now I lower it...*
(23) *Now I lay back. Now I close my eyes. Now I think of England.*

(24) *The pitcher glances over, winds up, and it's bunted, bunted down the third base line.*
(25) *Well, anyway, so Spike comes up and sees these people abusing me, and he shoves the twin on the shoulder and tells him to beat it, and before I knew it, the two of them had jumped on him.*

With respect to (22), Langacker observes that the bodily actions involved have approximately the "right length" (i.e., that of the speech event) for them to figure in a present-tense description. While this might be true for (22), I do not think it is a necessary condition for all such uses. Consider (23), where the two bodily actions do conform to this condition, but where the mental state described at the end hardly qualifies as the kind of instantaneous event that could be completed within the span of a single speech event ('thinking of England' for about one second is indeed conceivable — *Oh, I remember, I have to call London* —, but not in the present context).

What remains an important *temporal* facet in these examples, as in (24) and (25), is a general feeling of tempo created by this tense usage and linked to the explicitly serialized presentation of the events described. The vividness attributed to live reports and historical accounts such as (25) is undoubtedly attributable to the tense marking, but not necessarily because of a condition of temporal coincidence (with the speech event). Casparis (1975) hints at this conclusion as well. What he calls the "current report" meaning of the present tense reflects "the quality of perception reproduced with a minimum of cognitive analysis, or simply, perception before cognition" (Casparis 1975: 10). In other words, the characterization of a narrative strategy ("current report"), whereby a sequence of sense impressions is articulated almost simultaneously (as in first-person or eyewitness narration, but also in the narration of dreams, visions, and drug experiences), can naturally be undertaken in terms of their immediate, i.e., unmediated, epistemic status, or their direct availability for description ("telling without thinking"). The events in (24) are fairly stereotypical, if not wholly predictable, in the given context, and they can thus be presented as instantiating some of the normal things that may be expected to happen in a ballgame. Pragmatically, this routine-like quality of reporting standard event types that may occur in a given setting is the reason why the speaker can opt for a mode of narration that practically ignores the (first-person) vantage point grounding any act of description and that switches to a kind of god's-eye perspective. That, too, may be part of the use of the present tense, and the resulting descriptions have a "sourceless" feel to them, much like certain generic statements and the examples (19–21).

What is distinctive about examples (24) and especially (25), which involves some instances of the "historical present", is that they are set in a clearly narrative mode and accordingly exploit different aspects of the semantics of the present tense. In particular, the perfective verbs figuring in them typically profile very short actions that have none of the more structural implications we might still find in performative contexts, for example. In fact, these verbs illustrate some of the most ethereal states of affairs that one could imagine, and it is hard to see them contribute to any act of constituting the ground (or any new ground), in contrast with most of our previous examples. Therefore, it might be better to analyze these particular present-tense usages as exploiting the "immediacy", rather than the "givenness", of the presented states of affairs. In the examples, the speaker functions as an *animator* (Goffman 1979: 16–17), i.e., a "talking machine" that does not (even implicitly) engage in any interpretation or mediation of the reported events but "presentifies" them, in a Kantian sense, for immediate apprehension (cf. the discussion of example 11). In this sense, the opposite is happening of the kind of extreme subjectification that we have witnessed in previous examples. One could speak of a complete removal of subjectivity in these latter cases, creating an effect that highlights the mere presence of the events and producing (processual) objects that are not of a virtual but of a *hyper-real* nature. This hyper-reality is what prompts the vividness of such descriptions, and their occurrence in typically narrative contexts is not accidental. Narration differs from ordinary description in that it establishes a frame (that of a live broadcast, a fictive world, or a photographic reality, as in 16). It is this very frame that is in turn being negated in hyper-real uses of the present tense, as a temporary relief from the relevant modalities of the narrative medium, presenting objects — making them present — as if they happened right before our eyes. However, no strict grounding can be inferred from this, because the direct apprehension of hyper-real objects is a conceptual activity that is not mediated through a set of structuring beliefs (in reality or in the narrative space) and does therefore not require a qualification of these objects in modal terms, e.g., of necessity (givenness).

It is important, though, to realize that this type of exploitation does go back to the same semantic substrate. Indeed, the availability of two divergent paths of exploitation would suggest that the double present-tense meaning offered in section 3.1 has some analytical validity to it. I attribute the relatively marginal status of the hyper-real use of the present tense to its restricted attestation in explicitly narrative contexts. In simple description or reporting, it would make little sense to present an event as if it happened before our eyes, if it in fact does.

4. Conclusion

The present tense in English indicates that the designated process should be seen as constituting the ground. In this particular context, the ground is a modal conception, picturing what the/a world should be like or is necessarily like. In Table 1, I present the most palpable meaning types that can be distinguished for the simple and progressive present in light of the previous discussion.

Various types of scope and space building, as well as other forms of footing alignment within the epistemic domain defined by the ground, are responsible for the temporal (present and nonpresent) and nontemporal usage types that can be distinguished. Consequently, the temporal concerns that are taken to mark the use of the present tense do not instantiate what this construction is actually about. Such temporal meanings are, of course, empirically real but accidental, and they should emerge quite naturally from an account referring to the speaker's state of knowledge, which has analytic priority.

Table 1. Usage types for the present tense and progressive -*ing*

	Imperfectives	**Perfectives**
Present tense	*Constituting the ground*: from local to generic scope, and including the auxiliary form in progressives	*Constituting the ground* in general-validity statements *Performative* and other types of footing alignment
		Presenting hyper-real objects in narrative settings
Progressive –*ing*	*Contingency* (e.g., in temporally bounded contexts)	*Contingency* in "present-time" and other bounded contexts

I have thus outlined a schematic analysis of the English present tense that is, in a number of respects, meant to complement Langacker's previous accounts. In general, I have stressed the importance of an epistemic approach to tense, which I believe constitutes the essence of Cognitive Grammar's discussion of grounding. The elaborated epistemic model and notions of construal, such as immediate scope, mental-space construction, and subjectification, have therefore contributed significantly to the substance of the present analysis.

Instead of emphasizing the purely temporal function of the present tense, I have proposed a rather programmatic account of tense meaning that starts from an essentially epistemic (modal) approach. For the present tense in particular, this means that I have tried to explicate some of the ways in which nonpresent occurrences can nonetheless be available for immediate apprehension. This involves figuring out how the mental world we talk about (when using the present tense) can comprise far more than the direct observation of reality or actuality, much like previous analyses in Cognitive Grammar have proposed the postulation of virtual documents, including associated operations like projection (e.g., for futurates), mental replay (e.g., for the historical present), and fictive (temporal) vantage points (e.g., for a number of subclauses). The discussion, within the present paper, of "types", hypothetical spaces, photo captions where the world described is not the real one, and hyper-real uses fits directly into this concern with fictive or virtual constructs. I have posited mechanisms like accommodation, footing, and exploitation, which allow the analyst to locate effects of "special viewing arrangements" in strategies which the speaker has at her disposal to present, modulate, or even create an epistemic status for any given state of affairs on the spot. In other words, it is in the speaker's online attitude or orientation to knowledge about predicated events that I have looked for the source of many "extensions" of present-tense meaning. Technically, it seems as if the varied mental operations proffered by Langacker's accounts of the present tense are really to be situated at some processing level, whereas the ones discussed here are more about pragmatic interactions with context (given the highly schematic semantic content that is attributed to tense predications). I believe, though, that this analytical move does not go against the spirit of grounding theory in Cognitive Grammar, especially since it concerns clausal grounding, which is fundamentally thought to be dealing with the (non)reality of designated processes (and where I think actuality and even time are not per se significant factors).

Notes

1. The author is a Postdoctoral Fellow of the Fund for Scientific Research – Flanders (Belgium).

   I wish to thank Louis Goossens and Ron Langacker for going over some of the less obvious points in this analysis with me in the past. I also thank René Dirven for his valuable comments on an earlier version of this paper.
2. The term *English*, here and in the title, refers to a language, not a culture. Throughout this text I will be dealing with Standard English only. With respect to nonstandard varieties, Labov (1972: 51) provides a nice illustration of how a language like Black English Vernacular seems to be more precise (or "logical") in its treatment of *perfective* verbs and the various forms that are compatible with them. The sentence *He be working*, with invariant *be*, generally indicates so-called habitual (or iterative) behavior, so that we can conclude that the subject in question usually works or has a steady job. In contrast, the "elliptical" construction *He working* only indicates that the subject is

working at the time of speaking. Thus, Black English Vernacular presents more paradigmatic options for the marking of perfective verbs than Standard English does, and these options correspond to semantic functions (basically, those expressing general validity and coincidence with the time of speaking) that appear to be conflated in the single progressive form of Standard English.
3. Example (1) is adapted from Kress (1977). It figures in a discussion of the differentiation between various deictic and nondeictic concerns within the verb paradigm.
4. (Im)perfectivity is, strictly speaking, a matter of *Aktionsart*. In the present discussion, this aspectual notion is essentially treated as a semantic one in English, though grammatical operations may have effects that are describable in the same terms. Since perfective and imperfective processes are designated by different lexical "predication types", they should be conceptually distinguished from grammatical aspect marking, as in the contrast between progressive and simple forms of the past and present tense.
5. Nakamura (1991) rightly points out that Langacker's analysis of the English progressive bears many conceptual similarities with Jespersen's (1932: 180) "frame-theoretic" perspective on this construction.
6. An alternative way of putting this without resorting to morphological terminology would be to state that the higher-order process in question is obtained through a process of semantic extension.
7. "Experience" is the result of categorized perception and is therefore not to be equated with the latter. It is, in other words, perception that has passed through the "filter" of (grounded) knowledge.
8. In fact, the same meaning of nontypicality might even be difficult to realize in the context of example (4), which was supposed to indicate a habit and thus a typical trait of the person indicated by the subject. Notice, however, that the example involves a *temporary* habit, i.e., one that is in fact not part of the ground and that therefore constitutes something of a surprise against the backdrop of that person's more global patterns of behavior. The ground, I would like to maintain, is ultimately an atemporal notion, and any intimation of temporal boundaries, as in (4) or (10), will thus result in some degree of separation from it.
9. The (temporal) characterization of the present progressive with perfective verbs in Cognitive Grammar is somewhat involved but actually quite cogent as a first argumentative step. While the progressive marker imperfectivizes the perfective process, "zooming in" on that process and thus excluding the conception of its starting and endpoints, the present tense imposes a second scope ("IS_2") which selects part of the derived imperfective process and has that coincide with the speech event. See Langacker (1999b) for a related discussion of imperfectivized imperfectives (in generic contexts).

10. One might in principle wish to argue that expressions such as *be silly, be careful*, etc. have more of a perfective quality to them because of what they mean ('behave in a silly way, act carefully'), such that they can also appear in other, nonprogressive contexts where no apparent imperfectivization can be seen at work: *Try to be careful, Don't be so silly, He was repeatedly silly,* ... However, the principle does not seem to be limited to *"be*+adjective" constructions (*You're being an ass*), nor is it capable of precisely delimiting the class of predications that would be involved. Given the appropriate context, virtually any imperfective process may take the progressive form, regardless of the degree of control and volition it usually expresses: *I'm having difficulties with this, I'm seeing things lately*. The possibility of having imperfectives behave "perfectively" seems to be so widespread and productive that it would be preferable to see this as a grammatical phenomenon (with certain constructions, including the present tense, favoring more of an "active" construal of the process in question) rather than a lexical one.
11. I will not discuss plural generics here, which appear to have a number of special properties with respect to the present tense and progressive aspect. See Langacker (1997, 1999b).
12. Actually, it might seem as if so-called general-validity statements come in *three* varieties, because every generic or habitual expression may be imperfectivized regardless of the perfective or imperfective nature of the verb appearing in it, resulting in temporarily valid statements like *John is drinking heavily these days*, or *You're being very silly lately*. These are, first of all, obvious cases of scope building. And because of the explicitly temporal nature of the concrete scope builders involved, they may arguably be discussed in terms of the imperfectivizing procedure imposing a (higher-order) sense of temporal *boundedness* upon the predication (an effect of "zooming in"). This does not imply, however, that the epistemic properties that should come with such progressive constructions are lost. They remain in place and apply within the scope that is being predicated through the tense marker. The conclusion should thus be that, at the level of the content verb (as opposed to that of the auxiliary), general-validity statements lose their *absolute* validity in such contexts, even within the restricted temporal scope, and behave just like other progressive forms in general.
13. Habituals feature the same individual involved in the same type of event over time, while generics present the same type of subject with multiple distinct instantiations over time. It is a matter of analytical preference to assume, or not, that a generic or habitual reading necessarily construes multiple instances *over time* in the background (or maximal scope).
14. Naturally, this specification is not about the act of drinking in general but about the kind of heavy drinking that John engages in, i.e., it generalizes over a proposition instead of an isolated predication.

15. Consider the generic sentence *A cat plays with a mouse it has caught*, where the virtual event that is profiled captures what is common to an open-ended set of instantiations in actuality. Still, in Cognitive Grammar it is maintained that a fictive *instance* of the event type is profiled. The contrast crucially hinges on the fundamental definition of grounding as an act of singling out instances of a thing or process type. Accordingly, whenever there is talk of "arbitrary instances", what is invariably meant, it seems, is that the instance in question is to be situated at a fictive or virtual level of conceptualization.
16. The difference between a scope builder and a space builder is a relative one and basically depends upon the definition of "reality" that one assumes speakers are working with. Thus, the temporal subclauses (featuring *when, until*, etc.) adduced in Langacker (2001) to illustrate the temporal quality of mental-space building simply instantiate cases of scope building, insofar as the time stretches they indicate are set in "reality". I have already stressed that the scope (or space) built need not evoke the temporal domain.
17. I agree with Langacker (2001) that the type of reality involved is more likely to be projected than merely potential, because of the typically planned or scheduled nature of the events that are being "predicted" in this usage type. Thus, both *??Their plane arrives* (referring to an upcoming event that is anticipated but not precisely localizable in the future) and *??An earthquake strikes next week* are highly infelicitous, mainly due to the pragmatics involved.
18. I am not using the term "presupposition" in the sense of a representation that is part of a predication's "conceptual substrate", as in Langacker (2001), because that would imply that the presupposed content reside in the predication's maximal scope. It should be clear from the present discussion that the presupposition referred to here is very much part of the present tense's immediate scope (in fact, it defines that scope) and thus simply constitutes its semantic meaning. It acts as a presupposition with respect to potential pragmatic exploitations of that meaning.
19. Sentence (21) should be interpreted in a context where the speaker tells her apprentice what she *should* do in an actual instance of carcass processing. Notice that a progressive variant of (21), *"(What?) The rest of this carcass is going into sausages!"*, does not sound as "normal" and matter-of-fact as its simple counterpart. It could be said to express an element of surprise. Compare also *This bolt goes in there* vs. *The bolt is going in... (Hurray!)*.
20. Consider the possibility of turning these sentences into real directives, employing deontic modal verbs such as *should* or *must* or even the imperative mood.

References

Allen, Robert L.
1966 *The Verb System of Present-Day American English*. The Hague: Mouton.

Brisard, Frank
1997 The English tense-system as an epistemic category: The case of futurity. In: Marjolijn Verspoor, Kee Dong Lee and Eve Sweetser (eds.), *Lexical and Syntactical Constructions and the Construction of Meaning*, 271–285. Amsterdam: John Benjamins.
2001 *Be going to*: An exercise in grounding. *Journal of Linguistics* 37: 251–285.

Casparis, Christian Paul
1975 *Tense without Time: The Present Tense in Narration*. Bern: Francke.

Comrie, Bernard
1985 *Tense*. Cambridge: Cambridge University Press.

Fauconnier, Gilles
1994 *Mental Spaces: Aspects of Meaning Construction in Natural Language*. Cambridge: Cambridge University Press.
1997 *Mappings in Thought and Language*. Cambridge: Cambridge University Press.

Goffman, Erving
1974 *Frame Analysis: An Essay on the Organization of Experience*. Cambridge, MA: Harvard University Press.
1979 Footing. *Semiotica* 25: 1–29. Reprinted in: Erving Goffman [1981], *Forms of Talk*, 124–159. Philadelphia: University of Pennsylvania Press.

Goldsmith, John & Erich Woisetschlaeger
1982 The logic of the English progressive. *Linguistic Inquiry* 13: 79–89.

Goossens, Louis
1994 The English progressive tenses and the layered representation of Functional Grammar. In: Co Vet and Carl Vetters (eds.), *Tense and Aspect in Discourse*, 161–177. Berlin: Mouton de Gruyter.

Habermas, Jürgen
1998 Actions, speech acts, linguistically mediated interactions, and the lifeworld. In: Jürgen Habermas, *On the Pragmatics of Communication*, 215–255. Cambridge, MA: MIT Press.

Husserl, Edmund
1970 *The Crisis of European Sciences and Transcendental Phenomenology: An Introduction to Phenomenological Philosophy*. Translated, with an introduction, by David Carr. Evanston: Northwestern University Press.

Jespersen, Otto
    1932   *A Modern English Grammar on Historical Principles,* Part 4: *Syntax.* Volume 3: *Time and Tense.* London: Allen & Unwin.

Kochańska, Agata
    this vol.   A cognitive grammar analysis of Polish nonpast perfectives and imperfectives: How virtual events differ from actual ones.

Kress, Günther R.
    1977   Tense as modality. *University of East Anglia Papers in Linguistics* 5: 40–52.

Labov, William
    1972   *Language in the Inner City: Studies in the Black English Vernacular.* Philadelphia: University of Pennsylvania Press.

Langacker, Ronald W.
    1982   Remarks on English aspect. In: Paul J. Hopper (ed.), *Tense-Aspect: Between Semantics and Pragmatics, Containing the Contributions to a Symposium on Tense and Aspect, Held at UCLA, May 1979,* 265–304. Amsterdam: John Benjamins.
    1987   *Foundations of Cognitive Grammar,* Volume 1: *Theoretical Prerequisites.* Stanford: Stanford University Press.
    1991   *Foundations of Cognitive Grammar,* Volume 2: *Descriptive Application.* Stanford: Stanford University Press.
    1997   Generics and habituals. In: Angeliki Athanasiadou and René Dirven (eds.), *On Conditionals Again,* 191–222. Amsterdam: John Benjamins.
    1999a   Evidence for descriptive constructs. In: Ronald W. Langacker, *Grammar and Conceptualization,* 45–71. Berlin: Mouton de Gruyter.
    1999b   Generic constructions. In: Ronald W. Langacker, *Grammar and Conceptualization,* 247–259. Berlin: Mouton de Gruyter.
    1999c   Viewing in cognition and grammar. In: Ronald W. Langacker, *Grammar and Conceptualization,* 203–245. Berlin: Mouton de Gruyter.
    1999d   Virtual reality. *Studies in the Linguistic Sciences* 29: 77–103.
    2001   The English present tense. *English Language and Linguistics* 5: 251–272.
    2002   Extreme subjectification: English tense and modals. Manuscript.

Lewis, David
    1979   Scorekeeping in a language game. *Journal of Philosophical Logic* 8: 339–359.

Nakamura, Wataru
    1991   *Subjectification and the English Progressive.* (Papers, Series A, No. 318.) Duisburg: Linguistic Agency University of Duisburg.

Peirce, Charles S.
    1934   *Collected Papers*, Volume 5: *Pragmatism and Pragmaticism.* Cambridge, MA: Harvard University Press.

The preterit and the imperfect as grounding predications[*]

Aintzane Doiz-Bienzobas

Primarily, the contrast between the two past tenses in Spanish, i.e. the *pretérito indefinido* (henceforth, preterit) and the *pretérito imperfecto* (henceforth, imperfect), has been studied in the literature under three perspectives: temporal, aspectual, and discourse-oriented.[1] This paper takes a different perspective and characterizes the preterit and imperfect as grounding predications, as a result of which parameters other than aspectual, temporal, or discourse-oriented will be proposed as essential for the characterization of the two forms.

Grounding predications have the following three properties (Langacker 1991, this volume). (i) They are highly grammaticized elements which constitute the final step in forming a finite clause. (ii) They profile the grounded entity rather than the grounding relationship which provides their conceptual content. (iii) Their conceptual import relates the process they designate to the ground (i.e. the speaker and her circumstances).

The focus of this paper is to specify and articulate the way in which the conceptual import of the preterit and the imperfect relates a state of affairs to the ground. In order to do so, I work within Langacker's theory of grounding, whereby I refer to two idealized cognitive models, the timeline model and that of the structured world (Langacker 1991: 242). In addition, I analyze the role of the two predications as discourse tracking devices within the framework of Mental Spaces (Fauconnier [1985] 1994).

From an empirical point of view, the analysis I present here accounts for a wide range of data, which includes the following: (i) a number of semantic contrasts between the preterit (PRET) and the imperfect (IMPF) which have not been generally discussed in the literature (examples 1–3); (ii) the use of the imperfect for the description of nonpast situations, such as future scheduled situations (4); (iii) the use of the imperfect for the expression of irrealis, e.g. wishes, preludic, dreams (5); and (iv) the choice of the imperfect for the expression of past habituals and generics and of the preterit for repetitives and nongenerics (6).

(1) *Todas   las   mujeres cogieron   un tren   que*
   all   the   women   took   a train   which

   salió/salía   temprano.
   left-PRET/IMPF   early.
   a. PRET: 'All the women took a train which left early.' (the same train: wide scope)
   b. IMPF: 'All the women took a train which left early.' (the same/different train: wide, narrow scope)

(2) *El   coche me   costó/costaba   dos   millones.*
   the   car   me   **cost-PRET/IMPF**   two   millions
   a. PRET: 'The car cost me two million.' →(I bought it)
   b. IMPF: 'The car cost me two million.' →(maybe I bought it, maybe I didn't)

(3) *Oí   que   alguien   entró/entraba.*
   heard that   someone   **entered-PRET/IMPF**
   a. PRET: 'I heard someone entered.'
   b. IMPF: 'I heard someone enter/entering.'

(4) *Al año   siguiente   había   fiestas,   pero al final*
   to year   following   **were-IMPF**   festivities   but   at the end

   se   cancelaron.
   Reflx   canceled-PRET
   'The following year there were some festivities, but eventually they got canceled.'

(5) *Soñé   que   **ganaba/*gané**   el   premio Nobel de*
    dreamt that **won-IMPF/*PRET** the prize   Nobel of

literatura.
literature
'I dreamt that I won the Nobel Prize for literature.'

(6) *El   año pasado **iba/fui**   a nadar todos los*
    the year last   **went-IMPF/PRET** to swim   all   the

días.
days
a. IMPF: 'I used to go swimming every day last year.' (habitual)
b. PRET: 'I went swimming every day last year.' (nonhabitual repetitive)

The need to provide an accurate characterization of the preterit-imperfect contrast is further motivated by the realization that some of the uses of the Spanish imperfect that I consider in this paper are also shared by imperfective forms in other languages. A case at hand is provided by De Mulder and Vetters (this volume), who analyze the nonpast uses of the French *imparfait* (e.g. its occurrences in indirect speech), its modal uses (e.g. the politeness form, the preludic form, the expression of wishes and desires), and its occurrence in expressing imaginary events (e.g. conditional sentences with *si* 'if').[2]

From a theoretical point of view, I intend to generalize over all the uses of the imperfect by providing a comprehensive analysis. At a more specific level, I intend to explore the role of epistemic notions in the characterization of the preterit and the imperfect and to determine their role as discourse builders.

The core of the analysis is presented in the first three sections of the paper. Section 1 deals with the notion of *distance* within Langacker's (1991) timeline model. Section 2 centers around the notion of *structure of the world* within the model proposed by Langacker (1991, 1999). Section 3 introduces the cognitive function of the two forms as discourse tracking devices within the framework of Mental

Spaces (Fauconnier 1994). Finally, some concluding remarks are provided in section 4, where the parameters and notions introduced in the previous sections are brought together.

1. Distance: Past situation vs. past viewpoint

Past tense forms (*-ed* forms) indicate a "distance with reference to the time-line model, where non-immediacy is translated into past time exclusively" (Langacker 1991: 249).[3] Drawing on the notion of distance proposed by Langacker, I introduce the following two parameters for the characterization of the two past forms in Spanish: distance of the *situation* with respect to the ground, and distance of the *conceptualizer* to the ground. In particular, I will be arguing that:

(i) the preterit indicates distance of the situation with respect to the (surrogate) ground;
(ii) the imperfect evokes the presence of a distant conceptualizer apprehending the situation with respect to the ground.

1.1. Distance of the situation to the (surrogate) ground

The preterit designates a distal situation; its role is to indicate that the situation occurred in the past. In direct speech, in particular, the preterit designates situations which must be past or distant with respect to the ground, as shown by the ungrammaticality of the preterit in combination with the adverbs for 'now' and 'tomorrow' in (7).

(7) *Juan **estuvo**   aquí la   semana pasada, *ahora, *mañana.*
    Juan **was-PRET** here the week   last,   *now,   *tomorrow
    'Juan was here last week, *now, *tomorrow.'

In indirect speech, the preterit designates a situation removed from the surrogate ground, i.e. the time designated by the speech verb in the main clause, as illustrated by the grammaticality judgments of

(8), (9), and (10). Thus, the ungrammaticality of (8) is due to the occurrence of the situation designated by the preterit at a time posterior to the *SG*, as represented in Figure 1 (*SG* stands for "surrogate ground", *G* for "ground", *sit* for "situation" and *t* for "time axis").

(8) **Hace   dos   días   dijo   que   ayer   **estuvo**   en casa.*
     ago   two   days   said   that   yesterday   **was-PRET** in home
     'Two days ago he said that yesterday he was home.'

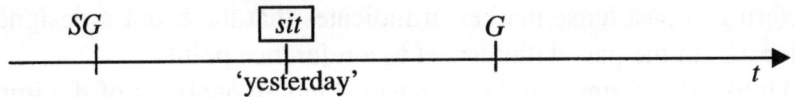

Figure 1. Sentence (8)

By contrast, in (9) and (10) the situations designated by the preterit are prior to the *SG*, and consequently, the sentences are grammatical.

(9) *Juan   nos   dirá   el   lunes   que   no   **estuvo**   aquí   hace*
    Juan   us   tell   the   Monday   that   not   **was-PRET** here   ago

dos   días.
two   days
'Juan will tell us on Monday that he was not here two days ago.'

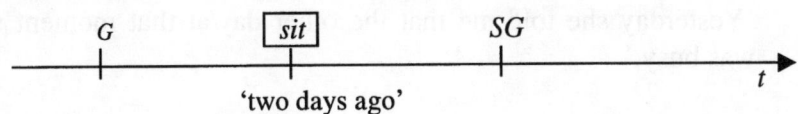

Figure 2. Sentence (9)

(10) *Juan   nos   dirá   mañana   que   hoy   no   **estuvo**   aquí.*
     Juan   us   tell   tomorrow   that   today   not   **was-PRET** here
     'Juan will tell us tomorrow that he was not here today.'

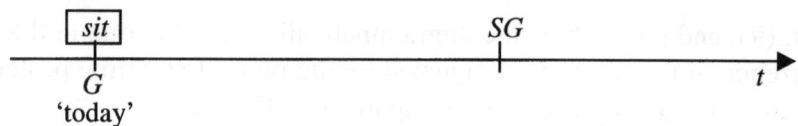

Figure 3. Sentence (10)

In the light of data such as (8–10), it can be concluded that the function of the preterit is to designate the distance of the situation to the ground or surrogate ground. Stated in more traditional terms, the preterit is a past tense marker; it indicates that the event it designates is located in the past with respect to a reference point.

Unlike the preterit, and counter to standard analyses of the imperfect, I propose that the imperfect is not a past time marker. That is, sentences occurring with the imperfect need not be removed from the ground or the surrogate ground in direct and indirect speech, respectively. In fact, situations designated by the imperfect may be prior to, simultaneous with, or posterior to the (surrogate) ground, as illustrated by the grammaticality judgments of sentences (11) through (13).[4]

(11) Ayer   me   dijo   que   el   otro día/en   ese
yesterday me   told   that the other day/in that

momento   **estaba**   ocupada.
moment   **was-IMPF** busy
'Yesterday she told me that the other day/at that moment she was busy.'

(12) Ayer   me   dijo   que hoy **estaba**   ocupada.
yesterday me   told that today **was-IMPF** busy
'Yesterday she told me that today she was busy.'

(13) Ayer   me   dijo   que mañana **estaba**   ocupada.
yesterday me   told that tomorrow **was-IMPF** busy
'Yesterday she told me that tomorrow she was busy.'

While the situations with the imperfect may have different temporal relationships with respect to the ground or surrogate ground, as illustrated by examples (11) through (13), situations with the imperfect convey some notion of pastness or conceptual distance that has led to the traditional characterization of the imperfect as a past tense marker. I will argue that the sense of pastness associated with (past and nonpast) events designated by the imperfect results from the presence of the second parameter characterizing the imperfect/preterit contrast, namely, distance of the viewpoint or conceptualizer apprehending the situation with respect to the ground. I consider this parameter next.

1.2. Distance of the conceptualizer or viewpoint with respect to the ground

The differences in the degree of distance or proximity between the ground and the viewpoint (i.e. the conceptualizer apprehending the situation) are responsible for the viewing arrangements which characterize the preterit and the imperfect. The following two characterizations will be argued for.

(i) Situations with the preterit are apprehended by a viewpoint which is *proximal* to the ground. That is to say, the preterit imposes a *present* viewpoint onto the situation it designates.[5]

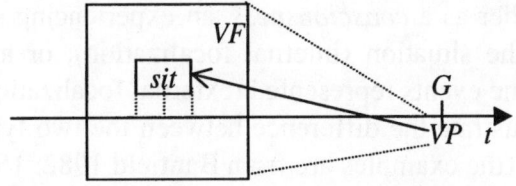

Figure 4. The preterit and proximal viewpoint

(ii) Situations with the imperfect are conceptualized by a viewpoint which is *distal* or removed with respect to the ground. That is, the imperfect imposes a *past* viewpoint onto the situation it designates. Generally, the past viewpoint is located *at* the situation time or at a time *prior to* situation time, as represented in Figure 5.[6]

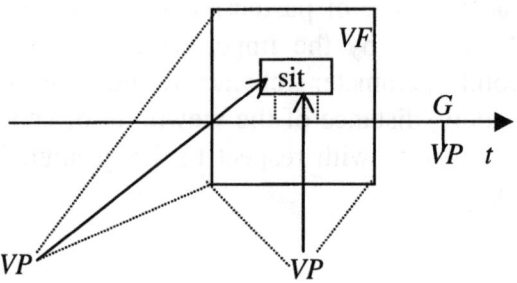

Figure 5. The imperfect and distal viewpoint

The role played by the tense-aspect categories in the conceptualization of situations has been dealt with in the literature previously, specifically in the study of narratives, where the role of tense-aspect categories has been considered to be distinct from their role in oral discourse situations. Thus, according to Fleischman (1990, 1991), in narratives tense-aspect categories are freed from their referential (aspectual) functions (i.e. to present the situation as bounded or unbounded) and take on pragmatic/expressive values. One of their expressive functions is to determine the nature of the situation's focalization (i.e. the way a situation is perceived): the speaker portrays herself or a character either as a *consciousness*, an experiencing self in the development of the situation (internal focalization), or as a *narrator* detached from the events represented (external focalization). The sentences in (14) illustrate the difference between the two types of focalization in French (the examples are from Banfield 1982: 157).

(14) a. *Elle vit la lune.*
    she **saw-passé simple** the moon
  b. *Elle voyait la lune maintenant.*
    she **saw-imparfait** the moon now

In (14a), where the *passé simple* (similar to the Spanish preterit) is used, the speaker is detached from the situation and reports its occurrence from an external point of view. There is an external "narrating self". In (14b), the use of the *imparfait* (similar to the Spanish imperfect) implies that the event of looking at the moon "has been experienced at some moment, and reports it by representing an experience of it" (Fleischman 1991: 301). There is an "experiencing self" which apprehends the situation from the past time in which it occurred, as reflected by the use of the adverb 'now' to refer to a past time.[7]

In this paper, I propose that the expression of a viewpoint is not just a pragmatic function of the preterit and the imperfect which surfaces in certain contexts only. Rather, I will be arguing that the expression of viewpoint as characterized in Figures 4 and 5 is one of the defining properties of the imperfect-preterit contrast. Evidence for the proposed viewing arrangements comes from the study of the interaction of the two forms with the temporal adverbial expression *al x siguiente* 'the following x' (e.g. 'the following year', 'the following month', etc.) and with the proximal deictic 'this'.

1.2.1. *Al x siguiente* 'the following x'

The adverbial expression *al x siguiente* 'the following x' may occur in combination with the preterit or with the imperfect (15). However, the reading of the sentence is very different with one or the other tense: when the preterit is used, the sentence designates a past situation (15a); when the imperfect is used, it designates an anticipated scheduled situation (15b).

(15) *Al año siguiente* **hubo/había** *fiestas.*
     to year following **were-PRET/IMPF** festivities
     a. PRET: 'The following year there were festivities.' → they took place
     b. IMPF: 'The following year there were festivities.' → maybe they took place, maybe they did not

The reading of the sentence with the preterit in (15a) is accounted for by the analysis of the preterit in terms of viewpoint, which states that the preterit provides a present viewpoint at the ground from where the situation is necessarily conceptualized as past. Figure 6 represents this reading of (15a).

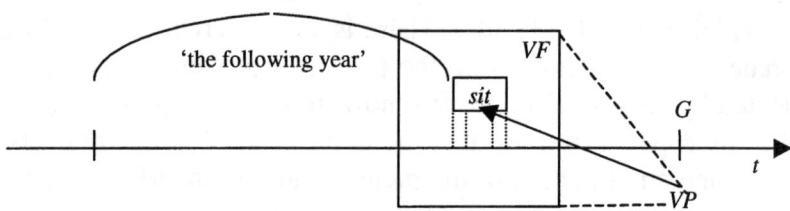

Figure 6. Sentence (15a)

The specific viewing arrangement imposed by the preterit accounts for the unacceptability of example (16), where the sentence 'but due to the rain they were canceled' is added.

(16) *Al   año   siguiente **hubo**   fiestas,   pero debido
     to   year following **were-PRET**   festivities but due

  a la   lluvia se   cancelaron.
  to the   rain   REFLX   canceled
  *'The following year some festivities took place, but due to the rain they were canceled.'

On the one hand, the clause 'some festivities took place' states that the festivities have taken place in the past as evidenced by the speaker's description of the situation from the ground. On the other hand, the second half of the sentence, 'due to the rain they were canceled', states that the festivities did not take place, contradicting the state of affairs depicted in the first part of the sentence. The presence of contradictory information accounts for the unacceptability of the sentence.

When the imperfect is used, the viewing arrangement associated with it states that the situation is apprehended through a past viewpoint prior to the situation time. This viewing arrangement accounts for the possibility of adding 'but due to the rain they were canceled' in (15), as illustrated in (17).

(17) *Al año siguiente* **había** *fiestas, pero debido*
to year following **were-IMPF** festivities but due

a la lluvia se cancelaron.
to the rain REFLX canceled
'The following year some festivities were going to take place, but due to the rain they were canceled.'

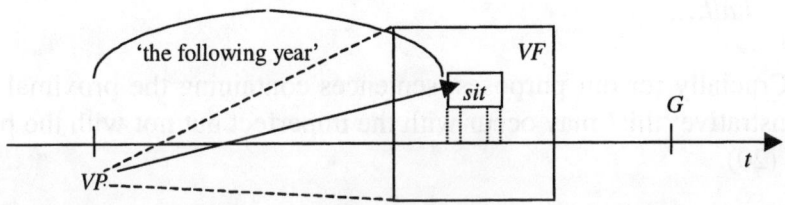

Figure 7. Sentence (17)

The apprehension of the situation by the viewpoint from a time prior to its occurrence prevents the speaker from portraying the situation as past. Consequently, the situation is construed as an anticipation, as reflected in the interpretation of the sentence in (17).[8]

1.2.2. The proximal demonstrative *este* 'this'

Deictic expressions, such as the demonstratives 'this' and 'that', "hinge on the position of the speaker rather than the subject" (Givón 1984: 121) with respect to some entity. Accordingly, the demonstrative in (18) below can only be interpreted as referring to the window which is close to the speaker but not to Sarah (example taken from Langacker 1991: 256).

(18) *Sarah said that **this** window is stuck.*

When the proximal deictic 'this' occurs in sentences with past tense verbs as in (19), Janssen (this volume: 180) proposes that the sentences are characterized by a sense of empathy between the speaker and the situation.

(19) *"They must go by the carrier," she thought; "and how funny it'll seem, sending presents to one's own feet! And how odd the directions will look! ..."*
Just at this moment her head struck against the roof of the hall....

Crucially for our purposes, sentences containing the proximal demonstrative 'this' may occur with the imperfect but not with the preterit (20).

(20)   (*Este era el   día de mi boda.) ¡Este día*
     this was the   day of my wedding this day

     fue/era   el   día más feliz de mi vida!*
     was-*PRET/IMPF the   day more happy of my life
     '(This was the day of my wedding.) This day was the happiest day of my life!'

As stated by the analysis proposed here, the preterit provides a viewpoint which apprehends the past situation from the ground. That is to say, the viewpoint is distant from the past situation, as reflected in the sense of a detachment between the occurrence of the situation and its description by the speaker. This sense of detachment characterizing the construal of the situation designated by the preterit clashes with the sense of empathy between the speaker and the situation created by the use of 'this' and results in the incompatibility of the preterit and 'this'. By contrast, our analysis states that the imperfect provides a past viewpoint from where situations are apprehended. That is to say, in (20) the speaker or conceptualizer is an experiencing self reliving her wedding day as it occurred at the time: she tells the reader about her wedding day and the description of her feelings as they crossed her mind at the time in the past. The sense of closeness between the viewpoint and the situation evoked by the imperfect is highly compatible with the empathy provided by the occurrence of 'this' in sentences with past tense verbs, thereby accounting for the acceptability of 'this' with the imperfect.

1.3. The preterit and the imperfect as distance markers of a different kind: Past situation vs. past viewpoint

The following statements summarize the main ideas presented in section 1. The preterit is a past tense marker; its role is to locate the situation it designates in the past. In addition, its viewpoint construes the situation from the ground, creating a sense of detachment between the speaker and the situation. By contrast, the role of the imperfect is to provide a past viewpoint from where the situation it designates is construed, and no specific temporal relationship between the situation and the ground is stated. This characterization accounts for the use of the imperfect in past and nonpast situations in sentences (11) through (13), repeated here under (21), and for the sense of pastness associated with them. Thus, in (21) the description of the situation through a viewpoint from the surrogate ground in the past confers a sense of pastness upon the situation.

(21) Me   dijo   que   ayer/   hoy/   mañana   **estaba**
     me   told   that yesterday/ today/   tomorrow **was-IMPF**

   ocupada.
   busy
   'She told me that yesterday/today/tomorrow she was busy.'

Finally, I have proposed that the past viewpoint may be at a time *prior* to the situation time as in (15, 17), or *at* the situation time as in (20). Whether the distal/past viewpoint is prior to or at the situation time is frequently determined by pragmatics, the context, and the semantics of the clauses themselves. Thus, the occurrence of the verb 'die' with the adverbial expression 'the following year', for example, is not likely to yield a scheduled or anticipated reading with the imperfect, because we do not tend to program the occurrence of death. The verb 'die' is more likely to be interpreted as a past (experienced) occurrence when modified by the imperfect. Translated into our terminology, the viewpoint is more likely to be at the situation time as illustrated by the sentence in (22), which represents the so-called *imperfecto de ruptura* ("imperfect of breakage").[9]

(22) *Cayó enfermo de repente y   al de dos días* **moría** *solo.*
     fell sick   suddenly and to of two days **died-IMPF**
                                                       alone
     'He suddenly felt sick and two days later he died alone.'

2. The structure of the world

Goldsmith and Woisetschlaeger (1982: 80) argue that there are two different ways to talk about the world, "by describing what things happen in the world, or by describing how the world is made that such things may happen in it". These correspond to two kinds of knowledge, phenomenal and structural, respectively.[10] Langacker (1991: 264) interprets this contrast as "reflecting an idealized cognitive world model", where certain events are direct manifestations of the way the world is and how it is expected to work, while others are "incidental, arising in ad hoc fashion from particular circumstances" (Langacker 1991: 264).

For representational purposes, Langacker (1991, 1999) distinguishes between an actual plane and a structural plane, corresponding to phenomenal and structural knowledge. The actual plane "comprises event instances that are conceived as actually occurring" (Langacker 1991: 251). These are anchored to the timeline and, accordingly, may express a past situation or a situation with future potentiality. On the other hand, the structural plane comprises event instances which characterize how the world is made but which do not have any existence outside of the structural plane. These event instances are arbitrary and, as Langacker (1999: 251; emphasis omitted) proposes, are ""conjured up" just for some local purpose, with no status outside the mental space ... thus created". Arbitrary instances may be found in numerous linguistic phenomena, as in the sentence in (23) provided by Langacker.

(23) *Zelda wants to buy a fur coat.*

On the nonspecific reading of (23), there is no particular coat that Zelda wants to buy: it is an arbitrary instance which is created with the only purpose of referring to Zelda's desire. Outside of the mental space of her desire, it has no existence. Along the same lines, events in the structural plane are "arbitrary instances conjured up just for purposes of characterizing the world's structure" (Langacker 1999: 251). Crucially, these arbitrary instances are not anchored to any particular point in time.

In this section, I will be arguing that:

(i) the role of the preterit is to include the situation it designates in the actual plane. That is, situations taking a preterit are actual and located at a specific moment in the past;

(ii) the role of the imperfect is to state that the situation it designates is interpreted in the structural plane. That is, sentences with the imperfect designate a state of affairs which does not have a direct link to the timeline and which portrays the way things work/are in the world.

The occurrence of correspondences similar to those between the Spanish preterit and the notion of an actual plane, and between the Spanish imperfect and a structural plane, can be observed cross-linguistically. A case at hand is provided by the study of the two types of future use of the nonpast tenses in Polish by Kochańska (this volume). In particular, Kochańska argues that while the nonpast perfective profiles a future actual event, the nonpast imperfective profiles a future event as a virtual document in the structural plane.

Language-internal evidence in support of the correspondences between the imperfect/perfective tenses and the two planes distinguished above comes from the consideration of three kinds of data in Spanish: (i) the expression of past habituals and generics; (ii) the grammaticality judgments of low-transitive sentences; (iii) the consideration of certain implicatures associated with the choice of the imperfect and the preterit.

2.1. The expression of past habituals and past generics[11]

In Spanish, the imperfect is used for the expression of past habitual situations (24a), the preterit for nonhabitual repetitives (24b).

(24) *El   año pasado **iba/fui**   a nadar   todos los*
  the   year last   **went-IMPF/PRET** to swim   all   the

  días.
  days
  a. IMPF: 'I used to go swimming every day last year.'(habitual)
  b. PRET: 'I went swimming every day last year.' (non-habitual repetitive)

In addition, the imperfect may be used to express generic statements (25a), i.e. statements in which a property is valid for all the members of the class the subject belongs to (Langacker 1999: 254), or statements which do not refer to a specific situation (Kuroda 1992).[12] When the preterit is used, a specific reading is more likely to occur, whereby reference is made to a specific event at a point in time (25b).

(25) Los   barberos   **sacaban/sacaron**   muelas.
      the   barbers   **took out-IMPF/PRET** teeth
      a. IMPF: 'Barbers took out teeth.' (generic reading)
      b. PRET: 'The barbers took out teeth.' (specific, nongeneric reading)

The correspondences between the imperfect and habituality/genericity on the one hand, and those between the preterit and nonhabituality/nongenericity on the other, follow from an analysis of these notions within the model of the structured world provided by Langacker (1991, 1999) and from the characterization of the preterit and the imperfect within this model, as I will show next.

Nonhabitual repetitives such as *John read his book every day last week* are part of the actual plane. Their structure is given in Figure 8 (the figure is provided in Langacker 1999: 252).

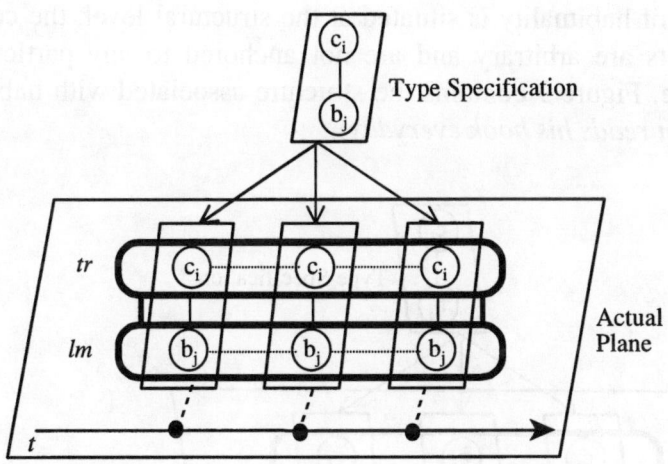

Figure 8. Repetitive

As schematized in Figure 8, a repetitive profiles a higher-order event which is represented by the lines in boldface surrounding and linking all trajectors (tr), *John*, and landmarks (lm), *his book*. The higher-order event comprises multiple-event instances of the same event type (e.g. 'John read his book'), and connects the higher-order trajectory, comprising the trajectors of all the component event instances, to the higher-order landmark comprising the landmarks of all the component event instances. The dotted correspondence lines linking the trajectors and the landmarks indicate that the subjects (*John*) and the objects (*his book*) are the same throughout. Finally, the event instances of 'John reading his book' are conceived of as being actual, and hence each one of these event instances is anchored to particular points in time, as indicated in Figure 8.

By contrast, habituals and generics "designate an imperfective process defined by its stable role as part of the scripts of how the world is expected to work" (Langacker 1991: 266), and are therefore part of the structural plane. In particular, a habitual profiles a higher-order event in the structural plane. The higher-order event is made up of component events of the same type in which the particular individuals (landmarks and trajectors) are the same, as indicated by the dotted lines linking all the trajectors and all the landmarks. Since the relationship of habituality is situated at the structural level, the component events are arbitrary and are not anchored to any particular point in time. Figure 9 contains the structure associated with habituals (e.g. *John reads his book everyday*).

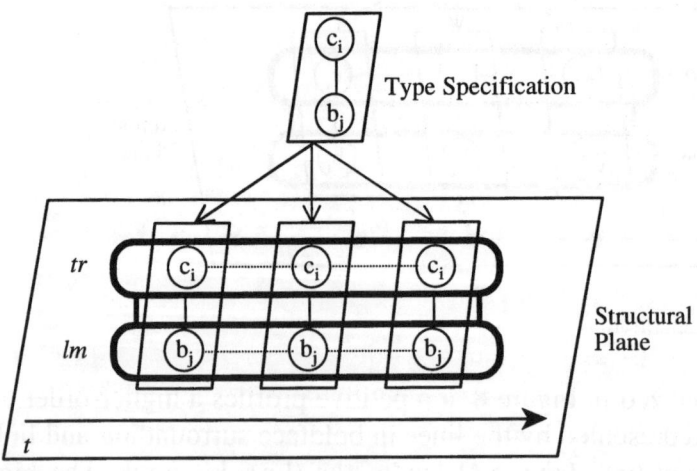

Figure 9. Habitual

Finally, a plural generic statement summarizes over arbitrary instances of potential trajectors and landmarks in the structural plane: for any entity which belongs to the class denoted by the trajector, the situation designated by the sentence follows. A sentence such as *Cats stalk birds* (Langacker 1999: 251) is a generic statement, and Figure 10 sketches its structure. It should be noted that the absence of a dotted correspondence line uniting all the trajectors (*cats*) and all the landmarks (*birds*) of the event type 'cat stalk bird' indicates that different instances of cats and birds are involved. Like in the case of habituals, the event instances are not anchored to points in time.

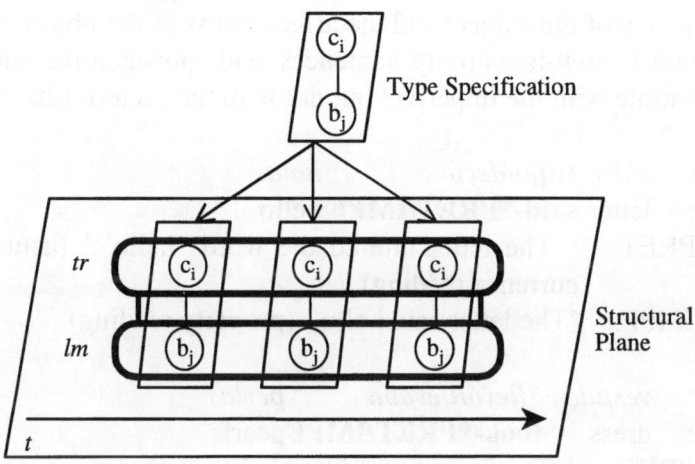

Figure 10. Plural generic

Based on the characterizations of habituals and generics, readings of habituality and genericity in sentences with the imperfect (24a, 25a) indicate that the role of the imperfect is to designate a situation within the structural plane.[13] Along the same line of reasoning, it may be concluded that the role of the preterit is to designate a past situation within the actual plane, since clauses with the preterit designate repetitives (24b) and nongeneric sentences (25b), that is, situations which are part of the actual plane.

2.2. Low-transitivity sentences: Nonagentive subjects and nonaffected objects

Hopper and Thompson (1980: 251) argue that "transitivity is traditionally understood as a global property of an entire clause such that an activity is "carried over" or "transferred" from an agent to a patient". Building upon this characterization, one of their objectives is to isolate the component parts of the *transitivity* notion, "each of which suggests a scale according to which clauses can be ranked" (Hopper and Thompson 1980: 251). Two of the multiple component parts of the notion of transitivity identified by Hopper and Thompson are the agency of the subject and the affectedness of the object.

In Spanish, low-transitivity sentences with nonagentive subjects are compatible with the imperfect but not with the preterit (26, 27).

(26) *La carta *dijo/decía hola.*
 the letter **said-*PRET/IMPF** hello
 a. PRET: *'The letter uttered the word "hello".' (actual occurrence reading)
 b. IMPF: 'The letter said hello.' (property reading)

(27) *El vestido *llevó/llevaba perlas.*
 the dress **took-*PRET/IMPF** pearls
 a. PRET: *'The dress carried pearls.' (actual occurrence reading)
 b. IMPF: 'The dress had pearls sewn into it.' (property reading)

When the preterit is used, the *actual occurrence* reading surfaces, designating actual events which have taken place at a specific point in time. Thus, in (26a) there is an instance of the event of saying hello (the letter said "hello"), and in (27a) there is an instance of the event of carrying pearls at some point in the past (the dress carried some pearls). Obviously, these situations are pragmatically unlikely, as reflected by the asterisk mark next to the examples. By contrast, when the imperfect is used the *property* reading surfaces; that is, the sentences designate a property ascribed to the subjects. Under this reading there is no activity involved in the events described and the subjects do not take on an agentive role: in (26b) the letter had the property of saying hello (I read it), in (27b) the dress had the property of having pearls sewn into it (I saw it or I was told about it).

The correlations between the property reading and the imperfect, and between the actual occurrence reading and the preterit, are reflections of the two different conceptions of the world imposed by the imperfect and the preterit, as stated within the analysis proposed here. On the one hand, the property reading associated with the imperfect describes the way the world or an entity in the world is in the structural plane. It describes a state of affairs which is not stated of a specific point in time, e.g. it is not the case that the letter said hello yesterday but not today (26a). On the other hand, the actual occurrence reading associated with the preterit portrays an event which is anchored to a specific past point in the actual plane. Under this construal, the subject takes an agentive role and it is held responsible for the occurrence of the situation, as evidenced by the unacceptability of (26b) and (27b).

Additional evidence for the characterizations of the preterit and the imperfect along the terms proposed here comes from the consideration of low-transitivity sentences of a different kind, namely, those with nonaffected objects. These sentences are characterized by the absence of a direct object in sentences which contain a transitive verb (28), or by the nonspecificity of the instance designated by the direct object (29). Like low-transitivity sentences with nonagentive subjects, sentences with nonaffected objects tend to occur with the imperfect. Consider the sentences in (28) and (29).

(28) *Juan oía/*oyó,   María   no.*
   Juan **heard-IMPF/*PRET**   María   not
   a. IMPF: 'Juan was capable of hearing, María was not.'
   b. PRET: *'Juan heard, María did not.'

(29) *Juan escribía/escribió*   una   novela   en dos   días.
Juan **wrote-IMPF/PRET** a   novel   in two   days
a. IMPF: 'Juan was able to write a novel in two days.'
b. PRET: 'Juan wrote a novel in two days.'

When the preterit is used in (28b), the sentence designates an actual occurrence of the event of hearing located at some point in the past. That is, the speaker portrays a situation in which the subject, *Juan*, carried out a conscious act of perception, e.g. Juan heard something at some point in the past. It is an actual event in the actual plane. However, since there is no object of perception, the sentence is unacceptable.[14] By contrast, when the imperfect is used (28a), the sentence does not describe an activity; it describes a property of the subject which is not located at a specific point in time. In the present case, the sentence states that Juan had the property of hearing, i.e. of being capable of hearing, a state of affairs which does not require the explicit presence of an object of perception. The situation describes the way things are in the structural plane.

Similarly, when the imperfect is used in (29a), reference is not made to one specific novel or to a specific 'novel-writing' event. In fact, it could be the case that Juan had never written a novel in his life, but we may be hypothesizing that he would have been able to write it in two days if he had wanted to. Thus, the property reading which is associated with the way things are in the structural plane surfaces.[15] By contrast, when the preterit is used (29b), the sentence designates an actual occurrence of the event anchored to a point in time: the speaker states that Juan actually wrote a novel in two days. The actual occurrence reading which belongs in the actual plane surfaces in this case.

As a summary of the previous discussion it may be stated that a low degree of transitivity correlates with the nonactualization of the situation designated by the sentences and hence, with the property reading within the structural plane. From a formal point of view, this reading is associated with the choice of the imperfect, as accounted for by the analysis proposed here. By contrast, the occurrence of the preterit with low-transitivity sentences results in the actual occurrence reading as stated by our analysis.

2.3. Presence and absence of implicatures with the preterit and the imperfect

The two different conceptions of the world imposed by the imperfect and the preterit (reflected in the property reading and the actual occurrence reading, respectively) are directly responsible for the presence or the absence of implicatures of a certain kind. Consider the sentences in (30) and (31).

(30) *El coche me **costó/costaba** dos millones.*
 the car me **cost-PRET/IMPF** two millions
 a. PRET: 'The car cost me two million.' → (I bought it)
 b. IMPF: 'The car cost me two million.' → (maybe I bought it, maybe I did not)

(31) *La película fue/era interesante.*
 the movie **was-PRET/IMPF** interesting
 a. PRET: 'The movie was interesting.' → (I saw the movie)
 b. IMPF: 'The movie was interesting.' → (maybe I saw it, maybe not)

When the preterit is used, the sentences designate situations which are anchored to a specific point in time in the actual plane, giving rise to the implicatures 'I bought the car' in (30a) and 'I saw the movie' in (31a). When the imperfect is used, the property reading surfaces and the situations are interpreted within the structural plane where no connection to the timeline is established. Thus, in (30b) the speaker states that the car had the property of being worth a certain amount of money. This property is not stated of a specific point in time, and consequently the interpretation that the speaker has bought the car does not surface. Similarly, in (31b) the speaker states that the movie has the property of being interesting, and since the property is not associated with a specific point in time, the implicature 'I saw it' does not appear.

2.4. The structure of the world and viewing arrangement

Based on the claims made in sections 1 and 2, the following characterizations of the preterit and the imperfect are proposed. On the one hand, the imperfect is used to describe the way things are in the world, as reflected in the property reading characterizing sentences with the imperfect. The properties ascribed to the subjects of sentences with the imperfect are apprehended through a past viewpoint which is responsible for the sense of pastness associated with the designated situations. Thus, the sentence *The letter said hello* designates the property of the letter 'saying hello' as apprehended by the speaker at a past time, for example, at the time in the past in which she read the letter. On the other hand, the preterit is used to talk about actual occurrences that happened in the world in the past, as perceived through a viewpoint which is distant from the situation.

3. Discourse tracking devices: Space accessibility

Language involves the construction of mental spaces, relations between them, and relations between elements within them (Fauconnier 1994: 2). Mental spaces are separate domains of referential structure which contain partial state descriptions conveyed by the discourse (Facounnier 1994: xi–xxxvi) and are built up in accordance with instructions provided by linguistic expressions. The default space in the organization of the information provided in a discourse is the speaker's reality space, R: "the speaker's mental representation of reality" (Fauconnier 1994: 15), which does not necessarily coincide with the real world. Additional spaces are created by space builders as the discourse progresses (e.g. prepositional phrases such as *in the movies*, which create a movie space; adverbs such as *probably* and *possibly*, which create a probability space; and subject-verb combinations such as *Max believes* ——, which create a belief space; Fauconnier 1994: 17).

Discourses may be characterized by the presence of several spaces such as the default space, R, and spaces different from R (e.g. a belief space, a probability space, an irrealis space, and so on), such that the linguistic elements in them may be interpreted in one or another space. Following Doiz-Bienzobas (1995) and Doiz-Bienzobas and Mejías-Bikandi (2000), I propose that the role of the preterit and the imperfect is to provide instructions which determine the identity of the space where the situations they designate are to be interpreted. In particular, the following two characterizations are argued for.

(i) The role of the imperfect is to render accessible a space M different from the speaker's reality space R for the interpretation of the situation it designates (Figure 11).

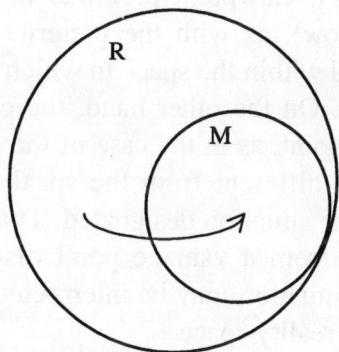

Figure 11. The imperfect

(ii) The role of the preterit is to state that the situation it designates is interpreted in the matrix clause, the speaker's reality space R. A space different from R is not accessible for the interpretation of the situation designated by the preterit (Figure 12).

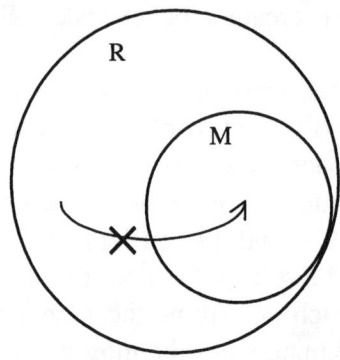

Figure 12. The preterit

The properties of space accessibility associated with the preterit and the imperfect, represented in Figures 11 and 12, are closely related to the viewing arrangements of the two forms. On the one hand, when a situation is perceived through a viewpoint proximal to the ground (e.g. the speaker's here-and-now), as with the preterit, the situation is more likely to be interpreted within the space in which the speaker is, the speaker's reality space. On the other hand, the construal of a situation from a distal viewpoint, as in the case of the imperfect, facilitates access into a space different from the speaker's reality space for the interpretation of the situation designated. That is to say, when a situation is construed from a vantage point distant from the speaker's here-and-now, the situation may be interpreted as part of a space other than the speaker's reality space.

Evidence for the characterizations of the imperfect and the preterit in terms of space accessibility as stated here comes from the consideration of four groups of linguistic phenomena: subject identification, determination of quantifier scope, the expression of irrealis, and the interpretation of sentences with perception verbs.

3.1. Subject identification

The choice of the imperfect or the preterit may determine the identity of the subject in sentences lacking an overt one. Thus, even though the second sentences in examples (32a) and (32b) do not have an overt subject, the identity of the subject of the event of smiling is clear to the hearer: María with the imperfect (32a), Juan with the preterit (32b).[16]

(32) a. *Juan vio   a María.   **Sonreía.***
       Juan saw-PRET to María   **smiled-IMPF**
       'Juan saw María. She was smiling.'

b. *Juan vio   a María.   **Sonrió.***
   Juan saw-PRET to María   **smiled-PRET**
   'Juan saw María. He smiled.'

Under a Mental Space representation, the sentence in (32) cues the construction of two spaces, the speaker's reality space and the embedded perception space created by the subject-verb combination 'Juan saw ____'. Accordingly, 'Juan saw María' is introduced into the base or the speaker's reality space, and the object of perception, *María*, into the perception space, as represented in Figure 13.[17]

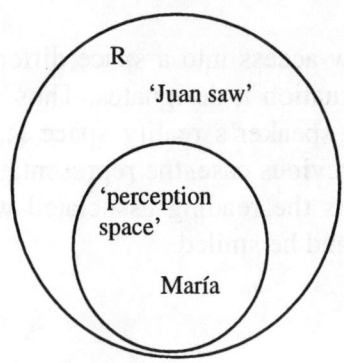

Figure 13. 'Juan saw María.'

The spatial configuration in Figure 13 is characterized by the presence of two spaces, both of which are accessible for the interpretation of the discourse.

The analysis proposed here states that the role of the preterit and the imperfect is to determine the space relevant for the interpretation of the sentence in configurations like the one provided in Figure 13. In particular, the imperfect allows access into a space different from R for the interpretation of the clause it modifies. Accordingly, the event of smiling designated by the imperfect in (32a) is interpreted in the perception space. Figure 14 represents this configuration, which automatically accounts for the interpretation of (32a), namely, Juan saw María and he saw her smiling.

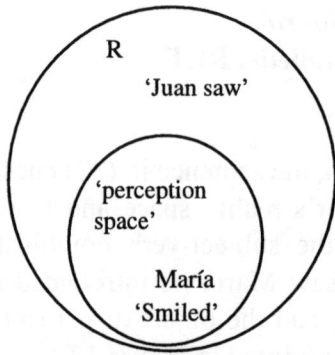

Figure 14. Sentence (32a) and the imperfect

By contrast, the preterit does not allow access into a space different from R for the interpretation of the situation it designates. Thus, the event of smiling is interpreted in the speaker's reality space R, as represented in Figure 15. Like in the previous case, the representation of (32b) provided in Figure 15 reflects the reading associated with the sentence, namely, Juan saw María and he smiled.

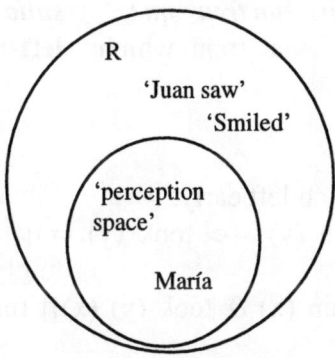

Figure 15. Sentence (32b) and the preterit

3.2. The determination of quantifier scope

The sentences in (33) and (34) illustrate the interaction between the imperfect and the preterit, and the determination of the scope of the quantifier. On the one hand, when the preterit is used (33), the wide scope reading surfaces. That is, the universal quantifier is within the scope of the existential quantifier, as reflected in the logical representation of the sentence. On the other hand, when the imperfect is used (34), the narrow scope reading is also given, whereby the existential quantifier is within the scope of the universal quantifier.

(33) *Todas   las   mujeres   cogieron   un tren   que*
     every   the   women   took   a train   which

  salió   temprano.
  left-PRET early
  'All the women took a train which left early.'
  $\exists x \ [\text{train} (x) \ \& \ \forall y \ [\text{woman} (y) \longrightarrow \text{took} (y) (x)]]$ (wide scope)

(34) *Todas las mujeres cogieron un tren que salía*
    every the women took a train which **left-IMPF**

temprano.
early
'All the women took a train which left early.'
a. ∃x [train (x) & ∀y [woman (y) —> took (y) (x)]] (wide scope)
b. ∀y [woman (y) —> ∃x [train (x) & took (y) (x)]] (narrow scope)

The logical representations for the wide and the narrow scope reading provided in (33) and (34) reflect the semantic differences between the two sentences. However, they do not account for the relationship between quantifier scope and the imperfect and the preterit, or for the specific correspondences that have been observed. Doiz-Bienzobas (1995) and Doiz-Bienzobas and Mejías-Bikandi (2000) show that an analysis of the data within the framework of Mental Spaces accounts for the existence of these particular correspondences.

Quantified expressions introduce a new embedded space Q (Fauconnier 1994: 166). The narrow and wide scope readings of quantified expressions differ with respect to the identity of the space, Q or R, into which an indefinite phrase introduces its element. Under the narrow scope reading, the indefinite phrase introduces its element directly into the quantifier space as in the case of (34b), schematized in Figure 16 (adapted from Fauconnier 1994: 166). The indefinite phrase 'a train' (t) is introduced directly in Q. *t* and *w* are roles, i.e. they do not have a fixed value in R.[18] Thus, when *w* is filled in by a counterpart in R, *t* takes some potentially different value in R. That is to say, for every woman who took a train, there is a train in Q, such that the trains are different in R (or at least not necessarily the same).

The preterit and the imperfect as grounding predications 329

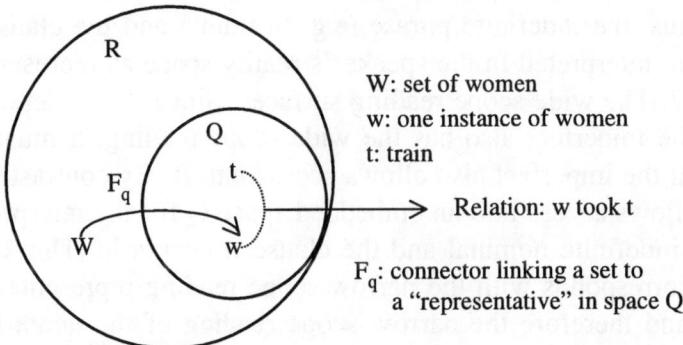

Figure 16. Narrow scope reading of the sentence in (34)

Under the wide scope reading of quantified expressions, the indefinite phrase introduces an element t_o ('train') in R, as represented in Figure 17. Since t has a counterpart in R (t_o), the indefinite phrase 'a train' gets a fixed value in R. This configuration is translated into the reading 'every woman took the same train'.

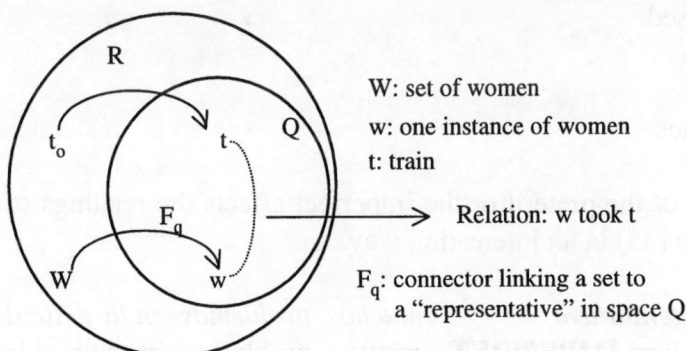

Figure 17. Wide scope reading of the sentence in (33)

The correspondences between the preterit and the wide scope reading and the imperfect and the narrow scope reading are automatically accounted for under the analysis of the imperfect and the preterit within the framework of Mental Spaces. According to our characterization, the preterit does not allow access into a space different from R. Thus, the indefinite phrase (e.g. 'a train') and the clause it occurs in are interpreted in the speaker's reality space as represented in Figure 17. The wide scope reading surfaces. Since the sentence in (34) with the imperfect also has the wide scope reading, it must be the case that the imperfect also allows access into R. By contrast, the imperfect allows access into an embedded space Q for the interpretation of the indefinite nominal and the clause it occurs in. This configuration corresponds with the narrow scope reading represented in Figure 16 and therefore the narrow scope reading of the quantified expression surfaces, as in the case of the sentence in (34).[19]

3.3. The expression of irrealis

In addition to the more frequently discussed use of the imperfect for the expression of children's pretend games, the following four contexts are considered for the notion of irrealis: the expression of movies, counterfactuals, dreams, and wishes. In all of these cases the imperfect is used.

3.3.1. Movies

The choice of the preterit or the imperfect affects the readings of the sentences in (35) in an interesting way.

(35)   *Juan **tenía/tuvo***   *muchos problemas en la película.*
      Juan **had-IMPF/PRET**   many   problems   in the movie
      a. IMPF: 'Juan had a lot of problems in the movie.' (it is part of the movie script)
      b. PRET: 'Juan had a lot of problems in the movie.' (e.g. in the movie-making process)

When the imperfect is used (35a), the situation 'had problems' is part of irrealis (i.e. the movie): the character played by Juan has a number of problems which are part of the movie script. When the preterit is used (35b), the situation is part of reality: Juan's problems are associated with the movie-making experience and are part of real life (e.g. remembering his lines, problems with the director and other actors).

Within the framework of Mental Spaces, linguistic expressions such as 'in the movie' cue the construction of an embedded space, the *movie space*. As stated above, the imperfect allows access into the embedded movie space for the interpretation of the situation it designates, namely, 'had problems', as a result of which Juan's problems are interpreted within the movie script, that is, as irrealis. On the other hand, the preterit does not allow access into the embedded space and it indicates that the situation 'had problems' belongs in the speaker's reality space. Consequently, Juan's problems are part of (his) reality.

3.3.2. Counterfactuals

The grammatical expression *if* cues the construction of an embedded *hypothetical space* (H). Given this configuration characterized by the existence of two spaces, H and R, our analysis predicts the grammaticality of the imperfect and the ungrammaticality of the preterit in the apodosis of the hypothetical sentence. The two predictions are borne out as illustrated by the grammaticality judgments of the sentence in (36).

(36) *Si tuviera   dinero, me   compraba/*compré una   casa.*
    if had-SUBJ money, me   **buy-IMPF/*PRET** a   house
    a. IMPF: 'If I had money, I would buy a house.'
    b. PRET: *'If I had money, I bought a house.'

As previously stated, the imperfect allows access into the embedded hypothetical space for the interpretation of the situation in the apodosis. Consequently, the situation is interpreted in the hypothetical space in accordance with the expectations set up by the hypothetical situation expressed in the protasis. By contrast, when the preterit is used the situation is interpreted in the speaker's reality space (running counter to the expectations created by the protasis) and thus, the sentence is ungrammatical.

Unlike in (36), the situation designated by the protasis of a hypothetical sentence may be part of R in some contexts. In such cases, the apodosis is also interpreted in R and our analysis predicts the grammaticality of the preterit. This prediction is confirmed by the grammaticality judgment and the interpretation of the sentence in (37).

(37) *Si Pedro estuvo en París, **robó**   el   banco.*
     if Pedro was   in Paris, **robbed-PRET** the bank
     'If Pedro$_i$ was in Paris, he$_i$ robbed the bank.'

In (37) the speaker does not know whether Pedro was in Paris or not. However, if it is the case that he was in Paris, it is also the case that he robbed the bank. That is, if the condition of being in Paris is met in R, the apodosis 'he robbed the bank' is also satisfied in the speaker's reality space (R), thereby accounting for the use of the preterit in the embedded clause.

3.3.3. Dreams

The description of dreams evokes the presence of two spaces, the reality space R and the *dream space* which is set up by the subject-verb combination 'I dreamt that ___'. As predicted by our analysis, dreams are described with the imperfect in Spanish, not with the preterit (38).

(38) *Soñé que   **ganaba/*gané**   el   premio Nobel de*
     dreamt that **won-IMPF/*PRET** the prize Nobel for

     literatura.
     literature
     'I dreamt that I won the Nobel Prize for literature.'

The imperfect allows access into the dream space and consequently, the situation it designates is interpreted as part of the speaker's dream. By contrast, situations designated by the preterit are directly introduced into R and are not interpreted as part of the dream.

The choice of the imperfect or the preterit in relative sentences describing the contents of dreams also affects the interpretation of the sentences, as illustrated in (39) (based on Mejías-Bikandi 1993).

(39) a. *En el   sueño,   la   señora que **trajo**   el*
        in the dream   the lady   who **brought-PRET** the

   libro   era   mi tía.
   book   was-IMPF   my aunt
   'In my dream, the lady who brought the book was my aunt.'

   b. *En el   sueño,   la   señora que **traía**   el*
        in the dream   the lady   who **brought-IMPF** the

   libro   era   mi tía.
   book   was-IMPF   my aunt
   'In my dream, the lady who brought the book was my aunt.'

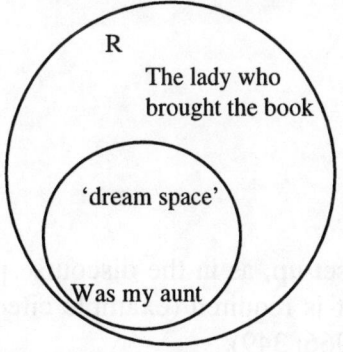

Figure 18. The preterit and the dream space

In accordance with the analysis proposed here, the situation designated by the imperfect 'was my aunt' in (39a) and (39b) is interpreted as part of the speaker's dream. That is to say, the lady is the speaker's aunt in her dream. However, the difference between (39a) and (39b) resides in the interpretation of the relative clause, 'the lady who brought-IMPF/PRET the book'. When the preterit is used (39a), the sentence is interpreted in R. That is, the lady was the speaker's aunt in her dream but she brought the book in reality, as represented in Figure 18. When the imperfect is used (39b), the embedded sentence is interpreted in the dream space, as represented in Figure 19. That is, the lady was the speaker's aunt in her dream and she brought the book in her dream as well.

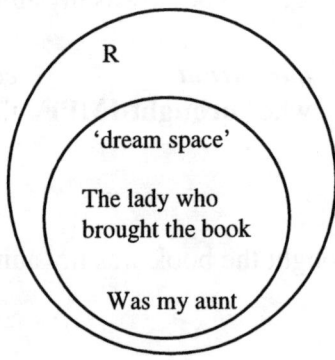

Figure 19. The imperfect and the dream space

3.3.4. Children's pretend games

In contexts where a *pretend space* is set up, as in the discourse provided in (40), the use of the imperfect is required (example cited in Fleischman 1989: 16, from Warnant 1966: 349).

(40) *Vamos a jugar a policías y ladrones: Yo **era** el jefe de la banda; éste **era** el que **abría** la caja fuerte; vosotros los que **dábais** el asalto y éstos los guardias civiles.*

Let's play cops and robbers: I **was-IMPF** the leader of the gang; this one **was-IMPF** the one who **opened-IMPF** the safe; you **gave-IMPF** the attack and these the police.
'Let's play cops and robbers. I'll be the leader of the gang; he'll be the one who opens the safe; you['ll be] the ones who carry out the attack and they['ll be] the police.'

The use of the imperfect in this context follows automatically from our analysis. The imperfect allows access into the pretend space, and the situations it designates are interpreted in this space. By contrast, the use of the preterit denies access into the pretend space and consequently, the situations are interpreted in the speaker's reality space.

3.3.5. Wishes

The imperfect is also used for the coding of wishes (41) where, in addition to the speaker's reality space, an embedded *wish space* is cued. As predicted by our analysis, the preterit may not be used.

(41) *¡De qué buena gana me*   ***bebía/*bebí***   *un vaso de*
     how gladly   me   **drank-IMPF/*PRET** a glass of

     agua!
     water
     'How gladly I would drink a glass of water!'

As a summary of this section on the irrealis, it can be stated that sentences expressing wishes, pretend games, dreams, counterfactuals, and movies create an additional irrealis space in which the situation designated by the imperfect is interpreted. In all these contexts the situations designated by the preterit are interpreted in the speaker's reality space. It should be emphasized that the analysis proposed here accounts for the grammaticality judgments as well as for the subtle semantic differences between sentences with the imperfect and the preterit.

3.4. The interpretation of perception verbs

The perception verb *hear* has two meanings, 'the thing heard' (42a) and 'the content of heard speech' (42b) (Sweetser 1990: 35).[20]

(42) a. *I heard John fall/falling.*
b. *I heard that John fell.*

Kirsner and Thompson (1976) and Barwise (1978) talk about the contrast in meaning between sentences such as (42a) and (42b) as a general property of *-ing* and "plain form" constructions with sensory verbs, and of "*that*-clause + sensory verb" constructions, respectively. In particular, Kirsner and Thompson refer to the meaning associated with the constructions in (42a) as "direct perception" and to that in (42b) as "indirect perception"; Barwise refers to sentences such as (42a) as containing an "epistemically neutral perception report" and, for (42b), as containing an "epistemically positive perception report".

In Spanish the distinction between direct and indirect perception, or epistemically neutral and positive perception reports, may be expressed through the choice of the preterit or the imperfect, as shown by the sentence in (43).

(43) *Oí que alguien **entraba/entró**.*
heard that someone **entered-IMPF/PRET**
a. IMPF: 'I heard someone enter/entering.'
b. PRET: 'I heard (that) someone entered.'

Under a Mental Space representation, perception verbs partition information into the base (or the speaker's reality space) and an embedded perception space. The base space contains the act of auditory perception; the perception space contains the object of perception itself. According to the analysis proposed here, in (43a) the choice of the imperfect renders the perception space accessible for the interpretation of the embedded clause 'that someone entered-IMPF'. That is to say, the embedded sentence with the imperfect designates the object of perception (e.g. feet shuffling or the slamming of a door) recognizable as the noises made by someone entering a house.[21] This interpretation is represented in Figure 20.

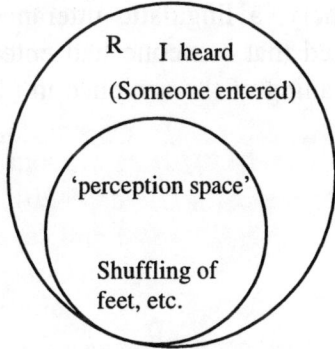

Figure 20. 'Hear' and the imperfect

By contrast, when the preterit is used our analysis states that the embedded clause it occurs in, 'that someone entered-PRET', does not belong in the perception space. That is, the embedded sentence does not designate the noises that are associated with someone entering a house, but rather a state of affairs in R, namely, 'someone entered', as represented in Figure 21.

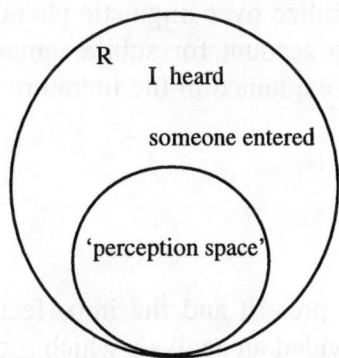

Figure 21. 'Hear' and the preterit

Figure 21 represents the occurrence of an act of perception which does not have a corresponding object of perception, an unlikely state of affairs given the acceptability of the sentence. However, the "hearsay" interpretation of the verb 'hear' in (43b) reveals the existence of an inferred object of perception, namely, a linguistic utterance: I heard a linguistic utterance which stated that someone had entered. Accordingly, Figure 22 reflects the meaning of the sentence in (43b) more accurately than Figure 21.

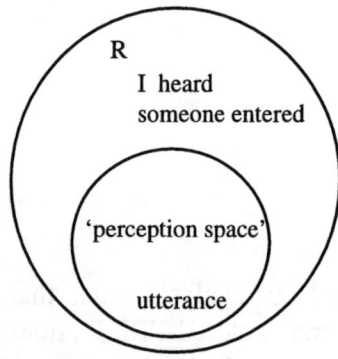

Figure 22. "Hearsay"

To conclude this section, I would like to emphasize the fact that the analysis of the preterit and the imperfect within the framework of Mental Spaces has allowed us to generalize over linguistic phenomena of quite a different nature, and to account for subtle semantic contrasts most of which have not been explained in the literature before.

4. Concluding remarks

In this paper I have characterized the preterit and the imperfect as grounding predications, and I have provided an analysis which establishes the way in which these predications relate a state of affairs to the ground. In order to do so, I have resorted to the use of epistemic notions, such as distance and viewpoint, within the timeline model and the model of the structured world (Langacker 1991, 1999). In addition, I have considered the role of the preterit and imperfect as discourse tracking devices (Fauconnier 1994), according to which the choice of the imperfect or the preterit determines the relevant domain for the interpretation of the situations they designate.

In particular, I have characterized the preterit and the imperfect as follows. On the one hand, the role of the preterit is to locate a situation in the past within the actual plane, where situations are descriptions of which things happen(ed) in the world. Situations designated by the preterit are construed through the speaker's viewpoint in the ground, creating a sense of detachment between speaker and situation. Finally, the presence of the viewpoint at speech time is directly related to the interpretation of the situations designated by the preterit within the speaker's reality space. On the other hand, the imperfect provides a past viewpoint removed from the ground from which the situation is construed, thereby providing a sense of pastness to the clauses modified by the imperfect. However, situations taking the imperfect are not temporally anchored; they describe the way things are in the world within the structural plane, as reflected in the property readings associated with these sentences. Finally, the presence of a distal conceptualizer apprehending the situation with respect to the ground is directly linked to the possibility of interpreting situations with the imperfect within a space that is different from the speaker's reality space.

The analysis I have provided does not include the aspectual, temporal, and discourse-related notions which have been traditionally proposed to characterize the two forms. While these notions provide partially correct descriptions, I believe that they are not fundamental for the characterization of the preterit and the imperfect. In fact, I propose that they are byproducts of the analysis I have presented in this paper. Thus, actual past situations which are viewed from the ground are necessarily bounded and anterior to a reference point, as stated under the aspectual and the temporal analyses of the preterit, respectively. Furthermore, actual past occurrences which are interpreted in a new matrix space tend to provide foregrounded information. By contrast, situations which are perceived through a past viewpoint located at situation time are likely to be interpreted as unbounded and simultaneous to a past point in time, as stated by the aspectual and temporal analyses of the imperfect, respectively. However, situations designated by the imperfect need not be unbounded or simultaneous with some temporal point at all times, as shown by some of the data considered here. Finally, situations that elaborate the embedded spaces in a discourse and describe the way things are, tend to provide background information. I believe that a characterization of a more abstract nature, such as the one proposed here, is more satisfactory in these respects.

Notes

* I would like to express my deepest gratitude to Gilles Fauconnier, John Moore, and especially to Ronald Langacker for their illuminating discussions of a previous version of the work presented in this paper. Special thanks also go to Frank Brisard and René Dirven for their insightful comments on this particular version of the paper. I would also like to thank Luis García Fernández for comments on some of the issues presented in this paper. Needless to say, any remaining errors or inaccuracies are my own responsibility. The research conducted for the paper was sponsored by a grant of the *Programa de Formación de Investigadores* from the *Departamento de Educación, Universidades e Investigación* of the Basque Government.
1. The aspectual approach is perhaps the most widely accepted analysis. Its main proponents are Alarcos Llorach (1970), Bennett (1981), Comrie (1976), Criado de Val (1972), Dowty (1979), Fernández Ramírez (1986), Fleischman (1990, 1991), Gili y Gaya (1948), Lamadrid, Bull, and Briscoe (1974), RAE (1983), and Smith (1983, 1986, 1991). The temporal approach is represented by Bello (1951), Rojo (1974, 1976, 1990), and Guitart (1978). Finally, the discourse approach includes several proposals of a different kind, such as the Anaphora approach (Partee 1973), Discourse Representation Theory (Kamp and Rohrer 1983, Kamp and Reyle 1993), and the analyses provided by Vet (1991), Silva-Corvalán (1983, 1984), and Hopper and Thompson (1980). See also Fernández Ramírez (1986) for an excellent descriptive account of the uses associated with the imperfect.
2. Unlike the analysis I present here, De Mulder and Vetters (this volume) propose an anaphoric analysis of the *imparfait* based on its aspectual imperfective value.

The preterit and the imperfect as grounding predications 341

3. At this point, there is no reference to the characterization of past forms within the elaborated/basic epistemic models, whose main idea is that the conceptualizer accepts certain occurrences as being real whereas others are not (Langacker, this volume). Within these models, the notion of distance is interpreted in the epistemic sphere, whereby the past tense may be used to indicate irrealis (e.g. *If I were you...*). I consider the choice of the imperfect (and not the preterit) for the expression of irrealis in section 3.
4. The behavior of the preterit and the imperfect in indirect speech is analyzed in more detail in Doiz-Bienzobas (1998), where the fact-prediction principle (Cutrer 1994) is shown to play a determining role.
5. The position taken by the viewer determines the "maximal field of vision" (*MF*). Within that field, the area which is the general locus of attention is called the "viewing frame" (*VF*); the specific object of perception, the target, is the "focus" (*F*) (*V* stands for "viewer", *VP* in my terminology) (Langacker 1995). In my examples, the situation is generally the focus.

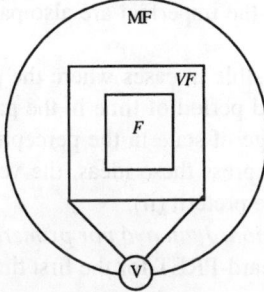

Figure i. Visual perception

6. For representational purposes I have located the situation in the past with respect to the ground, but as I have argued in section 1.1, situations with the imperfect need not be past. However, the viewpoint apprehending the situations, which is provided by the imperfect, must be located in the past.
7. A similar analysis is proposed by Lunn (1985: 57).
8. An alternative reading, whereby the festivities actually took place, is also possible with the imperfect. The occurrence of this reading is predicted by our analysis and surfaces when the viewpoint associated with the imperfect is located at situation time (Figure 5), as in the case of (14b). The "at" reading of the imperfect captures the presence of an experiencing self which describes the situation as it was taking place in the past. I discuss this alternative viewing arrangement in section 1.2.2.
9. The *imperfecto de ruptura* is normally included in a list of miscellaneous uses of the imperfect and is not generally accounted for.
10. Goldsmith and Woisetschlaeger (1982: 80) apply the distinction between the two kinds of knowledge to the semantic difference between the progressive and the simple present in sentences such as *The engine isn't smoking anymore*

vs. *The engine doesn't smoke anymore.* They argue that one value of the progressive is to provide phenomenal as opposed to structural knowledge. See Langacker (1987, 1999: 250) for comments on this analysis.
11. Habituals and generics have been studied in the literature from different perspectives. The majority of the analyses center around two issues that are nicely integrated in Langacker's (1999) account: (i) the abstract nature of the entity designated by the habitual/generic proposition (Brinton 1987: 205), although the issue regarding its exact nature is somewhat controversial (Lyons 1977: 716; Vendler 1967: 108; Brinton 1987: 210; Smith 1991: 42); (ii) the lack of a temporal setting for the designated situation, as proposed in the analysis of bare plurals (Carlson 1977; Diesing 1992; Kratzer 1989) and in the distinction between descriptions and predications (i.e. habituals and generics) proposed by Kuroda (1992).
12. A nonhabitual, specific reading of the subject is also possible with the imperfect in (25a). We are not interested in this reading at this point.
13. Nonhabitual situations with the imperfect are also part of the structural plane, as discussed in 2.2.
14. The preterit is not even possible in cases where the property of being able to hear is situated in a bounded period of time in the past, or in cases where the predicate designates a change of state in the perceptual capacities of the subject, as in (i). In order to express these ideas, the verb 'be able to' has to be used in combination with the preterit (ii):
    (i) *Después de la operación, Juan oyó por primera vez en su vida.*
    'After surgery, Juan heard-PRET for the first time in his life.'

    (ii) *Después de la operación, Juan pudo oir por primera vez en su vida.*
    'After surgery, Juan was-PRET able to hear for the first time in his life.'
15. Fernández Ramírez (1986: 275) refers to this reading as the *imperfecto de hecho virtual* "imperfect of virtual acts".
16. In addition to the difference in the identity of the subject, the sentences in (32) also differ with respect to the aspectual properties of the predicates 'was smiling' in (32a) vs. 'smiled' in (32b). In Doiz-Bienzobas (1995) I argue that the semantic import of the preterit leads to the construal of the situations as bounded: actual past situations construed from the ground are necessarily viewed as bounded. However, counter to the aspectual analysis of the imperfect and following Rojo (1974, 1976, 1990: 39), I argue that the imperfect in itself does not construe the situation as unbounded, as shown by the fact that situations with the imperfect may be bounded or unbounded (e.g. [21]), depending on the inherent aktionsart of the predicates themselves. In the present case, the predicate 'smile' is an activity (i.e. an intrinsically unbounded process) and it is construed as one in combination with the imperfect.

17. It is important to note that mental spaces are partial structures. Thus, in the example that concerns us here, the element *María* is also part of Juan's reality space although its occurrence in the perception space is more relevant for the interpretation of the sentence.
18. Roles are expressions such as *the President*, which may be filled in by a particular value, e.g. Reagan, Bush, Clinton, and so on.
19. Luis García Fernández (personal communication) has recently called my attention to the existence of sentences with the preterit with a narrow scope reading. He believes the correspondences between the referential reading and the preterit on the one hand, and between the nonreferential reading and the imperfect on the other, are responsible for the association of the wide scope reading with the preterit and of the narrow scope reading with the imperfect, respectively. A more detailed analysis of the phenomenon of quantifier scope and the choice of the imperfect and the preterit needs to be carried out.
20. See Sweetser (1990: 35) for a diachronic analysis of the semantic change of the verbs *hear* and *see* along the lines discussed here.
21. The imperfect also allows access into the speaker's reality space, as for example in the sentence in (i), where the embedded clause designates a habitual meaning and the main clause designates an act of indirect perception:
    (i) Oí   que   siempre entraba   por   la puerta principal.
        heard   that   always   entered-IMPF through the door   main
        'I heard that he always came in through the front door.'

References

Alarcos Llorach, Emilio
    1970   *Estudios de Gramática Funcional del Español*. Madrid: Gredos.
Banfield, Ann
    1982   *Unspeakable Sentences: Narration and Representation in the Language of Fiction*. Boston: Routledge and Kegan Paul.
Barwise, Jon
    1978   Scenes and other situations. *Journal of Philosophical Logic* 7: 47–80.
Bello, Andrés
    1951   *Gramática*. Caracas: Ediciones del Ministerio de Educación.
Bennett, Michael
    1981   Of tense and aspect: One analysis. In: Philip J. Tedeschi and Annie Zaenen (eds.), *Syntax and Semantics*, Volume 14: *Tense and Aspect*, 13–30. New York: Academic.

Brinton, Laurel J.
 1987 The aspectual nature of states and habits. *Folia Linguistica* 21: 195–214.
Carlson, Gregory
 1977 A unified analysis of the English bare plural. *Linguistics and Philosophy* 1: 413–457.
Comrie, Bernard
 1976 *Aspect*. Cambridge: Cambridge University Press.
Criado de Val, M.
 1972 *Fisonomía del Español y de las Lenguas Modernas*. Madrid: S.A.E.T.A.
Cutrer, Michelle
 1994 Time and tense in narrative and everyday language. Ph.D. dissertation, Department of Linguistics, University of California, San Diego.
De Mulder, Walter and Carl Vetters
 this vol. The French *imparfait*, determiners and grounding.
Diesing, Molly
 1992 *Indefinites*. Cambridge, MA: MIT Press.
Doiz-Bienzobas, Aintzane
 1995 The preterit and the imperfect in Spanish: Past situation vs. past viewpoint. Ph.D. dissertation, Department of Linguistics, University of California, San Diego.
 1998 Contrastes aspectuels dans le discours indirect. *Langues* 1: 114–124.
Doiz-Bienzobas, Aintzane and Errapel Mejías-Bikandi
 2000 El aspecto, la accesibilidad y el alcance de los cuantificadores. In: Ricardo Maldonado (ed.), *Estudios Cognoscitivos del Español*, 281–295. Castellón-Querétaro: Spanish Association of Applied Linguistics and The University of Querétaro, México.
Dowty, David R.
 1979 *Word Meaning and Montague Grammar*. Dordrecht: Reidel.
Fauconnier, Gilles
 1994 *Mental Spaces: Aspects of Meaning Construction in Natural Language*. Cambridge: Cambridge University Press. First published Cambridge, MA: MIT Press [1985].
Fernández Ramírez, Salvador
 1986 *Gramática Española: El Verbo y la Oración*, Volume 4. Madrid: Arco/Libros.
Fleischman, Suzanne
 1989 Temporal distance: A basic linguistic metaphor. *Studies in Language* 13: 1–50.

1990   *Tense and Narrativity: From Medieval Performance to Modern Fiction.* Austin: University of Texas Press.
1991   Verb tense and point of view in narrative. In: Suzanne Fleischman and Linda R. Waugh (eds.), *Discourse-Pragmatics and the Verb*, 26–54. London: Routledge.

Gili y Gaya, Samuel
1948   *Curso Superior de Sintaxis Española.* Barcelona: Spes.

Givón, Talmy
1984   *Syntax: A Functional-Typological Introduction*, Volume 1. Amsterdam: John Benjamins.

Goldsmith, John and Erich Woisetschlaeger
1982   The logic of the English progressive. *Linguistic Inquiry* 13: 79–89.

Guitart, Jorge M.
1978   Aspects of Spanish aspect: A new look at the preterit/imperfect distinction. In: Margarita Suñer (ed.), *Contemporary Studies in Romance Linguistics*, 132–168. Washington, D.C.: Georgetown University Press.

Hopper, Paul J. and Sandra A. Thompson
1980   Transitivity in grammar and discourse. *Language* 56: 251–299.

Janssen, Theo A. J. M.
this vol. Deictic principles of pronominals, demonstratives, and tenses.

Kamp, Hans and Uwe Reyle
1993   *From Discourse to Logic*, Parts 1 and 2. Dordrecht: Kluwer.

Kamp, Hans and Christian Rohrer
1983   Tense in texts. In: Rainer Bäuerle, Christoph Schwarze and Arnim von Stechow (eds.), *Meaning, Use, and Interpretation of Language*, 250–269. Berlin: Mouton de Gruyter.

Kirsner, Robert and Sandra Thompson
1976   The role of pragmatic inference in semantics: A study of sensory verb complements in English. *Glossa* 10: 200–240.

Kochańska, Agata
this vol. A cognitive grammar analysis of Polish nonpast perfectives and imperfectives: How virtual events differ from actual ones.

Kratzer, Angelika
1989   Stage and individual level predicates. In: *Papers on quantification*: NSF Grant Report, 1–73. Amherst: University of Massachusetts, Department of Linguistics.

Kuroda, S.-Yuki
1992   *Japanese Syntax and Semantics: Collected Papers.* (Studies in Natural Language and Linguistic Theory.) Dordrecht: Kluwer.

Lamadrid, Enrique, William E. Bull and Laurel E. Briscoe
1974   *Communicating in Spanish.* Boston: Houghton Mifflin.

Langacker, Ronald W.
   1987   Nouns and verbs. *Language* 63: 53–94.
   1991   *Foundations of Cognitive Grammar*, Volume 2: *Descriptive Application*. Stanford: Stanford University Press.
   1995   Viewing in cognition and grammar. In: Philip W. Davis (ed.), *Alternative Linguistics: Descriptive and Theoretical Modes*. (Current Issues in Linguistic Theory 102.) 153–212. Amsterdam: John Benjamins.
   1999   *Grammar and Conceptualization*. (Cognitive Linguistics Research 14.) Berlin: Mouton de Gruyter.
   this vol. Remarks on the English grounding systems.

Lunn, Patricia
   1985   The aspectual lens. *Hispanic Linguistics* 2: 49–61.

Lyons, John
   1977   *Semantics*, Volume 2. Cambridge: Cambridge University Press.

Mejías-Bikandi, Errapel
   1993   Syntax, discourse and acts of the mind: A study of the indicative/subjunctive contrast in Spanish. Ph.D. dissertation, Department of Linguistics, University of California, San Diego.

Partee, Barbara
   1973   Some structural analogies between tenses and pronouns in English. *Journal of Philosophy* 70: 601–609.

Real Academia Española (RAE)
   1983   *Esbozo de una Nueva Gramática de la Lengua Española*. Madrid: Espasa-Calpe.

Rojo, Guillermo
   1974   La temporalidad verbal en español. *Verba* 1: 68–149.
   1976   La correlación temporal. *Verba* 3: 65–89.
   1990   Relaciones entre temporalidad y aspecto en el verbo español. In: Ignacio Bosque (ed.), *Tiempo y Aspecto en Español*, 17–43. Madrid: Cátedra.

Silva-Corvalán, Carmen
   1983   Tense and aspect in oral Spanish narrative: Context and meaning. *Language* 59: 760–780.
   1984   A speech event analysis of tense and aspect in Spanish. In: Philip Baldi (ed.), *Papers from the 12th Linguistic Symposium on Romance Languages*, 229–251. Amsterdam: Benjamins.

Smith, Carlota
   1983   A theory of aspectual choice. *Language* 59: 479–501.
   1986   A speaker-based approach to aspect. *Linguistics and Philosophy* 9: 97–115.

1991   *The Parameter of Aspect.* (Studies in Linguistics and Philosophy 43.) Dordrecht: Kluwer.

Sweetser, Eve
1990   *From Etymology to Pragmatics.* Cambridge: Cambridge University Press.

Vendler, Zeno
1967   *Linguistics in Philosophy.* Ithaca: Cornell University Press.

Vet, Co
1991   The temporal structure of discourse: Setting, change, and perspective. In: Suzanne Fleischman and Linda Waugh (eds.), *Discourse-Pragmatics and the Verb: The Evidence from Romance*, 7–25. London: Routledge.

Warnant, Louis
1966   "Moi, j'étais le papa...": L'imparfait préludique et quelques remarques relatives à la recherche grammaticale. In: *Mélanges Maurice Grevisse*, 343–366. Gembloux: Duculot.

A cognitive grammar analysis of Polish nonpast perfectives and imperfectives: How virtual events differ from actual ones

Agata Kochańska

1. Introduction[*]

The present paper is meant as a preliminary analysis of selected issues in the semantics of the Polish nonpast tense, as well as of its interaction with perfective and imperfective aspect. More specifically, the considerations below focus on the meaning of nonpast tense clauses which contain either perfective or imperfective verbs and which are used in reference to future and temporally bounded events. The analysis is framed within the theory of cognitive grammar (cf. Langacker 1987a and b, 1991, this volume a,b, 1999a and b, 2001a and b, 2002). Additionally, it is also meant as an exercise in applying the methodological principle of looking for *converging evidence* from multiple sources, which has been formulated by Langacker (1998: 2) in the following way:

> A guiding principle is that language structure should be characterized relying only on mental abilities and phenomena that are either well known or easily demonstrated. This leads to a primary working strategy ... based on the convergence of three kinds of considerations. The objective is to find descriptions that simultaneously meet the conditions of being (a) reasonable from the psychological standpoint, (b) well motivated in purely semantic terms, and (c) optimal as a basis for analyzing grammar.

Thus, my aim in this study is to provide a detailed conceptual characterization for each of the two Polish tense-aspectual predications under consideration, a characterization which will not only pertain to the evoked conceptual content but also to the specific construal that is imposed on it. The next step is to see how the proposed analysis may account for the observed differences in the grammatical behavior of the structures under consideration.

In cognitive grammar terms, tenses are classified as clausal *grounding predications*, where the term grounding predication is understood as referring to those linguistic structures that combine the following properties: (i) they belong to "a small set of highly grammaticized elements, one of which has to be chosen as the final step in forming a full nominal or finite clause" (Langacker this volume b: 29); (ii) their function is to specify how the designated entity relates to the ground, that is, the speech event, its participants, and its immediate circumstances, in regard to such fundamental issues as time, reality, immediacy, and identification; and finally, (iii) they do not profile the grounding relation, but rather the entity they ground.[1]

Of course, every language has at its disposal different kinds of resource whose function is to situate conceived things and processes[2] relative to the ground. Not all linguistic structures which fulfill that role exhibit a substantial degree of grammaticalization and some of them actually put the epistemic relation of the conceived thing or process to the ground onstage. However, following Langacker (this volume a) and contrary to what is suggested by Nuyts (this volume), I believe that, among many kinds of expression with epistemic meanings, grounding predications, as defined above, have a special status and deserve a separate treatment. Obviously, the reason is not that they are the sole elements responsible for the epistemic qualification of what is being talked about. Instead, their special status derives from the fact that, on the one hand, they are necessary elements in the formation of a nominal or a finite clause and, on the other, they do not profile the grounding relation itself, but only the entity that is grounded. Therefore, they seem to convey those aspects of epistemic qualification which may be reasonably considered fundamentally indispensable or, in other words, which have to be signaled in any nominal or finite clause, even when they are not at all the explicit focus of attention.

Since the characterization of the role of grounding predications offered above is largely epistemic in nature, one of its consequences for clausal grounding is that it attributes not only temporal, but also, and more importantly, epistemic values to all clausal grounding predications, including "pure" tenses. Therefore, although the present study of the semantics of the Polish nonpast in its perfective and imperfective variants will deal with those uses of the structures under consideration which pertain to locating processes in time, the analysis will also be concerned with their epistemic import.

Summing up the discussion of the theoretical preliminaries, let me note that the present analysis of the Polish nonpast perfective and imperfective closely follows the lines of reasoning about clausal grounding that have originally been suggested by Langacker's work on the semantics of clausal grounding predications in English (Langacker 1987b, 1991, 1999b, 2001a, 2002) and that is being developed, e.g., by Brisard (1997, 1999, this volume) and Doiz-Bienzobas (1995, this volume).

The data to be discussed below comes from a Slavic language which is not widely known to the public. Let me therefore start my discussion with a few introductory remarks concerning the Polish tense-aspect system. Verbal lexemes in Polish commonly come in pairs (or even larger groups), whose members refer to more or less the same real-world situations, are related morphologically, and exhibit an aspectual contrast. The contrast in question is that between the perfective and the imperfective. Prototypically, the perfective is used to designate processes which are conceived of as completed, while the imperfective refers to processes viewed as ongoing. Note that the notions perfective and imperfective are used here in a way in which they are employed in Slavic studies, and that they are by no means equivalent to Langacker's use of the same terms. Langacker's perfective/imperfective contrast is strictly semantic in nature and pertains, respectively, to the temporal boundedness and unboundedness of a process within the immediate scope of a predication (cf. Langacker 1987a: 261, 1987b: 81). On the other hand, the aspectual opposition in Slavic languages is manifested morphologically. Despite the fact that the imperfective prototypically designates ongoing processes, that is, processes which are unbounded within their immediate scope of predication, while the perfective profiles temporally bounded processes, the semantic contrast between the two aspectual variants in Slavic languages does not always amount to the bounded/unbounded distinction. This may be illustrated by the examples in (1):

(1)a. *Piotr **otwierał** okno, ale ktoś je potem*
Piotr opened(Imperf.) window but somebody it later

zamknął.
closed
'Piotr opened the window but it was closed later on.'

b. *W pokoju jest zimno, bo Piotr **otworzył** okno.*
in room it-is cold because Piotr opened(Perf.) window
'It is cold in the room because Piotr has opened the window.'

In (1a), the imperfective verb, just like its perfective counterpart in (1b), designates a process which is viewed as completed, that is, temporally bounded. Thus, in cases analogous to (1), the semantic contrast between the perfective and the imperfective does not reside in the presence vs. the absence of temporal bounding. Instead, it may pertain, for example, to whether or not the final state of the profiled event is conceptualized as still obtaining at the time of speaking.

As far as its tense system is concerned, Polish has only two morphologically differentiated tenses: the past and the nonpast. One exception is the verb *być* 'be', which has past, present, and future forms.[3] Other Polish verbs do not have separate nonperiphrastic present and future tenses. Instead, present- and future-time meanings arise through the interaction of the nonpast tense with, respectively, imperfective and perfective aspect. Since the same tense may have either present- or future-time reference, depending on the aspect of the verb stem it is combined with, I have decided to use the term nonpast tense, rather than present or future tense. In addition to the nonperiphrastic nonpast tense, Polish also has a periphrastic future construction consisting of an appropriate future form of *być* 'be' plus an imperfective verb in the infinitive or in a form identical to the third person singular past. This construction is used to refer to future processes which are specifically conceptualized as temporally unbounded within the immediate scope of predication. However, if we limit our considerations only to temporally bounded process types, we may say that nonpast perfectives designate future instances of such processes, while nonpast imperfectives prototypically have present-time meanings. These prototypical meanings of the two tense-aspect variants in question are illustrated by the examples under (2):

(2)a. *Piotr je   śniadanie.*
     Piotr eat(Imperf.) breakfast
     'Piotr is eating his breakfast.'

   b. *Piotr zje   śniadanie.*
     Piotr eat(Perf.)   breakfast
     'Piotr will eat his breakfast.'

It may be observed that the two sentences in (2) differ formally with respect to just one parameter. Sentence (2a) contains an imperfective verb, while sentence (2b) contains its perfective counterpart. They are both grounded by the nonpast tense predication, yet each of them receives a different temporal interpretation. Sentence (2a) profiles a process simultaneous with the time of speaking, while sentence (2b) designates an event which is located in the future with respect to the time of speaking. Therefore, I would like to suggest that the Polish nonpast tense predication has two variants: one which combines with clauses containing a perfective verb, and the other with clauses containing an imperfective verb. The basic meaning of the nonpast perfective is that it profiles a process instance which is construed as located in the future relative to the ground. On the other hand, in its prototypical sense the nonpast imperfective designates a process which is coextensive with the time of speaking. However, as is illustrated by (3), in specific contexts the nonpast imperfective may also be used in reference to future events, just like its perfective counterpart:

(3)a. *Piotr jutro   je   śniadanie ze   swym*
Piotr tomorrow   eat(Imperf.)   breakfast with his

wydawcą.
publisher
'Tomorrow Piotr is having breakfast with his publisher.'

b. *Piotr jutro   zje   śniadanie ze   swym wydawcą.*
Piotr tomorrow   eat(Perf.)   breakfast   with his   publisher
'Tomorrow Piotr will have breakfast with his publisher.'

In the present study, I will focus on those uses of the nonpast perfective and imperfective which are analogous to those in (3). My aim is to look for answers to at least the following questions: (i) how do the two structures under consideration differ in meaning? (ii) Why is it at all possible to use the nonpast imperfective in reference to future events? (iii) What are the contexts that sanction the use of the nonpast imperfective with a future meaning? (iv) What is the epistemic import of, respectively, the nonpast perfective and the nonpast imperfective? However, before I turn to the main topic of the present discussion, let me first consider in the next section the problem of why Polish nonpast perfectives and imperfectives divide the labor of referring to the present and the future the way they do.

2. The interaction of the nonpast tense with perfective and imperfective aspect

There seem to be good reasons for the lack of a present-time interpretation for the nonpast perfective. Perfectives profile full instances of temporally bounded processes. As noted by Langacker, there are two problems with conceptualizing full instances of temporally bounded processes that are coextensive with speech events describing them. First of all, "the span of time required for a bounded process to occur has no inherent connection with the time required for a speech event describing it" (Langacker 1987b: 83; see also Langacker 1999b: 92

and Langacker 2001a: 263). This is what may be called a durational problem. There is also another problem, which is epistemic in nature. As Langacker (1987b: 83) notes, "[e]ven if the profiled process were the right length, the speaker could hardly describe it with a precisely coincident speech event: to do so, he would have to begin his description at exactly the instant when the process was initiated, before he had a chance to observe its occurrence and identify it. Once he observes a full instantiation of the process (including its endpoint), it is too late to initiate a temporally coincident description."

One situation in which the two problems do not arise is when explicit performatives are used (cf. Langacker 1987b: 83). An explicitly performative sentence profiles a process which is identified with the speech event. Such a process is temporally bounded, but at the same time its temporal span by necessity coincides with the speech event. Also, it is the speaker who is the trajector of the profiled event. Since she engages in the profiled process with prior intention, she has no problems identifying its nature. Thus, she can describe her speech act while performing it.

However, as illustrated by (4) and (5), the conventions of Polish do not allow the use of the nonpast perfective with a present-time meaning even in the case of explicit performatives:

(4) *Przyrzekam,* że nigdy cię nie opuszczę.
promise-I(Imperf.) that never you not leave-I
'I promise that I will never leave you.'

(5) *Przyrzeknę,* że nigdy cię nie opuszczę.
promise-I(Perf.) that never you not leave-I
a. ?'I promise that I will never leave you.'
b. 'I will promise that I will never leave you.'

Sentence (4) is an explicit performative containing an imperfective verb form. On the other hand, sentence (5), which contains the perfective counterpart of the verb in example (4), is unacceptable under the explicit performative interpretation given in (5a). It is only acceptable under the purely constative reading in which the profiled process instance fully follows the time of speaking, as in (5b).

The first step in explaining the unacceptability of the Polish non-past perfective in explicit performatives is the observation that, even if the durational and the epistemic problem mentioned above are disregarded, the viewing arrangement involved in conceptualizing process instances coextensive with the time of speaking is still far from optimal, at least in the temporal dimension. When the profiled process instance is coextensive with the time of speaking, the object of observation is maximally close (in time) to the observing subject. As Langacker (1993: 456) notes, the viewing distance

> shows a positive correlation with the size of the field of view. When the focus of visual attention is on a distant object, both the maximal field of view and the viewing frame (i.e. the general locus of attention) subtend large portions of the surrounding world. But if [we] look at something very close — e.g. the palm of [our] hand — [our] visual horizons shrink drastically and [we] see but a limited portion of [our] immediate environment. This correlation is mirrored in general conception.

Furthermore, "a decrease in [viewing] distance does not invariably enhance perception. As we approach an object, there is a point beyond which any further approximation actually makes it harder to observe — we are just too close to see it well." (Langacker 1993: 457)

In the case of conceptualizing a process instance identified with the speech event, the object of conception is so close to the observing subject that its endpoints coincide with the boundaries of the immediate scope delimited by the conceptualizer's viewing frame, instead of falling properly within them. Thus, the profiled process instance completely fills the conceptual onstage region. Since the processual endpoints fall at the fringes of the onstage region in a configuration of this kind, they are beyond the area of maximal conceptual acuity and are not clearly "visible" to the conceptualizer. This situation is analogous to the one in which we are approaching a cow and at some point come so close to the animal that its spatial expanse completely fills our visual field. At that point the animal's spatial boundaries are no longer clearly visible to us. In such a case our viewing experience should be more appropriately described as, e.g., "seeing a cowhide", rather than "seeing a cow".

It may thus be suggested that explicit performatives involve a conceptual configuration that is ambivalent in certain respects. On the one hand, the profiled process instance is identified with the speech event and, by its very nature, is conceptualized as temporally bounded. On the other hand, its endpoints — by the very nature of the process involved — are conceptualized as coinciding with the boundaries of the immediate scope, instead of properly falling within them. Therefore, they are at the fringes of the immediate scope adopted by the conceptualizer and beyond the region of her maximal conceptual viewing acuity. This kind of configuration is ambivalent in the sense that it simultaneously provides a motivation for coding both the performative's bounded character and the fact that its temporal boundaries are not clearly visible to the conceptualizer.

It seems that English conventionally focuses on the former factor. According to Langacker (1987b: 82; see also Langacker 2001a), the meaning of the English present tense predication is that "a full instantiation of the profiled process occurs and precisely coincides with the time of speaking". Due to the durational and epistemic problems discussed above, English verbs profiling temporally bounded processes do not normally occur in the present tense with the prototypical present-time meaning. One motivated exception to this pattern is the case of explicit performatives, which are coded in English by verbs in the present tense. What sanctions the use of such verbs in explicitly performative sentences is that the endpoints of the profiled process by definition coincide with the boundaries of the temporal viewing frame delimited by the time of speaking. Thus a full instance of a temporally bounded process is wholly contained in the onstage region (although not properly within it). Therefore, in English it is the bounded character of the process instance that is in focus.

On the other hand, Polish does not conventionally focus on the temporally bounded character of the profiled speech act, but rather on the poor visibility of its endpoints, which results from observing the event from a "close-up" perspective. There are good reasons to assume that in Polish the use of the perfective is only sanctioned when the endpoints of the profiled process fall properly within the conceptual viewing frame and are therefore clearly visible to the conceptualizer. Partial support for this claim comes from considering cases analogous to those in (6):[4]

(6)a. *Przez kwadrans* **wybierał** *pędzel.*
over quarter chose-he(Imperf.) brush
'It took him a quarter of an hour to choose a brush.'[5]

b. **Mył** *się przez pół godziny.*
washed-he(Imperf.) himself over half hour
'He spent half an hour washing up.'

c. **Czekał** *na nią pod bramą przeszło*
waited-he(Imperf.) for her under gate more-than

dwie godziny.
two hours
'He waited for her at the entrance for more than two hours.'

According to one reading, sentences like those in (6) may be understood as profiling the portion of processual states that is contained within the temporal viewing frame, whose span is specified by an adverbial consisting of either the preposition *przez* 'over' and a nominal, or a nominal alone. This profiled portion, in turn, is viewed as part of a whole process whose temporal expanse goes beyond the limits set by the adverbial in question. However, sentences of this kind are more commonly interpreted as referring to processes which started at the beginning of the period specified by the adverbial and were completed or terminated at the end of this period. In other words, they may be understood as profiling full instances of temporally bounded processes, whose endpoints coincide with the boundaries of the viewing frame adopted by the conceptualizer and specified by the temporal adverbial. They are used with this latter kind of meaning when the conceptualizer specifically focuses on the extended duration of the profiled process, which is often longer than expected. The important thing is that under such an interpretation, it is still imperfective verbs that have to be used in reference to temporally bounded process instances. The use of perfectives is unacceptable when the temporally extended character of the profiled process is specifically in focus.

It may be argued that focusing on the unexpectedly long duration of the profiled process involves conceptualizing its temporal expanse as completely filling the adopted temporal viewing frame. In other words, in a conceptualization of this kind, the processual endpoints have to be construed as coinciding with the boundaries of the immediate scope, rather than falling properly within them. In cases analogous to those in (6), it is past processes that are put in profile. Since they are conceptually viewed from a relatively distant, present-time vantage point, the reason for the coincidence is not the close-up perspective, which brings about a reduction of the locus of viewing attention in the case of explicit performatives. Instead, the responsible factor is a conception of the profiled event as maximally extended within the adopted immediate scope of predication. In both cases, however, the result is the coincidence of the processual endpoints with the boundaries of the viewing frame and hence, their poor visibility to the conceptualizer. In my view, this is what motivates the use of the imperfective in the case of both explicit performatives and past events whose duration was longer than expected.[6]

Let me now sum up the main points of what has been said so far. As mentioned above, with the exception of the verb *być* 'be' Polish verbs do not have separate present- and future-tense forms. Instead, present- and future-time meanings arise through the interaction of the nonpast tense with, respectively, imperfective and perfective aspect. The imperfective's temporal unboundedness within the immediate scope of predication is consistent with conceiving of a process as unfolding in front of the speaker's eyes "at present". Viewing an event from a zero distance in the temporal dimension results in the exclusion of its endpoints from the conceptualizer's viewing frame, or at least from the region of her maximal conceptual viewing acuity. On the other hand, since the perfective profiles process instances which are temporally bounded within the immediate scope of predication, the use of this aspectual variant makes the processual endpoints visible to the conceptualizer. This, in turn, can only be achieved by removing the profiled event from the speaker's immediate present. Thus, Polish nonpast perfectives may only have a future-time meaning.

After this longish digression, let me now turn to the main topic of the present paper, that is, to a semantic analysis of the nonpast perfective and imperfective in its nonprototypical future-time use.

3. The semantics of the nonpast perfective and imperfective in future-time uses: Actual and virtual events

While it may well be the case that a straightforward present-time reference is the prototypical meaning of the nonpast imperfective, a closer look at sentences such as (2a), as well as the corpus data in (7) below, immediately reveals that it is not the only one:

(7)a. *Poza   tym   jedna ciotka   **przyjeżdża**   do Allerod.*
    beside this   one   aunt   come(Imperf.) to Allerod
    'Besides, one of my aunts is coming to Allerod.'

   b. *O której   godzinie **przylatuje**   [Wanda Parker]?*
      at which   hour   arrive(Imperf.)   Wanda Parker?
      'What time is Wanda Parker arriving?'

It is clear that the events referred to in (7) are not yet in progress at the time of speaking and are expected to occur at some point in the future. As far as their objective content is concerned, the sentences in (7) seem to be equivalent to those in (8), where perfective verb forms are used, in line with the more prototypical pattern of expressing a future-time meaning:

(8)a. *Poza   tym   jedna ciotka   **przyjedzie**   do Allerod.*
     beside this one aunt   come(Perf.)   to Allerod
     'Besides, one of my aunts will come to Allerod.'

b. *O której   godzinie **przyleci**   [Wanda Parker]?*
   at which   hour   arrive(Perf.)   Wanda Parker?
   'What time will Wanda Parker arrive?'

In view of what has been said above with respect to the prototypical meanings of nonpast perfectives and imperfectives, the data in (7) may seem puzzling. It raises at least three questions: (i) why does Polish have two ways of referring to future, temporally bounded processes? (ii) Why, despite their prototypical present-time meaning, may nonpast imperfectives sometimes be used with a future-time reference, just like nonpast perfectives? (iii) What are the contexts that sanction the use of the nonpast imperfective with a future meaning?

My first step in an attempt at answering these questions will be to take a closer look at what the respective meanings of the two structures under consideration actually are. To this end, let me first consider the examples in (9):

(9)a. ***Spotkamy***   *się*   *dziś o szóstej?*
     meet-we(Perf.)   Reflex. today at six?
     'Will we meet at six today?'

b. ***Spotykamy***   *się*   *dziś o szóstej?*
   meet-we(Imperf.) Reflex. today at six?
   'Are we meeting at six today?'

It may be observed that the only formal difference between the two questions in (9) is that in (a) the verb form is perfective, while in (b) its imperfective counterpart is used. However, this small formal difference produces an important contrast in meaning. The two examples are in fact queries about quite different matters. In (9a) the speaker is asking about the possibility of making an appointment with her interlocutor. On the other hand, in uttering the question in (9b), she presupposes that some appointment has already been made. The aim of the question is only to make sure whether the speaker correctly remembers the plan for future action, which has already been made and agreed upon with the addressee of the query.

In my view, the semantic contrast between (9a) and (9b) may best be described in terms of Langacker's distinction between *actuality* and *virtuality*. Langacker (1999b: 79) characterizes actuality as our conception of the real world, or any conception of some imagined world whose status with respect to reality is at issue. On the other hand, virtuality may be defined as any departure from the direct conceptualization of actuality (cf. Langacker 1999b: 77). The claim that I would like to make in the present study is that in (9a) the speaker is asking the hearer whether the profiled future event will occur in actuality.[7] Thus the nonpast perfective in (9a) may be viewed as simply profiling a future event located in the *actual plane*. On the other hand, in uttering the question in (9b), the speaker is only indirectly concerned with actuality. Her primary aim is to confirm whether she correctly remembers the contents of the plan that she and her interlocutor have previously agreed upon. In other words, (9b) may be analyzed as a question about the contents of a mental representation of events that are supposed to occur in the future, as a matter of what the speaker and the hearer have planned to do. According to Langacker (1999b: 94; see also Langacker 2002), such a mental representation may be metaphorically understood as a kind of *virtual document*, whose entries represent the processes that are planned to occur in the future.

The virtual document involved in (9b) is that of a plan for future actions. The same type of document seems to be invoked in the case of the example in (7a) above (*Poza tym jedna ciotka **przyjeżdża** do Allerod* 'Besides, one of my aunts is coming to Allerod'). However, as illustrated by the examples in (10), different kinds of virtual document may be involved on different occasions:

(10) a. *Twój pociąg* **przyjeżdża** *za dwie godziny.*
     your train   come(Imperf.) in two hours
     'Your train comes in two hours.'

   b. *Śniadanie* **jem** *godzinę później.*
      breakfast eat-I(Imperf.) hour later
      'I have my breakfast an hour later.'

   c. *Zima* **zaczyna** *się za mniej więcej miesiąc.*
      winter start(Imperf.) Reflex. in less more month
      'Winter starts in about a month.'

Sentence (10a), as well as the one in (7b) above (*O której godzinie* **przylatuje** *[Wanda Parker]?* 'What time is Wanda Parker arriving?'), seem to invoke the document of a schedule. In turn, sentence (10b) has a habitual meaning. Hence, it invokes the mental representation of how things work in the world as a general rule (the latter kind of document is what Langacker [1997: 202–205] calls the *structural plane*; see also the discussion of the structural/phenomenal distinction in Goldsmith and Woisetschlaeger [1982]). Finally, sentence (10c) seems to require the activation of a record within our mental representation of the calendar cycle.

I suggest that the nonpast tense predication combined with a perfective verb stem profiles a future process in the actual plane. On the other hand, it seems that imperfective verb stems combined with the nonpast tense may only be used in reference to those future events that can be planned (cf. [7a] above) or are scheduled to occur in the future (cf. [7b] and [10a] above), or whose occurrence may be predicted on the basis of the "normal course of events" (cf. [10b] and [10c]). It may be claimed that each event of this kind is represented in the conceptualizer's mind as a "record" in a virtual document of an appropriate kind. Since virtual documents are mental representations, records within them may be accessed by the conceptualizer at any time. Each activation of a record in a document constitutes a virtual occurrence of the recorded event. Activating a record at the time of speaking results in the virtual occurrence of a process that is coextensive with the speech event. It is such a virtual occurrence of a process that the nonpast imperfective with a future-time meaning profiles.[8]

If the above analysis of future-time uses of the nonpast imperfective is on the right track, then the extended use of the tense-aspect form under consideration may be viewed as a straightforward extension from its prototypical meaning. In both cases, the imperfective profiles a process coextensive with the time of speaking and thus unbounded within the speaker's viewing frame. The only difference is that in the prototypical use, the profiled process is located in the plane of actuality. On the other hand, in the extended use the profile is shifted to the plane of a virtual document of a particular kind.

Assuming that the imperfective in the uses under consideration does indeed profile a virtual process whose temporal expanse is coextensive with the time of speaking, we may ask why such uses are taken as referring, at least in some sense, to the future. It seems to me that an answer to this question may be found in an idealized cognitive model describing the role that virtual documents of the abovementioned kinds have in shaping a future course of events. Our prototypical conception of plans, schedules, or what we view as natural patterns of how things are in the world, is that the existence of such documents either exerts a causal force with respect to future events (this seems to be the case with plans, for example), or else that it represents the conceptualizer's recognition of such causal forces in the outside world (this seems to be the case with the notion of structural knowledge). The future occurrence of actions that are planned is commonly taken as being nearly guaranteed by the very fact that somebody has made a plan to perform them. Scheduled events are also taken as bound to occur. Finally, our experience that certain patterns have so far been regularly recurring in reality leads us to the extrapolation that they are also bound to recur in the future. Thus, the present existence of virtual documents of the kinds discussed above is typically viewed as either providing reality with a particular *evolutionary momentum* (cf. Langacker 1991: 277; see also Langacker 2002), or else as reflecting the fact that we judge reality to have a particular evolutionary momentum independently of what we might wish or intend to be the case. In either situation, this evolutionary momentum is thought to be sufficiently strong to provide a basis for projecting the course of reality's future development with a confidence close to certainty. In this way, a future process which is planned, scheduled, or supposed to occur as part of the normal course of events may be conceived of in terms of what Langacker (1991: 276–278) calls *projected reality*, that is, those future states of affairs to which reality's development will be pushed by its present evolutionary momentum, unless "an extraordinary or wholly unanticipated input of energy" (Langacker 1991: 278) changes the evolution's predetermined path. In this respect, future events which may be referred to by means of nonpast imperfectives differ from those profiled by nonpast perfectives. The latter, unlike the former, may be conceived of as belonging either to projected or to *potential* reality (cf. Langacker 1991: 277), that is, to the set of all those future paths that reality is not precluded from following by its present evolutionary momentum. In contrast to what happens with future processes denoted by nonpast imperfectives, the inclusion of those future events profiled by nonpast perfectives into potential or projected reality is not determined by the choice of the tense-aspect form in question, but depends solely on contextual (linguistic and situational) factors.

The proposed meanings of the nonpast perfective and imperfective in their future-time uses are diagrammed, respectively, in Figures 1 and 2.

Figure 1 represents the meaning of the nonpast tense predication which grounds a process designated by a clause with a perfective verb. In the diagram, the immediate scope of predication (IS) and, thus, the profiled process (which is drawn in heavy lines) are located in the actual plane, in the future relative to the ground (the box labeled G). Figure 1 represents one possible use of the nonpast perfective, in which the conceptualizer is not fully certain of the profiled event's future occurrence. Hence, the process drawn in heavy lines is merely part of potential reality, that is, those paths of future evolution which reality may possibly follow, given its present evolutionary momentum. Evolutionary momentum itself is represented in the diagram by a double dashed arrow. Of course, it is also possible to use the nonpast perfective in reference to events whose future occurrence is viewed as nearly guaranteed by reality's present evolutionary momentum. In that case, the profiled process would be conceptualized as part of projected reality.

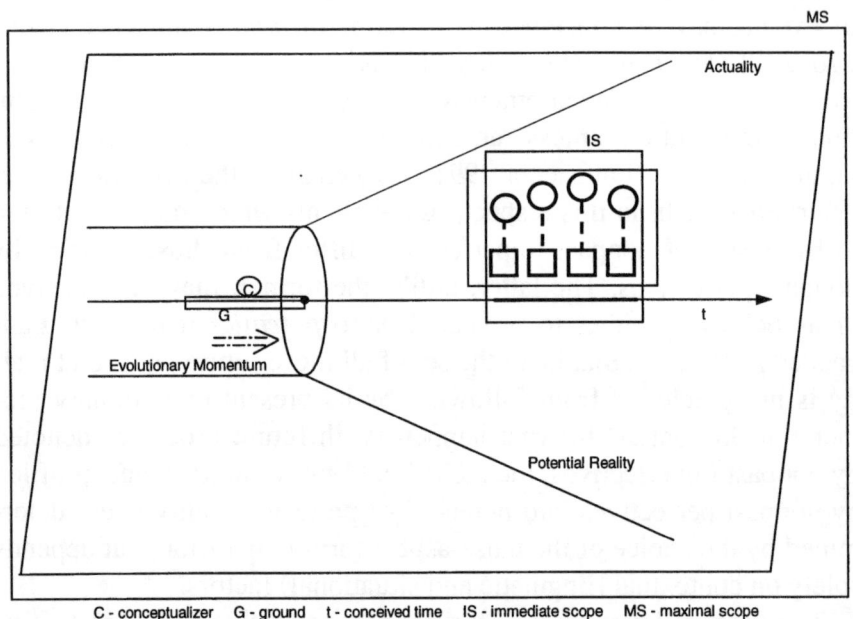

C - conceptualizer   G - ground   t - conceived time   IS - immediate scope   MS - maximal scope

Figure 1. The meaning of the nonpast perfective (the variant in which the profiled process is viewed as part of potential reality)

Figure 2, in contrast, represents the meaning of a clause containing an imperfective verb grounded by the nonpast tense predication and used in reference to a future event. In this case, the immediate scope of predication and the profiled process are located in the plane of a virtual document. The profiled virtual occurrence of a process consists in the conceptualizer's activating the relevant record from the virtual document at the time of speaking. This mental operation is represented by the dashed arrow linking C (the conceptualizer) with the profiled event. The dotted correspondence lines between the boundaries of the ground and those of the profiled process represent the fact that the temporal expanse of the latter is coextensive with that of the former. The component internal states of the profiled process are identical. This is because the process in question is viewed as simultaneous with the speech event and, therefore, as maximally close in time to the conceptualizer's vantage point.

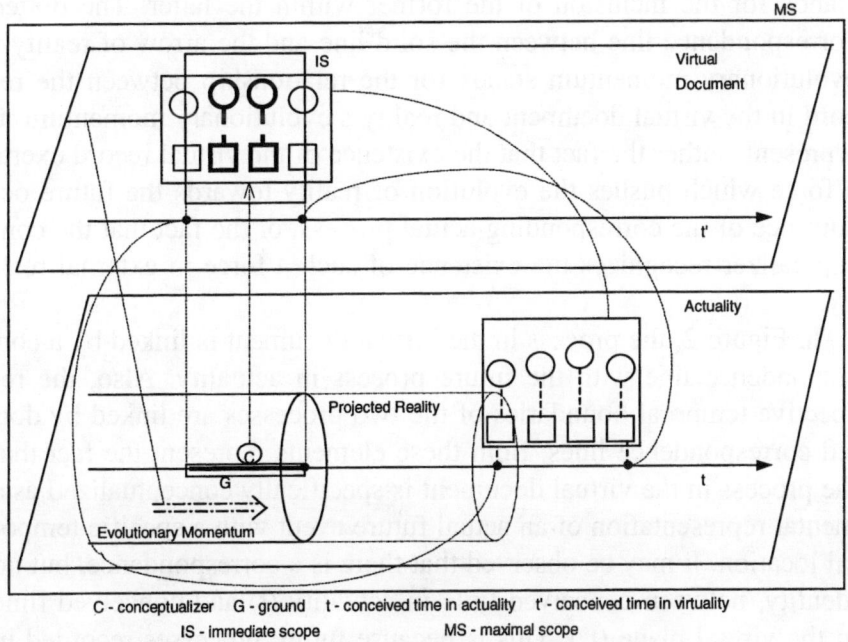

Figure 2. The meaning of the nonpast imperfective in its future-time use

Viewing a process from a zero temporal distance results in the coincidence between the endpoints of the process and the boundaries of the immediate scope. This coincidence results in the exclusion of the processual endpoints from the region of maximal conceptual viewing acuity. This, in turn, brings about the homogenization of the conceived event.

The existence of the activated record in the virtual document is understood as exerting a causal force on the evolution of reality, or at least as representing the conceptualizer's recognition of the existence of such a force in reality. It is this force which provides reality with an appropriate evolutionary momentum and brings about the future occurrence of a process in the plane of actuality. In Figure 2, reality's evolutionary momentum is represented by the double dashed arrow within the cylinder representing evolving reality. The solid line between the record in the virtual document and the document itself stands for the inclusion of the former within the latter. The dotted correspondence line between the solid line and the arrow of reality's evolutionary momentum stands for the relationship between the record in the virtual document and reality's evolutionary momentum. It represents either the fact that the existence of the virtual record exerts a force which pushes the evolution of reality towards the future occurrence of the corresponding actual process, or the fact that the conceptualizer recognizes the existence of such a force in external reality.

In Figure 2, the process in the virtual document is linked by a correspondence line with the future process in actuality. Also, the respective temporal boundaries of the two processes are linked by dotted correspondence lines. Both these elements represent the fact that the process in the virtual document is specifically conceptualized as a mental representation of an actual future event with a specific temporal location. It may be observed that there is a correspondence, but no identity, between conceived time in actuality (t) and conceived time in the virtual plane (t'). This is because future processes recorded in virtual documents are specifically conceptualized as having particular temporal locations in the future. On the other hand, virtual records in mental documents have their existence in the conceptualizer's mind at the time of speaking and are then accessible for activation. In the figure, this temporally ambivalent character of the virtual process is represented, on the one hand, by the coincidence of the process's temporal profile with the time of speaking and, on the other, by the correspondence between the process's endpoints on the axis of virtual conceived time (t') and the endpoints of the future event on the axis of conceived time in actuality (t).

To sum up the main points of the analysis offered above, I suggest that nonpast perfectives profile future processes in the actual plane. Depending on context, those processes may be viewed as belonging to either potential or projected reality. On the other hand, when imperfectives are used in reference to future processes, the profile is shifted from actuality to the plane of a virtual document of an appropriate kind. The profiled virtual event resides in the activation of a record in the virtual document at the time of speaking. Thus, in the future-time use of the nonpast imperfective, the process put in profile is coextensive with the time of speaking. In this respect, the use of the imperfective profiling an event in a virtual document is analogous to its prototypical use. In both cases the imperfective profiles a process coextensive with the time of speaking and thus unbounded within the immediate scope of predication. The main difference is that, prototypically, the process profiled by the nonpast imperfective is located in the plane of actuality. On the other hand, in the extended use the profile is shifted to the plane of a virtual document.

Although in the future-time use of the nonpast imperfective the profile is restricted to the present occurrence of a process in the mental space of a virtual document, the overall conceived scene incorporates (in its maximal scope) the conception of the future event in the plane of actuality as well. The occurrence of this event is viewed as being almost guaranteed by the existence of the virtual document under consideration. Hence, the event in question is conceptualized as belonging to projected reality. The relevant virtual document is understood as providing the conceptualizer with a measure of "mental control" over future events. The concept of mental control over future events is to be understood here in terms of whether or not the conceptualizer can provide reality with a particular kind of evolutionary momentum (as is the case when she makes plans with respect to the occurrence of the events in question) or, at least, in terms of whether or not she can recognize reality's present evolutionary momentum and make extrapolations with respect to what will happen in the future with a substantial degree of confidence. The latter kind of mental control is offered by virtual documents such as the conception of the calendrical cycle, or the conception of what is going to happen as a consequence of how the world is structured. In any case, it is this meaning of mental control that all uses of the imperfective in reference to future processes seem to share.[9]

4. Further evidence for the proposed analysis

As the next step in the present discussion, let me now turn to three selected examples of contexts in which the nonpast perfective is acceptable, while the extended use of the nonpast imperfective is not. The existence of such contexts provides further evidence that the two structures under consideration are semantically nonequivalent. It may also provide more clues with respect to the precise nature of the semantic contrast between them. My aim in considering the contexts in question is to see to what extent the observed differences in acceptability can be accounted for in terms of the analysis proposed above.

The first type of context in which the perfective is acceptable, while the imperfective is not, is illustrated by the contrast between, on the one hand, sentence (11a), where both the perfective and the imperfective are unproblematic and, on the other, sentence (11b), where the use of the imperfective is unacceptable:

(11) a. *Jutro   skończą   się   /kończą   się*
       tomorrow end(Perf.) Reflex. /end(Imperf.) Reflex.

   wakacje.
   vacations
   'Tomorrow our vacations will end/end.'

   b. *Jutro   skończy   się   /?kończy   się*
       tomorrow end(Perf.) Reflex. /?end(Imperf.) Reflex.

   nam herbata.
   to-us tea
   'Tomorrow we'll run out of tea.'

Future events may be divided into those that are planned, scheduled, or that regularly occur in the normal course of events, and those that just happen in an unpredictable, unanticipated way. While the process of vacations coming to an end (11a) belongs to the former group, that of running out of tea (11b) is clearly a member of the latter. Since in (11a) both the perfective and the imperfective are acceptable, while in (11b) the use of the imperfective is not, it may be concluded that nonpast perfectives may be used in reference to future processes of any kind, but that the use of nonpast imperfectives is restricted to events over which the conceptualizer can exert a measure of mental control.

The existence of such a difference between the two aspectual variants of clauses grounded by the nonpast tense seems to follow automatically from the analysis that has been proposed above. Since it lies in the very nature of certain events (like, for example, running out of tea in [11b]) that they are not amenable to any planning or scheduling, and they are not a matter of any structural properties of the world, we simply do not have any virtual documents allowing us to exert mental control over them. It is this absence of a virtual document in which the profiled event could be located that makes the use of the imperfective unacceptable in cases like (11b).[10]

Another kind of context in which the nonpast perfective is acceptable, while the nonpast imperfective is not, is illustrated by the sentences in (12):

(12) a. *Jeśli dostanę   pieniądze   za książkę, to   w*
       if   get-I(Perf.) money   for book,   then in

   przyszłym tygodniu kupię   /kupuję   samochód.
   next   week   buy-I(Perf.)/buy-I(Imperf.)   car
   'If I get the money for my book, I'll buy/I'm buying a car next week.'

   b. *Jeśli zechcę,   to   w przyszłym tygodniu kupię*
      if   want-I(Perf.), then in next   week   buy-I(Perf.)

   /?kupuję   samochód.
   /?buy-I(Imperf.) car
   'If I feel like it, I'll buy a car next week.'

Sentence (12a) is acceptable both with the perfective and with the imperfective. On the other hand, sentence (12b) sounds odd with the imperfective. To account for this, let me first consider in some detail the semantics of (12a) and (12b). In (12a) the conditional protasis describes a precondition on choosing a specific variant from an already existing plan for future actions. The variant in question is that described in the conditional apodosis. To be more specific, a future occurrence of the event of getting the money for the book is viewed as a precondition for choosing the buying of a car as that variant of a preexisting plan for future actions that is to be followed. A conceptualization of this kind presupposes that the virtual document of a plan is in existence at the time of speaking. Hence, there is nothing contradictory about situating the profiled event on the virtual plane. Consequently, the nonpast imperfective is perfectly acceptable in conditionals like (12a).

The situation is different in (12b). Here, the protasis profiles the future process of the trajector entering a state of willingness to engage in the process designated by the apodosis (that of buying a car). Thus, at the time of speaking, the trajector has not yet entered this state. A measure of willingness to perform an action seems to be a precondition for choosing that action as the variant of an already existing plan which is supposed to be followed. More importantly, however, it is also a precondition for the very making of a plan with respect to the action in question. Hence, in (12b), one of the preconditions for making a plan with respect to the event denoted by the apodosis is specifically conceptualized as not yet satisfied at the time of speaking. This means that in (12b), at the time of speaking, there is no virtual document of a plan where the event profiled by the main clause verb could be located. Thus, the unacceptability of (12b) with the nonpast imperfective follows from two things: (i) the fact that the nonpast imperfective profiles an event which is located in the virtual plane and is simultaneous with the time of speaking, and (ii) the fact that in (12b), at the time of speaking, the virtual document in which the profiled event could be located is conceptualized as nonexistent. On the other hand, (12b) is unproblematic with the nonpast perfective, since it profiles a future actual event and nothing blocks the possibility of conceptualizing both the process in the conditional protasis and that in the apodosis as future potential events in actuality.

The last example of a context in which the nonpast perfective may be used, while the nonpast imperfective is very doubtful, is illustrated by the sentences in (13):

(13) a. *Przypuszczam, że   za pół godziny **wyjdę***
      guess-I   that   in half hour   leave-I(Perf.)

    */?**wychodzę**   z   biura.*
    /?leave-I(Imperf.)   from office
    'I guess I'll leave the office in half an hour.'

  b. *Może   za pół   godziny **wyjdę**   /?**wychodzę***
     maybe   in half hour   leave-I(Perf.) /?leave-I(Imperf.)

    z   biura.
    from office
    'Maybe I'll leave the office in half an hour.'

Both sentences in (13) explicitly mark the speaker's uncertainty with respect to the epistemic status of the event profiled by the verb in bold. As both examples illustrate, nonpast imperfective verbs, as opposed to perfective ones, cannot be used in a context of this kind if the trajector of the bold verb is identified with the speaker.[11] I would like to claim that this is again a straightforward consequence of, on the one hand, the perfective designating a future event in the actual plane and, on the other, the extended use of the imperfective profiling an event in a virtual document of an appropriate type.

The absence of any restrictions in the case of perfectives is not surprising. Treating future events in the actual plane as epistemically uncertain seems to be a very sensible attitude — after all, when we talk about the future, we talk about what is not yet, and may in fact never be, realized. Thus, it is those cases where we feel certain of an event's future occurrence that seem to require more explanation than those where we have our doubts.

On the other hand, it may be observed that nonpast imperfectives are unacceptable in the context under consideration only in those cases in which the virtual document involved in the conceptualization is the speaker's plan for her own future actions. If nonpast imperfectives do indeed profile events residing in the activation of records in appropriate virtual documents, their unacceptability in a context of this kind is perfectly natural — by definition, no mentally sound speaker can have any doubts with respect to the contents of her own plans.

However, when the invoked virtual document is not that of the conceptualizer's personal plan, but one of a different nature, the restrictions on the use of the imperfective no longer remain in force. This is illustrated by (14):

(14) *Prawdopodobnie w przyszłym roku **idę** do wojska.*
 probably in next year go-I(Imperf.) to army
 'Probably next year I'll be joining the army.'

Sentence (14) is perfectly acceptable under an interpretation in which the relevant virtual document is not the speaker's personal plan, but rather a conception of what is going to happen as a consequence of "how things are in the world". In other words, the virtual document invoked in the case of sentence (14) is a prediction which is made with respect to a specific event and a specific individual, but which is nevertheless a direct extrapolation from the general knowledge of "how things are in the world" (the structural plane). In this case, there is nothing contradictory in the speaker's uncertainty with respect to whether or not a particular record should be included in the invoked virtual document. This is because the nature of the speaker's overall conception of how the world is structured may be such that it does not offer any basis for predicting future occurrences of specific processes with specific participants with any substantial degree of confidence. For example, in sentence (14), the speaker's conception of the world's structure is that not every single man is drafted every single year. Hence, the epistemic status of the record pertaining to the speaker himself being drafted the next year is, by the very nature of things, uncertain within the invoked virtual document.

It may also be observed that the sentences from (13) above, which are unacceptable when interpreted as invoking the virtual document of the speaker's personal plan for future actions, may be unproblematic under the assumption that they do not involve the document of a personal plan, but rather again profile events in the document representing the conception of what is going to happen as a consequence of the structural properties of the world. To illustrate this, let us once again consider sentence (13a), which is repeated below as (15):

(15) *Przypuszczam,   że   za pół   godziny **wychodzę**   z*
     guess-I   that   in half hour   leave-I(Imperf.)   from

   biura.
   office
   'I guess I'm leaving the office in half an hour.'

Let us imagine a context in which the speaker is spending her first day in a new workplace and is not yet fully certain of how things are in this environment. Let us further assume that her utterance does not pertain to what she is planning to do in the future, but rather to what she thinks she will be allowed to do by the rules operative in this new place. It seems to me that in a context of this kind sentence (15) is perfectly natural and acceptable.

Finally, I would like to consider one more piece of evidence for the analysis proposed above. As mentioned above, nonpast imperfectives are unacceptable in the context of explicit markers of the profiled event's uncertain epistemic status only in those cases in which the trajector of the imperfective verb phrase is identified with the speaker. On the other hand, no such restrictions seem to apply to sentences with other kinds of trajector. This is illustrated by sentence (16), which is perfectly acceptable, even if understood as referring to what the trajector of the imperfective verb personally plans to do:

(16) *Przypuszczam,   że   Piotr jutro   **wyjeżdża**   na*
     guess-I   that   Piotr tomorrow leaves(Imperf.) for

wakacje.
vacations
'I guess that Piotr is leaving on vacation tomorrow.'

I suggest that the virtual document involved in the conceptualization evoked by (16) is the speaker's conception of a personal plan of another person, the trajector of the bolded verb. When the speaker accesses a virtual document of her own plan, there is no way in which she can be uncertain about its contents. However, conceptualizing another person's plan for future actions is a different matter. Although in our Western culture we readily venture to imagine the contents of other people's minds, we are nevertheless sensible enough to realize, at least from time to time, that our ideas in this respect are nothing more than guesses. Thus, there is nothing contradictory in a conceptualization in which the profiled event is at the same time viewed as epistemically uncertain and as located in the virtual document of another person's plan.

In the present section, a number of contexts have been considered in which the use of the nonpast imperfective is doubtful, while the perfective is acceptable. The data that has been analyzed is claimed to provide further evidence for characterizing the semantic difference between the two structures under consideration in terms of the virtual/actual contrast. In the next section, let me turn to a brief consideration of the epistemic issues involved in the semantic characterization of the nonpast perfective and imperfective proposed above.

5. A note on the epistemic value of the nonpast perfective and imperfective

In the following brief discussion of the respective epistemic values of the perfective and the imperfective variant of the nonpast tense predication in Polish, I would like to comment first on how the epistemic import of the two structures under consideration has been treated in the present analysis. The claim made in this study is that the nonpast perfective profiles an event located in the future relative to the time of speaking. The nonpast imperfective, in turn, is characterized as designating a process whose temporal expanse is coextensive with the time of speaking. In the case of the basic meaning of the nonpast imperfective, this process is located in actuality. On the other hand, in the extended futurate use, the profiled event is virtual in nature. Importantly, under the proposed analysis, the common element in the two uses of the nonpast imperfective is that they both profile a process simultaneous with the time of speaking. It could be argued, then, that the above characterizations of the nonpast perfective and the nonpast imperfective concentrate almost exclusively on how each of the two structures under consideration locates the profiled process in time relative to the speech event. However, it has been convincingly argued by Brisard (1999, this volume) that the meanings of tense predications should ultimately be characterized in epistemic terms, rather than solely in terms of how they locate the profiled process in time relative to the speech event.[12] The present analysis could thus be accused of taking a "localist" perspective, that is, of concentrating on how the two grounding predications under discussion locate events in time relative to the time of speaking, at the expense of paying any attention to their epistemic import.

In my view, however, such an accusation is not completely justified. I believe that the respective characterizations of the nonpast perfective and the nonpast imperfective which have been proposed above can be straightforwardly interpreted in epistemic terms. To appreciate this, it should be noted first that when the speaker invokes virtual events in futurate uses of the nonpast imperfective, it is not in fact virtual processes that are at issue. Instead, the conceptualizer is concerned with their counterparts in actuality. Virtual documents and records within them are only invoked for purposes of thought and expression. Therefore, the temporal location of events that the speaker is really concerned with is not the same in the basic and in the futurate use of the nonpast imperfective: in the former case, the relevant process is located in the present, while in the latter, it is viewed as belonging to the future. The claim that in the futurate use of the nonpast imperfective the speaker activates an appropriate virtual record at the time of speaking is really equivalent to saying that, whenever the nonpast imperfective, instead of the perfective, is used in reference to future events, the events in question are conceptualized as those aspects of the future over which the speaker can exercise some kind of mental control. When the virtual document invoked by the conceptualizer is that of her personal plan, exercising mental control over a planned process is understood both in terms of the conceptualizer's effecting its future occurrence through the very making of the plan, and in terms of her being epistemically certain of that occurrence. In those cases in which the conceptualizer invokes other kinds of virtual document, such as various schedules or predictions made on the basis of structural knowledge, the conceptualizer does not think of herself as affecting the occurrence of future events that are scheduled or that are supposed to occur as a matter of how things are in the world. However, she still exercises some mental control over the events in question, in the sense that although they are not yet realized, she views their future occurrence as nearly guaranteed by what reality is like at present. She can also run through them mentally, as if they were immediately present and unfolding before her eyes. It could be argued that it is these epistemic parameters that the conceptualization involved in the futurate use of the nonpast imperfective shares with its basic present-time meaning. After all, it is only in the present that we sometimes have a chance to influence the course of reality's evolution, and it is only in the present that we can observe events as they actually unfold in time. Finally, it is only in the present that we can be immediately certain of what is happening before our eyes.

If we now compare the futurate use of the nonpast imperfective and the basic meaning of the nonpast perfective, we may observe that both these structures pertain to future processes in actuality and thus do not differ with respect to how they temporally locate those events which the conceptualizer is really concerned with. The main difference between the two structures lies in how the processes in question are construed in epistemic terms. In the case of the nonpast imperfective, they are thought to be under the conceptualizer's mental control. On the other hand, when the nonpast perfective is used, they are viewed as being both beyond the conceptualizer's sphere of influence and beyond what she can be epistemically certain of. In other words, those future processes which are referred to by means of the nonpast perfective are conceptualized as those aspects of the future over which the conceptualizer has no mental control.

Summing up this part of the present discussion, let me conclude that the semantic characterizations of the nonpast perfective and the nonpast imperfective proposed in the present paper seem to be very much epistemic in nature. I believe that the ultimate import of the structures under consideration is epistemic, despite the fact that I have described them as profiling, respectively, a future actual event and a process which is simultaneous with the time of speaking and is situated either in actuality or in a virtual document of some kind. On the surface, the above characterizations may be interpreted as pertaining only to temporal location. I would like to argue, however, that if they are interpreted in an appropriate way, their epistemic nature becomes apparent. I do believe that futurate uses of the nonpast imperfective really involve activations of appropriate records from virtual documents at the time of speaking. In my view, however, such activations amount to nothing more than attempts at exercising mental control over future actual events, and it is these actual events that the speaker is ultimately concerned with.

The second problem that I would like to consider briefly in the present section is the question why in the nonpast tense, the respective absence vs. presence of mental control are associated with the perfective and the imperfective variant of the nonpast tense predication. As observed by Fleischman (1995: 542), such an association, which is found in other Slavic languages as well, constitutes one type of counterevidence to her own hypothesis that there is a cross-linguistic "attraction" between the imperfective and the *irrealis* (Fleischman 1995: 539) or, in other words, that imperfectively marked verbs tend to be used, cross-linguistically, to signal a speaker's *lack of belief in* or *lack of commitment to* (a) the reality, realization, or referentiality of an event or a sequence of events predicated in an utterance; (b) the realization of an agent's wishes, hopes, or intentions, as expressed in the proposition of an utterance; (c) the authenticity of an utterance or chunk of discourse (i.e. a sequence of utterances); or (d) what for lack of a better term I will call the "canonicity" or normalcy of a discourse or of a communicative situation. (Fleischman 1995: 522; emphases in original)

In Polish, however, the association of the perfective with the absence of epistemic certainty/commitment, and of the imperfective with the presence of epistemic certainty/commitment, holds only in the non-past tense, as is illustrated by the examples in (17). In the past tense, the association seems to be reversed:

(17) a. *Lekarz* **powiedział** */?mówił* *mojej mamie, że w*
doctor told(Perf.) /?told(Imperf.) my mother that in

takich przypadkach to lekarstwo zwykle pomaga.
such cases this medicine usually helps
'A doctor told my mother that in such cases this medicine usually helps.'

b. *Sąsiadka* **powiedziała** */mówiła* *mojej mamie,*
neighbor-she told(Perf.) /told(Imperf.) my mother

że w takich przypadkach to lekarstwo zwykle pomaga.
that in such cases this medicine usually helps
'A neighbor told my mother that in such cases this medicine usually helps.'

Both sentences in (17) are reports of other acts of verbal communication. In (17a), the subject of the sentence, that is, the speaker in the profiled act of verbal communication, is a figure of authority with respect to what was communicated. This is supposed to guarantee an immediate acceptance of the contents of the message on the part of the conceptualizer. In a context of this kind, the use of the past perfective is much more felicitous than the use of the past imperfective. On the other hand, in (17b) the speaker in the profiled process of verbal communication is not a figure in authority and hence, the conceptualizer's immediate acceptance of what was said is possible but not guaranteed. In a context of this kind, both the past perfective and the past imperfective may be acceptable. The difference between them is that, while the perfective again signals an immediate acceptance of and commitment to the message contents on the part of the conceptualizer, the import of the imperfective is that the conceptualizer's mental stance with respect to what was communicated is still unsettled at the time of speaking. It may thus be concluded that in the past tense, Polish imperfective verbs profiling processes of verbal communication, unlike their perfective counterparts, may be used to signal an unsettled/uncommitted mental (e.g. epistemic) stance of the conceptualizer with respect to what was communicated in the designated speech acts. Hence, in the past tense, as opposed to the nonpast, the imperfective seems to be more attracted to *irrealis* than the perfective, in accordance with Fleischman's hypothesis.

This apparent inconsistency in the semantic behavior of the past and the nonpast imperfective may, at first sight, seem puzzling. However, it makes perfect sense once we take into consideration the fact that the past, the present, and the future have quite different statuses with respect to how events situated within them can be presented to the human mind. As observed by Brisard (1999: 11–12), "[k]nowing a thing from the past is not the same as experiencing it immediately, in the present, or as anticipating its future occurrence. In this sense, differences in temporal location are tantamount to variations in the way in which we construe a temporal object as fitting the established structures of our experience at any given point in time."[13] In other words, past events may, at least potentially, be known to us. Events located in the present may be in the process of becoming known to us. Finally, future events, by their very nature, cannot be known, since they are not yet realized.

The second important factor in the present considerations is the observation that in the past tense, the imperfective prototypically profiles a process which was in progress at some moment in the past. In other words, in the central meaning of the past imperfective, the designated process instance is conceptualized as a portion of a complete process, whose temporal expanse extends beyond the boundaries of the immediate scope and may well reach the present. In turn, the imperfective in the nonpast tense prototypically profiles a process instance which is simultaneous with the time of speaking. It could thus be argued that even in its extended uses the imperfective is a good candidate for coding conceptualizations in which the event the speaker is concerned with is portrayed as linked in some way with the present. I would like to claim that it is such a linking function that is fulfilled by both the past imperfective in uses like (17) above and the nonpast imperfective with a futurate meaning.

What kind of epistemic attitude on the part of the speaker is signaled by, respectively, the past and the nonpast imperfective follows directly from the imperfective's linking function, as well as the epistemic characterizations of the past, the present, and the future. In the epistemic dimension, construing the profiled past process of communication as linked to the present implies that the process in question was not immediately successful in settling the conceptualizer's mental stance with respect to what was communicated. In other words, when past imperfective forms of verbs of communication are used, the potential inclusion of the communicated contents into the speaker's conception of known reality is still treated as an open issue at the time of speaking. This nuance of an *irrealis* meaning is not conveyed by the past perfective, since in that case the profiled event of verbal communication is construed as completed in the past in any possible dimension. Consequently, it is also viewed as fully successful in settling the epistemic status of what was communicated immediately in the past, at the very moment of its occurrence. This is why in the past tense, it is the imperfective that is more attracted to *irrealis* than the perfective.

If we now turn to the epistemic attitude signaled by the two aspectual variants of the nonpast tense, we may observe that in the case of the perfective the profiled event is construed as being located within the future and wholly separated from the present. Since the future belongs to the realm of irreality, the nonpast perfective presents the profiled event as only potential, that is, not even on its way towards being realized. On the other hand, in the case of the imperfective, the profiled future event is construed as linked to the present. Epistemically, this means that the event in question is viewed, at least in some sense, as being under the speaker's mental control at the time of speaking. The speaker exercises mental control over a future event at the time of speaking in the sense that she activates a record of this event in a virtual document of a plan, a schedule, or a conception of how the world is structured. Virtual documents such as plans are viewed as giving reality the momentum which pushes its evolution towards the occurrence of the events recorded in them. Extrapolating the occurrence of specific processes with specific participants from our structural knowledge allows us to mentally run through the predicted events as if they were unfolding before our own eyes. In either case, the existence of the relevant virtual document is viewed as sanctioning the speaker's expectation of the occurrence of future processes with a confidence close to certainty. In this sense, the use of the nonpast imperfective carries at least a seed of some *realis* meaning. To put it differently, although in the case of both the nonpast perfective and the nonpast imperfective the future actual event is construed as nothing more than an unrealized potentiality, the use of the imperfective, as opposed to that of the perfective, implies that the future realization of this potentiality is largely determined by the evolutionary momentum of reality, produced by or recognized in the virtual document activated at the time of speaking.

5. Conclusions

The present paper has been concerned with analyzing the semantics of the Polish nonpast perfective and imperfective in their respective future-time uses. It has been argued that, despite their truth-conditional equivalence, nonpast perfective and imperfective sentences with future-time meanings are not semantically identical. The claim made in the present study is that, while the nonpast perfective simply profiles a future actual event, the profile of the nonpast imperfective is shifted to the plane of a virtual document of an appropriate kind. Within this virtual document, a record pertaining to a process is activated at the time of speaking and it this virtual occurrence of the process in question that is designated in the extended use of the nonpast imperfective.

Designating a virtual event coextensive with the time of speaking, the future-time use of the nonpast imperfective is similar to its prototypical meaning, in which an actual process simultaneous with the speech event is profiled. However, the temporal coincidence of the profiled process with the time of speaking is not the only commonality of the basic and the extended use. More importantly, both uses seem to share the same epistemic value, that of the conceptualizer exercising mental control over the designated event. When the future-time use of the nonpast imperfective is characterized in terms of profiling a virtual event coextensive with the time of speaking, this is another way of saying that, at the time of speaking, the speaker conceptualizes the virtual event's future actual counterpart as being under her mental control, in a way comparable to the mental control that can be exercised over actual processes unfolding before the speaker's eyes. In this respect, the nonpast imperfective differs from its perfective counterpart. When the latter is used in reference to a future actual event, this event is conceptualized as lying beyond any kind of mental control on the part of the conceptualizer. It is thus epistemic factors that motivate the speaker's choice of the perfective or the imperfective variant of the nonpast tense grounding predication in clauses referring to future processes in actuality.

As a final concluding remark, let me note that the analysis proposed above is supported by converging evidence coming from a number of sources, as has been postulated by Langacker (1999a: 26–27). The characterization of the semantic contrast between the nonpast perfective and imperfective which has been proposed above relies mainly on two psychological mechanisms: imagery (specifically, the mechanism of profiling) and the ability to conceive not only of actual processes, but also of processes within "virtual documents", such as plans for the future, predictions based on structural knowledge, etc. Both these abilities are not specifically linguistic. The former is a basic mental mechanism pervasive in all aspects of cognition. The latter is manifested whenever we look ahead into the future and plan or predict what is going to happen. Thus, the psychological phenomena invoked for the present analysis are either well known or easily demonstrated.

The presented analysis also seems to be well motivated in purely semantic terms. It elucidates the nature of the subtle meaning contrast between the nonpast perfective and the extended use of the nonpast imperfective, where the objective contents of the two structures are very similar. It also allows for establishing a straightforward link between using the imperfective in reference to future events and its prototypical present-time meaning.

Finally, the proposed analysis is also supported by grammatical considerations. It helps to account for the unacceptability of using the nonpast imperfective with a future-time meaning in a number of contexts. Thus, an important point that has been stressed in the present paper is that the semantic differences between the nonpast perfective and the extended use of the nonpast imperfective, though very subtle and pertaining only to construal, are nevertheless responsible for the fact that, in specific contexts, the two aspectual variants are not mutually interchangeable. This provides further support for the claim made in cognitive grammar that taking into consideration aspects of construal is not only relevant to a description of meaning in the narrow sense, but also to a revealing characterization of grammatical structure.

In my view, applying the research methodology suggested by Langacker may potentially lead to analyses of diverse linguistic phenomena in terms of a very restricted set of theoretical constructs. My hope is that the present application of this methodology to the study of the semantics of the Polish nonpast perfective and imperfective grounding predications has been at least partially successful, and that it has produced an analysis in which the mental representations of the two structures under consideration are tightly connected conceptual networks, unified by both temporal and epistemic factors.

Notes

* This study is a revised version of a paper read at the conference "Cognitive Linguistics in the Year 2001", which was held in April 2001 in Łódź, Poland. It is part of a larger study of the semantics of the Polish nonpast perfective and imperfective (cf. Kochańska 2002). The present work has greatly benefited from insightful comments by a number of people. I fully acknowledge and appreciate all their help. In the first place, I would like to express my deepest gratitude to Elżbieta Górska and to Ronald W. Langacker, who were very generous with their time and extensively commented on the analysis offered in Kochańska (2002). I would also like to thank René Dirven and Frank Brisard for their valuable comments on an earlier version of this paper. My understanding of the problems under consideration, as well as the clarity of my presentation, have greatly benefited from the comments and critical remarks of all these people. I wish to give my thanks separately to Frank Brisard for his extremely friendly, patient, and kind attitude, which was of great help in all those cases when I did not manage to meet my deadlines. My thanks are also due to Günter Radden, who has pointed out certain inadequacies in my translations of the Polish data into English. Last but not least, my thanks go to Aniela Korzeniowska, who kindly agreed to check and correct my English. Needless to say, all the remaining flaws of the present analysis are entirely my own.

1. In a grounding predication itself, the grounded entity is characterized only in schematic terms. However, when a full nominal or a finite clause are formed, this schematic element is elaborated by a more specific profile of the nominal or clausal structure with which the grounding predication is integrated.
2. Note that the terms "thing" and "process" are used here in a technical sense to refer, respectively, to "a region in some domain of conceptual space" (Langacker 1987a: 494) and to a "series of relational configurations that necessarily extend through conceived time and are scanned sequentially" (Langacker 1987b: 75).
3. What is here referred to as the future form of *być* 'be' is sometimes classified as the perfective present of the verb in question (cf. Vater 1995: 159). A classification of this kind makes it possible to think about the Polish system of nonperiphrastic verb forms in terms of two symmetrical divisions: a division between past and present forms, and for each tense, one between perfective and imperfective forms. However, it remains unclear why a verb denoting a state of future existence should be classified as a perfective present-tense form. It seems to me that the only possible motivation for advancing this is an attempt at imposing a symmetry on the Polish tense system that in fact is not there.

4. The examples in (6), as well as those in (7), come from a 180-utterance corpus that was collected for a larger study of the semantics of the Polish imperfective (cf. Kochańska 2002), extracted from two crime stories by Joanna Chmielewska, a contemporary Polish writer. The reason for choosing Chmielewska's works as a data source is that she uses good colloquial Polish which is not very different from the spoken language, at least as far as the grammatical patterns employed are concerned. The remaining examples discussed in the present paper are made-up sentences. My own intuitions concerning their (un)acceptability have all been checked with a number of other native speakers of Polish, who were kind enough to read earlier versions of the present analysis.
5. Note that the Polish example in (6a), unlike its English translation, does not explicitly state that some brush was ultimately chosen. The reason for choosing this translation of (6a) is that it reflects the meaning this sentence had in the context in which it was actually used. It is this meaning that is of interest to us here.
6. Although I had had certain intuitive ideas along the same lines about how to analyze the meaning of the Polish nonpast imperfective in explicit performatives, the present analysis was suggested to me by Ronald Langacker (personal communication), who helped me greatly in the journey from vague intuitions to preliminary understanding.
7. Of course, the speaker's question about the profiled future process in actuality in (9a) may also be viewed as an attempt at establishing a plan for future actions that the hearer would accept. Nevertheless, (9a) is primarily a query about what will happen in actuality.
8. Such an analysis of the nonprototypical, future-time use of the Polish nonpast imperfective is not at all original. Instead, it may be viewed as an application to the Polish data of the line of reasoning proposed in Langacker's discussion of the nonprototypical uses of the English present tense (cf. Langacker 1999b, 2001a, 2002).
9. The idea that the notion of mental control may be the key to understanding future-time uses of the Polish nonpast imperfective has been suggested to me by Ronald Langacker (personal communication).
10. The present account of the unacceptability of the Polish nonpast imperfective in examples like (11b) is precisely analogous to the one offered by Langacker for the oddness of sentences like *An earthquake strikes next week* (cf. Langacker 1999b: 93 and Langacker 2001a: 267).
11. It seems that for other kinds of subject, the restriction is either much weaker or altogether absent. I believe that there are good reasons for this, which will be considered in some detail later on.

12. Langacker expresses a similar view in his analysis of tenses in English, when he suggests that "their fundamental semantic characterization pertains to epistemic distance" (Langacker 1991: 249).
13. This observation has led Brisard to the idea that the grammatical expression of temporal concerns, that is tense marking, is not primarily a matter of situating an event in time relative to some reference point. Instead, its fundamental function is to provide the event's epistemological characterization. In Brisard's own words, "we might wish to question the analytical validity of linking the functions of so-called tense markers in any language with purely temporal considerations. Rather, it makes just as much sense to see the temporal correlations that are distinguished in English as resulting from more general epistemological characterizations which, for speakers of English, happen to prototypically correspond with certain firmly established time intervals (present, past, future)." (Brisard 1999: 38; cf. also Brisard 1997, this volume).

References

Brisard, Frank
    1997   The English tense-system as an epistemic category: The case of futurity. In: Marjolijn Verspoor, Kee Dong Lee and Eve Sweetser (eds.), *Lexical and Syntactical Constructions and the Construction of Meaning*, 271–285. (Current Issues in Linguistic Theory 150.) Amsterdam: John Benjamins.
    1999   A critique of localism in and about tense theory. Ph.D. dissertation, University of Antwerp.
    this vol.   The English present.

Doiz-Bienzobas, Aintzane
    1995   The preterit and the imperfect in Spanish: Past situation vs. past viewpoint. Ph.D. dissertation, Department of Linguistics, University of California at San Diego.
    this vol.   The preterit and the imperfect as grounding predications.

Fleischman, Suzanne
    1995   Imperfective and irrealis. In: Joan Bybee and Suzanne Fleischman (eds.), *Modality in Grammar and Discourse*, 519–551. (Typological Studies in Language 32.) Amsterdam: John Benjamins.

Goldsmith, John and Erich Woisetschlaeger
    1982   The logic of the English progressive. *Linguistic Inquiry* 13: 79–89.

Kochańska, Agata
    2002   Selected issues in the semantics of the Polish imperfective: A cognitive grammar account. Manuscript, Warsaw University.

Langacker, Ronald W.
1987a   *Foundations of Cognitive Grammar*, Volume 1: *Theoretical Prerequisites*. Stanford: Stanford University Press.
1987b   Nouns and verbs. *Language* 63: 53–94.
1991   *Foundations of Cognitive Grammar*, Volume 2: *Descriptive Application*. Stanford: Stanford University Press.
1993   Universals of construal. *Proceedings of the Annual Meeting of the Berkeley Linguistic Society* 19: 447–463.
1997   Generics and habituals. In: Angeliki Athanasiadou and René Dirven (eds.), *On Conditionals Again*, 191–222. (Current Issues in Linguistic Theory 143.) Amsterdam: John Benjamins.
1998   Conceptualization, symbolization, and grammar. In: Michael Tomasello (ed.), *The New Psychology of Language: Cognitive and Functional Approaches to Language Structure*, 1–39. Mahwah: Erlbaum.
1999a   Assessing the cognitive linguistic enterprise. In: Theo Janssen and Gisela Redeker (eds.), *Cognitive Linguistics: Foundations, Scope, and Methodology*, 13–59. (Cognitive Linguistics Research 15.) Berlin: Mouton de Gruyter.
1999b   Virtual reality. *Studies in the Linguistic Sciences* 29: 77–103.
2001a   The English present tense. *English Language and Linguistics* 5: 251–272.
2001b   Viewing and experiential reporting in cognitive grammar. In: Augusto Soares da Silva (ed.), *Linguagem e Cognição: A Perspectiva da Linguística Cognitiva*, 19–49. Braga: Associação Portuguesa de Linguística.
2002   Extreme subjectification: English tense and modals. Manuscript.
this vol. a   Deixis and subjectivity.
this vol. b   Remarks on the English grounding systems.

Nuyts, Jan
this vol.   Grounding and the system of epistemic expressions in Dutch: A cognitive-functional view.

Vater, Heinz
1995   The tense system of Polish. In: Rolf Thieroff (ed.), *Tense Systems in European Languages*, Volume 2, 153–165. Tübingen: Niemeyer.

Data sources

Chmielewska, Joanna
1998   *Wszystko czerwone [Everything red]*. Sixth edition. Konstancin-Jeziorna: Wydawnictwo "Vers".

1999   *Harpie [The harpies]*. Konstancin-Jeziorna: Wydawnictwo "Vers".

"Wieso sollte ich dich küssen, du hässlicher Mensch!" A study of the German modals *sollen* and *müssen* as "grounding predications" in interrogatives

Tanja Mortelmans

1. Introduction

The theme of this chapter — the possible "grounding" status of the German modals (especially *sollen* and *müssen*) in interrogatives — calls for an introductory discussion of at least four topics: first, the notion of grounding (and, in its wake, those of "grounding predication" and "subjectification"); second, a brief introduction to the German paradigm of verbal modal expressions (including both mood markers and modal verbs); third, the "meaning" of the interrogative sentence type in relation to grounding and subjectification; and fourth, the semantics of the German modals *sollen* and *müssen*.

1.1. Grounding predications and subjectification

The ground, referring to the speech event, its participants, and its immediate circumstances, plays a pivotal role with respect to the characterization of grounding predications, which can be regarded as a special class of deictic expressions. A grounding predication (also termed "epistemic predication") is defined as "a predication that locates a thing or process with respect to the ground in fundamental "epistemic" domains pertaining to reality and speaker/hearer knowledge" (Langacker 1991: 548). Nominal grounding in English is effected by the definite and indefinite articles, by demonstratives, and by relative quantifiers like *all*, *most*, *some*, and *no* (see Langacker

1991: chapter 3), whereas clausal grounding is taken care of by tense (present and past) and the modals (see Langacker 1991: chapter 6).

In the traditional Cognitive Grammar view, grounding predications stand out from the overall class of deictic expressions by virtue of two features. First, only grammaticalized[1] elements can function as grounding predications. Typical of grammatical elements is their schematic meaning and the fact that they tend to assume a "relativistic" character (Langacker 1990: 321), i.e. they do not locate the profiled entity in absolute terms but always relative to the ground. Second, the ground itself "receives a highly subjective construal despite its pivotal role" (Langacker 1990: 322). The terms "subjective" and "objective" are used by Langacker in a specific and rather technical way, referring to the construal of the ground. If the ground is put onstage and profiled, i.e. construed as a focus of attention, the ground is said to be objectively construed (examples are *I*, *you*, *here*, and *now*). Subjective construal, on the other hand, implies that the ground remains an unprofiled reference point, i.e. it is "offstage" and implicit. Subjectification, then, in Langacker's use of the term, refers to an increase of subjectivity (or conversely, a decrease of objectivity) from a diachronic point of view.

At this stage, a few comments seem to be warranted. First, it should be stressed that subjectivity (objectivity) is a gradient concept, often "a matter of degree" (Langacker 1990: 316). Second, Langacker's conception of subjectification has slightly changed over the years. Originally (Langacker 1990, 1991), subjectification was viewed in terms of replacement ("some relationship within the objective situation under description is replaced by a comparable but subjectively construed relationship inherent in the very process of conception", Langacker 1999: 298), whereas Langacker's (1999) view on subjectification focuses on the disappearance of an objective basis for the conceived relationship, leaving behind only a subjectively construed relation — which is already there in the objective construal. To put it bluntly, whereas Langacker (1990, 1991) stressed the increase of subjectivity in the process of subjectification, Langacker (1999) focuses on the decrease of objectivity.

Third, Langacker's definition of subjectification (both in the [1990, 1991] and in the [1999] versions) should not be confused, at least not on a theoretical basis, with Traugott's (1989, 1995) "pragmatic" use of the term. This issue — the possible confusion regarding the application of the term "subjectification" — will be taken up below.

The English modals (*shall, will, can, may,* and *must*) are discussed extensively by Langacker in the context of grounding and subjectification (see Langacker 1990, 1991, 1999). They are claimed to have gone through various processes of subjectification, from which they have emerged as full-fledged grounding predications. In his account of the diachronic development of the English modals, Langacker concentrates on two stages of subjectification. The first involves the evolution from an original main verb, where the subject functions as the locus of some kind of potency,[2] to a stage where the source of potency is shifted onto the speaker or some other entity whose potency the speaker can report on. Whereas the source of potency in the original configuration is well delineated and easily identifiable (as coincident with the subject), it becomes progressively more diffuse, implicit, and subjectively construed: "It may be the speaker but need not be... It is not necessarily any specific individual, but may instead be some nebulous, generalized authority." (Langacker 1999: 308) In this first stage, the modal relationship (the potency directed at the landmark process, which can be characterized in terms of obligation, permission, etc.) remains in profile.

In a subsequent stage, the verbal profile is shifted onto the landmark process. As a grounding predication, an English modal does not profile the grounding relationship (the modal relation of directed potency), but the grounded process expressed in the infinitive. Note that subjectification is not taken to affect the *content* of the modal verb: English *must* and German *müssen* both express some kind of necessity, but according to Langacker only the former has evolved into a grounding predication. This implies that *must* designates (or profiles) the landmark process, whereas *müssen* — in Langacker's view — by definition profiles the modal relation of necessity.

Langacker assigns grounding status to the English modals as a group, regardless of whether they have an epistemic[3] or a root meaning (Langacker 1991: 271). For both root and epistemic modals, not only the source but also the target of potency is diffuse, i.e. the source of potency is no longer identified with the subject, and the target of potency (the "entity" at which the modal relation is directed) need not be the subject or even a specific individual either. In the case of the root modals, "the force is simply directed toward realization of the target event, to be apprehended by anyone who might be in a position to respond to it" (Langacker 1999: 308).

Implicitly, however, Langacker seems to acknowledge that the modals in their epistemic use assume a higher degree of subjectivity than the root modals. As subjectification boils down to a process whereby the locus of potency becomes progressively less salient and well-defined, the epistemic use, in which the locus of potency is equated with reality's evolutionary momentum and hence maximally vague, presents a limiting case, in which "the force dynamics are inherent in the conceptualizer's mental activity, hence subjectively construed *in a strong sense*" (Langacker 1999: 309; emphasis mine). A similar argument can be put forward for the target of potency, which is *maximally* diffuse in the case of epistemic modality and always indicates a process rather than a concrete individual. In the case of root modality, however, the locus of potency can still be concrete and identifiable; in the case of *can*, the locus of potency may even coincide with the subject. Moreover, it is sometimes difficult to decide whether the subject of a root modal or the entire process is the target of the modal relation. This is particularly the case when the subject is a sentient agent capable of performing the action described by the verb in the infinitive, as in (1a): is the modal relation's target the (concrete, identifiable) subject 'you' or the (more diffuse) process of 'your going home right away'? In (1b), a case of what Talmy (1988: 79) has labeled "agonist demotion", a nonsentient patient is construed as the subject of the root modal; here it is undoubtedly the entire process ('the cake staying in the box') which the modal verb aims at.

(1)a. *You must go home right away — your wife insists.*
   b. *The cake must stay in the box.*

As Langacker distinguishes between weaker and stronger degrees of subjectification, one might want to assign grounding status only to those modals that have acquired a high degree of subjectification. The epistemic modals, "which are maximally diffuse in regard to the source and target of potency" (Langacker 1999: 309), unambiguously qualify for this. Incidentally, the epistemic modals' high degree of subjectification also corresponds to a higher level of formal grammaticalization. For one thing, they cannot be tensed anymore (Goossens 1996: 28–29). Moreover, whereas every English modal allows a root reading, only a subset of the modals can get an epistemic interpretation.[4] What about the grounding status of the root modals, then? In this respect, I side with Goossens (1996: 28; original emphasis), who only takes root modals to be grounding "in the case of *deontic* modalities where the authority for the permission or obligation is clearly in the ground, as a rule, when the speaker has or assumes authority", i.e. the grounding status is reserved for those modal uses in which the locus of potency can be equated with (an element of) the ground, as in (2).

(2) *You must go home right away (I insist).*

Note that the epistemic modals fulfill this requirement, as an assessment of reality's evolutionary momentum is by necessity an operation conducted by the speaker.[5] The status of grounding predication is therefore not attributed to the modals as a whole, but is made dependent on an actual (but implicit) link to the ground.

1.2. The German modals and mood

It is a well-established fact that the German modals have not acquired the same degree of formal grammaticalization as their English counterparts. This seems to be Langacker's main reason for calling the

German modals "periphrastic", which implies that, unlike their English counterparts, they profile the modal relationship (of necessity, obligation, ability, volition, and so on) instead of the process at which the potency expressed by the modal is directed. In other words, the German modals have not reached the second subjectification stage, which is claimed to be typical of the English modals. Langacker calls upon two criteria to arrive at this conclusion. First, the German modals "tolerate verb inflections whose specific effect is to render a verb nonfinite" (Langacker 1990: 335). They form infinitives (*können, sollen, wollen*, and so on) and past participles (*gekonnt, gemusst, gewollt*, etc.). Second, "the German modals themselves bear inflections for tense and person [mood could be added here as well, TM]" (Langacker 1990: 335), which are analyzed as grounding predications. So, instead of grounding a finite clause, the German modals are claimed to be grounded themselves — by tense and mood markers. For German, then, clausal grounding in the modal domain is effected by mood. The highly grammaticalized mood markers, indicative, present conjunctive (*Konjunktiv I*) and past conjunctive (*Konjunktiv II*), can therefore be claimed to function as grounding predications.

Diewald (1993, 1999), however, has convincingly shown that the German modals in their epistemic use have acquired a higher degree of grammaticalization than the nonepistemic ones. The epistemic modals generally do not allow nonfinite forms (neither infinitives nor past participles), past-tense inflections,[6] or variation as far as mood[7] is concerned. On the basis of both formal and semantic properties, Diewald sets the epistemic modals (which she terms "deictic") apart from the nonepistemic ones. For the epistemic modals, "die Enkodierung der (in der Kommunikationssituation objektiv vorliegenden) Verbindung zwischen Sprecher (Origo) und dargestelltem Sachverhalt ist definierender Bestandteil ihrer Bedeutung" [the coding of the connection between speaker (*origo*) and state of affairs, which is objectively there in the communicative setting, is a defining element of their meaning] (Diewald 1999: 15). Diewald goes on to claim that the German epistemic modals can be integrated into the German mood system, which she characterizes as a "deiktische Kategorie, die die sprecherbasierte Faktizitätsbewertung des dargestellten

Sachverhalts enkodiert" [a deictic category, which encodes a speaker-based assessment of the factuality of the state of affairs] (Diewald 1999: 245). In Diewald's view, the German moods (*Indikativ*, *Konjunktiv I*, and *Konjunktiv II*) *and* the epistemic modals have the same function: they attribute a speaker-based factuality value to a state of affairs. The indicative mood is taken to express an unmarked value, as it locates the state of affairs within reality, i.e. within the epistemic sphere of the speaker. The other ones (*Konjunktiv* and epistemic modals) are marked in some respect: *Konjunktiv I*, as a marker of indirect speech, signals a shift with respect to the *origo* that assesses the state of affairs, *Konjunktiv II* typically indicates nonfactuality, and the epistemic modals signal "daß der Sprecher nicht bereit ist, der Proposition einen definitiven Faktizitätsgrad, also den Wert [-nichtfaktisch] oder den Wert [+nichtfaktisch] zuzuweisen" [that the speaker is not willing to give the proposition a final degree of factuality, that is the value [-nonfactual] or the value [+nonfactual]] (Diewald 1999: 206).

Indikativ: *Sie ist in ihrem Zimmer.* 'She is in her room.'
Konjunktiv I: *Sie sei in ihrem Zimmer.* 'People say she is in her room.'
Konjunktiv II: *Sie wäre in ihrem Zimmer.* 'She would be in her room.'
Epistemic modal: *Sie muss in ihrem Zimmer sein.* 'She must be in her room.'
Sie dürfte in ihrem Zimmer sein. 'She's probably in her room.'

Note that the epistemic modals are obligatorily marked for mood as well: they are either in the *Indikativ* or in the *Konjunktiv II*. This mood marker, however, cannot be taken to ground the state of affairs anymore. An epistemic modal in the indicative does not locate a state of affairs within reality, whereas the past conjunctive in combination with an epistemic modal does not assume its usual meaning either.[8] In view of this, the assumption that in German, both mood and epistemic modals can be considered grounding predications seems to be warranted.[9]

Diewalds restricts the integration of analytic verb forms into the mainly synthetic German mood paradigm to the epistemically used modals. The root modal use, she argues, "stellt (typischerweise) einen Zustand des Satzsubjekts dar, wobei das Modalverb Bestandteil der dargestellten Szene ist" [(typically) presents a condition of the clausal subject, whereby the modal verb is part of the depicted scene] (Diewald 1999: 14). This clear-cut dichotomy between less grammaticalized, nonsubjectified root modals and strongly grammaticalized epistemic modals does not seem to match linguistic reality, though. Within the German root modals, some verbs (or verb forms) seem to be more strongly grammaticalized than others. The past conjunctive form *sollte*, which in declarative contexts has specialized as a deontic marker, is a case in point. Root *sollte*, in contrast to root *müsste*, does not occur in hypothetical contexts, in spite of its past conjunctive marking. This can be taken to signal that the mood marker (*Konjunktiv II*) does not assume its original meaning, a phenomenon that could also be observed for the epistemic modals. Moreover, *sollte* is a typical *speaker-oriented* marker. It is used by the speaker to express a personal assessment regarding a mode of action; the authority for the obligation (or recommendation) is therefore clearly in the ground (the speaker).

(3) *"Sie sind Nutznießer dieser Finanzpolitik, schämen sich aber nicht, sich hierherzustellen und diese Politik noch zu kritisieren. Sie **sollten** wenigstens den Anstand haben, ein schlichtes Dankeschön dafür zu sagen."* (WK, Bundestagsprotokolle, Sitzung Nr. 197, 15.02.1990, p. 15128)[10]
"'You are a beneficiary of this financial policy, but you are not ashamed to come here and even criticize it. You should at least have the decency to say a simple thank-you for it!'"

I have claimed (Mortelmans 2001, forthcoming) that this implicit reference to the speaker is not merely a matter of context, but has come to belong to the semantics of the form *sollte*. The observation that, with past conjunctive *sollte*, the speaker is automatically construed as an (implicit) locus of potency of the modal relation, can be taken as an argument in favor of attributing grounding status to this German root modal.

1.3. The interrogative as a basic sentence type

The interrogative is one of the three basic sentence types: declarative, imperative, and interrogative. Each of them "takes as its prototypical semantic value one of the three fundamental speech acts most plausibly regarded as archetypal" (Langacker 1991: 504). In the case of the interrogative, this speech act is questioning, which conventionally evokes a cognitive model "in which the speaker lacks but wants certain information, believes that the hearer possesses it, and directs the hearer to supply it" (Langacker 1991: 505). In a main-clause question, the context for interpreting an interrogative is a subjectively construed viewing arrangement "that subsumes both the actual speech event and the cognitive model of questioning" (Langacker 1991: 505), i.e. the positions of speaker and hearer are implicitly equated with those of the *actual* speaker and the *actual* addressee.

The cognitive model of questioning will be assumed to underlie all interrogatives, unless the linguistic or situational context provides clues that a given interrogative should be interpreted in a different way. The (prototypical) link between the grammatical form of the interrogative and the speech act of questioning can be "overruled" (see also Langacker 1991: 504).

Before we proceed, we must introduce a distinction between two basic types of question: yes-no questions on the one hand, and question-word questions on the other. The main difference between these two types pertains to the presuppositions they entail. In a yes-no question (4a), in which the finite verb occupies the sentence-initial position, the state of affairs is not presupposed, since "a yes-no question implies a lack of knowledge as to whether the event actually occurred" (Chafe 1995: 354). By contrast, with a question-word question, the speaker looks for information about the participants or accompanying circumstances of an event, the occurrence of which is presupposed (4b).

(4)a. *Ist er krank geworden?*
'Has he fallen ill?'

b. *Wer ist krank geworden? Wann ist er krank geworden? Warum ist er krank geworden?*
'Who has fallen ill? When did he fall ill? Why has he fallen ill?'

It can be expected that the difference regarding the epistemic status of the state of affairs will to some extent be reflected in the verbal mood of the finite verb, i.e. past conjunctive verb forms, which are associated with the expression of nonfactuality, are expected to occur more often in yes-no questions than in question-word questions.

1.4. The semantics of sollen and müssen

The semantic difference between German *sollen* and *müssen* is most often explained in terms of the locus of potency that both verbs evoke. *Sollen* is the more specific verb in this respect, since "die von *sollen* ausgedrückte Aufforderung in dem Willen einer Person oder Instanz gründet" [the request expressed by *sollen* is based on the will of a person or authority] (Duden 1998: 98), which entails that the locus of potency is typically animate, or to be more precise, it is an entity capable of communication ("eine der Kommunikation fähige Entität", Diewald 1999: 97).

An interesting and to some extent surprising feature of indicative *soll* is the fact that the "personal" source of potency is generally not equated with the speaker, i.e. the obligation expressed by the modal is ascribed to an "external" locus of potency, one that is neither the subject nor the speaker. At the same time, the locus of potency is usually available in the preceding context or can easily be reconstructed on the basis of it, such that the indicative of *sollen* can be claimed to have anaphoric properties (see also Glas 1984: 65; on the notion of anaphoricity, see Janssen, this volume; De Mulder and Vetters, this volume). This implies that with indicative *sollen*, the locus of potency is typically not highly diffuse, but a relatively objective participant in the modal relationship. Instances like (5), in which the locus of potency (*sie* 'she') appears onstage in the preceding context, are by no means rare.

(5) *"Gekündigt hat sie mir... ich soll gehen, gleich auf der Stelle, hat sie gesagt."* (MK1)
"'She has fired me... I must go, immediately, she has said.'"

With the indicative of *sollen*, a straightforward speaker-oriented interpretation only arises when the speaker repeats a previously uttered obligation, as in the following example. Again, this use of *sollen* can be claimed to be anaphoric, with the speaker in some way objectifying a previous personal command (here in the form of an imperative).

(6) *"Setz dich wieder hin. Ich sage, du sollst dich wieder hinsetzen!"*
(GR1, Torwegge, C.: *Liebe hat ihre eigenen Gesetze*, p. 9)
"'Sit down again. I say, you must sit down again!'"

Uses of indicative *sollen* in which the speaker can be taken to associate herself with an obligation that has not been previously communicated, are relatively rare.

(7)*Jetzt soll niemand sagen, das eine habe nichts mit dem anderen zu tun.* (WK, *Bundestagsprotokolle*)
'At this point no one should say that these things have nothing to do with one another.'

Elsewhere (Mortelmans, forthcoming) I have tried to show that in such cases, the past conjunctive *sollte* is preferred, which — at least in declaratives — seems to have specialized as a speaker-involved deontic marker. I will come back to the speaker-bound character of the past conjunctive *sollte* in a later stage.

With *müssen*, the specific nature of the locus of potency is undifferentiated, as it can be equated with all kinds of force. The German reference grammar *Duden*, for instance, lists six different causes that can give rise to the necessity expressed by *müssen* and adds that "die Aufzählung nicht vollständig sein kann, sind doch die Bedingungen für eine Notwendigkeit außerordentlich vielfältig" [the list cannot be exhaustive, since the conditions for a necessity to arise are extremely diverse] (Duden 1998: 96). The examples in (8) illustrate some of these possibilities, ranging from a natural force ("eine natürliche Kraft") in (8a), over emotional compulsion ("eine aus dem Gemüt, dem Gefühl kommenden inneren Zwang") in (8b), the laws of nature ("Naturgesetz") in (8c), a moral imperative ("Forderung der Sitte") in (8d), and a goal to be achieved ("Zweck oder Ziel") in (8e), to a command or an order ("Gebot oder Befehl") in (8f).

(8)a. *Die Kraft des Wassers war so stark, dass das Boot kentern musste.*
'The force of the water was so strong that the boat had to capsize.'

b. *Als er vom Tod seiner Schwester erfuhr, musste er weinen.*
'When he heard the news of his sister's death, he had to cry.'

c. *Der Stein muss notwendigerweise auf die Erde fallen.*
'The stone must necessarily fall down.'

d. *Wir müssen aus christlicher Nächstenliebe den Lot Leidenden helfen.*
'We must help the needy out of Christian charity.'

e. *Die Kartoffeln müssen mindestens 30 Minuten kochen, damit sie gar werden.*
'The potatoes must be cooked for at least 30 minutes until they are done.'

f. *An unserer Schule **mussten** sich die Schüler früher vor Schulbeginn in Reih und Glied aufstellen.*
'In our school pupils had to line up before classes began.'

Duden reserves a separate meaning variant for those uses of *müssen* in which the necessity "gründet in dem Willen einer Person, die an eine andere eine Forderung richtet" [is based on the will of a person, who issues a demand to someone else] (Duden 1998: 97).

(9) *Du musst mich lieben.*
'You must love me.'

In the case of such a "personal" locus of potency, nothing prevents the source of potency to coincide with the speaker. This possibility is only rarely explicitly mentioned in the relevant literature, although it is hinted at by Engel (1988: 466), who stresses the equivalence between the 2nd-person present-tense use of *müssen* and the imperative.

(10) a. *Lassen Sie sich sofort untersuchen!*
'Have yourself examined immediately!'

b. *Sie müssen sich sofort untersuchen lassen!*
'You must have yourself examined immediately!'

Indicative *muss* differs in this respect from indicative *soll*; with the latter verb, the locus of potency and that of the speaker do not so easily coincide.

2. *Sollen* and *müssen* in interrogatives

An analysis of *sollen* has to come to terms with the frequent use of this verb (especially its present indicative form) in interrogative contexts. Data from a written (Mannheimer Korpus)[11] and a formal spoken corpus (taken from the *Bundestagsprotokolle*, i.e. records from the German Parliament) reveal that indicative *soll* occurs in about 30% of its attestations in an interrogative environment.

Table 1. The syntactic contexts of indicative *soll*

	soll spoken	*%*	*soll written*	*%*
declarative main clause	50	38.7	67	51.2
interrogative main clause	*31*	*24*	*32*	*24.4*
interrogative subclause	*12*	*9.3*	*6*	*4.6*
other subclauses	36	28	26	19.8
Total number	*129*	*100*	*131*	*100*

These figures contrast sharply with the number of questions containing indicative *muss* in the same corpora.

Table 2. The syntactic contexts of indicative *muss*

	muss spoken[12]	*%*	*muss written*	*%*
declarative main clause	155	77.5	92	82.9
interrogative main clause	*2*	*1*	*4*	*3.6*
interrogative subclause	*2*	*1*	*0*	*0*
other subclauses	41	20.5	15	13.5
Total number	*200*	*100*	*111*	*100*

Interrogatives account for only 2% (in the spoken material) and 3.6% (in the written material) of all the occurrences of indicative *muss*.

Table 3. The syntactic contexts of past conjunctive *sollte*

	sollte spoken	*%*	*sollte written*	*%*
declarative main clause	77	72	52	63.4
interrogative main clause	*2*	*1.9*	*13*	*15.9*
interrogative subclause	*1*	*0.9*	*0*	*0*
other subclauses	27	25.2	17	20.7
Total number	*107*	*100*	*82*	*100*

Similarly, a comparison with the number of past conjunctive occurrences in interrogatives reveals that *sollte* appears considerably less frequently in interrogatives than its indicative counterpart *soll*. There is a considerable increase in written contexts, though. Quantitative data from larger text corpora confirm this tendency. Table 4 presents the number of cases in which (a) a particular interrogative pronoun is followed by *soll*, *sollte*,[13] or *muss*; and (b) the modal verb occurs sentence-initially, whereby the sentence ends in a question mark.

Table 4. General frequency of *soll*, *sollte*, and *muss* in interrogative environments

Public[14]	soll	sollte	muß/muss
warum 'why'	968	974	311
			(172+139)
was 'what'	3548	402	735
			(358+377)
wer 'who'	936	182	151
			(59+92)
wie 'how'	2818	686	306
			(119+187)
verb in sentence-initial position + question mark (as an interrogative signal)	1467	834	1052
			(537+515)
Total number	9737	3078	2555

Note that indicative *soll* clearly outnumbers indicative *muß/muss* in all these contexts. The situation is less straightforward for *sollte*, which on the whole occurs far less often than its indicative counterpart *soll*, but slightly more often than indicative *muss*. An interesting feature regarding *sollte* is its rather frequent occurrence in questions introduced by *warum* 'why', where *sollte* even outnumbers indicative *soll*. I will come back to this issue later on.

If we adopt a usage-based approach, in the sense of Barlow and Kemmer (1999), this quantitative difference between *sollen* and *müssen* on the one hand, and between *soll* and *sollte* on the other, should be accounted for and integrated into the semantic description of these verbs. *Sollen*'s higher frequency in interrogative contexts is taken to reflect a higher degree of entrenchment, and is thus regarded as an essential aspect in the makeup of the German modal system.

The question arises what element in the semantics of *sollen* makes its indicative so particularly eligible for an interrogative environment. On the basis of the meaning description given above, the answer presents itself right away: the cognitive model of questioning, in which the speaker directs herself to the *addressee*, fits in very well with the semantics of *sollen*, as the verb points to a locus of potency that is neither the speaker nor the grammatical subject. An analysis of corpus data (Mortelmans 1999) confirms this hypothesis. In real questions containing *sollen*, the addressee is implicitly equated with the locus of potency of the obligation expressed by the modal. The following question-answer pair (11) nicely illustrates this phenomenon, whereby the addressee can be taken to function as the source of potency. Note also that in his answer, the original addressee shifts to *müssen*, which is the "default" modal to express a speaker-oriented obligation in a declarative.

(11) *ja äh soll ich ehrlich sein — sie müssen ehrlich sein herr platte* (DSK)
'Yes, well do you want me to be honest? — You must be honest, Mr Platte.'

By contrast, the indicative of *müssen* is only rarely used in questions in which the addressee is the source of potency (Mortelmans 1999: 673–710). Rather, the addressee in *müssen* questions typically functions as some kind of expert, who knows about the necessity inherent in laws and regulations (12a,b), in the treatment of diseases (12c), in the evolution of nature (12d), or in social conventions (12e). The necessity at stake is one imposed by external forces, in which the addressee does not participate.

(12) a. *Da ich wegen der gleichen Symptome behandelt werde, habe ich die Absicht, ebenfalls die Akupunkturbehandlung durchführen zu lassen. **Muß** ich diese Behandlung — wie meine Freundin behauptet — selbst zahlen oder **muß** meine Krankenkasse eintreten? — Die gesetzlichen Krankenkassen übernehmen Akupunkturbehandlungen nicht, weil die*

Wirksamkeit solcher Behandlungen bisher wissenschaftlich nicht erwiesen ist. (Mannheimer Morgen, 16.03.85, p. 48)
'As I am being treated for the same symptoms, I am also thinking of taking the acupuncture treatment. Must I — as my friend claims — pay for this treatment myself or must my health care plan intervene? — Legal health care does not pay for acupuncture treatment, because up to now the effectiveness of such treatments has not been scientifically proven.'

b. *Was **muß** man tun, um Kindergeld zu bekommen? — Das Kindergeld muß schriftlich beantragt werden. Ein mündlicher Antrag ... genügt nicht. — Was **muß** man beachten, sobald man Kindergeld bezieht? — Sobald Sie Kindergeld beantragt haben, sind Sie verpflichtet,.... (H86, Merkblätter der Bundesanstalt für Arbeit, 01/85)*
'What does one have to do in order to obtain child benefit? — The child benefit must be applied for in writing. An oral application does not suffice. — What does one have to consider as soon as one receives child benefit? — As soon as you have applied for child benefit, you are obliged....'

c. *"Morgens und abends eine Spritze, in einer Woche, wenn die Augen wieder klar sind, nur noch abends eine Spritze". "Und wie lange **müssen** wir das beibehalten?" fragte Bernhard Körber. "Nun, sobald die Organe wieder normal arbeiten, können Sie mit den Spritzen Schluß machen." (MK2, Stephan, S.: Ihre Liebe gab ihr Leben, p. 48)*
'"One injection in the morning, one in the evening, in one week, when her eyes are clear again, only one injection in the evening". "And how long do we have to maintain this?" Bernhard Körber asked. "Well, as soon as the organs function normally again, you can stop the injections."'

d. *"Sie kennen die Krankheit? Mann, so reden Sie doch! Ist meine Frau zu heilen, oder **muß** sie sterben? Antworten Sie!"* (MK2, Stephan, S.: *Ihre Liebe gab ihr Leben*, p. 38)

"'Do you know the disease? Man, talk to me! Can my wife be cured or must she die? Answer me!'"

e. *"Wie soll ich wissen, wann es zwei Uhr ist?" stammelte Martha. "Hast du keine Uhr"? "Nein". Martha war betroffen. "**Muß** man eine Uhr haben? Warum?"* (MK2, Uhl, Y.: *Um Mitternacht im blauen Schloss*, p. 30)

"'How am I to know when it's two o'clock?" Martha stammered. "Haven't you got a watch then?" "No." Martha was upset. "Must one have a watch? Why?"'

In questions, indicative *sollen* has more or less specialized as the default verb to ask about obligations in which the addressee functions as the locus of potency. I take this to be an indication of the subjectification of *sollen*, as the addressee (an element of the ground) is implicitly construed as a pivotal participant (the source of potency) within the modal relationship. In line with the subjectified nature of indicative *sollen* in interrogatives, it is generally no longer anaphoric, i.e. the speaker can make use of *sollen* to ask a question about a "new" obligation, whereby the source of potency is construed within the given communicative setting and more or less by default equated with the addressee.

(13) *Bernhard seufzte tief auf und nickte. "Ich habe wohl ihr Vertrauen verloren." "**Soll** ich mal mit ihr reden?" fragte der Vater impulsiv. "Kommt nicht in Frage", antwortete Bernhard bestimmt.* (MK2, Stephan, S.: *Ihre Liebe gab ihr Leben*, p. 50)
'Bernhard gave a deep sigh and nodded. "I must have lost her confidence." "Shall I talk to her?" the father asked impulsively. "There's no question about it," Bernhard firmly replied.'

2.1. *A typology of indicative* sollen *questions*

Not every question containing indicative *soll* can be analyzed in the above fashion. Apart from real questions, in which the speaker seeks an answer from the addressee, indicative *sollen* also appears in deliberative and rhetorical questions, which both deviate from the prototypical model of questioning.

2.1.1. Indicative *soll* in deliberative questions

First, in a deliberative question, the speaker simply presents a state of affairs in the form of a question, without expecting an answer from the addressee. Deliberative questions can be linked to the distinction made by Lyons (1977: 754) between posing a question on the one hand, and asking one on the other. *Posing* a question is associated with the mere expression of the speaker's doubt or lack of knowledge, whereas *asking* a question combines the expression of doubt or ignorance with an appeal to the addressee to do away with it. A typical example of a deliberative *soll* question is presented in (14). Note that the question concerns the necessity of a particular mode of action, so that the modal verb can be said to retain its root meaning.

(14) *Nun gibt niemand mehr einen Plan vor,.... Reuter muß sich künftig seine Kunden selbst suchen, und er muß gegen Billigkonkurrenz aus dem Westen konkurrieren.* **Soll** *er sich auf Sonderanfertigungen spezialisieren, oder* **soll** *er expandieren, um durch Massenfertigung die Kosten zu senken? Abwarten. Die alte Sicherheit ist weg, mit der neuen Freiheit können sie nichts anfangen.* (WK, *Der Spiegel*, 25.06.1990, p. 22)
'Now nobody sets up a plan in advance anymore. Reuter must go and look for his customers himself, and he must compete with cheap products from the West. Should he specialize in custom-built design or should he expand to reduce the cost by mass production? Just wait and see. The old sense of security has gone, they [inhabitants of the former GDR] don't know what to do with their newly gained freedom.'

This need not be the case, however. In the following example, *sollen* is used to question the inevitability of a future development. Here, the speaker can be said to put the evolutionary momentum onstage: the speaker does not simply assess the likelihood of a future development, as his question concerns the threatening necessity of what might come.

(15) *Das Zimmer fing an, sich zu drehen, ihr wurde schwarz vor Augen — ohnmächtig fiel sie auf den Stuhl zurück. "Norma!" rief Bernhard erschrocken und sprang auf. ... "Um Gottes willen", rief Ludwig ängstlich aus.... "Jetzt fängt ihre Krankheit wieder an! **Soll** das denn immer so weitergehen?" knirschte er verzweifelt.* (MK2, Stephan, S.: *Ihre Liebe gab ihr Leben*, p. 62)
'The room began to turn, everything went black — she fainted and fell back onto the chair. "Norma!" Bernhard screamed in fright and jumped up. "For God's sake," Ludwig anxiously exclaimed. "Now her disease is starting again! Is this to go on for ever?" he ground desperately.'

In deliberative questions like (14) and (15), the modal relation (obligation, inevitability) is not grounded in the hearer, who does not function as a source of potency. This could explain why this type of question does not favor *sollen* to the same extent as the "real" questions discussed above in (11) and (13). The vagueness of the modal source seems to allow for the appearance of *müssen*, which is sometimes found to alternate with *sollen* within the same sentence.

(16) a. ***Muß** man dagegen, **soll** man dafür sein?* (*Die Zeit*, 05.04.85, p. 1)
'Must one be against it, or should one be in favor of it?'

b. *Unklar bleibt, was genau der Richter tun darf und wann. **Soll** er gleich bei der Scheidung eine befristete Regelung treffen? **Muß** er warten, bis ein Ehegatte kommt und eine Änderung beantragt?* (*Die Zeit*, 21.06.85, p. 14)
'It remains unclear what exactly the judge is allowed to do and when she can do it. Should she immediately arrange a

temporary settlement? Or should she wait until one of the spouses comes and demands a change?'

2.1.2. Indicative *soll* in rhetorical questions

A second type of question that deviates from the interrogative prototype is the rhetorical question, in which the speaker herself suggests an expected answer. Containing a concealed statement, rhetorical questions can be said to exhibit the illocutionary value of a declarative. A typical characteristic of rhetorical questions is the reversed polarity of the answer that is implied: questions containing a negative element generally imply a positive assertion, whereas questions without a negative element imply a negative answer (Meibauer 1986: 137; Herring 1991: 257). The role of the addressee in this type of questions should not be disregarded, as it is the addressee who has to recognize the rhetorical character of the question and work out the intended answer (Vandeweghe 1977: 284). Moreover, rhetorical questions are hearer-oriented to the extent that they "are intended to stimulate the involvement of the listeners in the story by making a direct appeal to their attention and evaluative processes" (Herring 1991: 259), for which reason they are given the label "appellative" by a number of scholars (Schmidt-Radefeldt 1977; Confais 1990). This appeal to the addressee may account for the fact that in rhetorical questions, (hearer-oriented) *sollen* is also generally preferred over (neutral) *müssen*. At the same time, a rhetorical question seems to be more speaker-oriented than an ordinary one, as the speaker tries to force her own point of view upon the addressee.

If one looks at rhetorical questions containing indicative *sollen*, it is important to dissociate the inherent speaker-bound character of the rhetorical question as a question type from the meaning of the modal verb as such. In the following example, the speaker "aa" refers to an existing prohibition (*"mein Vater meint das tut man nicht"*), the validity of which is questioned by the second speaker "bb". The modal *soll* takes up the prohibition referred to by the first speaker (for which the father is clearly the locus of potency) and can therefore be claimed to be anaphoric.

(17)   aa: *mein Vater meint das tut man nicht.*
       bb: *was heißt das tut man nicht ich finde warum **soll** man es nicht tun?* (DSK)
       - 'My father says one shouldn't do that.
       - What does that mean one shouldn't do that, I think why shouldn't one do that?'

It does not always seem feasible, however, to separate the semantics of the modal verb from the pragmatics of the question type. Especially in rhetorical questions introduced by *warum soll*, the rhetorical character of the entire utterance seems to affect the meaning of the modal as well. Even if the original source of the modal relation is located outside of the speaker (in a third person or in society as a whole), the speaker in a way construes herself as a new locus of potency. In the example above, the rhetorical question can be rephrased as 'I think that one should do that'. The originally "objective" *sollen*, which refers to an obligation that originated in someone else (the father), becomes secondarily subjective — because of the sentence type.[15]

Another feature of rhetorical *soll* questions (especially with *warum*) is the fact that deontic and epistemic meanings sometimes merge. Negating the necessity of a particular action, i.e. implying that something is not necessary, can boil down to locating the entire state of affairs in irreality, implying that it will not be realized. This is particularly interesting, given that neither indicative *soll* nor past conjunctive *sollte* have established a clear epistemic use in declaratives.

(18)   *Die Stiftung schätzte den Nachlaß ... auf 120 Millionen Dollar. Hayes hingegen, dem als Anwalt zwei Prozent des Nachlaßwertes zustehen sollten, kam auf 600 Millionen. "Warum **soll** irgend jemand einen Warhol kaufen", argumentierte er hintersinnig, "wenn die Stiftung selbst kein Vertrauen in den Wert seines Werks hat?"* (*Spiegel* 93, H41, p. 264)

'The foundation valued the works left by the artist at 120 million dollars. Hayes by contrast, who as a lawyer was to receive two percent of the estate, arrived at 600 million. "Why should anyone buy a Warhol," he argued subtly, "if the foundation itself has no confidence in the value of his work?"'

As far as questions introduced by *warum* 'why' in combination with a form of *sollen* are concerned, it has already been noted that the form *sollte* occurs much more often than in other question-word questions, which generally favor indicative *soll* (see Table 4 and Table 5, in which the results of Table 4 are spelled out for a number of smaller corpora).[16]

Table 5. Frequency of the forms *soll* and *sollte* following *wer, was, wie,* and *warum*

	soll			sollte		
	lit-pub	MMM	WK	lit-pub	MMM	WK
wer	8	142	27	7	34	6
was	150	514	83	37	70	6
wie	63	395	66	38	134	17
warum	32	136	17	45	141	19

This stronger preference for the past conjunctive could be accounted for if one takes the function of *warum soll(te)* questions into account. Very often, it seems, the speaker — by formally questioning the reason for an obligation (*warum soll*) — expresses her doubt regarding the state of affairs expressed in the infinitive. What is profiled, therefore, is the (nonrealization of the) infinitival process rather than the modal relation, which equals an epistemic assessment. This is precisely what happens in example (18) above. In the following section, we will see that an epistemic meaning and an outspoken orientation towards the speaker are typical traits of questions containing past conjunctive *sollte*.

With respect to indicative *soll* questions, then, a number of generalizations seem to be warranted. From a semantic/pragmatic point of view, indicative *soll* is compatible with various question types. In real questions, the addressee is implicitly equated with the locus of potency, which I regard as a symptom of subjectivity *à la* Langacker. Syntactically, indicative *sollen* most often occurs in question-word questions, whereby the most frequent interrogative pronouns are *was* 'what' and *wie* 'how'. The modal typically has a root meaning: the speaker asks a question about aspects of a (generally presupposed) obligation or necessity (*who* has to do it? *how* does it have to be done? *what* has to be done?), like in the following examples.

(19) a. *Was **soll** man wählen?* (WK, *Frankfurter Allgemeine*, 27.12.1989, p. 19)
'What should one vote for?'

b. *Was **soll** aus den Denkmälern und Gedenktafeln werden, die zur Zeit des SED-Regimes in Ost-Berlin und der weiteren DDR errichtet ... worden sind: erhalten — zerstören — verändern?* (WK, *Frankfurter Rundschau*, 24.08.1990, p. 11)
'What is to become of the monuments and commemorative plaques which have been put in place during the SED regime in East-Berlin and the rest of the GDR: keep them, destroy them, change them?'

c. *Eigentlich brauchen wir ... ein Gesamtkonzept für die Museumslandschaft in Berlin: Was kostet das alles? Wer **soll** das tragen?* (WK, *Bundestagsprotokolle*, Sitzung Nr. 216, 20.06.1990, p. 17061)
'Actually we are in need of an overall concept for the museums in Berlin: What does it all cost? Who is to pay for it?'

d. *Die Frage ist: Wie **soll** der Prozeß gestaltet werden, der nun offenkundig von immer mehr Menschen dringend gewünscht wird?* (WK, *Bundestagsprotokolle*, Sitzung Nr. 197, 15.02.1990, p. 15149)
'The question is: How should one shape the process, which more and more people obviously strongly call for?'

2.2. A typology of past conjunctive sollte *questions*

Before we tackle the use of past conjunctive *sollte* in questions, it should be stressed that questions containing *sollte* occur much less frequently than their indicative counterparts. The conclusions drawn from the analyses to come therefore only apply to a limited range of instances. Still, questions containing past conjunctive *sollte* are particularly interesting, as they generally contain highly subjectified and grammaticalized instances of *sollte*.

A general characterization of *sollte* questions in terms of the question type immediately reveals a clear opposition between *soll* and *sollte* interrogatives. Past conjunctive *sollte* hardly occurs in real questions, in which the addressee is treated as a locus of potency. By contrast, *sollte* questions are either rhetorical or deliberative, so in any case much more speaker-oriented than real (i.e. addressee-oriented) questions.

Syntactically, questions containing *sollte* are predominantly either of the yes-no type or introduced by *warum*, as the following table shows.[17]

Table 6. Questions containing *soll(te)*

Wendekorpus	sollte	soll
yes-no question	43	22
warum/wieso ('why')	21	5
wie ('how')	13	*30*
was ('what')	7	*28*
wer ('who')	7	*11*
welch ('which')	3	*1*
other (*wo* 'where', *wohin* 'whereto', *woher* 'wherefrom', *wann* 'when', *wieviel* 'how much')	3	*3*
Total number	*97*	*100*

This observation does not come as a surprise, given that the past conjunctive — as a marker of irreality — seems to be more compatible with the fact that the state of affairs in a yes-no question is not presupposed (and therefore in some way not real). By the same token, *sollte* is less compatible with question-word questions, whose epistemic status should be described in terms of givenness. Another characteristic of questions containing *sollte* is the fact that, more often than indicative *soll* questions, they express doubt or ignorance as far as the epistemic status of a state of affairs is concerned, rather than ignorance concerning a possible mode of action.

Based on an analysis of various *sollte* questions (both question-word and yes-no questions), I have set up a typology of *sollte* interrogatives (see Mortelmans 1999: 617–655), which will be presented in the remainder of this chapter. For reasons of simplicity, I will restrict myself to yes-no questions introduced by *sollte*, which can be divided into three main types: *sollte* appears in rhetorical questions, in deliberative questions with a root meaning (in which case *sollte* alternates with *soll*), and in deliberative questions with an epistemic-like meaning. Note that real questions are absent from this typology, as real questions containing past conjunctive *sollte* hardly occur. Let us now have a closer look at the various question types.

2.2.1. Past conjunctive *sollte* in deliberative questions

A first type of *sollte* question is illustrated in (20). Here, we are dealing with a deliberative question, in which the speaker presents a possible course of action, without taking a personal stance. As the obligation is not anchored in any of the participants of the speech event (neither speaker nor addressee), it does not come as a surprise that *sollte* can be replaced by *soll* (and sometimes even by *muss*).

(20) a. *Die USA haben in den 80er Jahren mit Druck auf Moskau die Sowjetunion gesprengt.* **Sollte** *man dies auch mit China versuchen und was wird die dann unweigerliche Unordnung und das Chaos für die 1,2 Milliarden Chinesen bedeuten? Mit solchen Fragen gilt es sich jetzt ernsthaft zu beschäftigen.* (*Mannheimer Morgen*, 10.7.1995)

'In the eighties the United States have blown up the Soviet-Union by exerting pressure on Moscow. Should one try this with China as well, and what will the inevitable disorder and chaos mean for 1.2 billion Chinese? Such questions should be dealt with seriously now.'

b. *Morgen wird sich die Regierung mit dem Problem befassen. Wie könnten notwenige Entscheidungen aussehen?* **Sollte** *man subventionierte Erzeugnisse nur noch mit Ausweis kaufen können?* **Sollte** *man die Grenze zu Polen zeitweilig schließen?* **Sollte** *man die Preise für bestimmte Waren erhöhen und dafür die Löhne bzw. das Kindergeld heraufsetzen? (Berliner Zeitung,* 22.11.1989, p. 1)

'The government will deal with the problem tomorrow. What could necessary decisions look like? Should it only be possible to buy subsidized products by showing an identity card? Should the border with Poland be closed temporarily? Should one raise the prices of particular commodities and in return raise wages or child benefit?'

The question arises as to what the import of the past conjunctive is here. In other words, what is the difference between *soll* and *sollte* in this type of deliberative question? Obviously, the past conjunctive cannot be taken to signal the speaker's personal stance (see the following section 2.2.2), as she simply presents possible ways of acting without suggesting any answer at all. An (admittedly conjectural) way of interpreting the use of the past conjunctive here would be to view the mood marker as affecting the *speech act* of questioning as such. The past conjunctive could then be taken to signal that the question itself is problematic and deviates from an ordinary question, to the extent that the speaker does not expect an answer from the addressee.

2.2.2. Past conjunctive *sollte* in rhetorical questions

Second, past conjunctive *sollte* with a root meaning appears in rhetorical questions.[18] This use of *sollte* resembles its use in declaratives (see Mortelmans, forthcoming), to the extent that the speaker presents a personal point of view with respect to the action described, i.e. it is the speaker who functions as the source of potency. A typical feature of rhetorical *sollte* questions is the appearance of the negation marker *nicht*, which in this particular context seems to function more like a discourse particle (termed "*Modalpartikel*" or "*Abtönungspartikel*" in the German literature), indicating the emotional involvement of the speaker (see Duden 1998: 724; Helbig 1988: 181).[19]

(21) a. *In der Bundesrepublik gibt es rund 2,1 Millionen Ehen, die seit 43 Jahren halten. Sollte darüber **nicht** genausoviel geredet werden wie über zerbrochene Bindungen?* (Meibauer 1986: 212)
'In the Federal Republic about 2.1 million marriages have been lasting for 43 years. Shouldn't we talk about this as much as about divorces?'

b. *Neu 1990 ist ... die Rekonstruktion der Kongreßhalle am Zoo, was bedeutet, daß ursprünglich geplante Rekonstruktionen von Wohnhäusern in der Seeburgstraße nicht begonnen werden. ... Beides ist wichtig, aber **sollte** die Lösung der Wohnungsfrage **nicht** einmal das Prä haben?* (WK, *Leipziger Volkszeitung*, 04.01.1990, p. 3)
'New in 1990 is the renovation of the conference hall near the zoo, which implies that originally planned renovations of private homes in the Seeburgstraße will not be initiated. Both things are important, but should the housing problem not be solved first?'

If we compare rhetorical *sollte* questions with rhetorical *soll* questions, the absence of *nicht* in the latter strikes the eye.

Table 7. The appearance of the modal particle *nicht* in rhetorical questions

H85, H86, WK	*soll*	*sollte*
nicht	1	11
without *nicht*	45	2

An analysis that treats *nicht* as a speaker-oriented modal particle can easily come to terms with the general absence of *nicht* in a rhetorical question containing the indicative of *sollen*. Recall that indicative *sollen* in rhetorical questions is often anaphoric, as it refers to pre-existing obligations or intentions, whose source is not to be equated with the speaker but with an external locus of potency. The insertion of *nicht* would create the impression that the speaker sides with the obligation or intention expressed by the modal, which is exactly the opposite of what the speakers in (22) want to achieve.

(22) a. *"Ich halte nichts von einer Verschärfung des Demonstrationsstrafrechts. Sollen Tausende von Demonstranten in die Untersuchungshaft abgeführt werden?" Mit diesen Worten wandte sich der Präsident des Bundesgerichtshofes (BGH), Gerd Pfeiffer, gegen entsprechende Gesetzesvorhaben Bonns.* (Meibauer 1986: 227)
'"I don't believe in tightening the criminal law on demonstrations. Are thousands of demonstrators to be held on remand?" With these words the president of the Federal Court, Gerd Pfeiffer, opposed corresponding bills of the federal government.'

b. *Die DDR ... hält auch uns einen Spiegel unserer Versäumnisse vor, gerade weil wir einander so ähnlich sind. In diesem Spiegel sehen wir als drohende Möglichkeit ein riesiges deutsches Land mit 80 Millionen Menschen, ... mit einer Autobahnpiste dreimal um die Erde, mit einem horrenden Verbrauch an Wäldern und mit einer goldenen Mauer gegen Flüchtlinge aus der Dritten Welt. Soll so das unökologische Prinzip unseres Wirtschaftens in die DDR überspringen? Wollen wir das wirklich?* (WK, *Bundestagsprotokolle*, Sitzung Nr. 176, Bd. 151, 16.11.1989, p. 13374)

'The GDR keeps a mirror before us, in which we see our sins of omission, precisely because we resemble one another so much. In this mirror we see the threatening possibility of a gigantic German country with 80 million people, a motorway three times around the earth, with a shocking consumption of woods, and a golden wall against refugees from the Third World. Is our nonecological way of doing business to be taken over in the GDR? Do we really want that?'

Interestingly, rhetorical questions with past conjunctive *sollte* can also be used to question the epistemic status of the state of the affairs in the infinitive. In the following instance, the author wants to convince her readers that it *is* possible for Reagan (*"dem greisen Herrn im Weißen Haus"*) to look for less military ways of achieving world peace.

(23) *Michail Gorbatschow und Ronald Reagan sagen ... übereinstimmend, daß Amerika und Rußland in dieser Welt zusammenleben müssen. Dem jungen Kremlchef ist die Kraft zuzutrauen, neue Zugänge zur Friedenssicherung aufzuspüren, ohne sowjetische Interessen zu mißachten.* **Sollte** *es da dem greisen Herrn im Weißen Haus nicht möglich sein, aller technischen Besessenheit zu entsagen und, ehe er Hunderte von laserproduzierenden Atomkraftwerken an den Himmel hängt, lieber zu erforschen, ob es nicht direktere ... Wege zum Weltfrieden gibt?* (*Die Zeit*, 20.09.1985, p. 1)
'Michael Gorbatchow and Ronald Reagan say in mutual agreement that America and the USSR have to live together in this world. The young head of the Kremlin can be believed to be capable of finding new ways of peacekeeping without ignoring Soviet interests. Wouldn't it therefore be possible for the old man in the White House to renounce all technical obsessions and, before he hangs hundreds of laser producing nuclear power stations in the sky, to find out whether there are not more direct ways to world peace?'

A number of speaker-oriented mechanisms seem to join forces here — the rhetorical question, the discourse particle *nicht*, and the past conjunctive *sollte* as such — to produce a highly subjectified utterance, in which the meaning of the modal can be characterized as inferential: the speaker draws an inference, which she more or less forces upon the addressee. The adverb *da* underscores the inferential nature of *sollte*, as it points to the available premises in the preceding context: given that Gorbatchow has the power to look for new ways to secure peace, it should be possible for Reagan to look for such new ways as well. The utterance is highly subjectified, both in terms of the locus of potency (the speaker) and the target (the process expressed by the infinitive).

2.2.3. Mirative *sollte* in deliberative questions

Finally, past conjunctive *sollte* also occurs in deliberative questions, in which the speaker brings up a state of affairs for further consideration.

(24) a. ***Sollte** ich etwa bisher am eigentlichen Leben vorbeigelebt haben? Der Verdacht liegt nahe. Ich dachte lange nach.... Und ich begann, meinen Alltag umzukrempeln.* (*Mannheimer Morgen*, 30.06.1989)
'Have I perhaps until now rushed by real life? It seems like it. I thought hard about it. And I began to change my daily life radically.'

b. *Der 22jährige Mann steckt in einem eleganten dunklen Anzug.... Wenn sich sein klassisch geschnittenes Gesicht entspannt, gleicht er einem levantinischen Verführer. **Sollte** er tatsächlich ein Mörder sein?* (*Mannheimer Morgen*, 30.06.1995)
'The twenty-two year old man wears an elegant dark suit. When his face with its classical features relaxes, he looks like a Levantine seducer. Would he really be a killer?'

The latter use of *sollte* has puzzled many scholars, who generally tried to link it with the "normal" uses of the modal. In fact, the meaning of *sollte* in this context seems very hard to pinpoint, as it can hardly be said to have any deontic or even epistemic import. Moreover, it cannot be dissociated from the syntactic context in which it is used, as this specific use seems to be restricted to yes-no questions, or perhaps more accurately to constructions with *sollte* in sentence-initial position.[20] In his discussion of this type of deliberative *sollte* question, Kaufmann (1962) distinguishes between two kinds. For both types, the speaker's conjecture is crucially based on her confrontation with the "here and now", the immediate circumstances accompanying the speech event. It is the speaker's observation of a given state of affairs which seems to make a particular conjecture inevitable. The conjecture forces itself on the speaker, as it were.

> Das Modalverb SOLLEN im Konjunktiv + *(etwa) doch* begegnet uns in zweifelnden Fragen. Der Zweifel hat sich dem Sprechenden aus eigener nachträglicher Überprüfung eines Sachverhalts ergeben. ... Das Modalverb SOLLEN im Konjunktiv II (in der Regel in Verbindung mit *etwa*, *wirklich* oder *tatsächlich*) erscheint in erstauntem oder in ungläubigem Ton vorgebrachten Fragen. Der Sprechende ist darüber verwundert, daß seine Erwartungen nicht durch den tatsächlichen Verlauf des Geschehens bestätigt werden. (Kaufmann 1962: 171)
> [The modal verb *sollen* in the conjunctive + *(etwa) doch* occurs in conjectural questions. The conjecture arises out of the speaker's retrospective verification of a state of affairs. The modal verb *sollen* in the past conjunctive (normally in combination with *etwa*, *wirklich*, or *tatsächlich*) occurs in questions which are uttered in a surprised or disbelieving tone. The speaker is surprised that her expectations are not confirmed by the actual course of history.]

Kaufmann's second type differs from the first to the extent that the speaker is *surprised* to find that a particular state of affairs holds: the speaker's observation clashes with her own expectations, causing surprise or disbelief. The element of surprise calls to mind Delancey's (1997: 35) grammatical category of mirativity, marking statements "for which the speaker had no psychological preparation", the proposition at issue being one "which is new to the speaker, not yet integrated into his overall picture of the world" (Delancey 1997:

36). This new and unexpected information is exactly what seems to be at stake in this type of deliberative question. Note that the inferential moment is rather weak: it is not so much a process of inference, but the mere perception of a particular state of affairs, which brings up the conjecture introduced by *sollte*.

In the same paper, Delancey also briefly discusses Akatsuka's (1985) examples of (nongrammaticalized) mirativity in English, which pops up in a conditional context. So, according to Akatsuka, the *if* clause in (25) can get a mirative-like, nonconditional reading, if it contains newly acquired information. An interesting structural parallel with the German construction suggests itself, as the German deliberative *sollte* question formally equals an (asyndetic) conditional protasis.

(25) *Well, if John is going to the meeting, I'll go, too.* (The speaker just heard that John is going.)

This use of *sollte*, then, can be taken to be maximally subjective, both in terms of the source of potency (the implicit speaker) and the target of the modal relation (a state of affairs). Note that the meaning of the modal cannot very well be described in terms of epistemic modality, but rather in terms of information status (see also Nuyts, this volume), i.e. the speaker does not so much assess the factuality of a state of affairs but rather its degree of newness or unexpectedness.

3. Conclusion

The question whether a modal verb functions as a grounding predication, is in need of a more qualified answer than the one suggested by Langacker. I have argued that a number of parameters, functional as well as formal, determine the grounding status of a modal. This is particularly the case for the German modals, which as a group have not acquired the same degree of formal grammaticalization as their English counterparts, a reason for Langacker to deny them the status of grounding predication. If one investigates the individual members of the German modal verb category, though, finer distinctions can be made. Thus, it can be argued that the German epistemic modals function as grounding predications, a claim implicitly made by Diewald (1999). Second, among the German root modals, some seem to have acquired a special status as well, again both from a semantic and from a formal point of view (see Mortelmans 2001 for a short discussion of *sollte* in declaratives). In this paper, another parameter is brought in: the sentence type in which the modal verb occurs. The reason for this particular perspective lies in the notably frequent occurrence of indicative *sollen* in interrogatives. Interrogative instances of indicative *soll* account for about 30% of all occurrences of indicative *soll*. As far as real questions are concerned, i.e. questions in which the speaker seeks an answer from the addressee, *sollen* typically appears in contexts in which the addressee is implicitly construed as a locus of potency.

(26) *Wir müssen etwas unternehmen.* **Soll** *ich mal nachsehen?*
 (MK2)
 'We have to do something. Shall I have a look?'

This use is grammaticalized to the extent that indicative *soll* is by and large the only possible form in this context, i.e. *soll* cannot normally be replaced by the past conjunctive *sollte* or by *muss*. This, then, can be interpreted as a loss of paradigmatic variability, one of the parameters used by Lehmann (1985: 307) to determine the degree of grammaticalization for a particular linguistic item: "Within the paradigm, choice among its members becomes constrained by grammatical rules." Indicative *soll*, therefore, can be regarded as a grammaticalized item in real questions in which the addressee is regarded as source of potency. I take this use of *sollen* to be grounding, as the reference to the ground element (the addressee) is generally implicit and the modal relation itself cannot be grounded anymore by tense or mood. Past conjunctive *sollte* favors other interpretations, whereas past indicative *sollte* (which cannot be formally distinguished from the past conjunctive) mainly occurs in questions within free indirect speech, in which the past tense seems to mark an alternative ground rather than a genuine past tense.

Not every occurrence of *soll* can be analyzed in the above way, though, as *soll* is also frequently found in "deviant" question types (deliberative and rhetorical questions), which on the whole are less addressee-oriented. For *soll* in deliberative questions, I have argued that the modal relation is less anchored in the immediate speech situation: the speaker simply poses or even "describes" a question, without expecting an answer.

(27) *Über den Vollzug der deutschen Vereinigung ist eine Diskussion entbrannt...: **Soll** die DDR als ganzes, sollen ihre wiederbelebten Länder der Bundesrepublik beitreten?* (WK, *Rheinischer Merkur*, 09.03.90, p. 3)
'A discussion has arisen about the way in which the German unification is to be carried out: Should the GDR in its entirety, or should its resurrected *Länder*, join the Federal Republic?'

Not surprisingly, past conjunctive *sollte* and indicative *muss* can take over here, albeit for different reasons. The use of the past conjunctive in this context takes the "abnormality" of the question type into account, whereas *muss* expresses a vague kind of necessity.

For rhetorical questions, it is important to distinguish between the intuitively subjective nature of the question type as such, and the modal verb, whose meaning can be described in more objective terms, as the modal relation is often anchored in a previously mentioned, onstage entity.

If we concentrate on the past conjunctive uses of *sollen* in questions, a different image emerges. For one thing, *sollte* questions are not normally used to obtain an answer from the addressee (real questions hardly occur), but are instead highly speaker-oriented. Root meanings are found to prevail (both in rhetorical and in deliberative questions); compared to indicative *soll* questions, however, epistemic-like meanings occur more often. In rhetorical *sollte* questions, the speaker typically recommends a particular way of action (28a), whereas deliberative *sollte* questions simply present it, without the speaker taking a particular stance (28b).

(28) a. ***Sollte** sich die Gewerkschaft nicht erst einmal finden..., bevor zum letzten aller Streikmittel gegriffen wird?* (WK, *Berliner Zeitung*, 02.02.90, p. 1)
'Shouldn't the trade union first come to terms with itself, before it turns to the ultimate strike action?'

b. *Morgen wird sich die Regierung mit dem Problem befassen. Wie könnten notwendige Entscheidungen aussehen? ... **Sollte** man die Grenze zu Polen zeitweilig schließen?* (WK, *Berliner Zeitung*, 22.11.89, p. 1)
'Tomorrow the government will deal with the problem. What could necessary decisions look like? Should one close the border with Poland for the time being?'

Particularly interesting is the deliberative-mirative *sollte* question, which provides a case of high grammaticalization (note that the meaning of *sollte* is highly abstract here) and subjectification. On the basis of her observation of the surrounding world, the speaker arrives at a particular supposition (which often causes surprise). In this particular use, modal verb and sentence type (only yes-no questions) seem to reinforce each other, which also implies that one cannot dissociate this use of *sollte* (and its possible grounding status) from the sentence type in which it occurs.

(29) *Erst vor 6000 Jahren zog sich die letzte große Eisdecke vom kanadischen Festland zurück. Wodurch werden diese Kälteperioden ausgelöst? Sollte es einen festen Zyklus geben, eine Art kosmischen Puls, der alle 250 Millionen Jahre einmal schlägt?* (*Mannheimer Morgen*, 15.03.85, p. 3)
'Only 6,000 years ago, the last big icecap retreated from the Canadian mainland. What causes these spells of cold weather? Is there perhaps a fixed cycle, some kind of cosmic pulse that beats every 250 million years?'

Finally, the foregoing has shown that I find it very difficult *not* to confuse subjectification *à la* Langacker with Traugott's more pragmatic interpretation of the term.[21] In the case of the German modals, stronger grammaticalization, leading to attenuation of the locus and the target of potency (Langacker's subjectification), seems to go hand in hand with a stronger orientation towards the speaker or the addressee (Traugott's subjectification). The more grammaticalized uses of *sollen*, for instance, feature both attenuation (the locus of potency is no longer an identifiable third person, but can be equated with either the speaker or the addressee) and a development towards interpersonal or pragmatic functions, for which the mirative reading of *sollte* in deliberatives provides an excellent example.

Notes

1. Nuyts (this volume) explicitly challenges the assumption that grounding predications have to be grammaticalized. From an onomasiological perspective, there seem to be valid reasons to look for grounding elements outside of the verbal complex. If one concentrates on the modal auxiliaries, though, the assumption that grammaticalization and grounding are linked, in that a higher degree of formal grammaticalization generally reflects more subjectification, seems to be warranted as well.
2. With the verbs *will*, *can*, and *may*, the subject's potency seems to be intuitively clear (*will*=volition; *can*=mental ability; *may*= physical ability). The determination of the subject's potency seems to be less straightforward for *shall* (originally meaning 'to owe'; see Birkmann 1987: 87) and *must* (originally meaning 'to have space'; see Birkmann 1987: 114).
3. Langacker (1991: 272): "A modal is regarded as epistemic when its sole import is to indicate the likelihood of the designated process. In a root modal, there is additionally some conception of potency directed toward the realization of that process, i.e. some notion of obligation, permission, desire, ability, etc."
4. It seems generally accepted that neither *shall* nor *can* allow an epistemic use.
5. Langacker (1991: 274): "The speaker is involved in any case as the primary conceptualizer and the person responsible for assessing the likelihood of reality evolving in a certain way."
6. See Diewald (1999: 26): "die Opposition zwischen Präsens und Präteritum ist im deiktischen Gebrauch stark modifiziert und dient nahezu ausschließlich zur

Kennzeichnung "erlebter Rede", d.h. dem Bericht über die Faktizitätsbewertung einer erzählten Person in der Vergangenheit." [In the epistemic use, the opposition between present and preterite is highly modified and serves almost exclusively for marking "free indirect speech", i.e. reporting about the factuality assessment of a narrated person in the past.]

7. See Diewald (1999: 26): "bei einigen Modalverben [können] nur eine oder zwei Formen zur Faktizitätsbewertung verwendet werden." [With some modal verbs only one or two forms can be used to assess factuality.] The epistemic meaning of *mögen* is only possible in the indicative, whereas *dürfen* only has an epistemic reading in the past conjunctive (*dürfte*). By the same token, the epistemic reading of *können* has a strong preference for the past conjunctive (*könnte*), whereas *müssen* prefers the indicative (see Diewald 1999: 219). The quotative readings of *wollen* and *sollen* are tied to the indicative as well (for *sollen*, see Mortelmans 1999).

8. Diewald (1999: 286) describes the meaning of the *Konjunktiv II* in terms of "phorisch verankerte bedingte Nichtfaktizität" [phorically anchored conditional nonfactuality], i.e. the nonfactuality indicated by the past conjunctive is typically conditional ("*bedingt*") to the extent that it refers to a condition, the nonfulfillment of which entails the nonfactuality of the process the past conjunctive designates. This condition is typically textually available, and thus "phorically anchored".

9. Diewald explicitly states that her semiotic-functional approach is compatible with Langacker's, but does not pursue this link (Diewald 1999: 15).

10. Note that word-by-word translations will not be provided for the German examples to come. The English translations are mainly intended to capture the intended meaning of the entire utterance rather than to exactly render the German original.

11. A total number of 348 tokens of *sollen* in the Mannheimer Korpus were analyzed. Note that *soll* can be both 1st- and 3rd-person singular.

12. The form *muss* occurred 439 times in this corpus (WK, *Bundestagsprotokolle*, "Hj. 89"). I only looked at the first 200 occurrences, though.

13. Note that not all occurrences of *sollte* are past conjunctive, as it can also function as a past indicative form. Earlier research on smaller text corpora (see Mortelmans 1999) has shown that *sollte* has to be interpreted as an indicative rather than a past conjunctive in about one quarter of its occurrences. This does not strongly affect the interpretation of the data in Table 4, though. Compared to the frequencies of *was sollte*, *wer sollte*, and *wie sollte*, there is a rather dramatic increase of *sollte* in combination with *warum*, even if not every instance can be interpreted as conjunctive.

14. "Public" refers to all the written corpora within the COSMAS system, the online corpora provided by the *Institut für deutsche Sprache* (Mannheim). As

these corpora are regularly updated, it should be added that the search was conducted in March 2002.
15. Note that the speaker's involvement is also objectified (or put onstage) by the phrase *ich finde*, a typical mental state predicate (see also Nuyts, this volume).
16. The corpora are taken from the COSMAS system. Three corpora were searched: "lit.pub." contains a collection of (older and recent) literary texts, "MMM" refers to the newspaper *Mannheimer Morgen* (mainly between 1989 and 2001), and "WK" to the *Wendekorpus*, a collection of (written and formal spoken) material collected in 1989 and 1990.
17. Data are drawn from the *Wendekorpus*. I looked at all interrogatives containing *sollte* (97 instances) and compared them with questions containing indicative *soll*. The latter form occurred over 300 times in an interrogative environment — I only took the first 100 occurrences into consideration.
18. I take Schmidt-Radefeldt's (1977: 382) remark that the conjunctive mood in German is an indicator of rhetorical import to be somewhat overstated, in view of the fact that past conjunctive *deliberative* questions are by no means rare.
19. Hentschel (1998: 205) rejects the analysis of *nicht* as a "*Modalpartikel*" and claims that *nicht* is used to negate the sentence type "interrogative", which by itself signals a diminished likelihood as far as the validity of the proposition is concerned. The particle *nicht* in a way reduces the interrogative character of the question, so that the question has a more positive tendency than its equivalent without *nicht*.
20. More in particular, this use of *sollte* could be related to its use in conditionals of the type *Sollten Sie noch Fragen haben, so wenden Sie sich an den Vorsitzenden* 'Should you have any questions, please turn to the chair'. The formal and semantic/functional resemblance between conditionals on the one hand, and the interrogative sentence type on the other, has been commented on earlier. Werth (1997: 251), for instance, points out that inversion constructions (yes-no questions, exclamatives, conditionals) share a basic property: "Rather than simply depicting [=asserting, TM] a situation, they all take some situation and hold it up for inspection." This is in line with Traugott (1985: 294), who describes how interrogative markers can develop into conditional ones: "Interrogatives such as *whether* ask about truth in ways that can be answered by *yes* or *no*. They therefore ask about alternative possible worlds, and are questions about the epistemic status of a proposition." A similar argument is put forward by Hentschel (1998: 186–187), who argues that the asyndetic conditional (i.e. one that is not introduced by a conjunction like *wenn* 'if' but has the finite verb in clause-initial position) is one of the secondary functions of the interrogative sentence type. Given the resemblance of these syntactic environments, it does not come as a surprise that this use of *sollte* bears some similarities to its use in conditional protases.

21. See Traugott (1995: 32): "'Subjectification in grammaticalisation' is the development of a grammatically identifiable expression of speaker belief or speaker attitude to what is said. It is a gradient phenomenon, whereby forms and constructions that at first express primarily concrete, lexical, and objective meanings come through repeated use in local syntactic contexts to serve increasingly abstract, pragmatic, interpersonal, and speaker-based functions."

References

Akatsuka, Noriko
    1985   Conditionals and the epistemic scale. *Language* 61: 625–639.
Barlow, Michael and Suzanne Kemmer (eds.)
    1999   *Usage-Based Models of Language*. Stanford: Center for the Study of Language and Information.
Birkmann, Thomas
    1987   *Präteritopräsentia: Morphologische Entwicklungen einer Sonderklasse in den altgermanischen Sprachen*. (Linguistische Arbeiten 188.) Tübingen: Niemeyer.
Chafe, Wallace
    1995   The realis-irrealis distinction in Caddo, the Northern Iroquoian languages, and English. In: Joan Bybee and Suzanne Fleischman (eds.), *Modality in Grammar and Discourse*, 349–365. (Typological Studies in Language 32.) Amsterdam: Benjamins.
Confais, Jean-Paul
    1990   *Temps-mode-aspect: Les approches des morphèmes verbaux et leurs problèmes à l'exemple du français et de l'allemand*. Toulouse: Université de Toulouse-Le Mirail.
De Mulder, Walter and Carl Vetters
    this vol.   The French *imparfait*, determiners and grounding.
Delancey, Scott
    1997   Mirativity: The grammatical marking of unexpected information. *Linguistic Typology* 1: 33–52.
Diewald, Gabriele
    1993   Zur Grammatikalisierung der Modalverben im Deutschen. *Zeitschrift für Sprachwissenschaft* 12: 218–234.
    1999   *Die Modalverben im Deutschen: Grammatikalisierung und Polyfunktionalität*. (Germanistische Linguistik 208.) Tübingen: Niemeyer.

Dudenredaktion (eds.)
  1998   *Grammatik der deutschen Gegenwartssprache.* Revised by Peter Eisenberg et al. 6th, newly revised edition. (Der Duden in 12 Bänden 4.) Mannheim: Dudenverlag.
Engel, Ulrich
  1988   *Deutsche Grammatik.* Heidelberg: Groos.
Glas, Reinhold
  1984   *"Sollen" im heutigen Deutsch: Bedeutung und Gebrauch in der Schriftsprache.* Tübingen: Narr.
Goossens, Louis
  1996   *English Modals and Functional Models: A Confrontation.* (Antwerp Papers in Linguistics 86.) Antwerp: University of Antwerp.
Helbig, Gerhard
  1988   *Lexikon deutscher Partikeln.* Leipzig: Enzyklopädie.
Hentschel, Elke
  1998   *Negation und Interrogation: Studien zur Universalität ihrer Funktionen.* Tübingen: Niemeyer.
Herring, Susan C.
  1991   The grammaticalization of rhetorical questions in Tamil. In: Elizabeth Closs Traugott and Bernd Heine (eds.), *Approaches to Grammaticalization,* Volume 1, 253–284. Amsterdam: John Benjamins.
Janssen, Theo A. J. M.
  this vol. Deictic principles of pronominals, demonstratives, and tenses.
Kaufmann, Gerhard
  1962   Der Gebrauch der Modalverben *sollen, müssen* und *wollen*: Definition ihrer Bedeutungen unter Berücksichtigung des für den ausländischen Deutschlernenden besonders schwierigen idiomatischen Gebrauchs. *Deutschunterricht für Ausländer* 12: 154–172.
Langacker, Ronald W.
  1990   *Concept, Image, and Symbol: The Cognitive Basis of Grammar.* Berlin: Mouton de Gruyter.
  1991   *Foundations of Cognitive Grammar,* Volume 2: *Descriptive Application.* Stanford: Stanford University Press.
  1999   *Grammar and Conceptualization.* Berlin: Mouton de Gruyter.
Lehmann, Christian
  1985   Grammaticalization: Synchronic variation and diachronic change. *Lingua e Stile* 20: 303–318.
Lyons, John
  1977   *Semantics,* Volume 2. Cambridge: Cambridge University Press.
Meibauer, Jörg
  1986   *Rhetorische Fragen.* Tübingen: Niemeyer.

Mortelmans, Tanja
1999   Die Modalverben *'sollen'* und *'müssen'* im heutigen Deutsch unter besonderer Berücksichtigung ihres Status als subjektivierter 'grounding predications'. Ph.D. dissertation, Department of Germanic linguistics and literature, University of Antwerp.
2001   An introduction to Langacker's 'grounding predications': Mood and modal verbs in German. In: Heinz Vater and Ole Letnes (eds.), *Modalität und mehr/Modality and More*, 3–26. (Fokus 23.) Trier: Wissenschaftlicher Verlag Trier.
forthcom.   The 'subjective' effects of negation and past subjunctive on deontic modals: The case of German *dürfen* and *sollen*. In: Friedrich Lenz (ed.), *Deictic Conceptualisation of Space, Time and Person*. Amsterdam: John Benjamins.

Nuyts, Jan
this vol.   Grounding and the system of epistemic expressions in Dutch: A cognitive-functional view.

Schmidt-Radefeldt, Jürgen
1977   On so-called 'rhetorical' questions. *Journal of Pragmatics* 1: 375–392.

Talmy, Leonard
1988   Force dynamics in language and cognition. *Cognitive Science* 12: 49–100.

Traugott, Elizabeth Closs
1985   Conditional markers. In: John Haiman (ed.), *Iconicity in Syntax*, 289–307. Amsterdam: John Benjamins.
1989   On the rise of epistemic meanings in English: An example of subjectification in semantic change. *Language* 65: 31–55.
1995   Subjectification in grammaticalisation. In: Dieter Stein and Susan Wright (eds.), *Subjectivity and Subjectivisation: Linguistic Perspectives*, 31–54. Cambridge: Cambridge University Press.

Vandeweghe, Willy
1977   Fragen und ihre Funktionen: Versuch einer Typologie auf pragmatischer Basis. In: Konrad Sprengel, Wolf-Dietrich Bald and Heinz Werner Viethen (eds.), *Semantik und Pragmatik: Akten des 11. Linguistischen Kolloquiums, Aachen 1986*, Volume 2, 277–286. Tübingen: Narr.

Werth, Paul
1997   Conditionality as cognitive distance. In: Angeliki Athanasiadou and René Dirven (eds.), *On Conditionals Again*, 243–271. Amsterdam: John Benjamins.

Grounding and the system of epistemic expressions in Dutch: A cognitive-functional view

Jan Nuyts

0. Introduction[1]

In this chapter I will use the case of the linguistic system of expressions of epistemic modality in Dutch to reflect on the nature of grounding in language. By epistemic modality I mean an estimation of the chances (the likelihood) that some state of affairs is "true" or applicable in "reality".[2] In Dutch (like in many other languages), this semantic category can be expressed by a wide variety of linguistic forms. And there appear to be good reasons for this: as an investigation of the functional organization of this "semantic paradigm" reveals, the alternatives are required to suit the various demands on expressing an epistemic evaluation in different circumstances. The term grounding is coined by Langacker (1987) to refer to the (linguistic) process of situating an object or event in the speaker's and hearer's knowledge by means of certain grammatical elements. Epistemic modality (as defined above) is a dimension which squarely falls within the range of meanings involved in this phenomenon. But the present view on the status of epistemic modality and its expressions deviates from Langacker's view on grounding in ways which will hopefully get clearer in the course of the paper. The differences are probably the result of differences in the perspective on (some aspects of) language and grammar, as I will try to show.

This paper is organized as follows. As a preamble, section 1 introduces some elements of the approach to linguistic analysis adopted here. Section 2 relates Langacker's notion of grounding to analytical dimensions used in the present framework, and specifically to the notion of "qualifications of states of affairs". In section 3 the empirical facts regarding the system of epistemic expressions in

Dutch are presented, and section 4 discusses some of the most important consequences of these facts for the points made in sections 1 and 2.

1. Theoretical preamble

Let me start by briefly introducing some essentials of the theoretical background for the present analysis, as it differs from Langacker's Cognitive Grammar in ways which appear relevant for understanding the discussion of grounding below. To what extent these differences are due to fundamentally different concepts of language and linguistics is a matter which I will have to leave for another occasion (compare, e.g., Nuyts 2001a: 16–19 with Langacker 2000), but in any case, the resulting frameworks look very different.

The present view is situated in the context of what may be called a "cognitive-pragmatic" or "cognitive-functional" approach (Nuyts 1992, 2001a). Its basic principle is simple: starting from the observation that language is (primarily) a means of communication, it considers the goal of language research to find out what this means in terms of the organization of the cognitive infrastructure responsible for producing and interpreting language, and how it is situated in the human mind in general. Assuming the basic "functional plausibility" of the analysis of linguistic structure in the "classical" functionalist tradition in linguistics, grammatical description is conceived of in terms of (versions of) the basic notions that are common there, such as lexically represented predicate-argument structures, (types of) semantic role functions, syntactic functions (subject, object), information-structural notions (theme vs. rheme, contrastivity, topic vs. focus), word ordering procedures, etc. (the details of which do not matter here). But — in the spirit of the work of cognitively oriented functionalists such as Givón (1984, 1990, 1995) and Chafe (1994) — this kind of analysis is embedded in, and often heavily adjusted to, an explicit concern with the question how the cognitive systems for language must be organized so as to allow the production and understanding of linguistic utterances as communicative acts. And since communication essentially involves the transmission of information (in a very broad sense),[3] this crucially involves a concern with the question how the linguistic systems relate to other cognitive systems involved in communicative behavior, including, very importantly, the central conceptual system responsible for storing and processing general world knowledge.

The present framework does not only deviate from the Cognitive Grammar analysis, then, in terms of the grammatical apparatus which is being employed, but also in (explicitly) assuming more types of meaning and meaning representation, and in postulating a more complex (and more distal) relationship between conceptual meaning and linguistic form.[4] The basic philosophy behind this is the following.

At a very general level, the human cognitive apparatus can be considered one major (de)contextualization device. The adaptive strength of such a sophisticated cognitive system is its ability to store information about particular "encounters" with reality on a long-term basis. This includes forming generalizations over (aspects of) information acquired in several similar (or even not so similar) encounters at different points in time. By discovering analogies and correspondences between objects or events across those encounters, particular tokens of these objects and events get stripped from unessential features which are due to accidental properties of specific contexts — i.e., they get decontextualized. This results in abstract types which can be used in new, previously unmet situations. But using them in new situations then obviously means recontextualizing them in view of the specifics of the new context.

Now, perceiving and applying information in context is obviously done in a variety of ways. It is, first of all, acquired through the different sense organs — the visual, acoustic, tactile, olfactory, etc. — and applied through motor activity of a wide variety of types. And, secondly, there is, of course, language and other types of symbolic behavior, perceptive and productive. But contrary to the former types of information processing, which are (biologically) primary or basic, symbolic behavior is actually a "superimposed" or "derivative" type, both functionally and physiologically. It is so physiologically, since it taps into the basic possibilities of one or more primary sense organs (the acoustic, the visual) and motor systems (the vocal tract, the hands) by applying certain patterns based on their "basic operational possibilities" as codes to convey information. And it is so functionally, because it is a conventional type of behavior: the patterns just mentioned are conventionalized ones. As such, symbolic systems allow information to be conveyed between cognitive systems even out of its context, and at considerable levels of abstraction (or schematicity, in Langacker's terms). But the cost is that only certain aspects of elementary conceptual information can be conveyed, viz. only those aspects which can be encoded in the symbolic system's representational repertoire.

The conceptual system, then, is obviously a necessary "partner" to all perceptive and behavioral systems involved in information processing, primary and superimposed alike, since they must all somehow draw on a representation of information about "the world". One may thereby reasonably assume that there is just one central conceptual system, which is shared by all "peripheral" systems, i.e., that there is one core system coordinating and integrating all knowledge acquisition, and feeding into and coordinating all types of knowledge-driven actions. Otherwise, it is hard to see how human behavior as a whole could be (more or less) coherent, and how a human being could be perceived as a (mentally) integrated, unified organism. But this would seem to imply that conceptualization is done in a format which is not determined by any one specific perceptive or behavioral system (and especially not by language, as a superimposed behavioral system), but rather in a more abstract format which can "talk to" the different kinds of perceptive and behavioral system.[5]

In the context of this global view, then, it seems natural to make a distinction between conceptual meaning and linguistic meaning — or, in other words, to differentiate between "thinking in general" and (using a term adopted from Slobin 1996) "thinking for speaking", whereby (from the speaker's perspective) the latter forms an intermediary stage in the process of converting conceptual information into a linguistic string. Langacker (this volume a: 3) states that "meaning is critically dependent on construal, i.e. on our capacity for conceptualizing the same situation in alternate ways. Owing to construal, expressions that describe the same objective situation and convey the same conceptual content (or have the same truth conditions) can nevertheless be semantically quite distinct." In essence, this claim is perfectly compatible with the view adopted here. But in fact, the cited statement contains two senses of "conceptual": one is contained in "the same conceptual content" (in the second sentence), the other in "conceptualizing the same situation in alternate ways" (in the first sentence of the quote). (When presenting my own view, I am using the term "conceptual[ize]" exclusively in the former sense.) These two uses correspond to the two levels of semantics assumed in the present analysis:[6] a decontextualized, conceptual level pertaining to one's global knowledge of (in Langacker's words) "the same situation" or "the same conceptual content", which is probably quite independent from language, also in its representational format; and a language-related level pertaining to the way this situation or content is construed (recontextualized) by the speaker in view of the actual communicative circumstances. This view is perfectly in line with the assumption that using language to convey conceptual information is already a contextual choice, determined by the local circumstances. In a way, language is a contextualization device, and so linguistic meaning is a contextual adaptation of conceptual meaning (or, in Langacker's terms, "conceptual content"). Thus, one cannot but agree with Langacker's argument in the above quote, that "expressions that convey the same conceptual content can nevertheless be semantically quite distinct", for linguistic expressions do not only code the conceptual meaning as such, but also the effects of the functional conditions of the communicative context. The paradigm of expressions of epistemic modality in Dutch actually offers a nice illustration of this. In fact, it even offers an excellent empirical argument in favor of the global concept of multiple levels of semantics developed above, as I will show in section 4.

2. Grounding

Langacker (1987: 126) uses the term "ground" to refer to "the speech event, its participants, and its setting". This term thus appears to correspond to what has been called the "communicative situation" elsewhere in the functionalist literature (and above). A traditional functionalist not familiar with Cognitive Grammar, then, might take the term "grounding" at face value to be equivalent to what is often called (and has been called above) "contextualization", i.e., as involving any feature of a linguistic expression which serves to relate its contents to the specific properties of the communicative situation. This is not so, however, or at least not entirely so. As one may have inferred from the previous section, many dimensions which functionalists would think of in the first place as elements of contextualization are not part of Langacker's notion of grounding but belong to his notion of "construal". For instance, information structuring — dimensions such as the thematicity/rhematicity or topicality/focality of information — appears to relate to notions such as profiling and figure/ground or trajectory/landmark organization, and these belong in the domain of construal in Cognitive Grammar.[7] According to Langacker (1987: 489), "an entity is epistemically grounded when its location is specified relative to the speaker and hearer and their spheres of knowledge".[8] His notion of grounding, then, rather pertains to the situation "in the world" (as interpreted by the language user — see note 2) of an object or a state of affairs talked about, in function of the position "in that world" of the speaker and hearer in their actual situation. It is not (or in any case not primarily) a matter of adjusting the presentation of objects or states of affairs to the actual communicative conditions, but of specifying the "ontological" situation or status of those objects or states of affairs relative to the "ontological" situation of the speech event (although, as the analysis of epistemic expressions will show, this specification as such is also subject to adjustments of the former type).[9]

As Langacker (this volume b: 29) states, grounding pertains to "some very basic notions reasonably considered "epistemic" in nature: notions such as time, reality, immediacy, and identification". In terms of the traditional functionalist literature, then, this notion obviously relates to the issue of "tense-aspect-modality marking", which is currently a hot topic among others in linguistic typology and the grammaticalization literature (e.g., Bybee, Perkins, and Pagliuca 1994). And in more theoretical terms this leads us to the proposals in the context of a few grammatical frameworks (Role and Reference Grammar and Functional Grammar) to treat such markers in terms of a layered representational system (e.g., Foley and Van Valin 1984; Hengeveld 1989; Van Valin 1993; Dik 1997).

The basic idea behind these proposals is that semantic dimensions such as aspect, time, deontic and epistemic modality, and evidentiality — which I will henceforth call "qualifications" of states of affairs (or of objects, of course, but I will concentrate on the level of the state of affairs)[10] — are not mutually unrelated. They appear to stand in a fairly strict and probably universally valid hierarchical relationship, which reflects their relative extension of scope. This hierarchical relationship reveals itself semantically, in terms of which meaning extends over the other if two of them are combined in one utterance. For instance, in (1a), the quantificational aspect marking achieved by *once* is obviously caught by the time marking expressed in *yesterday*, but not vice versa. Or in (1b), the epistemic marker *probably* concerns 'her mother's calling yesterday', i.e., including the time marking, but the time marker obviously does not affect the epistemic marking in any way (the estimation of the probability of the event is not situated yesterday, it is valid at the time of speaking).

(1)   a. *Her mother only called once yesterday.*
        b. *Her mother probably called yesterday.*

The hierarchical relationship also reveals itself grammatically, albeit often in very complex ways. For example, in languages which use affixation for expressing these kinds of meaning, the ordering of affixes on the verb tends to reflect the semantic ordering of their meanings directly; or the ordering of adverbials is at least to some extent constrained by the relationship between the meanings (cf. Van

Valin and LaPolla 1997: 164). In other words, the linguistic organization of these qualificational forms is often iconic vis-à-vis the semantic hierarchy in the qualifications.

How all of this works in any detail is far from well established, and the specific proposals mentioned (which actually differ substantially, even in a few very basic respects) are certainly vulnerable to criticism (cf. Nuyts 2001a: 304 for discussion). But in strongly simplified and theory-neutral terms, the following semantic relationship between the major categories appears to apply:

> \> evidentiality
>   \> epistemic modality
>   \> deontic modality
>   \> time
>   \> quantificational aspect (frequency)
>   \> phasal aspect (internal temporal constituency)[11]
>   ∨ (elements of the) STATE OF AFFAIRS

Figure 1. The semantic hierarchy of qualifications

It is not clear to me whether Langacker would consider (the different types of) aspect to belong to the range of meanings (potentially) involved in the phenomenon of grounding.[12] But otherwise this kind of hierarchy might offer a good starting point for a more precise semantic characterization of it.

Langacker's notion of grounding cannot simply be equated with just any kind of linguistic realization of (some part of) this hierarchy, however. The individual qualificational dimensions in it share the property that each can be expressed by quite different linguistic form types, both cross-linguistically and within languages. In English, e.g., most of these categories can be expressed by at least two, and some by several more, linguistic types, including at least morphological (affixal) and/or auxiliary or auxiliary-like forms, as well as one or more types of lexical form (including, most often, adverbs and prepositional phrases, and in a few cases also predicative adjectives and even full verbs). Langacker's notion of grounding only involves grammatical devices, however, as "grounding predications constitute a small set of highly grammaticized elements, one of which has to be chosen as the final step in forming a full nominal or finite clause" (Langacker this volume b: 29). Thus, at the clause level, only tense and the modals are grounding devices in English (cf. Langacker 1987: 126, this volume a,b). And for German, Langacker (1991) even questions the grounding status of the modals, because they are less grammaticalized than the English ones (but see Mortelmans, this volume, for discussion). He would no doubt argue the same for Dutch, since the degree of grammaticalization of its modals is comparable to that in German.

If one accepts this view, however, one would be facing a quite peculiar situation in Dutch. Let us focus on the semantic category of epistemic modality (in the narrow sense used in this paper), which, as indicated, is quite central to Langacker's concept of what grounding is about (in terms of its functionality/semantics). Although Dutch does have plenty of expressive devices for this category, in actual practice none of these, or at least none of the frequently used ones, would be considered real grounding devices. Dutch does not have any other grammatical devices which are systematically dedicated to, or used for, expressing epistemic modality (the subjunctive, which is still available in German, is obsolete in Dutch since the late Middle Ages).[13] (The same observation could be made for deontic modality.) From a commonsense functionalist perspective, this sounds suspicious, as it would mean that Dutch speakers have available, and use, plenty of epistemic (or deontic) modal forms, but never (or hardly ever) use them to really ground what they are saying.

One alternative would be to loosen the requirement on the degree of grammaticalization of a form for it to qualify as a grounding device, and/or to follow Mortelmans (this volume) in differentiating between different uses of a form — some of which are more grammaticalized than others — as to their grounding status. In that case, some uses of the Dutch auxiliaries might possibly fall within this category, including the epistemic ones. But, as the following analysis of the system of epistemic expressions in Dutch will show, this does not appear to resolve the above objection. Moreover, the analysis will turn out to offer very few reasons to see the auxiliaries as more central than, or as functionally special in comparison with, other epistemic expression types. Let us now turn to the empirical facts.

3. The system of epistemic expressions in Dutch

As suggested above, Dutch, like several other European languages, has a remarkable variety of linguistic forms for expressing epistemic modality, including, most importantly, adverbs, predicative adjectives, auxiliaries, and full verbs (especially mental state predicates).[14] They are illustrated in (2), with, for the mental state predicates and auxiliaries, an indication of the alternative syntactic patterns in which they can occur.

(2)   a. Modal sentence adverbs:
*Jan komt **waarschijnlijk** morgen terug naar huis.*
'John probably returns home tomorrow.'
b. Predicative adjectives:
*Het is **waarschijnlijk** dat Jan morgen terug naar huis komt.*
'It is probable that John returns home tomorrow.'
c. Mental state predicates:
*Ik **denk** dat Jan morgen terug naar huis komt.*
'I think (that) John returns home tomorrow.' (complementing)
*Jan komt morgen terug naar huis **denk** ik.*
'John returns home tomorrow, I think.' (parenthetical)
d. Modal auxiliaries:
*Jan **kan** morgen terug naar huis komen. / Jan **zou** morgen terug naar huis **kunnen** komen.*
'John may/might return home tomorrow.' (default)
*Het **kan** (zijn) / Het **zou kunnen** (zijn) dat Jan morgen terug naar huis komt.*
'It may/might be that John returns home tomorrow.' (complementing)

It is clearly no accident that this variety should exist. A functional analysis of the use of these forms reveals that there are a few dimensions beyond the epistemic meaning per se which play a crucial role in expressing this semantic dimension. The presence of these additional dimensions and the way they work are clearly motivated by the epistemic evaluation. Still, most of them impose their own requirements on form, beyond the epistemic meaning. Hence, the different expression types (and their syntactic variants) offer alternative "solutions" (each more or less adequate in different kinds of circumstance) for this complex "functional problem space". In the present context I cannot present the full details of this investigation (see Nuyts 2001a), but here is a summary overview of the relevant findings.

The data for this investigation are drawn from a few corpora of spoken and written Dutch.[15] The written materials (more than 700,000 words) predominantly involve expository prose taken from journals, magazines, and popular scientific publications, next to a small portion of literary prose. The spoken data (more than 210,000 words) involve different kinds of public interview and debate, mainly taken from Dutch and Flemish television.[16] In these, I have concentrated on the occurrences of one representative "lemma" per expression type mentioned, viz. *waarschijnlijk* 'probable/probably' as an adverb or a predicative adjective (in Dutch there is no morphological difference between the adverbial and adjectival form), *denken* 'think' as a mental state verb, and *kunnen* 'can/may' as an auxiliary.[17] Table 1 gives an overview of the average frequencies of (the epistemic use of) these forms in written and spoken Dutch (in terms of occurrences per 10,000 words).[18]

For the mental state predicate, these frequencies only cover its qualificational (epistemic) use, illustrated in (2c) above (both complementing and parenthetical; the latter represent slightly more than 17% of the epistemic uses), but not its nonqualificational use (as in *Ik ben erover aan het denken* 'I am thinking about it').

For the auxiliary, too, only its epistemic use, illustrated in (2d) above, is covered. Such uses are actually a minority. Next to the epistemic use, *kunnen* also has a very dominant dynamic modal use, indicating an ability or potential, comparable to the equivalent use of English *can*, as illustrated in (3a).

Table 1. Frequencies per 10,000 words of alternative epistemic expressions

		WRT	SPK	AVR
Adverb		1.89	2.58	2.22
Adjective		0.37	0.05	0.28
MS predicate		1.95	25.65	7.60
Auxiliary	max	5.16	2.62	4.28
	min	0	0.33	0.11

This use accounts for (on a minimal count) more than 77% of the occurrences of this modal. And it also has a deontic modal meaning, as illustrated in (3b), which accounts for nearly 15% of its occurrences and which is still twice as frequent as the epistemic use.

(3) a. *Hij kan die job wel de baas.*
    'He can do/master the job.'
  b. *Je kan iemand niet zomaar ontslaan.*
    'You cannot/it is morally unacceptable to fire someone just like that.'

The epistemic use is actually problematic (much more so than Dutch native speakers might assume on an intuitive basis), in the sense that unambiguous occurrences of it are extremely rare in the data: the figures are given under "min" in Table 1. The figures under "max" also include a much larger number of cases which are undecidably ambiguous between a dynamic and an epistemic reading (these cases are not included in the 77% dynamic uses mentioned above). The example for the "default" pattern in (2d) above is illustrative in this regard: it can be taken to mean either that there is a chance that John is returning home tomorrow ('he *may* return'), or that John is able to return home tomorrow ('he *can* return'). This is an example out of context, but in the ambiguous cases in the corpus data, even the context offers no decisive clues to figure out which of the two meanings was actually meant by the speaker/writer (see Nuyts 2001a: 192–201 for an elaborate discussion of this problem). The fact that the overwhelming majority of (seemingly) epistemic cases in the data is of this kind corresponds with the diachronically very late appearance of the epistemic meaning in this modal (Nuyts 2001a: 228): it probably only dates back to the second half of the nineteenth century. Another interesting observation is that there is one syntactic pattern in which the modal does seem to be exclusively and unambiguously epistemic, viz. the "complementing" pattern in (2d) above. So this construction appears to be specializing for the epistemic reading. Quite a few Dutch epistemic adverbs and adjectives have developed out of a pattern with an auxiliary (or an auxiliary-like element) in a comparable complementing position. *Misschien* 'maybe' and *mogelijk* 'possible/possibly' derive from a complementing construction with the modal *mogen* 'may' as a central element, and *waarschijnlijk* 'probable/probably' originates in a similar pattern with the evidential auxiliary-like predicate *schijnen* 'seem' (cf. also English *maybe*). So, maybe the current appearance of the complementing use of *kunnen* is the first step in a process of "relexicalization" of the epistemic form.[19]

In terms of the usage properties of these forms, then, the data suggest that there are four additional functional dimensions at work in a speaker's choice of one among the alternative expressions. The match between these dimensions and the different expression types is summarized in Figure 2. In this figure, a dash means that the dimension is absent, "(+)" means that it is marginally present, "+" means that it is fully present, and "++" means that this is the major factor determining the speaker's use of the expression type.

	epistemic qualification (probability of the state of affairs)			
	↙	↓	↓	↘
performativity:				
descriptive use	–	(+)	+	–
(inter)subjectivity:				
intersubjective use	–	+	–	–
subjective use	–	+	++	–
information structure:				
focalized use	–	++	(+)	–
discourse strategy:	+	–	+	+
	↓	↓	↓	↓
	adverb	adjective	ms-predicate	auxiliary

Figure 2. Functional properties of epistemic expressions

Here is a brief explanation of these dimensions.

(i) *The performativity vs. descriptivity of the epistemic qualification.* Epistemic forms can be used to express an epistemic evaluation of a state of affairs which is made by the speaker herself at the moment of speaking and to which she is therefore fully committed while expressing it. This kind of usage can be called "performative". Or they can be used to report on someone else's epistemic evaluation of a state of affairs, on the speaker's own evaluation at a time other than the moment of speaking, or to advance a possible/hypothetical evaluation, yet without the speaker herself being committed to this evaluation at the moment of speech. This kind of usage can be called "descriptive".[20] Performative uses are the default for epistemic expressions, both in the sense that all form types mentioned in (2) can be used in this way (in fact, all examples in [2] are performative), and in the sense that even those forms which allow descriptive uses are nevertheless by far most frequently used performatively. In Dutch, only the mental state predicates and the adjectives can be used descriptively[21] — this usage is illustrated in (4).

(4)   a. *Jan denkt dat Piet morgen naar huis komt.*
      'John thinks that Piet is coming home tomorrow.'

b. *Jan acht het waarschijnlijk dat Piet morgen naar huis komt.*
'John considers it probable that Piet is coming home tomorrow.'

The position of epistemic modality in the hierarchy in Figure 1 only applies to the performative cases. Descriptive cases are obviously within the reach of, e.g., time marking — in fact, in such cases the epistemic evaluation is rather (part of) a state of affairs the speaker is talking about, which is thus situated at the bottom of the hierarchy.

(ii) *The subjectivity vs. intersubjectivity of the epistemic qualification*. This involves an issue which is clearly related to the traditional distinction between subjective and objective epistemic and deontic modality (e.g., Lyons 1977: 797). But, as I have argued elsewhere (see Nuyts 2001a: 33–39, 2001b), this opposition is better not interpreted as something inherent to these types of modality as such, but rather as an independent, evidential-like dimension. What this involves in the present case, then, is an indication of whether the speaker is solely responsible for the epistemic evaluation of the state of affairs — i.e., subjectivity — or, alternatively, whether she shares this evaluation with others, possibly including the hearer — i.e., intersubjectivity. The adverbs and auxiliaries, then, are in principle completely neutral in this respect. The predicative adjectives are either subjective or intersubjective, depending on the construction in which they appear: the default pattern illustrated in (2b) above is intersubjective, but the pattern in (5) is subjective.

(5) *Het lijkt me eerder waarschijnlijk dat Piet morgen naar huis komt.*
'It seems rather probable to me that Piet is coming home tomorrow.'

Obviously, the (inter)subjective value is not due to the adjective itself, but to its syntactic "environment". Yet to the extent that the adjective necessarily takes either one or the other environment, this dimension is inextricably interwoven with it. The mental state predicate *denken* 'think', finally, is always subjective,[22] and this is very clearly the predominant reason for a speaker to choose this expression type among alternatives. This also explains the predominance of this expression type in the spoken data (see Table 1). As compared to written language, conversation is characterized by a much higher degree of spontaneity, and a speaker is more often forced to produce opinions (also epistemic ones) on the spot, without preparation, which are therefore more tentative, impressionistic, and personal: hence, the predominant use of a "subjective" expression type in this context.

The present notion of "subjectivity" is clearly not to be confused with Langacker's (1990, this volume a) notions of "subjectivity" and "subjectification". The only obvious connection between the two is that both notions have to do with the presence of the speaker in the utterance. But otherwise, there appear to be no links between them whatsoever.

(iii) *The informational status of the epistemic qualification.* More specifically, this concerns the question whether the epistemic expression is focalized in the utterance or not. Focus is hereby defined as the element in the utterance which is informationally most salient, as an effect of one or more underlying (discourse) factors, such as its newness, its rhematicity, or its contrastivity with other elements in the discourse context. It turns out that — in line with assumptions formulated, e.g., by Langacker (1974), Lötscher (1985), and Chafe (1994) — epistemic expressions rarely ever occur in focus. If they do, then this is exclusively for reasons of contrastivity with an alternative epistemic assessment of the state of affairs in the discourse context. In those circumstances, however, only the complementing mental state predicates and the predicative adjectives can be used. The adverbs and auxiliaries and the parenthetical mental state predicates are not only never used focally, they even turn out not to allow such a use at all (as appears from a series of grammatical properties, including their inability to be contrasted in an utterance or to be questioned, or their behavior in the context of negation — see Nuyts 2000, 2001a). Even focal uses of the complementing mental state predicates are very rare, however. Only the adjective is quite systematically used this way. This is clearly the predominant reason for using the latter expression type in Dutch, which at once explains its very low frequency in corpus data (cf. Table 1).

These corpus findings are actually fully corroborated by the results of a separate experimental investigation into this issue, reported in Nuyts and Vonk (1999) and Nuyts (2001a: 235).

(iv) *Interaction strategy*. Some epistemic expressions are clearly used by speakers to achieve certain kinds of "strategic" effect vis-à-vis the hearer.[23] Specifically, the mental state predicate *denken* 'think' is quite frequently used to hedge a statement, often for reasons of politeness (this adds to its high frequency in the spoken data). In such cases it is sometimes even quite obvious that the speaker is not really expressing an epistemic judgment regarding the state of affairs, in the sense that, given the contextual conditions, she can be assumed to be very certain about its reality status (e.g., when someone hedges a statement about something she has done herself — see Nuyts 2001a: 163 for specific examples). The auxiliary *kunnen* 'may' is sometimes used for purposes of argument management, viz. to indicate that the speaker is not rejecting a suggestion by the interlocutor but is not endorsing it or its consequences either (i.e., a use of the type: *He may be a good scientist, but he's a lousy teacher*). The adverb under consideration in the present investigation, *waarschijnlijk* 'probably', is not used for this kind of strategy (nor for any other type which might have emerged from the corpus data), but its semantically weaker cousin *misschien* 'maybe', which is equivalent in epistemic strength to the auxiliary *kunnen* 'may', clearly is (cf. *Maybe you're right that he's a good scientist, but he's a damned lousy teacher*).

Among these four dimensions, then, the latter two are clearly a matter of "contextualization processes" in the traditional functionalist sense (in Langacker's terms, they are related to construal — or at least information structure is). The former two are more profound, as they relate (each in a quite different way) to the conceptual status of epistemic modality. But all four of them are perfectly expectable in view of the basic nature of epistemic modality. Space does not allow me to explain this in much depth (see Nuyts 2001a: chapter 6), but here is a very brief sketch of the relations. The two additional conceptual dimensions can both be related to the fact that making an epistemic judgment means explicating one's degree of (one type of) commitment to a state of affairs. Hence, it is no accident that these two dimensions also appear to play a major role in expressing deontic modality and evidentiality, but not in expressing time or any other qualificational dimension lower in the hierarchy in Figure 1. Evidentiality and deontic modality also involve an explicit concern with the degree to which one can be committed to some state of affairs (each in a different way), but qualifications from time downwards do not (they involve issues regarding where/how to situate a state of affairs within the boundaries of some possible world, usually the real world). Obviously, if one is talking about degrees of commitment, one must be able to make it abundantly clear whether that commitment is one's own or not. And a concern with one's degree of commitment to something no doubt easily triggers an additional concern with whether one is alone in one's judgment, or whether others share it. As for the "contextualization" dimensions, information structure is obviously a pervasive dimension in any kind of language use. But the special status of epistemic expressions in this regard should not come as a surprise. As Plank (1981) states, epistemic evaluations do not show up for their own sake but only so as to assess the status of some state of affairs — and it is the state of affairs which is therefore usually at the center of attention (cf. also Steele 1975). And that epistemic expressions should be used strategically is obviously related to the kind of semantics they express, viz., in the case of the mental state predicate, the fact that it expresses a "subjective uncertainty", and in the case of the auxiliary, the fact that it admits, but only to a very moderate degree, the possibility of some state of affairs.

How, then, can the linguistic variation in the range of epistemic expression types be related to these various functional dimensions? The variety of epistemic expression types and their alternative syntactic realizations are summarized in Figure 3 (see Nuyts 2000: 106 and 2001a: 262):[24]

	Complementing structure:		Flat structure:
Adj./Adv.:	*Het is waarschijnlijk*	*dat SoA.*	*S waarschijnlijk oA.*
	'It is probable	that SoA.'	'S probably oA.'
MS-Pred.:	*Ik denk*	*dat SoA.*	*S, denk ik, oA.*
	'I think	(that) SoA.'	'S, I think, oA.'
Modals:	*Het kan zijn*	*dat SoA.*	*S kan oA.*
	'It may be	that SoA.'	'S may oA.'

Figure 3. The system of alternative epistemic expressions in Dutch (and English)

These alternatives appear motivated by the functional dimensions as follows. Epistemic modality as such is, conceptually, a meta-representational notion (cf. the hierarchy in Figure 1). In view of the fact that linguistic form shows a tendency to be "iconic", i.e., to reveal underlying (conceptual) semantic relations as clearly and directly as possible, this conceptual status is perfectly rendered in a complementing structure, with the epistemic expression "dominating" the clause expressing the state of affairs. It is not surprising, then, to find this pattern recurrently among the expression types, as shown in Figure 3. If the adverbs and adjectives are considered one basic expression type with alternative syntactic realizations, then each major expression type appears with a complementing pattern (even the modals "enforce" it, though that is not a prototypical pattern for an auxiliary to occur in). Yet such a structure is disadvantageous in view of the fact that an epistemic expression is usually nonfocal, since syntactic subordination tends to correlate with information-structural subordination: the main clause, and not the embedded clause, prototypically carries the most salient or focal information (cf. Givón 1984; Tomlin 1985; Brandt 1994). This explains the systematic occurrence of noncomplementing variants across the epistemic expression types (including the mental state predicates), even if that is a nonstandard pattern for such a type of verb. As I have argued at length elsewhere (see Nuyts 2000, 2001a: 261–272 for a detailed discussion of all these function-form correlations), the tension between these two aspects of epistemic expressions (iconicity vs. discourse status) goes a long way towards explaining several of the more detailed (and often quite divergent) behavioral properties of the different expression forms, as well as their diachronic development. Descriptivity and (inter)subjectivity, then, create another niche for (linguistically independent) predicative expressions — specifically, for the adjectives and the mental state predicates —, since both dimensions (in different ways) require an expression type which can somehow be altered in terms of person and time. Descriptivity requires an explicit indication of the fact that the person committed to the epistemic evaluation is not the speaker herself, and that is most efficiently done by a predicative form licensing a (grammatical) subject which can be set to non-first person and/or non-present tense. In the same vein, (inter)subjectivity is most clearly expressed by a predicative form which sanctions a first-person subject (for subjectivity) or which allows an impersonal subject (for intersubjectivity).[25] (Interaction strategy is the only functional dimension which does not appear to correlate with any special structural aspects of the expression types.)

Let us now return to the issues raised in sections 1 and 2 and see what our observations regarding the system of epistemic expressions in Dutch reveal about them.

4. Some implications

4.1. Conceptual vs. linguistic semantics

Let me first return to the argument in section 1, namely that a cognitive theory needs to distinguish clearly between a level of conceptual semantics and a level of linguistic semantics, which are probably quite substantially different. As suggested there, the epistemic paradigm offers a clear — and actually fairly simple — empirical argument for this assumption. Here it is.

Since the different epistemic expression types all involve the same notion of epistemic modality, they must all have their cognitive origins in one and the same core level, which is the site or locus of the speaker's epistemic evaluation of a state of affairs. Claiming otherwise would mean giving up meaning as a coherent cognitive category. This is what I would call the level of conceptual meaning. When producing an epistemic expression, then, a speaker works her way from this conceptual level down to an expression form via procedures sensitive to the different functional factors mentioned. This, then, produces linguistic meaning. Now, it is quite obvious that the major types of expression in the epistemic paradigm (or at least the categories of adverbs/adjectives, verbs, and auxiliaries) are lexically or grammatically basic, hence basic in terms of their linguistic representation and processing. That is, they cannot be productively derived from each other in a grammar. For instance, imagine that one would take the adverbs as the core forms. One can easily see that it would require very radical transformational operations, including lexical exchanges (i.e., the deletion of one lexical form and its replacement by another), to go from this form to an expression with a clause-internal auxiliary or a complementing mental state predicate. Probably no one in present-day (functional) linguistics or language psychology would consider such operations theoretically acceptable. But if so, the conclusion must be that at the conceptual level the epistemic evaluation cannot have the format of any of these linguistic alternatives, or, going one step further, that it even cannot have a format using lexical items of the language, or anything closely resembling it, as a representational device at all.

This kind of argument is clearly not restricted to epistemic modality. As indicated in section 2, most or all qualificational dimensions have several basically different expression types, and, presumably, the same kind of analysis applies to them. But even in the range of linguistic expressions of states of affairs (of the "object world", broadly defined), there are "semantic paradigms" — i.e., paradigms of alternative expression types for one core conceptual notion or cluster — which are open to such an analysis. One of the most famous ones is Fillmore's (1977) "commercial event" scene, but there are many more (cf. Fillmore 1977, 1985; Nuyts 1992: 223; Kay 1996 for further examples).

This argument actually suggests very far-reaching consequences for modeling conceptualization. It not only militates against clearly linguistic models of it but even appears to go against more abstract models, such as Jackendoff's (1983, 1990) predicate-argument style propositional conceptual representations. Although these are nonlinguistic (they do not contain lexical items of a language), they are still clearly language-related (cf. the "grammatical constraint on semantic theory", Jackendoff 1983: 13). One consequence is that the conceptual structures pertaining to alternative commercial event predicates such as *buy*, *sell*, and *pay*, though similar, remain different. So, a "real" conceptual representation (in the sense intended here) must be more abstract. (An interesting question in this respect is whether a comparable line of reasoning also applies to the semantic parts of the "symbolic structures" — hence, to semantic or conceptual representations in general — in Cognitive Grammar, even if they look quite different from Jackendoff's.) However, the argument does not provide ammunition for the proponents of image-based conceptual representations either. There is nothing perceptual or imagistic to an epistemic judgment, so how could the conceptual structure of epistemic modality be imagistic (or 3D-structural, in Jackendoff's terms)? Rather, the argument pushes us in the direction of a more abstract type of conceptual representation (even if it is presently not clear what this may look like), in line with the expectations formulated in section 1. Dwelling further on these issues is unfortunately beyond the present paper — see Nuyts (2001a: 294–303).

Another possible implication concerns the status of linguistic meaning in a cognitive model. Obviously, conceptual meaning can be assumed to be more or less stable and long-term (although it is changeable, too, as one constantly acquires new knowledge and adjusts old knowledge due to new experience or to reasoning processes).[26] But linguistic meaning is something which is "forged" each time anew in a process of adjusting conceptual information to the local conditions of communicative situations, which are quite specific and more or less unique. In other words, it looks as if linguistic meaning is not something which has a stable, long-term cognitive representation (beyond the basic meaning representation of individual lexical elements and standard or fixed constructional patterns, of course). It is rather a temporary structure which is formed in the course of producing and interpreting linguistic expressions, and which is erased from short-term memory as soon as all relevant operations (articulation in production, conceptual interpretation in understanding) have been performed. To what extent this view has implications for — or is reconcilable with — radically constructionist views of grammar and linguistic meaning is a matter which needs further consideration.

4.2. Grounding, again

Let us pick up the loose thread of grounding where we left it in section 2. The corpus data indicate that the epistemic use of *kunnen* 'may' in Dutch is rather unstable. The status of most (potentially) epistemic modal uses is uncertain, and in the worst interpretation of the data (the minimal count in Table 1) it is, together with the adjective, by far the least frequent epistemic expression type. In addition, the epistemic use of the auxiliary appears to move away from a rather grammaticalized status and towards a more lexical, predicative, or possibly even adverbial status (cf. its complementing use).[27] (Exactly the same situation emerges from the experimental investigation which was briefly mentioned earlier — see Nuyts and Vonk 1999; Nuyts 2001a: 252–256.) If only highly grammaticalized forms are grounding, then epistemic modal grounding in Dutch appears to be a fairly marginal thing (at least in the range of epistemic judgments with a fairly low strength).[28] As mentioned in section 2, this is somewhat suspicious in view of the range of means available for making epistemic statements, as well as their frequent use. In fact, Figure 2 also shows that the auxiliary is functionally perfectly comparable to the adverb. They are both quite neutral expression forms, unlike the predicative adjective and the mental state predicate, which are used for more special or functionally marked purposes.

In the view adopted here, then, grounding would be considered a primarily conceptual phenomenon, rather than a linguistic one. In terms of the argument developed in section 4.1, epistemic modality must obviously be considered a conceptual dimension, and the same argument can no doubt be made for other qualificational dimensions and for the entire hierarchical system in Figure 1 (*pace* what current proposals in the functionalist literature, and particularly those mentioned in section 2, do with it — see Nuyts 2001a: chapter 6 for discussion). In fact, judging the likelihood or veridicality of a state of affairs is probably something which plays a role in any kind of perception and behavior, as it is crucial to survival (when you are about to cross a street, before acting you had better judge the chances of making it to the other side before that speedy car over there gets to you). In terms of conceptual knowledge, then, and in line with Chafe's (1994: 129) adage that "consciousness cannot function without being oriented in space, time, society, and ongoing background events", it seems reasonable to assume that for each state of affairs which an individual (gets to) know(s) about (with different degrees of schematicity), she needs to develop in one way or another a full qualificational system of the kind sketched in Figure 1, with a value set for all dimensions involved. For knowledge about events (and objects) is probably not fully anchored in one's conceptual system until all dimensions of its status are clear, in terms of how it relates to other conceptual information, its frequency (aspect), its spatial and temporal situation,[29] its social value (deontic modality), its reality status (epistemic modality), and how one got to know about it (evidentiality). As long as some of those dimensions are not clear, the cognitive system will no doubt strive to resolve the remaining gaps. (This is a strongly simplified and overly simplistic rendering of a highly complex matter, though — see Nuyts 2001a: chapter 6 for more subtle considerations.)

This conceptual anchoring is obviously a matter of relating a state of affairs to the ground as defined by Langacker, but not to the ground as a communicative event per se. It is a matter of relating it to the ground in the sense that the values for these different dimensions are necessarily set relative to the moment of consciousness (cf. the above quote from Chafe) of the "conceptualizing individual", that is, to her *hic et nunc*, at any time. But this is irrespective of whether or not she includes these dimensions in (a) linguistic expression(s). Of course, as soon as a "conceptualizer" starts bringing them up (in whichever way) by means of language, then these dimensions as such are also related to the ground in a communicative sense. First of all, deciding which dimensions to address at all involves a consideration of the ground. Speakers rarely bring up more than one or two qualifications of a state of affairs in an utterance, and what is addressed in a specific utterance is a matter of what is relevant in terms of the speaker's goals vis-à-vis the hearer in the local communicative situation (e.g., a qualificational dimension may be verbalized because it is required for the hearer to uniquely identify a state of affairs, or because the status of the state of affairs in terms of the qualificational dimension requires some clarification which may be obtained in the actual communicative situation).[30] And how the dimensions are linguistically realized, then, is due to considerations such as (for epistemic modality) those revealed in the system presented in Figure 2. But in any case, on this view, all epistemic expressions, and expressions of any other qualificational dimension (grammatical and lexical alike), can be considered grounding elements if they are used as a means to indicate the current status of the state of affairs in the speaker's conceptualization of the world (just like any nonverbal acts — such as gestures — which are used as such would also be considered grounding elements).

Of course, one question which remains unanswered in this discussion is why there should be auxiliaries next to adverbs to express epistemic modality, especially since the two are functionally nondistinct in terms of the dimensions mentioned in section 3. A more profound question is why, in languages across the world, (certain rudimentary distinctions within) dimensions such as those involved in the hierarchy of qualifications in Figure 1 should tend to be coded grammatically (as optional devices, or in some cases even as obligatory devices, i.e., more or less necessarily present in each singular expression, such as tense in most Western languages), while dimensions of the object world clearly do not (or at least not in the same way). I will not take issue with Langacker's (this volume a: 10) construal of the special status of grammatical as opposed to lexical expressions of qualificational dimensions, as this would require a concern with dimensions of Cognitive Grammar — such as profiling — which are beyond the present scope. But there are no reasons to think that the essence of Langacker's analysis (or of most of it) might not in principle be compatible with the above considerations (except for his view of how all this relates to the concept of grounding per se, of course).

In the context of the present framework, I have tried to formulate an explanation for these two questions as follows. For the first question (why there are two functionally apparently identical expression types, viz. adverbs and modals), the reason may be found in the principle of expressibility: given the (relatively) minimal mutual combinability of adverbs, and especially of auxiliaries, one may need those alternatives to allow the simultaneous, functionally neutral expression of several qualificational dimensions in one utterance. For the second question (why languages tend to grammatically code qualificational dimensions, but not dimensions of the "object world"), we might, in the spirit of earlier considerations by Talmy (1988), turn to the conceptually fundamental nature, yet at the same time the conceptually fairly "simple" structure, of these dimensions. Unlike the range of possibilities in the "object world", which is virtually infinite, most qualificational dimensions are "closed classes" in the sense that they are fairly limited in the possible (major) values they can take. And since these same dimensions are applied time and again to ever-changing states of affairs, their major values are conceptually deeply entrenched. That is why they may tend to enter the structure of language itself.[31] (For the details of these explanations, I can refer the reader to Nuyts 2001a: 228 and 268–270.)

5. Conclusion

In this paper I have tried to relate the Cognitive Grammar notion of "grounding" to that of "qualifications" of states of affairs in the current functionalist literature. I have thereby argued for a nonlinguistic view of grounding, i.e., for a view in which grounding is a matter of conceptual semantics, irrespective of the specific expressive device a speaker decides to use when she brings up certain grounding dimensions in communication. That is, grounding so conceived is not restricted to grammatical(ized) devices only. I have argued this against the background of a discussion of some theoretical differences between the present view and the Cognitive Grammar view, including a possible difference in assumptions regarding the distinction between a level of conceptual semantics and a level of linguistic semantics.

Notes

1. Thanks to Frank Brisard for inviting me to participate in this volume, in spite of the fact that I am an outsider to Cognitive Grammar. Also thanks to him and to the series editors for their useful feedback on an earlier version of this paper.
2. The notion of truth as used in this paper is not meant in a logical or truth-conditional sense, but as a "folk-psychological" concept figuring in everyday, commonsense reasoning. In the same vein, when I use the notions of "reality" or "the object world" in this paper, I am always referring to "reality/the world as perceived by the speaking subject", i.e., not to what is actually the case out there in the world, but to what is the case in the subject's personal interpretation of the world.
3. Obviously, communicative language use is also a vehicle for social contact and everything that belongs to it. But that is an essential subpart of a wider concept of "information transmission".
4. This difference may actually, at least in part, be due to a much more outspoken — or at least more explicit — concern with processing in the present framework (like in most other "traditional" functionalist frameworks), but going into this basic discussion is beyond the present concern.
5. This obviously does not rule out that there is also information storage in terms of mode-specific representations, in support of the central conceptual system. One's knowledge of physical objects, for instance, no doubt includes information about their perceptual properties. Thus, one's knowledge about cats no doubt includes a vision-based schematic image of a prototypical instance of the category. And one's knowledge about garlic no doubt includes a representation of its smell and taste. In other words, one's abstract representation in the central conceptual system of information about things

such as pets, or food, includes a reference to mode-specific representations of such items. A comparable dimension in the range of language is the long-term storage of the linguistic labels used to name concepts, that is, of the lexical items of one's language.
6. These two levels of semantic representation are no doubt an abstraction. There is rather a continuum of levels of semantic representation in converting a conceptual structure into a linguistic expression (see Nuyts 2001a), but this fact is of no import for the present discussion.
7. The precise correspondences between the traditional functionalist and these Cognitive Grammar notions are actually not entirely obvious to me, but going into this matter is beyond the present paper.
8. The term "epistemic" in this quote is obviously used with a much wider meaning than in my notion of "epistemic modality", as defined above. I will always use the term in the latter, narrower, sense.
9. Again, "ontological" does not refer to "situation in the outer world", but to "situation in the world as interpreted by the language user".
10. In Cognitive Grammar terms, this means that I will only be concerned with clausal grounding, not with nominal grounding.
11. On the difference between phasal (or "qualificational") and quantificational aspect, see, e.g., Hengeveld (1989).
12. Aspect markers such as the perfective auxiliaries *hebben* in Dutch and *have* in English are, of course, not grounding predications in Langacker's view, since they require tense marking in order to become finite forms. But my question here concerns the semantic dimension as such. In languages with, e.g., affixal aspect markers (i.e., fully grammaticalized forms, which is an essential feature for a linguistic element to qualify as a grounding device — see below on this issue), would these be considered grounding devices?
13. Dutch "morphological" tense — specifically the past tense, as the only morphological form next to the present — is in some circumstances used with what might be called an epistemic meaning, but this is highly infrequent (in absolute terms, and relative to other epistemic expression forms). The auxiliary *zullen* 'will, shall', which is central to the Dutch "periphrastic" future tense, is even more clearly used epistemically, and much more frequently so than the past tense. But its status as a grounding device would in Langacker's view probably be in doubt again, since its grammatical status is perfectly comparable to that of other modals such as *kunnen* 'can/may' or *moeten* 'must' (in fact, it requires morphological tense marking, as present or past, in order to be finite).
14. That these are in fact the most important epistemic expression types in Dutch is very obvious from the data obtained in an experiment eliciting epistemic evaluations (see Nuyts and Vonk 1999; Nuyts 2001a: 235). Next to these four form types, only modal particles are relatively frequently used by participants.

I will leave the particles (which are actually very close to adverbial forms) out of consideration in this paper, however, because they bring up special problems which are irrelevant for our present concern.
15. A parallel corpus investigation has been performed for German, with perfectly comparable results, but I will not go into the German part here. See Nuyts (2001a).
16. The corpora used are Uit den Boogaert (1975) and Vandenbosch (1992). For details about how these have been used in the investigation, see Nuyts (2001a).
17. For practical reasons, not all corpus data have been used for all forms. Specifically for the mental state predicate and the auxiliary, this would have produced far too many instances to be workable, but the details of this do not matter for the present. See Nuyts (2001a).
18. Abbreviations: "WRT" = written data; "SPK" = spoken data; "AVR" = global average for written and spoken data together; "max" = maximum count; "min" = minimum count.
19. Even if the Dutch modals — including *kunnen* — are not as strongly grammaticalized as, e.g., their English counterparts, they are nevertheless much higher on the scale of "grammatical" forms than adverbs, which are probably quite far towards the "lexical" end of the grammaticalization scale.
20. This issue of performativity vs. descriptivity is obviously reminiscent of, yet not identical to, distinctions made elsewhere in the literature, such as Sweetser's (1990) "imposing" vs. "reporting/describing" uses of modals, or the "use" vs. "mention" distinction (Sperber and Wilson 1981), or "performativity" in speech act theory (Searle 1989). See Nuyts (2001a: 40–41) for a discussion of similarities and differences.
21. This is true except in reported speech contexts, in which all form types can be used. But reported speech is obviously a special kind of context: the actual speaker can be said to "re-perform" (or "recycle") the evaluation of the reported speaker.
22. Most other statements about functional properties of epistemic expressions in this section do not only apply to the specific form investigated in this corpus analysis but, presumably, to the expression type represented by it as a whole. But here I am confining this particular statement to *denken* 'think' specifically. Other mental state predicates with a qualificational usage, such as *believe*, *suppose*, *guess*, and *know* (or equivalents in Dutch) do not necessarily also have a subjective meaning, although they always do express an evidential one (some, such as *geloven* 'believe', even appear to combine a subjective with another evidential meaning). The situation for these other predicates is actually fairly complicated — see Nuyts (2001a: 109, 122) for a preliminary discussion (but much more empirical research is needed here). Of course, Dutch *denken*, quite like its English counterpart *think*, is by far the

most frequently used among the mental state predicates with a qualificational meaning (see Thompson and Mulac 1991 on [American] English), hence it could even be argued to make up a category of its own.
23. The specific effects mentioned here are, however, probably bound again to the individual linguistic forms considered in this investigation, and they do not extend to the expression type to which these forms belong in general: the mental state predicates, the modals, the adverbs.
24. In the figure, "SoA" stands for "State of Affairs".
25. The epistemic modals are predicative, too, of course, but they are not actually "controlling" the subject of the clause (epistemic modals, unlike dynamic ones, relate to the speaker, and not to the subject of the clause), hence they are not suitable means for expressing these two functional dimensions.
26. Nothing in the foregoing implies in any way that conceptualization is universal, either. While one may reasonably assume that what humans can conceptualize is universal, there is no reason to believe that what actually gets conceptualized is also universal. For conceptualization is essentially a generalization over contextual variation. But this variation is unavoidably limited by the physical, cultural, and social environments to which one happens to be exposed. And that is quite different for people from different cultures in different places, and to a lesser extent even for different people within similar cultures in one small area (cf. differences in social and educational background).
27. This might thus be an instance which runs counter to the widely accepted assumption that grammaticalization is always and unavoidably unidirectional (e.g., Heine, Claudi, and Hünnemeyer 1991; Hopper and Traugott 1993; Bybee, Perkins, and Pagliuca 1994). Admittedly, the situation is complicated by the fact that the development involves "univerbation", i.e., an (originally) syntactically organized combination of separate forms, or a "phrase" (Hopper and Traugott 1993: 135). But the problem remains that the modal auxiliary is the core element in the univerbation, rather than a subsidiary element which is cliticized onto some other, more central element in the (original) phrase. See Nuyts (2001a: 267–268) for further discussion.
28. There is, of course, also the modal *zullen* 'will, shall', which can be used to express a judgment that is high on the epistemic scale. And there is possibly also *moeten* 'must', which has uses that could be considered to render a strong epistemic judgment (though one could argue that this involves an evidential and more specifically an inferential, rather than an epistemic, meaning). Although these modals have not been included in the present investigation, there are no indications that their situation is substantially different from that of *kunnen* 'can/may'.
29. Space is not included in the hierarchy in Figure 1, but it no doubt does belong to it. I have not included it because the discussion regarding its precise

position is far from simple (e.g., one needs to distinguish between directionality and location).
30. The status of "obligatory" expressive devices for qualificational dimensions, such as tense in finite clauses, is obviously very special in this regard, but I cannot go into this matter here.
31. This may also explain why, in many languages, the qualificational dimension of space is not encoded in the (clausal) grammatical system (i.e., in auxiliaries or in verb morphology), while most or all other qualificational dimensions in the hierarchy in Figure 1 are. Space is much more complex in its structure than any of these other dimensions.

References

Brandt, Margareta
    1994   Subordination und Parenthese als Mittel der Informationsstrukturierung in Texten. *Sprache und Pragmatik* 1994: 1–37.
Bybee, Joan, Revere Perkins and William Pagliuca
    1994   *The Evolution of Grammar: Tense, Aspect and Modality in the Languages of the World.* Chicago: University of Chicago Press.
Chafe, Wallace
    1994   *Discourse, Consciousness, and Time.* Chicago: University of Chicago Press.
Dik, Simon
    1997   *The Theory of Functional Grammar.* Berlin: Mouton De Gruyter.
Fillmore, Charles
    1977   Topics in lexical semantics. In: Roger W. Cole (ed.), *Current Issues in Linguistic Theory*, 76–138. Bloomington: Indiana University Press.
    1985   Frames and the semantics of understanding. *Quaderni di Semantica* 6: 222–254.
Foley, William and Robert Van Valin
    1984   *Functional Syntax and Universal Grammar.* Cambridge: Cambridge University Press.
Givón, Talmy
    1984   *Syntax: A Functional-Typological Introduction,* Volume 1. Amsterdam: Benjamins.
    1990   *Syntax: A Functional-Typological Introduction,* Volume 2. Amsterdam: Benjamins.
    1995   *Functionalism and Grammar.* Amsterdam: Benjamins.

Heine, Bernd, Ulrike Claudi and Friederike Hünnemeyer
 1991 *Grammaticalization: A Conceptual Framework.* Chicago: University of Chicago Press.

Hengeveld, Kees
 1989 Layers and operators in functional grammar. *Journal of Linguistics* 25: 127–157.

Hopper, Paul and Elizabeth Closs Traugott
 1993 *Grammaticalization.* Cambridge: Cambridge University Press.

Jackendoff, Ray
 1983 *Semantics and Cognition.* Cambridge, MA: MIT Press.
 1990 *Semantic Structures.* Cambridge, MA: MIT Press.

Kay, Paul
 1996 Intra-speaker relativity. In: John Gumperz and Stephen Levinson (eds.), *Rethinking Linguistic Relativity*, 97–114. Cambridge: Cambridge University Press.

Langacker, Ronald W.
 1974 Movement rules in functional perspective. *Language* 50: 630–664.
 1987 *Foundations of Cognitive Grammar,* Volume 1. Stanford: Stanford University Press.
 1990 Subjectification. *Cognitive Linguistics* 1: 5–38.
 1991 *Foundations of Cognitive Grammar,* Volume 2. Stanford: Stanford University Press.
 2000 A dynamic usage-based model. In: Michael Barlow and Suzanne Kemmer (eds.), *Usage-Based Models of Language*, 1–63. Stanford: Center for the Study of Language and Information.
 this vol. a Deixis and subjectivity.
 this vol. b Remarks on the English grounding systems.

Lötscher, Andreas
 1985 Akzentuierung und Thematisierbarkeit von Angaben. *Linguistische Berichte* 97: 228–251.

Lyons, John
 1977 *Semantics.* Cambridge: Cambridge University Press.

Mortelmans, Tanja
 this vol. "*Wieso sollte ich dich küssen, du hässlicher Mensch!*" A study of the German modals *sollen* and *müssen* as "grounding predications" in interrogatives.

Nuyts, Jan
 1992 *Aspects of a Cognitive-Pragmatic Theory of Language.* Amsterdam: Benjamins.
 2000 Tensions between discourse structure and conceptual semantics: The syntax of epistemic modal expressions. *Studies in Language* 24: 103–135.

2001a   *Epistemic Modality, Language and Conceptualization.* Amsterdam: Benjamins.
2001b   Subjectivity as an evidential dimension in epistemic modal expressions. *Journal of Pragmatics* 33: 383–400.
Nuyts, Jan and Wietske Vonk
1999   Epistemic modality and focus in Dutch. *Linguistics* 37: 699–737.
Plank, Frans
1981   Modalitätsausdruck zwischen Autonomie und Auxiliarität. In: Inger Rosengren (ed.), *Sprache und Pragmatik: Lundner Symposium 1980,* 57–71. Lund: CWK Gleerup.
Searle, John
1989   How performatives work. *Linguistics and Philosophy* 12: 535–558.
Slobin, Dan
1996   From "thought and language" to "thinking for speaking". In: John Gumperz and Stephen Levinson (eds.), *Rethinking Linguistic Relativity,* 70–96. Cambridge: Cambridge University Press.
Sperber, Dan and Deirdre Wilson
1981   Irony and the use-mention distinction. In: Peter Cole (ed.), *Radical Pragmatics,* 295–318. New York: Academic.
Steele, Susan
1975   On some factors that affect and effect word order. In: Charles Li (ed.), *Word Order and Word Order Change,* 197–268. Austin: University of Texas Press.
Sweetser, Eve
1990   *From Etymology to Pragmatics.* Cambridge: Cambridge University Press.
Talmy, Len
1988   The relation of grammar to cognition. In: Brygida Rudzka (ed.), *Topics in Cognitive Linguistics,* 165–205. Amsterdam: Benjamins.
Thompson, Sandra A. and Anthony Mulac
1991   A quantitative perspective on the grammaticization of epistemic parentheticals in English. In: Elizabeth Traugott and Bernd Heine (eds.), *Approaches to Grammaticalization,* Volume 2, 313–329. Amsterdam: Benjamins.
Tomlin, Russell
1985   Foreground-background information and the syntax of subordination. *Text* 5: 85–122.
uit den Boogaart, P. C. (ed.)
1975   *Woordfrequenties in geschreven en gesproken Nederlands [Word Frequencies in Written and Spoken Dutch].* Utrecht: Oosthoek, Scheltema & Holkema.

Van Valin, Robert
  1993   A synopsis of role and reference grammar. In: Robert Van Valin (ed.), *Advances in Role and Reference Grammar*, 1–164. Amsterdam: Benjamins.
Van Valin, Robert and Randy LaPolla
  1997   *Syntax: Structure, Meaning and Function.* Cambridge: Cambridge University Press.
Vandenbosch, Luc
  1992   Aspekten van passiefvorming in het Nederlands [Aspects of passivization in Dutch]. Ph.D. dissertation, University of Antwerp.

Subject index

accessibility, xii–xiii, xx, xxii, xxix, 16, 42, 44, 48–51, 54, 56, 58–63, 65, 67–68, 70–73, 76–77, 92, 96–97, 104, 119, 122–123, 125, 135–138, 152, 163, 174, 176–177, 274, 278, 363, 368, 376

actual occurrence reading, 312, 318–322

actual plane, xx, xxii, 312–313, 315, 317, 319–321, 339, 362–365, 368–369, 373

actuality, 117–120, 122, 124–127, 130, 133, 138–139, 254, 256, 266, 268, 271–272, 274–276, 278–279, 281–282, 286, 290–291, 314, 316, 318, 320, 339, 360, 362, 368–369, 372–373, 376–379, 383–384, 397, 399–400, 423, 459

agreement, *see* tense

anaphora, xx, 12, 45, 49, 54, 58, 113, 133, 136–138, 174, 176–179, 181, 340, 401, 408, 412, 419

article, xii, xvi–xvii, xix, 7, 30, 33, 43–44, 54, 57, 63–65, 68, 72, 74–76
– definite, xix, 10, 30, 33–34, 41–63, 65–68, 70–77, 97, 99–100, 102, 105, 113, 135–136, 138, 153, 155–157, 161–162, 165–166, 168, 391
– indefinite, 30–31, 34–37, 54, 56, 61, 63–64, 97, 99–100, 102, 241, 276, 280, 328–330, 391
– partitive, xix–xx, 129–130, 138

aspect
– grammatical, xvii, xx–xxii, 113, 120, 127, 131–132, 138, 198, 204–205, 211, 245, 257–258, 279, 299, 306, 339–340, 349, 351–354, 359–360, 364–365, 371, 382, 385, 439–440, 456
– lexical, xxi–xxii, 252, 256, 351

aspectual categories
– habitual, 138, 220, 257–258, 262, 274, 300–301, 314–317, 363
– iterative, 258, 292
– perfect, 121, 199, 204–205, 218, 281
– progressive, xxii, 182, 252, 256–258, 260, 263, 266, 270–272, 280, 282, 290–291

atemporal relation, 12, 299

attention, xv, xxx, 15–16, 19, 29, 33, 36, 41, 43–44, 53, 59, 65, 88–89, 92, 104, 411
– focus of viewing, xxix, 9, 13, 15–16, 18, 42, 75, 120, 174, 186, 214, 223, 257–258, 260, 269, 350, 356, 392, 450
– locus of viewing, 15, 75, 120, 269, 356, 359

background (knowledge), xvi, xxv–xxvi, xxix–xxx, 4, 42, 48, 50, 58–60, 62, 67, 71–72, 174, 186, 265–266, 280, 340, 456

base (space), xxxii, 325, 336

basic epistemic model, 31, 123, 126, 207, 210

Subject index

billiard-ball model, 31–32
boundedness, 4, 127, 130–131, 252–254, 260, 270–271, 290, 306, 339–340, 349, 351–361, 364, 366–369, 382

clause, *see* finite clause
conception, xxviii, 16, 356, 392
- subject of, 2, 17, 75
- object of, 2, 17, 75, 356

conceptual archetype, 31
conceptual content, 3–4, 5, 8, 11, 29, 299, 349, 360, 385, 437
conceptual occurrence, 277, 363–364, 366, 369, 384
conceptual reference, *see* designation
conceptualization, 3–4, 17, 19, 41, 75, 119–120, 123, 134, 138, 266, 277, 306, 436–437, 453
construal, xiii–xiv, xix, xxiv, xxviii–xxix, 1, 3–6, 9–11, 14–21, 23–24, 35–36, 64–65, 75–76, 151–152, 173–174, 183–184, 214–219, 229–230, 244–245, 256–257, 262–263, 269–274, 278–282, 309–311, 381–383, 392–394, 437–438
context, xiii–xiv, xxi–xxiii, xxix, 3, 33, 35–36, 42–43, 46–52, 55–60, 70–72, 127–128, 229–230, 239–241, 243–244, 252–255, 257–259, 261–263, 273–274, 276–278, 280–282, 284–285, 287–291, 334–335, 353–354, 370–371, 373–376, 380–381, 398–401, 403–405, 421–425, 434–439, 448–450
control, xvii–xviii, xxv, 33–34, 74, 76, 211–212, 229, 245, 271, 285–286, 369, 371, 378–379, 383–384

current discourse space, 44, 49, 173–176, 182

definiteness, xiv–xv, xvii–xix, 7, 10–11, 13, 30–31, 36, 41, 43–45, 49–50, 73–75, 97, 105, 153–154, 157–158, 175, 185, 241
deictic center, xii, 20, 83–84, 183, 258, 396–397
deixis, xi–xiii, xv, xvii, xix–xx, xxvi–xxvii, xxix, 1–2, 8–9, 24, 29, 45, 49, 54, 67, 74, 95, 117, 151–152, 157–158, 162–165, 167, 169, 172–179, 181–186, 258, 307, 310, 391–392, 396–397, 427
demonstrative, *see* pronoun
designation, xi, xiv–xv, xviii, xx, xxii, xxvi, xxviii–xxix, 3–4, 6–9, 13, 29, 33–35, 42–44, 253–255, 259–261, 267–271, 275, 302–307, 310–311, 313, 316–324, 326, 331–337, 339–340, 350–353, 372–373, 381–382, 384
determiner, xiii–xiv, xix–xx, xxvii, 74, 76, 84, 99, 104, 120, 129, 161, 163
discourse role, 153–155, 157–160, 164, 167–169
discourse tracking device, xxii, 299, 301, 322, 339
distance, xv–xvi, xviii, 10, 30–31, 34–35, 92, 122, 126, 161–162, 169, 172, 217, 268, 301–302, 304–306, 310–312, 322, 324, 339, 356, 359, 367, 435
dominion, 143, 211, 214
dynamic evolutionary model, xiv, xx, 32, 123, 134, 208–209, 211

Subject index

elaborated epistemic model, 32, 252, 290
epistemic commitment/effort, xviii, xx, 33–34, 49, 71, 76, 212, 221, 223, 225, 229, 235, 244, 380–381, 450, 452
epistemic stance, 85, 102, 262, 284, 381–382
event time, 122, 175, 183–185, 218–220, 231, 233, 306, 309, 312, 340
evolutionary momentum, 32–33, 208, 221, 364–369, 383, 394–395, 410

factuality, *see* actuality
familiarity, xxvi, 45, 47, 54, 62, 64, 68, 73–74
field of vision, xx, 120, 151, 154–155, 165, 172–174, 181, 183–184, 356
finite clause, xi–xii, xviii, 2, 6–9, 12–13, 15, 17, 19–20, 23–24, 29–31, 33, 84, 198, 299, 350, 396, 441
footing, xxvii, xxx, 85, 88, 93, 95–96, 100, 102–105, 282–283, 289–291
force dynamics, 32–33, 208, 364, 367–368, 394
frame, 42, 47, 60–65, 67–70, 137, 151–155, 157, 159–160, 162, 175, 281, 285, 288
framing, *see* participation framework

general validity, 261–263, 274–276, 278, 290
genericity, xxii, 34, 71–72, 138, 241–242, 254, 261–262, 264, 274, 277, 288, 290, 300, 314–317

grammaticalization / grammaticization, xii, xiv, xxi, xxiii, 22, 29, 34, 84, 99, 106, 299, 350, 392, 395–396, 398, 415, 423–424, 426–427, 439, 441, 455, 459
ground, xi–xii, xiv–xvi, xx–xxii, xxiv–xxvi, xxviii–xxx, 5, 7–11, 13–14, 17–19, 23, 29–30, 34, 41–44, 83–84, 88–89, 95–96, 103–106, 122–123, 258–259, 265–273, 278–280, 284–286, 288–290, 302–305, 310–311, 338–339, 365–366, 391–392, 424–425, 456–457
grounded entity, xv, 7, 13, 18, 20, 23, 29, 35, 75, 199–200, 241, 270, 278, 299, 350, 393, 396, 410, 424, 438
grounding relationship, xiii, xv, 7, 13, 18, 20, 23, 29–30, 43, 51–52, 60, 65, 68, 72, 75, 122, 128, 197, 269, 299, 305, 311, 350, 393

higher-order entity, 11, 29, 260–261, 315–316
hypothetical, *see* sentence type, conditional

iconicity, xviii, 33, 125, 281, 440, 451
idealized cognitive model (ICM), 31, 123, 207, 299, 312, 364
identifiability, *see* uniqueness
illocutionary force, 204, 227, 411
immediacy, xxiv–xxvi, 7–8, 10, 29, 34, 42, 83, 125–126, 172, 174, 197, 240, 244, 255, 263–270, 273–274, 276, 278, 287–288, 290, 302, 350, 356, 360, 378, 380–381, 391, 422, 425, 439

470 *Subject index*

imparfait, xix–xx, 113–120, 122, 124–128, 130–138, 205, 211, 301, 306–307
imperfect, xxii, 120, 122, 138, 203–205, 211, 223, 225–227, 299–302, 304–307, 309–340
imperfectivity, xxi–xxii, 113, 127, 132, 252–254, 256–257, 259–264, 269–272, 274, 290, 301, 314, 316, 349, 351–355, 359–361, 363–367, 369–385
indefiniteness, *see* definiteness
indexicality, xix, xxvi, 73–74, 83–84, 88–89, 93, 95–97, 102–105, 153, 175–177, 181, 183–184
instance, xi, xiv, xvi, xviii, 7, 29, 32–37, 42–44, 63–64, 198–200, 241–243, 253–254, 258–259, 274–276, 278–279, 312–313, 315–319, 353–354, 356–359
irrealis, 115, 123, 125, 132, 300, 323–324, 330–331, 335, 379, 381–382, 412, 415

knowledge structure, *see* frame

landmark, 5–6, 9, 18, 21–23, 315–317, 393, 438

mental contact, xv, 7, 10, 29, 43–44, 97, 99, 152
mental experience, *see* conceptualization
mental space, xvi, xx, xxii, xxviii, 48–49, 62, 67–68, 70, 72, 122, 197, 215, 217, 245, 279, 290, 299, 301, 313, 322, 325, 328–329, 331, 336, 338, 369

metaphor, 4, 62–63, 76, 126, 268, 362
modal (auxiliary), xii, xvii, xx–xxi, xxvii, 8, 10–12, 30–31, 33–34, 124, 244, 391–396, 398, 400, 405–406, 409, 411–412, 414, 419, 421–427, 441–442, 444–445, 451, 458
modality, xvi–xvii, xxii–xxv, 113–114, 118–119, 126, 131–132, 138, 185, 205–206, 220, 244, 252–255, 268, 286, 289, 301, 393–396, 399, 401, 405, 408, 410, 412–413, 418–419, 423–425, 439, 442, 447
– deontic, 395, 398, 402, 412, 422, 439–441, 444, 447, 450, 456
– dynamic, 443–444
– epistemic, xviii, xxi, xxiii, 10–11, 13, 19–20, 29, 33, 290, 391, 394–398, 400, 412–413, 416, 420, 422–425, 433, 437–457
– root, 33, 394–395, 398–399, 409, 414, 416, 418, 424–425
mood, xvii, xx, xxvii, 197, 199–200, 204–207, 211, 214–216, 223, 228–230, 240, 244–245, 286, 391, 395–398, 400, 417, 424
– conditional, 197, 199–200, 203–206, 214, 220–223, 225–230, 233, 235, 244–245
– imperative, 399, 401–403
– indicative, 197, 199–206, 210–220, 223, 229, 231, 233–235, 237, 239–241, 243–244, 396–397, 400–401, 403–406, 408–409, 411–413, 415–416, 419, 424–425
– past conjunctive, 396–402, 404–405, 412–413, 415–418, 420–422, 424–425
– present conjunctive, 396–397

– subjunctive, 197, 199–203, 206, 210, 214–219, 229–230, 233, 235, 241, 243–245, 441

negation, 201–202, 214, 229, 243, 411–412, 418, 448
nominal, xi–xv, xvii–xix, xxvii–xxx, 2, 5–9, 12–15, 17, 19, 24, 29–37, 41–47, 49–51, 53–57, 59–60, 66–72, 74–76, 83–84, 96–97, 161–162
nonimmediacy, *see* immediacy; reality
noun
– count, 128–129
– mass, 128–130

objectification, xxvi, 16, 18, 401
objective content/scene, *see* conceptual content; objectivity; scope
objectivity, xii–xiii, xix, xxv, xxix–xxx, 3, 15–19, 21–22, 41, 55, 64–65, 74–75, 131, 207, 253, 258, 262–263, 267, 269, 276–278, 281, 283–286, 392, 396, 401, 412, 425, 437, 447
obligation, 33, 93, 393, 395–396, 398, 400–401, 406, 408, 410, 412–414, 416, 419
offstage region, xii, 9–10, 13, 16, 18, 23, 30, 75, 269, 392
onstage region, xxvi, 9–10, 13, 15–19, 30, 75, 262, 269, 283, 286, 350, 356–357, 392, 401, 410, 425
origo, *see* deictic center

participation framework, xxx, 84–86, 88–89, 93, 97, 100, 283
participation status, *see* footing

passé composé, 121, 131
passé simple, 113, 119, 121, 126–127, 130, 135, 211, 306–307
past situation, xxii, 113–114, 116–117, 119, 121, 124–127, 133, 179, 233, 299, 302, 304–305, 307–313, 317–320, 322, 339–340
perception, xxviii, 14–17, 118, 120, 123, 125, 174, 181–182, 263–266, 273, 277–279, 284, 287, 306, 320, 322, 324–326, 336–338, 356, 423, 435–436, 454, 456
– subject of, 15
– object of, 15–16, 266, 320, 325, 336–338, 356
perfectivity, xvii, xxi–xxii, 127, 252–254, 256–257, 259–264, 270–272, 274, 279, 281, 283–284, 288, 290, 314, 349, 351–356, 358–363, 365–366, 368, 370–373, 376–385
performative, 9, 73, 277, 282–286, 288, 290, 355–357, 359, 446–447
permission, 33, 393, 395
person, 197, 199–200, 396, 452
perspective, xix, 1, 4, 6, 19–20, 23, 25, 66, 70–71, 83, 159–161, 164–171, 180, 260, 267, 272, 288, 357, 359, 436
plane, *see* actual plane; structural plane; virtual plane
point of event, *see* event time
point of reference, *see* reference point
point of speech, *see* speech event; time of speaking
point of view, *see* perspective; vantage point; viewpoint
potency, 393–396, 399–403, 406, 408, 410, 412–413, 415, 418–419, 421, 423–424, 427
potentialis, 115

472 Subject index

pragmatics, xvii, xxvi–xxvii, xxx, 1, 3, 59, 73–74, 85, 253, 256, 279, 288, 291, 306–307, 312, 318, 393, 412–413, 427, 434

presupposition, xii, xiv, 4, 11, 34, 102, 120, 199, 215, 281, 284, 362, 372, 399–400, 414, 416

preterit, xxii, 120–122, 175, 177–185, 299–305, 307–308, 310–311, 313–315, 317–339

process, *see* finite clause

profile, xii, xiv–xv, 4–10, 12–13, 17–20, 23, 29–30, 33–35, 252–253, 255–259, 269–270, 272–273, 314–316, 350–360, 362–366, 368–369, 371–377, 380–384, 392–393

prominence, 4–5, 44, 46–47, 50, 52–59, 62, 68–69, 72, 74, 76

pronoun, 5, 49, 83–85, 96–97, 162
- demonstrative, xii, xvi–xvii, xix–xx, xxvii, 7, 10–11, 12, 14–15, 29–30, 33–35, 43, 89, 92, 99, 103–104, 151–153, 157, 161–172, 174–182, 184–185, 309–310, 391
- interrogative, 95, 405, 414
- personal, xix–xx, 9, 14, 85, 88, 93, 95–96, 102, 119, 136, 151–158, 161–163, 166–168, 171
- relative, 95, 216

property reading, 314, 318–322, 339

proposition, xx, xxiv, xxvi, 197, 209, 211–216, 218–221, 223, 229, 233, 239–241, 244, 397, 422, 454

proximity, xv–xvi, xviii, 10–11, 13–14, 29–31, 34–35, 92, 161–162, 172, 265, 268, 305, 307, 309–310, 324, 356

qualification, xiii–xiv, xix, xxiii, xxix, 42, 271, 276, 289, 350, 433, 439–440, 443, 446–448, 450, 453, 456–458

quantification, xii, xiv, xvii–xix, xxvii, 7, 12, 30–31, 33, 35, 43, 198–199, 276, 391, 439–440

quantifier scope, 300, 324, 327–330

realis, 383

reality, xii–xv, xix–xx, xxix, 8, 10, 29, 31–34, 123–126, 206–215, 217–219, 221–229, 233–235, 239–241, 253–254, 265–266, 268–269, 272–274, 278–286, 288–291, 330–331, 364–369, 394–395, 449–450
- alternative to, 66, 197, 220–222, 225–229, 235, 245, 425
- basic, 207–211, 214, 245
- elaborated, 207–213, 215–216, 218, 245
- hyper-, 288–291
- immediate, 34, 123, 125, 210–211, 213, 216, 259
- known, 123–125, 133, 231, 382
- potential, xxii, 125, 208, 223, 281, 313, 365–366, 369
- projected, xxii, 124, 180, 208, 211, 214, 220–221, 226, 233, 281–282, 365–366, 369
- virtual, xxii, 132, 275, 314, 362, 376

reality space, 122, 322–326, 330–332, 335–336, 339

reference, xii–xiv, xvi, xxii, 8, 12, 24, 33, 41–48, 50–59, 61–62, 65–71, 73–76, 85–86, 92–93, 95–97, 99–100, 102–105, 128–129, 135–137, 177–180, 216–217, 279–

Subject index 473

280, 352–354, 359–361, 365–366, 384–385
– coordination of, xvi, xix, 42–45, 48, 76, 97
reference frame, 20, 137, 153, 155, 174–176, 185
reference point, xiii, xv, 5, 9–10, 13–14, 18, 21, 23, 34, 120–121, 133–134, 136–137, 183–185, 304, 339, 392
referential concern, xvi, xx, 173–174, 182–183, 185, 277
referentialism, xxvii–xxviii, 41, 45–47, 73–75
relationship, 5–6, 8–9, 12, 15, 18–19, 22, 392–394, 412–413, 423–425
rhetorical question, 409, 411–412, 415–416, 418–421, 425
role, xix, 42, 44, 46–48, 60–64, 68–71, 74, 76, 97, 328

salience, xv, xviii–xix, 5, 9–11, 16–18, 20, 47, 64, 68, 74–75, 97, 119, 173–174, 184–185, 394, 448, 451
schema, xii, xiv–xvii, xxiv, xxix, 3–4, 10, 13, 30, 48–49, 126, 163, 166–169, 254–255, 258, 267–268, 278, 290–291, 392, 436, 456
scope, 4, 8–10, 17–19, 23, 75, 263–264, 268–273, 275–276, 278–279, 282, 284, 289–290, 439
– immediate, 4, 17, 253, 258, 269–270, 273, 275, 290, 351, 353, 356–357, 359–360, 365–367, 369, 382
– maximal/overall, 4, 17, 275, 369
semantics, xiv–xv, xvii, xxi, xxvii, xxx, 1–3, 279, 291, 312, 349, 351–352, 385, 412–413, 433, 437, 439–441
– conceptualist, xiv, xxi, 435–437, 451–454, 459
– linguistic, 1, 3, 436–437, 452–455, 459
sentence type
– conditional, 204, 206, 220–223, 227, 280, 290, 301, 331–332, 372–373, 398, 423
– counterfactual, 204, 221–223, 330–331, 335
– declarative, 398–399, 401, 404, 406, 411–412, 418, 424
– interrogative, xxi, 114, 201–202, 391, 399, 403–406, 408, 411, 415–416, 424
situation time, *see* event time
source, 16, 62–63, 291, 393–395, 400, 403, 406, 408, 410, 412, 418–419, 423–424
space, xii, xv–xvii, xxiv–xxv, xxvii, 31–32, 35, 153, 456
space accessibility, 48–49, 68, 122, 322–324, 326, 330–331, 333, 335–336
space building, 48–50, 72, 279–282, 284–285, 289–290, 322–323
speech event, xi, xxviii–xxix, 7, 9, 14, 20, 29, 42, 83–85, 89, 93, 122–123, 151–154, 157, 159, 162, 175, 210, 252–253, 259, 276, 278, 284, 287, 350, 354–357, 364, 367, 377, 384, 391, 399, 416, 422, 438, 456
structural plane, xxii, 312–314, 316–317, 319–321, 339, 363, 374
structure of the world, xx–xxi, xxix, 123, 208, 221, 260–269, 274–277, 286, 299, 301, 312–313, 315, 322, 339, 364, 369, 371, 374–375, 378, 381, 383–384

subjectification, 20–23, 276, 284–286, 288, 290, 391–396, 398, 408, 415, 421, 426–427, 448

subjectivity, xiii, xviii–xix, xxiii–xxvi, xxix, 2, 6, 11, 15–21, 23–24, 41–42, 44, 52, 54–55, 64–65, 73–76, 83, 269, 278, 284, 288, 392–394, 399, 412–413, 423, 425, 446–448, 450, 452

target, xviii, 16, 62–63, 120, 394–395, 421, 423, 427

tense, xii–xiii, xv–xvii, xix–xxi, xxvii, 8, 10, 30, 123–124, 132–133, 151–152, 175–176, 180–185, 199–200, 204–206, 209–211, 213–214, 251–252, 257–258, 262–264, 267–273, 276–277, 279–280, 290–291, 349–353, 364–365, 395–396

– future, 23, 203, 205–206, 208, 214, 220–221, 223–224, 227, 230, 243–244, 251, 278, 280, 282, 349, 352, 359

– nonpast, xxii, 299, 301, 305, 311, 314, 349, 351–356, 359–385

– nonpresent, 452

– past, xix, xxii, 8, 10–11, 13, 30, 34, 113–114, 117–119, 122, 124–127, 133, 175, 181–182, 184, 206, 211, 214, 227, 245, 252, 268, 278, 280, 299, 302, 304–305, 307, 310–311, 352, 380–382, 392, 396, 424–425

– pluperfect, 204, 281

– present, xxi–xxii, 8, 30, 67–68, 105, 124–125, 175, 177, 179, 181–185, 199, 206, 211, 213, 223–225, 251–259, 261–291, 352, 357, 359, 392, 403

thing, *see* nominal

time, xii, xv–xviii, xxiv–xxv, xxvii, 10, 29, 31–32, 198–199, 210–211, 220, 251, 253, 265–267, 273–277, 286, 291, 302, 350–351, 354, 367–368, 377–378, 439–440, 450, 452, 456

time of speaking, xxvi, 8, 11, 13–14, 23, 113, 120–121, 183–185, 199, 209–210, 251–252, 254–262, 265–267, 271–273, 277, 282, 285–286, 339, 352–353, 356–357, 360, 363–364, 366, 368–369, 372, 377–379, 381–384, 439, 446

timeline, 123, 126, 208, 210–211, 256, 299, 301–303, 313, 321, 339

trajector(y), 4–6, 9, 18, 21–22, 199, 315–317, 355, 372–373, 375–376, 438

truth conditions, *see* conceptual content

type, xi, xiv–xv, 7, 19–20, 29, 32–33, 35, 43–44, 46, 54, 56, 61, 63–64, 71, 74, 198–200, 241, 243, 253, 259, 261, 273–276, 278–279, 288, 290, 315–317, 353

unification, xxvii, xxx, 1, 42, 48, 76, 253, 255, 263, 385

uniqueness, xii, xv–xvi, xviii, 33, 36, 41, 44–47, 50–51, 54, 60, 64, 67–69, 72–74, 76, 153–155, 165, 174, 176, 181–182, 184–185, 241, 457

value, xix, 42, 44, 47, 60–62, 68, 74, 76, 97, 328–329

vantage point, 2, 6, 19–20, 83–84, 96, 105, 123, 151, 154, 172–174,

180–185, 210, 288, 290, 324, 359, 367
viewing arrangement, xxviii, 15–17, 20, 123, 269, 305, 307–309, 322, 324, 356, 367, 399
– canonical, 15–16
– special, 16, 66, 283, 291
viewing frame, 120, 356–359, 364
viewpoint, xx, xxii, xxviii, 42, 44, 50, 65–70, 76, 84, 97, 117–122, 125–127, 132–133, 138, 281, 284, 305–312, 322, 324, 339, 411, 418
– past, 120–122, 302, 306, 309, 311–312, 322, 339–340
virtual plane, xxii, 254–255, 262, 274–275, 279, 285–288, 290–291, 314, 362–364, 366–369, 371–379, 383–384

Cognitive Linguistics Research

Edited by René Dirven, Ronald W. Langacker and
John R. Taylor

Mouton de Gruyter · Berlin · New York

This series offers a forum for the presentation of research within the perspective of "cognitive linguistics". This rubric subsumes a variety of concerns and broadly compatible theoretical approaches that have a common basic outlook: that language is an integral facet of cognition which reflects the interaction of social, cultural, psychological, communicative and functional considerations, and which can only be understood in the context of a realistic view of acquisition, cognitive development and mental processing. Cognitive linguistics thus eschews the imposition of artificial boundaries, both internal and external. Internally, it seeks a unified account of language structure that avoids such problematic dichotomies as lexicon vs. grammar, morphology vs. syntax, semantics vs. pragmatics, and synchrony vs. diachrony. Externally, it seeks insofar as possible to explicate language structure in terms of the other facets of cognition on which it draws, as well as the communicative function it serves. Linguistic analysis can therefore profit from the insights of neighboring and overlapping disciplines such as sociology, cultural anthropology, neuroscience, philosophy, psychology, and cognitive science.

1. Ronald W. Langacker, *Concept, Image, and Symbol. The Cognitive Basis of Grammar.* 1990.
2. Paul D. Deane, *Grammar in Mind and Brain. Explorations in Cognitive Syntax.* 1992.
3. *Conceptualizations and Mental Processing in Language.* Edited by Richard A. Geiger and Brygida Rudzka-Ostyn. 1993.
4. Laura A. Janda, *A Geography of Case Semantics. The Czech Dative and the Russian Instrumental.* 1993.
5. Dirk Geeraerts, Stefan Grondelaers and Peter Bakema,*The Structure of Lexical Variation. Meaning, Naming, and Context.* 1994.
6. *Cognitive Linguistics in the Redwoods. The Expansion of a New Paradigm in Linguistics.* Edited by Eugene H. Casad. 1996.
7. John Newman, *Give. A Cognitive Linguistic Study.* 1996.

Cognitive Linguistics Research

Edited by René Dirven, Ronald W. Langacker and
John R. Taylor

Mouton de Gruyter · Berlin · New York

---

8 *The Construal of Space in Language and Thought.* Edited by Martin Pütz and René Dirven. 1996.
9 Ewa Dąbrowska, *Cognitive Semantics and the Polish Dative.* 1997.
10 *Speaking of Emotions: Conceptualisation and Expression.* Edited by Angeliki Athanasiadou and Elżbieta Tabakowska. 1998.
11 Michel Achard, *Representation of Cognitive Structures.* 1998.
12 *Issues in Cognitive Linguistics. 1993 Proceedings of the International Cognitive Linguistics Conference.* Edited by Leon de Stadler and Christoph Eyrich. 1999.
13 *Historical Semantics and Cognition.* Edited by Andreas Blank and Peter Koch. 1999.
14 Ronald W. Langacker, *Grammar and Conceptualization.* 1999.
15 *Cognitive Linguistics: Foundations, Scope, and Methodology.* Edited by Theo Janssen and Gisela Redeker. 1999.
16 *A Cognitive Approach to the Verb. Morphological and Constructional Perspectives.* Edited by Hanne Gram Simonsen and Rolf Theil Endresen. 2001.
17 *Emotions in Crosslinguistic Perspective.* Edited by Jean Harkins and Anna Wierzbicka. 2001.
18 *Cognitive Linguistics and Non-Indo-European Languages.* Edited by Eugene Casad and Gary B. Palmer. Forthcoming.
19.1 *Applied Cognitive Linguistics I: Theory and Language Acquisition.* Edited by Martin Pütz, Susanne Niemeier and René Dirven. 2001.
19.2 *Applied Cognitive Linguistics II: Language Pedagogy.* Edited by Martin Pütz, Susanne Niemeier and René Dirven. 2001.
20 *Metaphor and Metonymy in Comparison and Contrast.* Edited by René Dirven and Ralf Pörings. 2002.